lonely planet

American Rockies

Rocky Mountains
p48

Southwest USA
p124

Christopher Pitts, Anthony Ham, Liza Prado

Grand Teton National Park (p96)

CONTENTS

Plan Your Trip

Mountain biking, McDowell Sonoran Preserve (p144)

The Guide

Toolkit

Storybook

MARGARET.WIKTOR/SHUTTERSTOCK

Hiking Emerald Lake (p64)

THE AMERICAN ROCKIES

THE JOURNEY BEGINS HERE

Like so many people, I first fell in love with the Rockies on a family road trip. I remember the exact moment: sitting next to a campfire in Colorado and gazing up at the stars, and seeing the transcendent arc of the Milky Way for the very first time. It was a moment of recognition not unlike *Voyager 1*'s famous shot of earth, taken from the edge of our solar system and labeled: You are here.

Everything else that followed lived up to that moment: the unreal desert landscapes, the howling coyotes and shaggy bison roaming beneath big cobalt skies, and the wild and untamed River of No Return Wilderness in Idaho where we embarked on a weeklong rafting trip the following year. All reasons why I finally chose to make the West my home.

Christopher Pitts

christopherpitts.net

Chris writes about the Rockies, Southwest USA, China and France. When he's not outdoors or overseas, he also enjoys writing fiction.

My favorite experience is backpacking the Maze in the **Canyonlands** (p190). I love the off-trail desert adventure and the simplicity of unrolling your sleeping bag on a ledge high above the canyon walls.

WHO GOES WHERE

Our writers and experts choose the places which, for them, define the American Rockies.

CHRISTOPHER MOSWITZER/SHUTTERSTOCK

Hiking the Rim Trail in **Bryce Canyon National Park** (p192), I had one of those moments that only seem to happen in the parks of this remarkable state. All of a sudden, the earth fell silent, there was no-one else around, and it felt like this special landscape was holding its breath. I stood still, doing the same, looking around me in wonder. And then, somewhere high on the rock walls, a single chickadee started to sing.

Anthony Ham

anthonyham.com

Anthony writes about the wild places of our planet from the deserts of Africa to the Amazon. In the US, he writes regularly about the West and the Great Plains. He has written two books of narrative nonfiction, including The Last Lions of Africa.

ZACK FRANK/SHUTTERSTOCK

I'm not sure what I expected to find as I was headed to **Craters of the Moon National Monument** (p120) in Idaho. But standing in the middle of a blackened lava field, small volcanoes dotting the horizon, I felt like I was on the Big Island in Hawaii. Until it started to snow. The volcanic landscape dusted in white was a reminder of just how wildly diverse the Rocky Mountain region is.

Liza Prado

@liza.prado

Liza is a corporate lawyer turned travel writer and the author of more than 60 books.

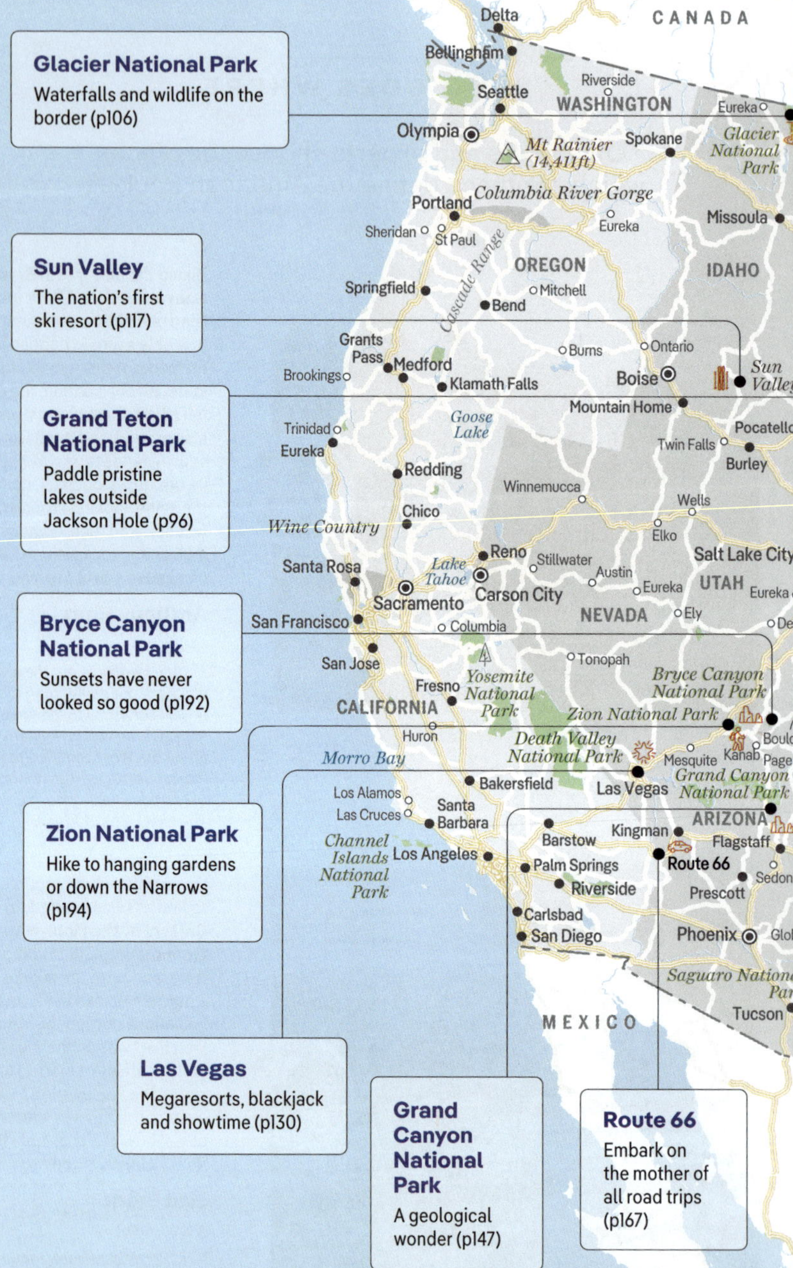

Glacier National Park
Waterfalls and wildlife on the border (p106)

Sun Valley
The nation's first ski resort (p117)

Grand Teton National Park
Paddle pristine lakes outside Jackson Hole (p96)

Bryce Canyon National Park
Sunsets have never looked so good (p192)

Zion National Park
Hike to hanging gardens or down the Narrows (p194)

Las Vegas
Megaresorts, blackjack and showtime (p130)

Grand Canyon National Park
A geological wonder (p147)

Route 66
Embark on the mother of all road trips (p167)

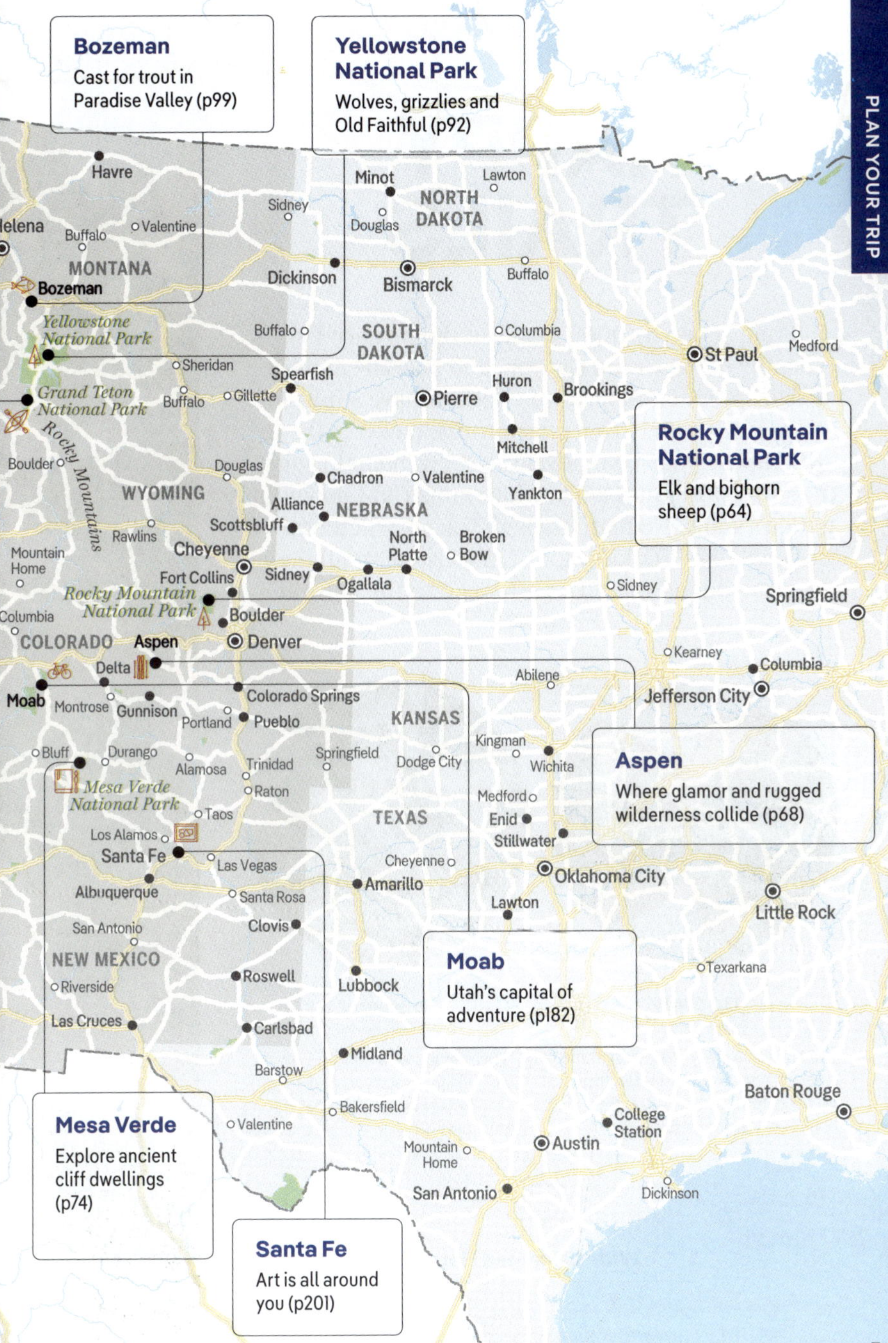
Bozeman
Cast for trout in Paradise Valley (p99)
Yellowstone National Park
Wolves, grizzlies and Old Faithful (p92)
Rocky Mountain National Park
Elk and bighorn sheep (p64)
Aspen
Where glamor and rugged wilderness collide (p68)
Moab
Utah's capital of adventure (p182)
Mesa Verde
Explore ancient cliff dwellings (p74)
Santa Fe
Art is all around you (p201)
MONTANA
NORTH DAKOTA
SOUTH DAKOTA
WYOMING
NEBRASKA
COLORADO
KANSAS
TEXAS
NEW MEXICO
Rocky Mountains
Yellowstone National Park
Grand Teton National Park
Rocky Mountain National Park
Mesa Verde National Park
Havre
Helena
Buffalo
Valentine
Bozeman
Sidney
Minot
Lawton
Douglas
Dickinson
Bismarck
Sheridan
Spearfish
Gillette
Pierre
Huron
Brookings
Mitchell
Yankton
St Paul
Medford
Columbia
Boulder
Chadron
Alliance
Scottsbluff
Rawlins
Cheyenne
North Platte
Broken Bow
Mountain Home
Fort Collins
Sidney
Ogallala
Boulder
Denver
Aspen
Delta
Moab
Montrose
Gunnison
Colorado Springs
Portland
Pueblo
Springfield
Kearney
Abilene
Jefferson City
Bluff
Durango
Alamosa
Trinidad
Raton
Taos
Dodge City
Kingman
Wichita
Medford
Enid
Stillwater
Los Alamos
Santa Fe
Las Vegas
Cheyenne
Oklahoma City
Albuquerque
Santa Rosa
Amarillo
Lawton
Little Rock
San Antonio
Clovis
Riverside
Roswell
Lubbock
Texarkana
Las Cruces
Carlsbad
Midland
Barstow
Bakersfield
Valentine
Baton Rouge
College Station
Austin
Mountain Home
San Antonio
Dickinson

HAPPY TRAILS

From snowy 14,000ft peaks to the furnace-like depths of the Grand Canyon, and lakeside ambles to slickrock scrambling, the Rockies have a hike for you. Trails range from quarter-mile paved paths to the choose-your-own-adventure Continental Divide (roughly 2700 miles long), which runs right down the nation's spine. No matter where you go, whether it's a national park, national forest, big city or small town, you're bound to find a pathway into the natural world.

Go Early

You need an early start to beat the desert heat, avoid thunderstorms and, most importantly, get a parking space.

Footwear

Trailrunners with Vibram soles: yes. Hiking boots: yes. Flip-flops and tennis shoes: no. Wear the right shoes on your feet for the hike at hand.

Wide-Brimmed Hat

Embrace your inner cowboy or girl and wear a wide-brimmed hat. The UV rays are far stronger at elevation: protect yourself.

FROM LEFT: MICHAEL RYNO/SHUTTERSTOCK, MILJAN ZIVKOVIC/SHUTTERSTOCK, PETER KUNASZ/SHUTTERSTOCK

Fiery Furnace (p189)

BEST HIKING EXPERIENCES

Shimmy through slots and pull yourself over fins in the natural labyrinth known as the ❶ **Fiery Furnace** (p189), in Arches National Park.

Walk back into the prehistoric past at ❷ **Yellowstone**'s (p92) Black Sand Geyser Basin, where the steaming pools and spouting geysers evoke an era long before this one.

Scramble up to the saddle of ❸ **Cathedral Rock** (p157) and watch the sunset turn Sedona red. Don't forget your headlamp for the way down.

Climb to the summit of a pitch-black cinder cone at the ❹ **Craters of the Moon** (p120) on the short but otherworldly Inferno Cone Trail.

Put a crick in your neck while enjoying the views from the Bear Lake trailhead in ❺ **Rocky Mountain National Park** (p64).

SCENIC DRIVES

Welcome to the land of the road trip. Route 66. The Million Dollar Hwy. Going-to-the-Sun Rd. The Rockies are full of epic ribbons of asphalt that shoot like an arrow in between desert mesas or climb like a sidewinder over precipitous mountain passes. As you progress from one scenic byway to the next, even the critics in the backseat will fall under the spell. 'Did we just pass a bighorn sheep?' 'Is it snowing in summer?' Yes, kids, it really is that good.

Fuel Up

In remote areas, gas stations are few and far between. Fill up the tank when you get the chance.

Road Conditions

Weather can change in the blink of an eye, and some high-altitude roads are closed from October through May or June. Check ahead.

Cell Service

Remember the days of yore, before there were cell phones? Well, many places out West still have zero service. Take a paper map.

FROM LEFT: JENLOB/SHUTTERSTOCK, STEVE BOWER/SHUTTERSTOCK, AMEHIME/SHUTTERSTOCK

BEST DRIVING EXPERIENCES

Embark on one of the most spectacular drives in the US, ❶ **Going-to-the-Sun Road** (p106) in Glacier National Park. It's only open for four months of the year.

Get your kicks on the original Route 66 near ❷ **Seligman** (p168), Arizona.

Take it slow on the hairpin bends of the ❸ **Million Dollar Highway** (p73) outside of Ouray, Colorado. White-knuckle driving at its best.

Experience rural New Mexico, from old adobe houses to Catholic pilgrimage towns, on the ❹ **High Road to Taos** (p202).

Climb the highest paved road in the country, ❺ **Trail Ridge Road** (p65; 12,183ft) in Rocky Mountain National Park.

St Elmo (p71)

THE OLD WEST

Miners, gunslingers and cattle rustlers: life on the frontier was a hardscrabble existence, where justice was meted out by the best shot, treaties were broken and those who struck gold sometimes wound up penniless. And yet, the era of the 'wickedest town in the West' continues to resonate in the public imagination.

Ghost Towns

Boom-and-bust mining towns litter the Rockies: such settlements could have had up to 15,000 residents for a decade or two before disappearing.

Small Museums

Don't skip the local museums. These share the stories of everyday townsfolk, not just the gunslingers, and display a host of quirky artifacts.

BEST OLD WEST EXPERIENCES

Have a drink at hillside ❶ **Jerome** (p160), and then decide if it's the Sliding Jail that's moving... or is it you?

Learn how Lewis and Clark navigated the rushing cascades of the Missouri River at a ❷ **historic trail interpretive center** (p108) in Montana.

Spend a night in the Ghost Town Guest House, in 1880s ❸ **St Elmo** (p71) in Colorado's Collegiate Peaks.

Sink a drink at the ❹ **Palace Saloon** (p160) in Prescott, just like old-timers Wyatt Earp and Doc Holliday.

Brush up on all your fur-trapping skills and Oregon Trail lore at Wyoming's ❺ **Museum of the Mountain Man** (p88).

ANCESTRAL HOMELANDS

Today, some 732,000 Native Americans live in the Rocky Mountain states and the Southwest, representing over 50 distinct tribes, from the Crow to the Navajo. New Mexico and Arizona account for the bulk of the Native population, with over half a million enrolled members and the largest tribal lands in North America.

FROM LEFT: GARY YIM/SHUTTERSTOCK, RED HERRING/SHUTTERSTOCK

Ancient Ties

Throughout the region, you'll encounter traces of those who came before, from the Ancestral Puebloans to the Hohokam. Do not touch pottery sherds or disturb ancient structures.

Guided Tours

The best way to gain insights into culture and traditions when visiting a Native American reservation? Join a guided tour led by a member of the tribe.

Powwows

Powwows are intertribal celebrations of Native heritage, with music and dancing. They are held annually across the US and many are open to the public.

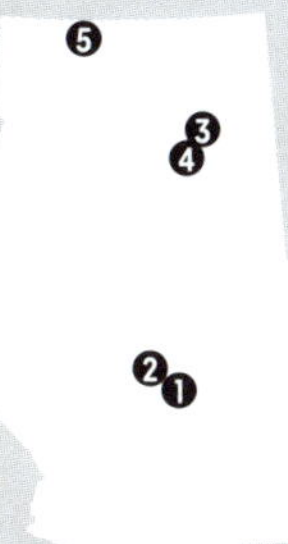

BEST NATIVE AMERICAN EXPERIENCES

Visit the largest collection of cliff dwellings in the US, ❶ **Mesa Verde** (p74, pictured far left), the home of the Ancestral Puebloans over 1000 years ago.

Hike to smaller granaries and cliff dwellings scattered amid ❷ **Bears Ears** (p185), a patchwork of protected sacred lands in the canyons of the Colorado Plateau.

Attend the ❸ **Crow Fair** (p102) near Billings, Montana. Over a century old, this is the largest Native celebration in the northern Great Plains.

Cross the high plains to Wyoming's Bighorn Range to see the ❹ **Medicine Wheel National Historic Landmark** (p89), an ancient site sacred to many Native nations.

Learn more about the Crow, Cree, Sioux, Cheyenne and the Blackfeet at the ❺ **Museum of the Plains Indians** (p108) in Montana.

NAGEL PHOTOGRAPHY/SHUTTERSTOCK

Grizzly bear, Yellowstone National Park (p92)

CALL OF THE WILD

You don't have to be in a national park to catch a glimpse of wildlife, big or small. Antelope bound by the side of the interstate, and bears can wander right into camp – keep those smellables secure! Smaller creatures, from hummingbirds to rattlesnakes, will keep you alert and engaged across the Rockies.

Keep Your Distance

Bison, elk and moose are truly massive animals that have been known to charge when approached. Always stay at least 50yd away.

Don't Feed the Animals

No matter how cute a wild animal looks, do not feed it; you will not be doing them any favors.

BEST WILDLIFE EXPERIENCES

Spot wildlife in ❶ **Yellowstone** (p92), where sightings are a guarantee and the Lamar Valley has been called the American Serengeti.

Hunker down at dusk or dawn with a spotting scope or binoculars at Oxbow Bend or Willow Flats in ❷ **Grand Teton** (p96).

Listen for bugling elk at ❸ **Rocky Mountain National Park** (p64). There are plenty of other critters here too, from moose to black bears.

Keep your eyes peeled: grizzlies and wolves are part of the natural landscape at ❹ **Glacier National Park** (p106).

Look for roadrunners, Mexican spotted owls and reptiles of all stripes and colors in the desert of ❺ **Saguaro National Park** (p174).

EPIC OUTDOORS

Canyoneering, mountain biking, white-water rafting and backcountry skiing. When it comes to outdoor adventures, go big or go home. And with dramatic, super-sized backdrops – cactus-filled deserts and snow-covered peaks that stretch into the horizon – your photos will amaze. Even if your face is frozen in terror.

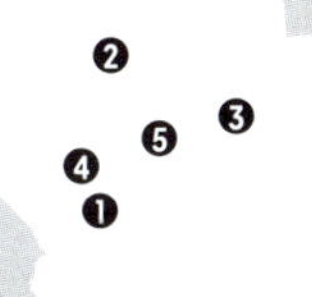

FROM LEFT: JACOB BOONSMA/SHUTTERSTOCK, BOB POOL/SHUTTERSTOCK

Ski the Steeps

Many of the best ski resorts are located in the Rockies, where the combination of feather-light snow and big peaks make even in-bounds skiing wild.

Rafting

A river trip will take you to places that are otherwise inaccessible, like the River of No Return Wilderness area (pictured) in Idaho.

Play It Safe

Don't bite off more than you can chew: always factor elevation gain and weather conditions into your plans for the day.

BEST ADVENTURE EXPERIENCES

Crash through white water, hike narrow canyons and whoosh down turquoise-blue waters on a ❶ **Grand Canyon rafting trip** (p151).

Feel the thrill of first tracks as you plunge through deep powder at one of a dozen world-class ski resorts, like ❷ **Park City** (p181).

Get your cardio on when you mountain bike up to the Continental Divide – and then race back down – on the ❸ **Monarch Crest Trail** (p70).

Find out what the word 'commitment' really means after you rappel into deep, dark pools and squeeze-you-tight slot canyons in ❹ **Zion National Park** (p194).

Go off the grid in some of the harshest, most demanding terrain in the lower 48 while backpacking through the Maze in the desert ❺ **Canyonlands** (p190).

DRAMATIC OVERLOOKS

You just can't go wrong here. From the rim of the Grand Canyon to the pastel-colored hoodoos of Bryce, and the majestic, sharp-toothed Tetons to the untrammeled wilderness of Glacier, your camera app will be working overtime no matter where you are. For the best lighting conditions, try to time your photo-taking sessions for the golden hour: the moments just after sunrise or right before sunset. This will enhance your pictures with a soft, reddish glow.

FROM LEFT: OLEG KOVTUN HYDROBIO/SHUTTERSTOCK, KYLE J LITTLE/SHUTTERSTOCK, SEAN XU/SHUTTERSTOCK

Deserts

The red-rock landscapes of the Southwest are like a real-life fantasy land: crumbling spires, lonely mesas and over 2000 natural arches.

Mountains

Chairlifts, heart-in-your-throat roads and your own two feet will take you to some of the most outrageous mountain scenery in the lower 48.

Dark Skies

Light pollution is minimal and the elevation is high: drag yourself out of bed on a moonless night to contemplate the universe in all its glory.

Maroon Bells (p70)

BEST SCENIC EXPERIENCES

Hike to the striated peaks of the ❶ **Maroon Bells** (p70) outside Aspen, one of the most quintessential Rocky Mountain landscapes.

Drive one of the most gorgeous ribbons of asphalt in the entire US: ❷ **Going-to-the-Sun Road** (p106) in Montana. Big views abound.

Enjoy the sunset amid the castle-like spires and surreal hoodoos of the surreal Fairyland Loop Trail in ❸ **Bryce Canyon** (p193).

Paddle out onto ❹ **Jenny Lake** (p96) for gasp-worthy views of the Grand Tetons.

Cycle out to ❺ **Hopi Point** (p152), which juts further into the Grand Canyon than any other South Rim overlook, making it an excellent choice at dawn or dusk.

URBAN COOL

While you may not have come to the Rockies for a city break, you'd be remiss not to tack on some extra days for an urban adventure or two, whether it's catching a concert at Red Rocks (Denver), following the Margarita Trail in Santa Fe or enjoying cut-rate prices at a luxury resort in Vegas. There are more than enough fantastic eats and cultural adventures (three incarnations of Meow Wolf) to keep you busy.

Art

Santa Fe (pictured), Phoenix and Las Vegas lead the pack when it comes to public art, fire-breathing sculptures and fun museums.

Music

There's Red Rocks in Denver, of course, but other outdoor music shows are staged in Las Vegas, Telluride, Tucson and Phoenix. Keep your eyes on the calendar.

Cuisine

Yes, the cities sprawl shamelessly and getting around on foot isn't a thing, but if you're willing to drive, you'll find great under-the-radar eats.

FROM LEFT: JHVEPHOTO/SHUTTERSTOCK, MICHAELA MOULAISON/GETTY IMAGES, LUCKY-PHOTOGRAPHER/SHUTTERSTOCK

The Strip (p131), Las Vegas

BEST URBAN EXPERIENCES

Find inspiration in ❶ **Santa Fe** (p201), the most distinctive city in the West and a wellspring of traditional art and culture.

Indulge in the no-holds-barred fun in ❷ **Vegas** (p130), but don't forget about all the public art, foodie fun and mesmerizing spectacles, too.

Rock out at legendary ❸ **Red Rocks** (p61), one of the world's most scenic concert venues.

Enjoy the museums, urban hiking trails, cacti and stylish lowriders in ❹ **Phoenix** (p142), one of the country's fastest-growing cities.

Stop over in ❺ **Salt Lake** (p179) for small-town charm and big-city fun. It might just be the coolest and friendliest little destination in the Rockies.

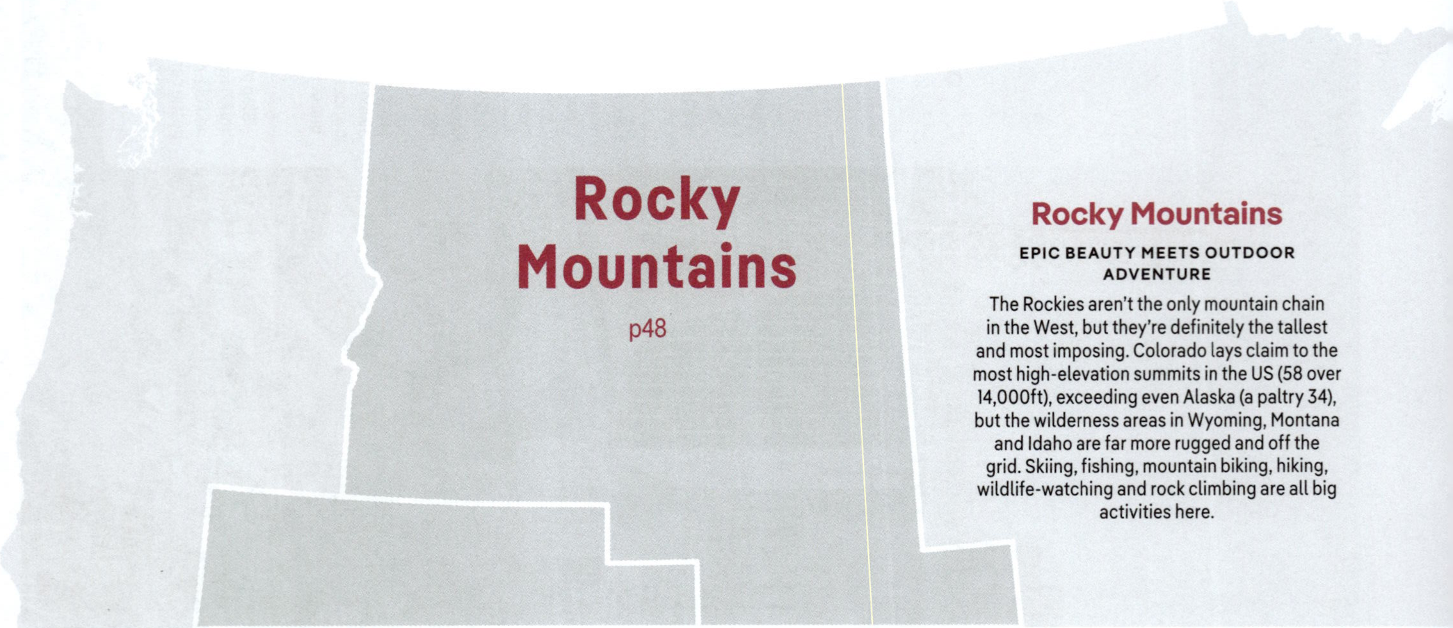

Rocky Mountains

EPIC BEAUTY MEETS OUTDOOR ADVENTURE

The Rockies aren't the only mountain chain in the West, but they're definitely the tallest and most imposing. Colorado lays claim to the most high-elevation summits in the US (58 over 14,000ft), exceeding even Alaska (a paltry 34), but the wilderness areas in Wyoming, Montana and Idaho are far more rugged and off the grid. Skiing, fishing, mountain biking, hiking, wildlife-watching and rock climbing are all big activities here.

REGIONS

Find the places that tick all your boxes.

Southwest USA

p124

Southwest USA

ONE OF AMERICA'S GRAND EPICS

The land of deserts – the Sonoran, Mojave, Chihuahuan, Great Basin and the wild Colorado Plateau – the Southwest is a unique geographical and cultural jigsaw puzzle, spread across four states: New Mexico, Arizona, Utah and Nevada. Expect great chile-driven cuisine, surreal red rock landscapes and the oldest continuous-y inhabited villages in North America.

ITINERARIES

Yellowstone to Glacier

Allow: 8 days **Distance:** 615 miles

If you've been a-hankerin' for some time in the Rockies, where the geysers spout and the bison roam, then Wyoming and Montana are for you. This epic journey takes in some of the last great wilderness areas in the lower 48, where sharp-toothed grizzlies and howling wolves are part of the landscape.

Castle Geyser, Yellowstone National Park (92)

❶

JACKSON HOLE ⏱1 DAY

Completely unlike anywhere else in Wyoming, **Jackson Hole** (p95) is rich, exclusive and oh-so hip. But just look at those craggy peaks! If you're already feeling their magnetic pull, then hop on the aerial tram, which will whisk you up to the top of Rendezvous Mountain (10,450ft) in just 12 minutes. Or keep your feet on the ground and ease into the excellent **National Museum of Wildlife Art** (p91).

❷

GRAND TETON NATIONAL PARK ⏱1 DAY

Let the adventure begin! For a truly memorable experience in **Grand Teton National Park** (96), rise at dawn and look for moose and elk at Oxbow Bend, or rent a canoe and quietly paddle across String Lake. Or beat the crowds for Grand Teton's most popular day hike up Cascade Canyon. Follow up with a bike ride around Mormon Row for iconic views of barns and bison.

❸

YELLOWSTONE NATIONAL PARK ⏱2 DAYS

Day one: explore the southern reaches of **Yellowstone** (p92), beginning with Yellowstone Lake, followed by geyser country and Old Faithful. Then it's on to Grand Prismatic Spring and the Grand Canyon of the Yellowstone. On day two, head straight to the Lamar Valley for sunrise sightings of wolves and bears, followed by Dunraven Pass, Norris Geyser Basin and Mammoth Hot Springs.

FROM LEFT: BENNY MARTY/SHUTTERSTOCK, JEFF R CLOW/GETTY IMAGES, IDAHO STATESMAN/GETTY IMAGES

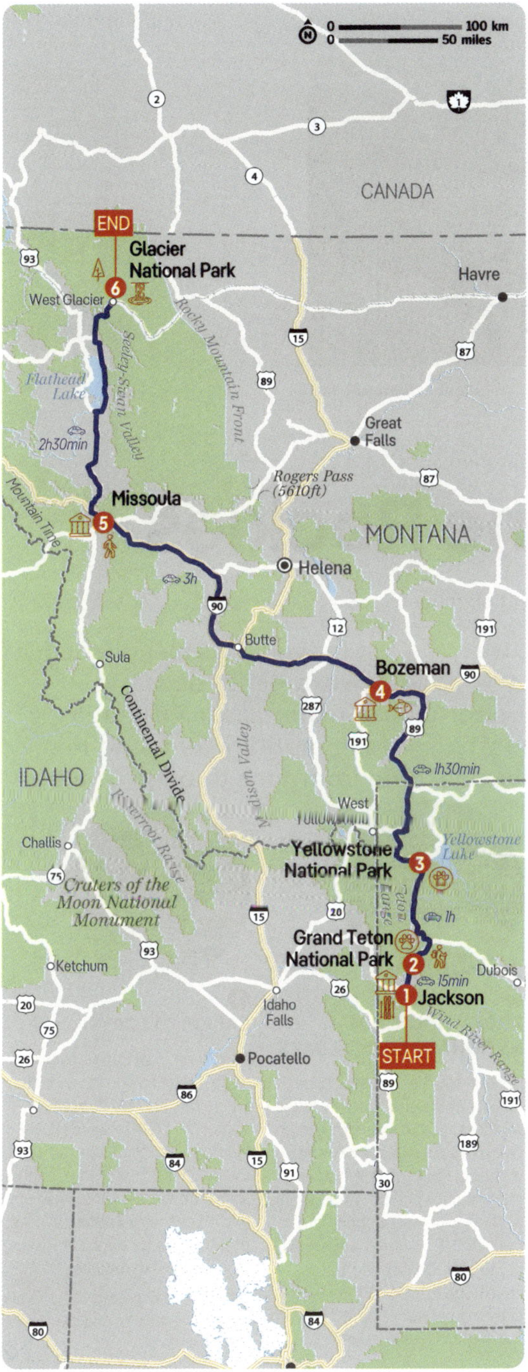

4

BOZEMAN ⏱ 1 DAY

Montana's most popular town, **Bozeman** (p99) is your base for transcendent fly-fishing on the Gallatin and Yellowstone Rivers in – actual name – Paradise Valley. Hiking, rafting trips and rock climbing round out the outdoorsy fun. Wait, there's more: don't miss the **Museum of the Rockies** (p99) with its stellar dino exhibits (including the largest *T rex* skull in the world) and Native American history.

5

MISSOULA ⏱ 1 DAY

Home to the University of Montana, the low-rise city center in **Missoula** (p103) and riverside walking trails make for a welcome break from too many hours spent in the car. Top sights include the **Smokejumper Visitor Center** (p104), which includes a tour of a base where the firefighters who parachute into remote wildlands live and train. Also nearby is the **Garnet Ghost Town** (p103), with more than a dozen abandoned gold-rush buildings.

6

GLACIER NATIONAL PARK ⏱ 2 DAYS

Even though **Glacier National Park**'s (p106) giant ice cubes are melting, this is still a spectacularly pristine and monumental destination. If there's one place that sums up the park, it's Going-to-the-Sun Rd, which surely contains some of the most vertiginous drop-offs of any paved road in America. Be warned – this drive is usually only open from mid-June or July through September.

JURGAR/SHUTTERSTOCK

Independence Pass

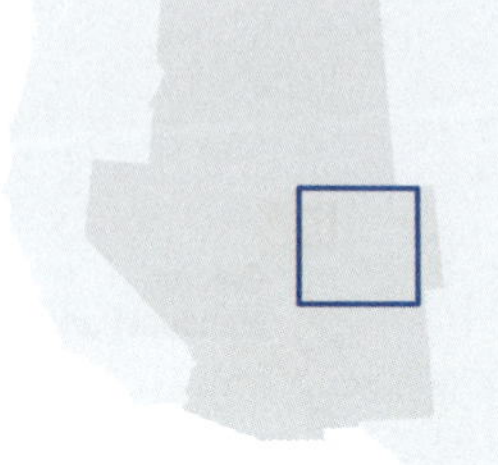

ITINERARIES

Top of the Rockies

Allow: 9 days **Distance:** 560 miles

Love mountains? Have we got a trip for you. This meandering route takes in some of the highest peaks – and roads – in the US, with plenty of opportunities to partake in Coloradan delights, whether it be rafting, wildlife-spotting or hiking the trails. You can only drive this route from June through October.

1

BOULDER 1 DAY

Start your trip in the uber-fit university town of **Boulder** (p62). Acclimatize with a hike in **Chautauqua Park** (p66), wending your way through sun-dappled ponderosa forest to the signature Flatirons, or hop on an e-bike for a leisurely ride along Boulder Creek. Or maybe join the crowds of students tubing the rushing waters. Stock up on outdoor gear on Pearl St while street performers entertain.

2

ROCKY MOUNTAIN NATIONAL PARK 2 DAYS

Here an elk, there an elk... Lace up your boots and join the prolific wildlife amid the majestic glacier-shorn cirques of **Rocky Mountain National Park** (p64). Whether you summit a peak or amble along the half-mile loop around Bear Lake, RMNP is sure to leave you breathless. On day two, follow Trail Ridge Rd, the country's highest continuous paved road, to overnight in Grand Lake.

3

SALIDA 2 DAYS

Drive past Gore Range, over Mosquito Range and on to Leadville, where the Rockies' two tallest summits – Mt Elbert and Mt Massive – dominate the horizon. Continue south, with the Collegiate Range now coming into view, until you reach lovely **Salida** (p70) – the perfect base for Arkansas River white-water adventures.

Detour: *After Leadville, climb over Independence Pass for a gorgeous side trip to Aspen.*

FROM LEFT: PAGE LIGHT STUDIOS/SHUTTERSTOCK, KELLY VANDELLEN/SHUTTERSTOCK, JACOB BOOMSMA/SHUTTERSTOCK

4

CRESTED BUTTE ⏱ 2 DAYS

Nowhere says Colorado quite like the wildflower-bedecked mountain town of **Crested Butte** (p71), beloved by mountain bikers and ski bums in equal measure. Its remote location has helped it maintain a renegade charm over the years, and hundreds of miles of hikes and singletrack through lupine-strewn meadows await.

Detour: *Peer into the 2000ft chasm of the Black Canyon of the Gunnison.*

5

TELLURIDE ⏱ 1 DAY

Spend a glorious day in the box canyon town of **Telluride** (p77) – ahem, 'to hell you ride' – where you can splurge on a luxe hotel or camp right in town. Admire Colorado's highest cascade, Bridal Veil Falls, or push your comfort zone on the via ferrata. Post-adventure, good food and drink abound. Time your visit for festival season...just book tix and accommodations early!

6

MESA VERDE ⏱ 1 DAY

Plan on a full day exploring the magnificent **Mesa Verde National Park** (p74), the best-preserved Native American archaeological site in the US and one-time home of the Ancestral Puebloans. Brimming with stunning cliff dwellings, surface sites and trails, the best way to experience it is via a ranger-led tour or two. Book online well in advance to guarantee a spot.

FROM LEFT: KRISTI BLOKHIN/SHUTTERSTOCK, DEB SNELSON/GETTY IMAGES, ZACK FRANK/SHUTTERSTOCK

ITINERARIES

Route 66

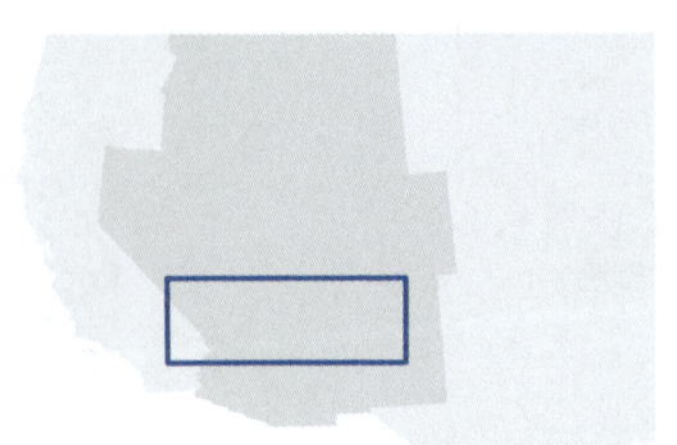

Allow: 8 days **Distance:** 795 miles

A gigantic green head. Burma Shave signs. A giant hole in the ground. And concrete tipis. You'll be sure to get your kicks – as well as your kitsch – on this storied stretch of the Mother Road through New Mexico and Arizona. Finish with dazzling displays of neon.

1

SANTA FE 2 DAYS

The Southwest's most enchanting **city** (p201) is one-of-a-kind: Georgia O'Keeffe paintings, historic adobe architecture, blue corn enchiladas, Native American crafts and the trippy Meow Wolf art installations. At more than 7000ft above sea level, Santa Fe is both the nation's oldest (1610) and highest state capital.

Detour: *Stop by the Indian Pueblo Cultural Center in Albuquerque on your way west through New Mexico.*

2

PETRIFIED FOREST NATIONAL PARK 1 DAY

From Santa Fe, drive west through Albuquerque and into Navajo country at Gallup. In eastern Arizona is the **Petrified Forest National Park** (p166), situated in the midst of the spectacular Painted Desert. Marvel at the giant fossilized logs (225 million years old) and ancient petroglyphs, take in the desert sunsets and pitch a tent. Or drive on to Winslow to stay at the historic La Posada.

3

FLAGSTAFF 1 DAY

The roadside kitsch starts to kick into high gear west of Winslow (what is up with those jackrabbit billboards?) and before you know it you'll be in the mountain town of **Flagstaff** (p161), where Route 66 is Main St. Go line dancing at the **Museum Club** (p163) to celebrate your arrival.

Detour: *Spend a day clambering over spectacular red-rock formations in Sedona, accessed via Oak Creek Canyon.*

4 GRAND CANYON 2 DAYS

This is it: America's supersized **canyon** (p150). Enter through the east entrance (Hwy 64), which takes you past the Desert View Watchtower and the Inter-Tribal Cultural Heritage Site. Follow the scenic Desert View Drive along the South Rim until you reach the main village area. Enjoy stargazing and a hike down the **Bright Angel Trail** (p151), which leads you into the magical world beneath the rim.

5 KINGMAN 1 DAY

The longest and best preserved stretch of Route 66 in the country is coming up, right after you pass through tiny Seligman, the inspiration for *Cars*. This is where **Angel Delgadillo** (p168), a small-town barber, saved the road from obscurity in 1987. Pass through pinion and juniper landscape on the twisty two-lane ribbon of pavement until you reach the Route 66 Museum in **Kingman** (p167).

6 LAS VEGAS 1 DAY

Where else but **Vegas** (p130) can you see Paris, Venice and Egypt all in the same day? Or maybe you'd rather be bedazzled by all the signage at the **Neon Museum** (p135)? Follow it up with a gourmet feast, and then get ready for showtime: choose one of five dazzling Cirque du Soleil acrobatics extravaganzas. Finish up your trip by tying the knot with Elvis at the Graceland Wedding Chapel.

KNELSON20/SHUTTERSTOCK

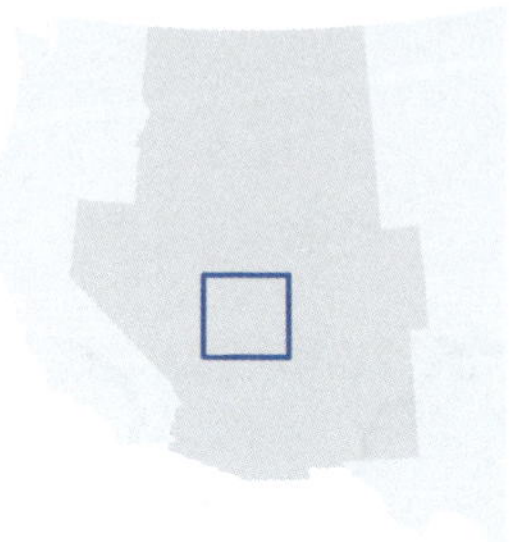

Bryce Amphitheater, Bryce Canyon National Park (p192)

ITINERARIES

Red Rock Circle

Allow: 8 days **Distance:** 845 miles

Desert spires. Claustrophobic canyons. Delicate arches, crumbling mesas and waves of slickrock. Utah is a place of geological wonders and surreal experiences. Take a loop around this often overlooked state, passing through Navajo country on the way, for a geological extravaganza. It's easiest to access from Las Vegas.

1

ZION NATIONAL PARK 2 DAYS

It may be relatively small, but **Zion** (p194) is biblical in scope. Sandstone cliffs shoot up 1500ft in the Narrows, where hikers wade through the Virgin River, backpacks above their heads. The climb to Angels Landing ascends a narrow ridge, where steel chains and the encouragement of strangers are your only friends. Got a wetsuit and a rope? Clip in for a heart-racing slot-canyon adventure.

2

MONUMENT VALLEY 1 DAY

Race across desert landscapes worthy of an old Western on the way to Arizona's **Monument Valley** (p163), an epic wonderland of crimson towers on the Navajo Reservation, and take a horseback ride with a local guide. At night, watch the shooting stars arc across the sky. On the way here, stop off in Page for a glimpse of the Colorado River's Horseshoe Bend.

3

BEARS EARS NATIONAL MONUMENT 1 DAY

Back in Utah, **Bears Ears** (p185) protects sites of significance to five Native American nations, with ancient rock art, dwellings, ceremonial sites and granaries in a big-sky landscape of mesas and desert canyons. Hike to 700-year-old kivas (ceremonial enclosures), Ancestral Puebloan granaries and other sites like the **Moon House** (p186). You'll need a day-use permit to visit many places in Bears Ears.

FROM LEFT: CHRISTINEMINATO/SHUTTERSTOCK, XAMNESIACX84/SHUTTERSTOCK, ROBERT HARDING VIDEO/SHUTTERSTOCK

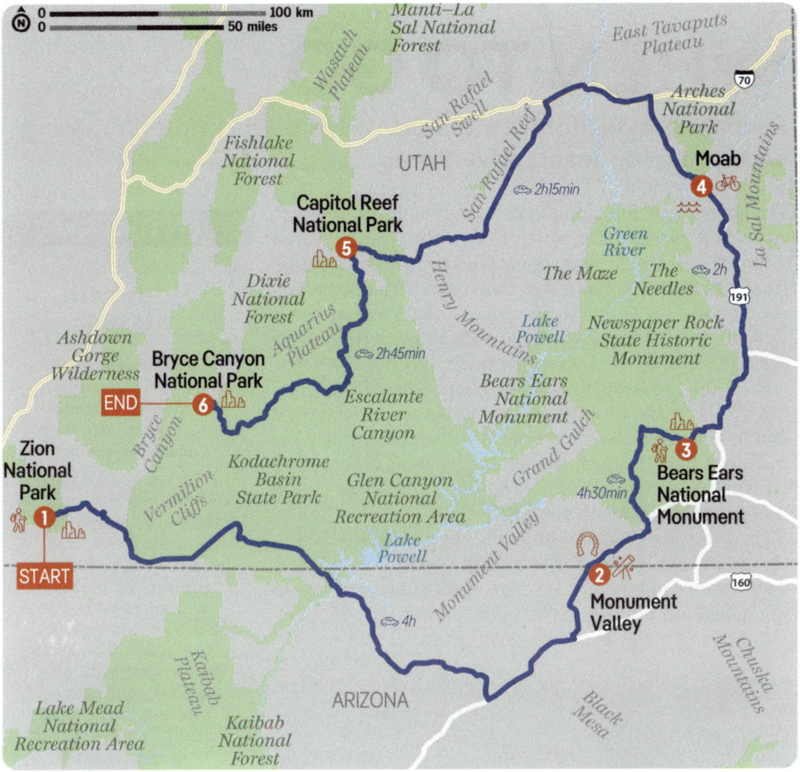

0 100 km
0 50 miles
Manti–La Sal National Forest
East Tavaputs Plateau
Wasatch Plateau
70
Arches National Park
San Rafael Swell
Fishlake National Forest
UTAH
Moab
4
San Rafael Reef
2h15min
La Sal Mountains
Capitol Reef National Park
5
Green River
Dixie National Forest
Henry Mountains
The Maze
The Needles
2h
191
Aquarius Plateau
Lake Powell
Newspaper Rock State Historic Monument
Ashdown Gorge Wilderness
Bryce Canyon National Park
2h45min
END
6
Escalante River Canyon
Bears Ears National Monument
Bryce Canyon
Zion National Park
Kodachrome Basin State Park
Grand Gulch
3
Bears Ears National Monument
Vermilion Cliffs
Glen Canyon National Recreation Area
4h30min
1
Lake Powell
Monument Valley
START
2
160
Monument Valley
4h
Kaibab Plateau
Chuska Mountains
ARIZONA
Black Mesa
Lake Mead National Recreation Area
Kaibab National Forest

4

MOAB ⏱ 2 DAYS

An adventurer's paradise, **Moab** (p182) is where mountain bikers, river runners and over 2000 natural arches converge. You could stay busy here for days, but if time is limited, make the most of it hiking in **Arches National Park** (p188) or **Canyonlands** (p190) – reservations required – followed by a day biking the desert rock or rafting the Colorado or Green Rivers outside of town.

5

CAPITOL REEF NATIONAL PARK ⏱ 1 DAY

Capitol Reef National Park (p187) is smack in the middle of nowhere, Utah, and that's a good thing – it sees far fewer visitors than elsewhere in the state. The park's centerpiece is Waterpocket Fold, a 100-mile-long monocline (a buckle in the earth's crust) that blocked explorers' westward migration. Native Americans called it the Land of the Sleeping Rainbow.

6

BRYCE CANYON NATIONAL PARK ⏱ 1 DAY

Hwy 12 traverses 124 remote miles, passing colossal domes, cool stands of aspen and the razor-thin Hogback Ridge on the way to **Bryce Canyon National Park** (p192), a place that might have been dreamt up by Dr Seuss. Fairyland hoodoos form a natural labyrinth for hikers and the improbable spires reflect an ethereal orange glow at sunrise and sunset.

WHEN TO GO

Summer and fall for high-altitude adventures, winter for skiing and spring for desert adventures.

The most important factor in deciding when and where to go is the elevation. The North Rim of the Grand Canyon (8000ft) will still be snowbound in May, while Phantom Ranch (2400ft) in the Inner Canyon is already averaging highs of 92°F, and in Phoenix (1086ft), the mercury may already be topping 100°F. Meanwhile, wildflowers are blooming in the Denver foothills and the Utah deserts (4000ft to 5400ft), and most ski resorts from Colorado to Montana (8000ft and up) will have already shut down for the year for 'mud season,' which is exactly what it sounds like. In short, the weather depends most of all on what elevation you're at, and then to a lesser extent how far north or south you are.

The good news is that within all the regional variations, there's always a time for something, whether it's crisp desert walks or bluebird ski days in February, or refreshing mountain breezes in the high country in mid-July.

I LIVE HERE

MOUNTAIN BIKING

Kyle McKendree is the general manager of Absolute Bikes in Flagstaff. *absolutebikes.net*

For me, July through September is the best time to ride around Flag, because there's more moisture and the trails are wet. Some people might be scared away by the afternoon thunderstorms, but as long as you get out in the morning and are back before noon, the riding is excellent. In spring and late fall, it's easy to hop on down to Sedona.

Mountains outside Salt Lake City

FROM LEFT: SILENTSKYPHOTOGRAPHY/SHUTTERSTOCK, WIRESTOCK CREATORS/SHUTTERSTOCK

SUMMER STORMS

Summer afternoons often bring powerful, localized thunderstorms in both the deserts and the high country. If you're hiking, beware lightning strikes (best advice is to turn around by noon), and in canyons be mindful of deadly flash floods.

Weather Through the Year (Denver, Colorado)

JANUARY	FEBRUARY	MARCH	APRIL	MAY	JUNE
Avg. daytime max: **49°F**	Avg. daytime max: **49°F**	Avg. daytime max: **58°F**	Avg. daytime max: **65°F**	Avg. daytime max: **73°F**	Avg. daytime max: **86°F**
Days of precipitation: 6	Days of precipitation: 7	Days of precipitation: 5	Days of precipitation: 7	Days of precipitation: 8	Days of precipitation: 4

SUNNY DAYS

Sunshine is the operative word in the Rockies: many states experience over 300 days of sun a year. Even in the winter, the sun can cut through the chill and make daytime temps surprisingly pleasant. Always wear sunblock.

Film, Music & Art Festivals

An annual indie film celebration, **Sundance Film Festival** has been held in Utah, primarily Park City (p181), since 1978. In 2027 it'll relocate to Boulder, Colorado (p62). **January and February**

Acoustic music aficionados and nature appreciators spend four days camping and jamming out during the **Telluride Bluegrass Festival** (p77) in Colorado. Headliners include virtuosos like Béla Fleck, Alison Krauss and Gillian Welch. **June**

Free classical music performances are staged outdoors at Idaho's **Sun Valley Music Festival** (p118). Going strong for over 40 years. **July and August**

Each year, about 80,000 people attend **Burning Man** (p140) in Nevada, an outdoor celebration known for its elaborate art displays, commerce-free ethic, blowing sand and the final burning of the man. This temporary city rises in the desert 100 miles north of Reno. **August**

Smaller Events

Count the stars in the Bryce Canyon night sky during the **Astronomy Festival** (p193), which is held annually for three days during a new moon in summer. Events include a free astrophotography workshop and telescope viewing. **June**

For an honest-to-goodness Western rodeo, head to the Wyoming state capital for the 10-day **Cheyenne Frontier Days** (p85). **July**

Don't miss the largest gathering of Native Americans in the northern states at the **Crow Fair** (p102), near Billings, Montana. Expect one week of competitive dancing, over 1200 tipis and a Plains Indian rodeo. **August**

Other Native American powwows and festivals are held throughout the year in most states. New Mexico has the largest concentration of events, in particular around Taos (p204), which holds **torchlight Christmas processions** and traditional dances at San Ildefonso on the feast day. **December and January**

I LIVE HERE

BIRDS OF A FEATHER

Tim Meehan is a wildlife biologist based in Boulder, Colorado. *boulderaudubon.org*

As a birder, my favorite time of the year is spring, when the migrants return to Colorado in vibrant breeding plumage. The creeks running out of the foothills are great places to find eye-catching warblers, grosbeaks, buntings and orioles, and the Flatirons make ideal breeding sites for cliff-nesting predators like eagles and falcons. At the edge of the Rockies, we get a cool mix of birds from eastern and western North America.

Golden eagle

SNOW

The flip side of the coin is snowfall, which can occur at almost any time in the mountains. The dry air makes snow light and fluffy, however, which is perfect for skiing. At lower elevations, the snow rarely lingers long.

JULY	AUGUST	SEPTEMBER	OCTOBER	NOVEMBER	DECEMBER
Avg. daytime max: **92°F**	Avg. daytime max: **90°F**	Avg. daytime max: **82°F**	Avg. daytime max: **68°F**	Avg. daytime max: **57°F**	Avg. daytime max: **47°F**
Days of precipitation: 6	Days of precipitation: 4	Days of precipitation: 4	Days of precipitation: 5	Days of precipitation: 4	Days of precipitation: 7

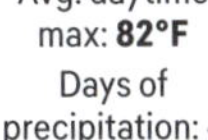

FROM LEFT: MARGARET.WIKTOR/SHUTTERSTOCK, FLIXPIX/ALAMY

Emerald Lake trail, Rocky Mountain National Park (p64)

GET PREPARED FOR THE AMERICAN ROCKIES

Useful things to load in your bag, your ears and your brain

Clothes

Layers Lightweight layers are a must. You should be prepared for heat, cold, rain, snow and intense sun...all on the same day. Even in summer, nights in the high country can be chilly, and afternoon thunderstorms can leave you drenched. Cotton traps moisture and does not insulate when wet; it may be fine on a hot day, but not in the rain or at night. Useful all-season clothing includes a lightweight outer shell, fleece, down puffy, quick-dry shirts (long-sleeve UV-resistant hoodies are popular) and quick-dry pants or shorts.

Dinner Oh wait, you're leaving camp to eat? No worries, jeans and a T-shirt is the attire of choice.

Manners

Take only pictures, leave only footprints. Litter comes in various forms: graffiti, plastic water bottles, energy bar wrappers, toilet paper. Do not remove rocks, plants, pottery fragments or anything else that is a part of the landscape.

Don't feed the wildlife. They might look cute, but you're not doing anyone any favors – least of all the animals – by exchanging food for a picture.

Shoes Lightweight trail-running or approach shoes are a good choice. Heavier hiking boots also work. On river trips, take closed-toe sandals.

READ

Blood and Thunder (Hampton Sides; 2006) The Navajo, Kit Carson and life in the West in the mid-1800s.

Close Range (Annie Proulx; 1999) 'Brokeback Mountain' and other short stories paint a vivid picture of rural Wyoming.

House of Rain (Craig Childs; 2007) All about the Ancestral Puebloans, with archaeology and adventure baked in.

A River Runs Through It (Norman Maclean; 1976) Classic Montana family tale of fly-fishing on the Big Blackfoot River.

Reservation Etiquette

- Visitors are usually welcome on Native American reservations, as long as they behave in an appropriately courteous and respectful manner. Tribal rules are often clearly posted at the entrance to each reservation, but here are some general guidelines.
- Most reservations ban the sale and use of alcohol and other drugs.
- Many tribes ban all forms of recording, be it photography, videotaping, audiotaping or drawing. Others permit these activities in certain areas only if you pay the appropriate fee (usually $5 to $10). If you wish to photograph a person, do so only after obtaining his or her permission. A posing tip is usually expected. Photographers who disregard these rules can expect tribal police officers to confiscate their cameras and then escort them off the reservation.
- Don't enter private property unless invited. Don't climb on ruins or remove any kind of artifact from a reservation or historical site. Kivas (ceremonial chambers) are always off-limits to visitors. Off-road travel is not allowed without a permit.
- As a rule of thumb, don't bargain.
- Ceremonies and powwows are either open to the public or exclusively for tribal members. Ceremonies are religious events, and applauding or trying to talk to the performers is rude. Photography and other forms of recording are rarely permitted. While powwows also hold spiritual significance, they are usually more informal.
- Activities such as backpacking, fishing and hunting require tribal permits. On Native American lands, state fishing or hunting licenses are not valid.

WATCH

American Primeval (Peter Berg; 2025; pictured) 1857: Fort Bridger, Wyoming. Where fugitives, Mormons and the Shoshone collide.

The Hateful Eight (Quentin Tarantino; 2015) Wild West thriller set in Wyoming; filmed near Telluride.

The National Parks: America's Best Idea (Ken Burns; 2009) Documentary on the foundation of the park system.

Temple Grandin (Mick Jackson; 2010) Inspiring true story of a woman with autism who revolutionized the livestock industry.

Yellowstone (2018–24) Property conflicts and family drama on a Montana ranch and the Broken Rock Reservation.

LISTEN

Colorado River in Crisis (LA Times; 2023) Six-part podcast on the water crisis gripping the Western states.

Dirtbag Diaries (2007–) OK, they're based in Seattle, but this podcast is the perfect fit for all your favorite outdoor activities.

Paralyzed by a Scorpion in the Grand Canyon (Outside; 2022) Riveting account of the aftermath of a scorpion sting on a rafting trip.

Up and Vanished: Season 3 (2021) True crime podcast investigates the disappearance of Ashley Loring HeavyRunner in northwest Montana.

TAYLORBANKS/SHUTTERSTOCK

Arches National Park (p188)

TRIP PLANNER

NATIONAL PARKS

Listen to the spine-tingling howl of a wolf at dusk. Watch two elks lock antlers in a battle for supremacy. Walk beneath shimmering gold aspen leaves or clamber up the spine of a narrow ridge 14,000ft high. Sleep beneath the Milky Way and awaken to a desert sunrise. This, and so much more, is the reason these parks exist.

Planning Your National Park Trip

In 2024, 331.9 million visited national park sites across the US, up from 237 million in 2020. Conversely, Trump administration budget cuts in 2025 meant that the National Park Service permanent staffing was reduced by 25% that same year, while 45% of seasonal positions remained unfulfilled. Some of the information presented here may have changed by the time you read this, including possible entry-fee increases for non-Americans.

TIMED-ENTRY RESERVATIONS

First things first: make sure you can enter the park that you want to visit. As visitor numbers increase and the number of park staff continues to decrease, more and more parks (both national and state) have been turning to timed-entry reservations to manage overcrowding. This means that you must plan your trip carefully. Always check the latest requirements on park websites.

Timed-entry reservations are good for one vehicle. The easiest way to reserve your slot is on recreation.gov; note that this is not an entry fee, which is separate. If you have already reserved a campground or a room in a park lodge, or you have a backcountry permit, you should not need a timed-entry slot. Park passes only grant entry; they cannot be used for timed entries.

In the Rockies and Southwest, there are currently five parks that use timed-entries of some kind. These include the following.

Arches Between 7am and 4pm, from April through early July and late August through October, you must have a timed-entry reservation in order to visit Arches. Slots

THE 10 ESSENTIALS

What to pack on your trip depends on whether you're flying or driving to your destination – and, of course, whether you plan on camping. But even if you don't have the luxury of stashing an air mattress, stove and camp chairs in the back of your car, you can still plan accordingly. Some gateway towns (eg Estes Park, Flagstaff) have gear rental options, so you don't have to incur extra airline baggage fees if you want to pitch a tent. Just make sure you call ahead and book.

Flying or driving, you should always have the 10 essentials stashed in your daypack. Remember, it's unlikely you will have cell service in most parks.

- **Water**
- **Sun protection: hat, sunglasses and sunscreen**
- **Rain jacket**
- **Basic first-aid kit**
- **Map and compass**
- **Headlamp**
- **Matches or lighter**
- **Food**
- **Pocket knife and duct tape**
- **Extra layer of clothing**

open up six months in advance. A small number of last-minute slots are released the night before at 7pm.

Carlsbad Caverns You must reserve your cave tour in advance.

Glacier The two most popular sections of the park, Going-to-the-Sun Rd and North Fork, require timed entries between 7am and 3pm, from mid-June through September. Slots are released four months in advance. A small number of last-minute slots are released the night before at 7pm.

Rocky Mountain Has two separate timed-entry options. The regular entry grants you access to the entire park, with the exception of Bear Lake, between 9am and 2pm, from late May to mid-October. The coveted Bear Lake Corridor entry is more restrictive: it is in place from 5am to 6pm. If you don't have a permit, a park shuttle does run to Bear Lake from Estes Park; however, this also requires reservations. Slots are released on the first day of the month prior to your visit (so May 1 for a June visit). A small number of last-minute slots are released the night before at 7pm.

SEAN XU/SHUTTERSTOCK

Bear Lake (p64)

WHERE TO GO FOR...

Hiking

- **Rocky Mountain (CO)** Alpine lakes and windswept summits.
- **Zion (UT)** Hanging gardens and slot canyons in the Utah desert.
- **Canyonlands (UT)** Incredible swath of rugged desert backcountry.
- **Great Basin (NV)** Solitude and high peaks.

Wildlife

- **Yellowstone (WY, MT, ID)** Heartland of the American Serengeti.
- **Glacier (MT)** Grizzlies, wolves and moose.
- **Grand Teton (WY)** Spot raptors and megafauna at Oxbow Bend.

Sunrise, Sunset

- **Grand Canyon (AZ)** Best sunsets in the US, no contest.
- **Arches (UT)** Sublime geological wonderland.
- **Bryce Canyon (UT)** See the hoodoos take on an ethereal glow.
- **Saguaro (AZ)** The land of the wild and weird cacti.
- **Petrified Forest (AZ)** Watch shadows creep across the Painted Desert.

History

- **Mesa Verde (CO)** The site of over 600 cliff dwellings.
- **White Sands (NM)** Where the first atomic bomb was detonated.

Off the Beaten Track

- **Capitol Reef (UT)** The Land of the Sleeping Rainbow.
- **Great Sand Dunes (CO)** One of the quietest places in the US.
- **Black Canyon of the Gunnison (CO)** For 2000ft cliffs and dark skies.

Zion The park's most popular hike, Angels Landing, requires a permit that can only be secured through a lottery. There are four lotteries per year, one for each season. Lotteries are held two months before the start of each season (so January 1 for spring, which runs from March through May). A next-day lottery for last-minute tickets is held the night before at 7pm.

PARK PASSES

Entry for most national parks is $35 per vehicle and is valid for seven days. If you're planning on visiting several national parks and monuments on your trip, an **America the Beautiful Pass** ($80) is an excellent investment. It's valid for one year. Other passes include the **Senior Pass** ($20), which is valid for those 62 and older; and the **Access Pass** (free), which is available for US citizens with a permanent disability. All children in the 4th grade in the US qualify for a free park pass as well, which can be used for the entire family. You can buy park passes at entry kiosks or online *(store.usgs.gov)*. In 2026 the fees for both single entries and park passes are expected to increase for international visitors.

BACKCOUNTRY PERMITS

In addition to timed-entry reservations, parks also require permits for popular backcountry hikes and campgrounds. For instance, if you're planning to summit Longs Peak and would like to sleep at the Boulderfield campground, you will need a permit. If you are organizing a backpacking trip to Yellowstone or the Canyonlands, you will also need a permit. The most popular sites, like the Bright Angel campground at the bottom of the Grand Canyon, are only available via a lottery, but remember: you don't have to do what everyone else is doing. National parks are enormous and chances are you will be able to find a backcountry permit or campsite of some kind, somewhere, even if it's not the one you had your heart set on. Just make sure to plan ahead of time so you know how to navigate the red tape in each park. Permits and lottery entries can be secured on recreation.gov.

SLEEPING OPTIONS

A handful of parks have historic lodges where you can stay the night. Rooms are comfortable enough, but usually basic. The draw, of course, is the fantastic location. Lodges offer something akin to VIP access: that same spot that was thronged with people at midday might be utterly deserted after the sun sets. It is not easy to get a room in a historic lodge; you'll need to book months ahead. Frontcountry campsites – aka car camping or a place to park your RV – are more common than lodges, and often have the same spectacular locations. No surprise, then, that they are even more difficult to reserve. Backcountry campsites, which are only accessible on foot, are usually easier to reserve, outside of a few extremely popular areas like the Grand Canyon or the Chesler Park Loop in the Canyonlands.

By and large, the vast majority of park visitors wind up staying at a hotel, motel or private campground in a gateway town outside the park. Although these accommodations are less appealing than in-park options, they are generally far more likely to have a vacancy and suit a wider range of budgets.

FOOD

Some of the most popular parks have restaurants, cafeterias and even a grocery store on site (we're looking at you, Grand Canyon). For the most part, however, when it comes to replenishing your calories, you'll be on your own. If you're staying in a gateway town, eating breakfast and dinner is a cinch. For lunch, some sandwich shops specialize in boxed lunches to go if you can't be bothered. The healthiest and most economical option will always be to buy your groceries and snacks ahead of time. If you don't have a cooler or a hotel fridge, plan on stocking up on nonperishable protein-rich items like peanut butter, hard salami and energy bars. Remember: you need more calories when hiking at elevation than you do at home. Online resources like **Backcountry Foodie** *(backcountryfoodie.com)* will help you estimate exactly how many calories you do need, in addition to providing an assortment of meal ideas, including 'no-cook' favorites.

Camping in the Maze, Canyonlands National Park (p190)

HOW TO... Find a Campsite

Camping in the Rockies is one of the best ways to experience the region's diverse natural beauty. In most Western states, enormous tracts of land are public (eg 64.5% of Utah, 62% of Idaho, 43% of Colorado), which is good news for campers looking to pitch a tent under the stars.

Decide on Your Camping Experience

Public Campgrounds A convenient option, these drive-in campsites are suitable for both RV (no hookups) and tent campers. They have amenities like picnic tables, tent pads, firepits and bear-proof storage lockers. There are public restrooms, from pit toilets to bathrooms with showers. Sites range in cost ($18 to $40 per night).

Private Campgrounds Less appealing locations but convenient for RVs as they usually have full hookups and many other amenities like wi-fi and cell service. Usually not a great choice for campers in tents.

Dispersed Camping Pitch your tent or park your rig on national forest or Bureau of Land Management (BLM) land. Typically, it's off a back road; sites can be up to an hour away from your destination. Plan on packing everything in and out, including all water. Camping is free; there are no facilities so you have to bury all human waste appropriately. Ask at national forest or BLM offices for guidance on where you can legally camp.

Backcountry Camping For serious campers, this is the best option as you can access remote locations with no vehicles around for miles. Backcountry camping means you are backpacking – everything you need is on your back. Permits are often required.

Reservations & Red Tape

Developed Campgrounds Most are reservation only; but there are always a few campsites that are first come, first served.

- National forests and parks: recreation.gov
- State parks: check state government websites
- Private campgrounds: check hipcamp.com

Dispersed Camping Public lands have designated dispersed camping areas. Call or drop in to the local ranger station to find out where they are.

- National forests: fs.usda.gov
- BLM land: blm.gov
- Check thedyrt.com for reviews

Backcountry Camping The most popular areas require backcountry permits. Check requirements, especially in national parks.

WHAT TO PACK

Regardless of your camping spot, here are some must-haves.

Shelter

- Tent or tarp
- Sleeping bag rated for the season
- Sleeping pad or air mattress

Food & Drink

- Water or water filtration system
- Easy-to-cook meals
- Bear canister (required for backcountry campers)
- Stove and fuel
- Camping cookware
- Matches or lighter

Safety

- Headlamp plus extra batteries
- First-aid kit
- Multitool
- Maps
- Hand sanitizer and soap

Navajo tacos (p40)

THE FOOD SCENE

Cuisine in the Rockies is heavily influenced by the Southwest. When it comes to regional cooking, green chiles and blue corn set the trends.

Whoever advised 'moderation in all things' has clearly never eaten in the Southwestern states. From green-chile cheeseburgers to Sonoran dogs and huevos rancheros to red-chile posole, the regional specialties are pleasingly diverse. Sampling local fare is a big reason to get excited about a trip to New Mexico or Arizona.

Colorado and Las Vegas, meanwhile, are the standard bearers for more contemporary fare. With a rapidly growing population and an A-list clientele in the ski resorts and casinos, you can expect plenty of gourmet offerings in all the big-ticket destinations.

In most places, however – whether you're on the road in the mountains or the deserts – the pickings will be slim. Our best advice is to bring a cooler and fill it up with groceries whenever you can. While there might not be much to eat on the Beartooth Hwy or in the Arizona Strip, you better believe that the scenery is outrageous and the picnic spots are divine.

Southwestern Cultural Influences

Three ethnic groups – Native American, Hispanic and cattle-country Anglo – influence Southwestern food culture. Traditional Native American crops are the foundation of Southwestern cuisine, providing the main ingredients: corn, beans, squash and, of course, chiles.

Spain and Mexico controlled territories from Texas to California well into the 19th

Best American Rockies Dishes

BLUE CORN ENCHILADAS
Stuffed corn tortillas smothered with chile sauce.

STEAK
Juicy slabs of beef are the specialty throughout the Rockies.

HUEVOS RANCHEROS
Breakfast of tortillas, eggs, cheese, beans and chile sauce.

GREEN-CHILE CHEESEBURGERS
A New Mexico classic; beef, American cheese and Hatch chiles.

century. After the US took over, most inhabitants – and their cooking styles – simply stayed put. The American miners, cowboys and pioneers who subsequently streamed into the formerly Mexican territories also contributed to the Southwest style of cooking. Much of the West is cattle country, and whether you are in Phoenix, Denver or Jackson, you can expect a good steak.

New Mexican Chiles

Chiles are Capsicum peppers that are native to the Americas. In the Southwest, they are infused into everything, from chocolate to beer, and typically served as a sauce. Chili, on the other hand, is a Tex-Mex meat-and-bean dish. Let's be clear: chile and chili are not the same thing.

Although there are many different varieties of chiles, all with different heat indexes, in New Mexico people tend to break them down into two kinds: green and red. Easy, right?

Green chiles are long and pale green, and they are often grown in the Hatch Valley in southern New Mexico. They have a sharp heat evoking a vegetable flavor and often have more of a kick than red chiles. Red chiles are typically grown in northern New Mexico and have a sweeter flavor, some tartness and a slow burn. 'Red or green?' references your choice of sauce – and it's the official state question. Ordering a dish Christmas-style means it will come with a half-and-half mix of red- and green-chile sauce. Vegetarians note: chile sauces are usually made with pork.

Dried chiles

Roasting green chiles

FOOD FESTIVALS

Hatch Chile Festival Events at this early-September ode to the green chile include a chile-eating contest.

Santa Fe Wine & Chile Fiesta *(santafewineandchile.org)* Five days of food and wine tastings with 60+ participating restaurants in September.

Street Eats Food Truck Festival Sample pizza, crepes, seafood, Cajun specialties and more at this two-day round-up of mobile eats in January in Phoenix.

Great American Beer Festival (p61) The nation's largest beer celebration brings craft-beer fans to Denver to taste almost 9500 brews, all competing for gold in 109 different categories.

Food & Wine Classic *(classic.foodandwine.com)* An epic Aspen fest, filled with tastings, cooking demonstrations and panels with celebrity chefs and beverage connoisseurs.

FRY BREAD TACOS
Fried dough with a soft center that's layered with toppings.

ELK BRATS
Gourmet sausages, often mixed with cheddar and jalapeño.

SONORAN DOGS
Bacon-wrapped hot dogs slathered with tomatillo salsa and pinto beans.

ROCKY MOUNTAIN OYSTERS
Bull testicles, breaded and deep fried, served with dipping sauce.

BREAKFAST BURRITOS
Eggs, cheese, beans, veggies and hot salsa – perfect breakfast on the go.

VEGETARIANS & VEGANS

Most metro-area eateries offer at least one veggie dish, although few are devoted solely to meatless menus. Almost every larger town has a natural-food grocer but you may go wanting in smaller hinterland towns, where beef still rules. In that case, your best bet is to assemble a picnic from the local grocery store.

Vegetarians will be happiest in New Mexico and Arizona, where they will have no problem finding something delicious on most menus, even at drive-throughs and tiny dives. In Phoenix, try Green New American Vegetarian.

One potential pitfall? Traditional Southwestern cuisine uses lard in beans, tamales, sopaipillas (deep-fried puff pastry) and flour (but not corn) tortillas, among other things. Be sure to ask – often, even the most authentic places have a pot of pintos simmering for vegetarians.

Farm to Table in Colorado

Colorado takes great pride in sustainable dining, and with close to 40,000 farms and ranches in the state, there are plenty of opportunities to buy locally grown and sourced foods. There are terrific farmers markets, most bustling from May to October with rows of vendors selling fresh fruits and vegetables, plus ethically produced meat like lamb and bison. The explosion of food halls, too, showcase Colorado's offerings with aspiring chefs testing their recipes and new concepts. And in towns like Denver, Boulder, Aspen, Telluride and Vail, auteur restaurants increasingly feature flavorful local ingredients as the new gold.

Native American Food

Modern Native American cuisine bears little resemblance to the diet eaten before the Spanish conquest, but it is distinct from Southwestern cuisine. Navajo tacos – fried bread usually topped with beans, meat, tomatoes, chile and lettuce – are readily available. Chewy horno bread is baked in the beehive-shaped outdoor adobe ovens (hornos) using remnant heat from a fire built inside the oven, then cleared out before cooking.

Most other Native American cooking is game-based and usually involves squash and locally harvested ingredients such as berries and piñon nuts. Though becoming better known, it can be difficult to find, especially outside of New Mexico and Arizona. Your best bets are festival food stands, powwows, rodeos, pueblo feast days, casino restaurants or people's homes at the different pueblos.

BRENT HOFACKER/SHUTTERSTOCK

Margaritas

Margaritas

Margaritas are the alcoholic drink of choice and synonymous with the West. Margaritas vary in taste depending on the quality of the ingredients used, but all are made from tequila, a citrus liquor (Grand Marnier, triple sec or Cointreau), freshly squeezed lime and possibly agave nectar or simple syrup.

Santa Fe has made margarita sampling easy for die-hard fans with its **Margarita Trail** *(santafe.org/margaritatrail)*. Download the app, then flash your margarita passport at more than 50 participating restaurants and bars for discounts. You might even earn margarita swag.

TOP RIGHT: STANISLAV71/SHUTTERSTOCK; BOTTOM FROM LEFT: ABEAUTIFULWORLD/SHUTTERSTOCK, CACTUSPILOT/SHUTTERSTOCK, BRENT HOFACKER/SHUTTERSTOCK, ARFIN STUDIO/SHUTTERSTOCK

Specialties

Southwest

Breakfast burritos Flour tortilla stuffed with scrambled eggs, bacon or chorizo, cheese, chile and potatoes.

Calabacitas Sautéed squash (or zucchini), corn and green chile; often topped with cheese.

Carne adovada Slow-cooked pork in red-chile sauce.

Carne seca Beef that's sun-dried before cooking.

Chile verde Green-chile pork stew; New Mexican comfort food.

Chimichanga Deep-fried burrito possibly created in Arizona during a kitchen accident.

Frito pie Chili and cheese piled on corn chips.

Posole Stew made from hominy (dried corn).

Sopaipilla Deep-fried puff pastry with honey.

Native American

Fry bread Deep-fried, doughy Native American bread.

Horno bread Chewy bread baked in beehive-shaped outdoor adobe ovens.

Carne adovada

Hiking Staples

Energy bars Grab-and-go bars with loads of protein and (ideally) minimal processing.

Electrolyte packets Powder or tablet added to water bottle to replenish minerals.

Jerky Dried, flavored meat, typically beef, bison or turkey. Lightweight.

Stinger Shot of honey for a quick energy boost.

Tortillas and nut butter Indestructible, easy lunch. Hard salami and cheese works, too.

Trail mix Protein- and calorie-rich combo of nuts, seeds and dried fruit (caution: chocolate will melt on hot days and become totally gross). Prep it from bulk food.

MEALS OF A LIFETIME

Gun Barrel Steak and Game House (p91) Mesquite-grilled steaks, wild game and taxidermied decor in Jackson.

Kai Restaurant (p145) Traditional Native American fare reaches new heights in Arizona at the Sheraton Wild Horse Pass Resort.

Pine Creek Cookhouse (p69) Cross-country ski or take a sleigh ride to this intimate log cabin in the Aspen wilderness.

La Choza (p200) Blue-corn burritos, a festive interior and an extensive margarita list make La Choza a long-standing local favorite.

Shan (p99) Bozeman might not be the most obvious choice for a pan-Asian restaurant sourcing local bison and lamb, but this is one to remember.

THE YEAR IN FOOD

SPRING

Spring is marked by the appearance of leafy greens like spinach, arugula and lettuce. Asparagus, radishes and turnips are in season too. Though available year-round, Colorado lamb is especially popular for Easter and Passover meals.

SUMMER

Farmers markets are rife with local produce: Palisade peaches and Olathe corn, Rocky Ford cantaloupes plus zucchini, tomatoes and cucumbers from the Arkansas Valley. Fresh rainbow trout is a menu go-to.

FALL

Things heat up in late August and September as it's Hatch green-chile season. Expect a crazy array of green-chile fare. Apples and pears figure big in pies and cider. Farm-raised venison and elk also appear on menus.

WINTER

Winter brings a shift to root vegetables like potatoes, carrots and onions plus winter greens like kale and Swiss chard. Locally raised beef and bison are often the base of hearty dishes and stews.

FROM LEFT: CSNAFZGER/SHUTTERSTOCK, ASKARIO PHOTOGRAPHY/SHUTTERSTOCK

Sawtooth National Recreation Area (p118)

THE OUTDOORS

Catch big air on a snowboard, paddle furiously through class V white water or spot western tanagers in the ponderosas – for every season, terrain and elevation, there's an activity just for you.

The Rockies have 'adventure playground' written all over them, and visitors from back East or overseas may find themselves rubbing their eyes in disbelief: people get to *live* here? Wilderness areas are vast, untamed and full of unbelievable landscapes: the Grand Canyon, Yellowstone, the Canyonlands, the Sawtooth Mountains. You will see bears and antlered elk, shaggy bison and bighorn sheep. And while you won't see a mountain lion, a mountain lion may see you. There are countless ways to explore the Rockies, and every one will stay with you for a lifetime.

Hiking & Backpacking

Whether you're a day hiker, through hiker or peak bagger, you can bet there are dozens of bucket-list trails waiting for you. And you don't need to be an ultrafit endurance athlete to enjoy them: experiences like the paved Rim Trail at the Grand Canyon are easy, accessible and *Wow! Look at those views!* Zion has trails under a mile that lead to secret hanging gardens in the desert, and at Rocky Mountain you can experience the alpine tundra without having to climb three hours and 3000 vertical feet to get there.

However, if you do want a little adventure, the hardest part will be deciding where to

Adventure Sports

RAFTING
Crash through the rapids on the **Arkansas River** (p70) or the Middle Fork of the **Salmon River** (p119).

FLY-FISHING
Leave the world behind while you cast for trout on the **Gallatin River** outside Bozeman (p100).

CANYONEERING
Sign up for a guided canyoneering trip – rappelling, cold pools and tight spaces – in **Zion** (p194).

FAMILY ADVENTURES

Enjoy a leisurely mule ride (p152) down the **North Kaibab Trail** at the North Rim of the Grand Canyon. Reservations here are far easier to get than on the South Rim.

Float downstream on an inner tube or in a kayak on the **Boise River** (p113) in Idaho.

Let your kiddos experience the thrill of dogsledding (p91) in **Jackson Hole** with a former Iditarod racer.

Observe everyone's favorite predators from a safe distance at the **Grizzly & Wolf Discovery Center** (p101) near Yellowstone's west entrance.

Climb four ladders to a ceremonial cave, combining education with adventure at **Bandelier National Monument** (p204).

Explore the universe during an evening program at the **Lowell Observatory** (p163) in Flagstaff.

go. One thing is for sure: backpackers often need a permit. Some permits are so hard to get that they are only distributed by lottery or require booking ahead months in advance. Always make sure you do your research long before your trip.

Skiing & Snowboarding

Say goodbye to icy trails and long lift lines and hello to soft powder and bluebird skies. Once you ski the Rockies, there's no going back; it doesn't matter if you're in Park City, Vail, Sun Valley, Jackson Hole or Big Sky. Beginners can cruise for an eternity on easy groomers while experts slalom the trees or drop off precipitous cornices into pristine back bowls. All the superlatives are right here: the highest ski lift in North America, the most extreme in-bounds skiing in North America, the steepest runs in North America – heck, the Rockies even have the highest restaurant in North America (it's at A-Basin if you're curious). And then there are the monster terrain parks, the SUV-sized moguls, snow so deep you'll need a snorkel, and the legendary backcountry runs, huts and yurts that you can only reach on foot, AT skis, snowcat or helicopter.

Snowboarding, Park City (p181)

Mountain Biking & Cycling

Mountain biking is everywhere, and the terrain varies wildly from place to place: slam over the slickrock in Utah, slalom through prickly cacti in Arizona, flow through the aspen groves on Crested Butte singletrack... it's all out there, and trail networks keep getting bigger. At ski resorts, you can catch a chairlift up the mountain, fly down the hill in style, and jump and bank to your heart's content on the freeride trails. Elsewhere, going uphill is on you – but that's part of the fun, right? All mountain towns have bike rental shops, where staff will be able to dole out suitable advice for your level.

And you don't have to go mountain biking for two-wheeled fun. Paved bike paths make for great family excursions, from the Grand Canyon rim to the Hiawatha Scenic Trail in Idaho and Montana.

ROCK CLIMBING
Feel the exposure as you ascend ever higher up Boulder's **Flatirons** (p66) or at **Rocky Mountain National Park** (p64).

VIA FERRATA
Make your way, hand over hand, across a sheer mountain face in **Telluride** on an 'iron way' (p77).

HOT-AIR BALLOONING
Soar skyward at dawn in a hot-air balloon during annual **balloon festivals** (p199) in Albuquerque.

SANDBOARDING
Slide down the tallest dunes in North America at Colorado's **Great Sand Dunes National Park** (p82).

National Parks

1. Yellowstone National Park (p92)
2. Grand Canyon National Park (p150)
3. Rocky Mountain National Park (p64)
4. Glacier National Park (p106)
5. Mesa Verde National Park (p74)
6. Arches National Park (p188)
7. Zion National Park (p194)

Walking/Hiking

1. Canyonlands National Park (p190)
2. Maroon Bells (p70)
3. Grand Teton National Park (p96)
4. Great Basin National Park (p141)
5. Telluride (p77)
6. Sedona (p155)
7. Bears Ears National Monument (p185)

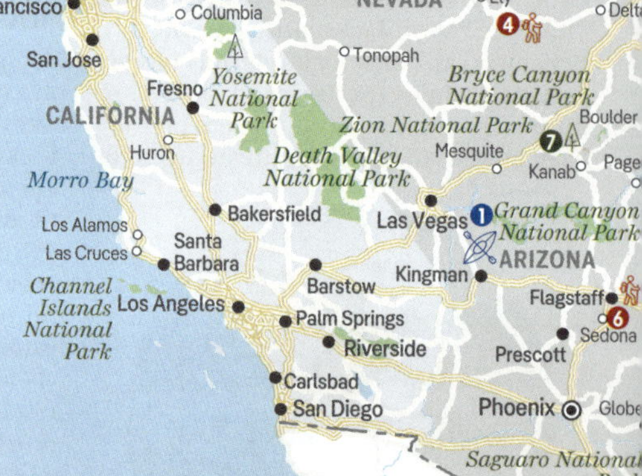

Cycling

1. Moab (p182)
2. Monarch Crest Trail (p70)
3. Crested Butte (p71)
4. Route of the Hiawatha (p117)
5. Rio Grande del Norte (p207)
6. Ridge to Rivers Trails (p116)
7. Deer Valley (p181)

N 0 — 500 km
0 — 250 miles

ACTION AREAS

Where to find the American Rockies' best outdoor activities.

AMERICAN ROCKIES

THE GUIDE

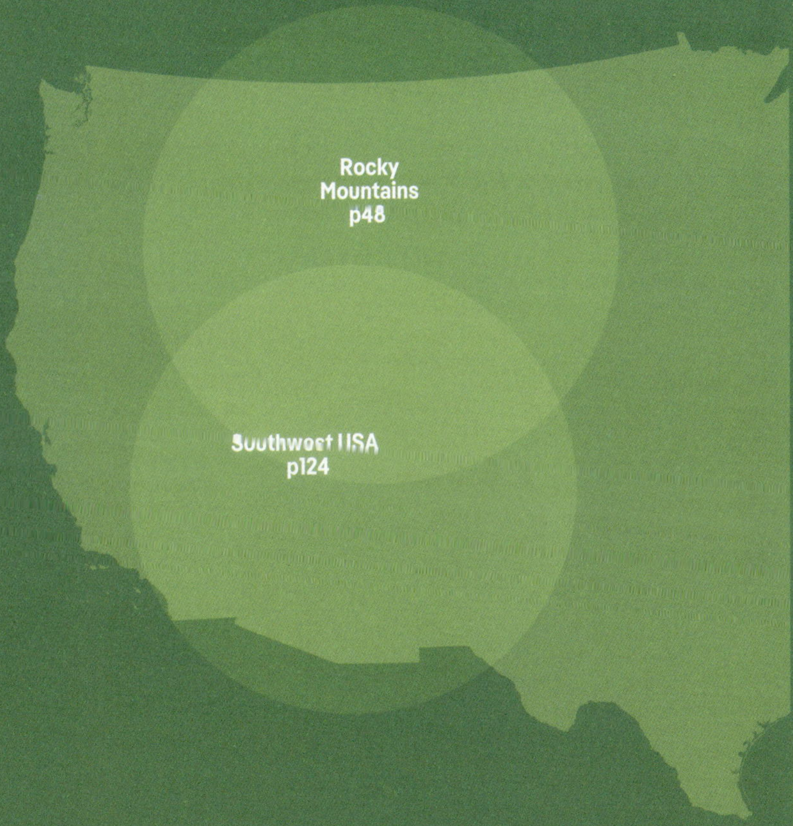

Bison, Yellowstone National Park (p92)

THEBROOKEMARK/SHUTTERSTOCK

Researched and curated by Liza Prado

Rocky Mountains

EPIC BEAUTY MEETS OUTDOOR ADVENTURE

A four-state wonderland of mountains, rivers and alpine forests, renowned for outdoor adventuring and rich in history, arts, small-town life and urban centers.

Welcome to the Rocky Mountains, where the Great Plains meet the rugged backbone of the continent. It's a vast region, rife with towering peaks and glacial lakes, dense forests and rushing rivers. Also red-rock canyons and sand dunes, volcano-scapes and hot springs. It's a veritable playground for outdoors enthusiasts, with eight national parks and over 100 million acres of public land. World-class skiing? Check. Epic rafting and fly-fishing? Check. Hiking, climbing and mountain biking? Check, check, check. The ways and places to get an adrenaline rush are nearly endless.

But there's more to the Rockies than the outdoors. History is visible everywhere – cliff dwellings, battlefields, ghost towns and trading posts turned forts...even some of the world's best dinosaur sites. Collectively, they tell the multilayered history of the West: one of survival and conflict, fortune-seeking and possibility.

And the Rocky Mountain region continues to evolve. Today, it has a wealth of terrific cities, from Denver to Boulder, Missoula to Boise, each with engaging museums and performing arts, plus nightlife, craft breweries and culinary excellence (hello Michelin stars). Prefer something smaller? Check out historic towns turned glitzy destinations like Aspen, Jackson and Ketchum.

To visit the Rocky Mountains is to have at your fingertips spectacular landscapes, rich history, and thriving urban and small town life – the hard part is deciding where to go.

HARRY HAYASHI/SHUTTERSTOCK

THE MAIN AREAS

COLORADO
Year-round outdoors options and great cities. p54

WYOMING
Yellowstone, Indigenous sites and rural life. p83

MONTANA
Mountains, rivers and a youthful vibe. p97

IDAHO
Underrated destination with stunning landscapes. p111

For places to stay in the Rocky Mountains, see p122

YEGOROV/SHUTTERSTOCK

Bison, Yellowstone National Park (p92)

Find Your Way

The Rocky Mountain states cover a vast and varied region, extending 1100 miles from the towering sand dunes of southern Colorado to the stunning glacial-carved peaks of northern Montana. The Rocky Mountains themselves are the backbone of it all.

Idaho, p111

A secret stash of stunning landscapes, with evocative names like Sawtooth Mountains and Craters of the Moon, plus charming towns like Boise and Ketchum.

Wyoming, p83

A place of contrasts, from the captivating beauty of Yellowstone and Grand Tetons to stark high plains, windblown towns and compelling Indigenous sites.

CAR

To fully explore the region, you'll need a car. It'll give you freedom to stop in small towns, explore national parks and forests, tour archaeological zones, and access trailheads and ski resorts, all at your own pace. In winter, consider a 4WD vehicle.

BUS

Bus service is limited. Greyhound travels between the bigger cities in the Rocky Mountain region (and beyond), while smaller companies like Bustang, Jefferson Lines and Salt Lake Express provide service to a handful of small towns in each state.

PLANE

Flying within the region cuts down your travel time tremendously – a plus if you're short on time or hate long-haul drives. Denver has the only major international airport in the Rocky Mountain region, but there are several small airports scattered around each state.

Montana, p97

Everything here is big – the mountains, rivers, even the skies. Glacier National Park is a must-see, while Missoula and Bozeman have a fun college-town feel.

Colorado, p54

The true one-stop shop of the Rocky Mountains, with remarkable all-season outdoors options, rich historical sites and modern cities, all within easy reach.

Plan Your Time

Travel options vary immensely by season, and few top attractions are available year-round. Decide on the main thing you want to do – hiking, skiing or visiting archaeological or dino sites – and base your trip around that.

VOLKY/SHUTTERSTOCK

Old Faithful (p92), Yellowstone National Park

Pressed for Time

- Head straight to the country's first national park: **Yellowstone** (p92), known for its otherworldly geothermal features and wildlife. Start at **Old Faithful** (p92), the park's famously reliable geyser, before taking in the other gushing geysers and smoke-belching fumaroles that dot **Geyser Country** (p92). Don't miss the **Tribal Heritage Center** (p93) to learn more about local tribes and their ancestral connections to the park. Later, check out the astounding views of thundering falls through the **Grand Canyon of the Yellowstone** (p93) – **Artist Point** (p93) is a must see.

- Around dusk, look for bison, elk and other big wildlife in the **Lamar Valley** (p93). If you have another day, drive to Cody's **Buffalo Bill Center of the West** (p90), a remarkable complex of museums all about the West.

SEASONAL HIGHLIGHTS

Winter is ski and snow season, while spring is muddy and green. Summer is best for hiking, especially with the appearance of wildflowers. Fall brings golden colors and cooler weather.

JANUARY

Winter storms dump powder across the Rockies, and ski season is in full gear. Head to resorts like **Vail**, **Sun Valley** and **Big Sky**. If you're in Denver, stop in the **National Western Stock Show** (p60).

MARCH

Treefort Music Fest (p113) takes over Boise, showcasing hundreds of indie bands and the city's artsy spirit. In Jackson's **National Elk Refuge** (p91), take a sleigh-ride to observe one of the largest elk herds on the continent.

JUNE

Telluride Bluegrass Festival (p77) kicks off summer along with **PrideFest** in Denver and **Eastern Shoshone Indian Days** (p87), Wyoming's largest powwow. Drives along **Trail Ridge Rd** (p65) and **Going-to-the-Sun Rd** (p106) open.

A Weeklong Road Trip

● With some room to breathe, start in **Mesa Verde National Park** (p74), known for its impressive cliff dwellings, and take a ranger-led tour – prepare to climb ladders and crawl through tunnels. Next drive to **Telluride** (p77), a charming mountain town tucked into a box canyon, and hike to Colorado's tallest waterfall, **Bridal Veil Falls** (p77).

● Bright and early, straight-shot it to **Black Canyon of the Gunnison National Park** (p78) for the spectacular canyon vistas along South Rim Rd. From there, drive to **Dinosaur National Monument** (p79), making sure to see the Quarry Wall, with some 1500 dino bones embedded in it. Next, spend time in **Grand Teton National Park** (p96), taking in its jagged peaks and shimmering lakes before ending your trip in **Yellowstone** (p92).

Two Weeks to Travel Around

● Begin your Rocky Mountain odyssey in **Denver** (p58), soaking in its urban energy. From there, head to **Rocky Mountain National Park** (p64) for epic hiking on alpine trails and wildflower-filled meadows. Take **Trail Ridge Rd** (p65) through the park before crossing into Wyoming.

● Continue to cowboy chic **Jackson**, making time to visit **National Museum of Wildlife Art** (p91) before exploring the majestic **Grand Teton National Park** (p96). Drive into Idaho though the gorgeous **Teton Valley** to the volcanic landscapes of **Craters of the Moon** (p120). From there, cross into Montana – big sky country – stopping at the vibrant **Missoula People's Market** (p105) before exploring **Glacier National Park** (p106) on foot, wheels or boat. Wrap up your trip at iconic **Yellowstone** (p92).

JULY

Crested Butte's **Wildflower Festival** (p72), Cheyenne's **Frontier Days** (p85) and **Sun Valley Music Festival** (p118). The mountains fill with hikers and campers, and paddlers take on the rivers.

SEPTEMBER

Cooler days begin and crowds disperse – a good time to visit national parks like **Yellowstone** (p92), **Glacier** (p106) and **Mesa Verde**. Listen for the bugling elks in **Rocky Mountain National Park** (p64).

OCTOBER

Aspen paints the region in brilliant yellows; **Grand Teton National Park** (p96) and **Million Dollar Hwy** are beautiful. **Colorado National Monument** (p80) and **Craters of the Moon** (p120) cool off, optimal for outdoor adventure.

DECEMBER

Powder hounds hit the slopes, though the snow can be hit or miss (discounted lift tickets make up for it). Hot springs like **Strawberry Park** (p67) and **Ouray** (p76) provide an easy way to warm up.

Colorado

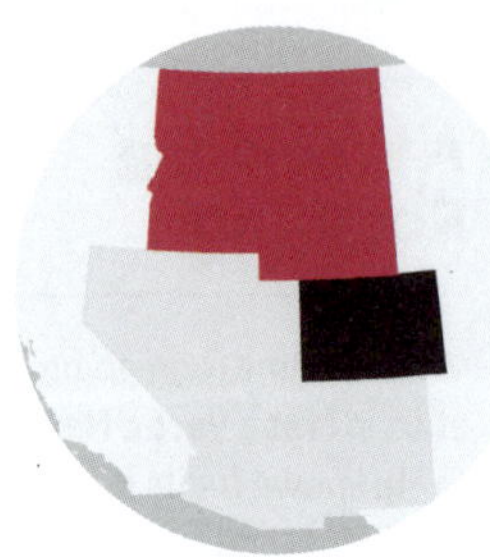

EPIC LANDSCAPES | URBAN ENERGY | SPORTS

Places

Colorado is a place of striking contrasts and seemingly endless adventure. Towering peaks, red-rock canyons, dense forests and surreal sand dunes make for a landscape that's as diverse as it is beautiful. In winter, world-renowned ski resorts like Aspen and Vail draw powder hounds from near and far, while summer brings hikers and mountain bikers to alpine trails and meadows awash in wildflowers. Off trail, you can unwind in natural hot springs or explore ancient cliff dwellings at Mesa Verde National Park. Add to all that the creative energy of cities like Denver and Boulder – with their vibrant food and craft-beer scenes, street art and museums – and the mountain chic of historic mining towns, and you've got a destination that blends outdoor adventure, layered history, cultural depth and laid-back urban cool. All that under big, bluebird skies.

TOP TIP

Altitude sickness is a real thing in Colorado. Stay hydrated, take it easy and allow a few days to acclimatize. A little light-headedness, slight headaches and sluggishness are normal. But if you experience severe and continued nausea, headache and dizziness, consult a doctor and/or get to lower altitudes.

GETTING AROUND

Most visitors arrive through **Denver International Airport** (DIA) though regional airports dot Colorado. **Bustang** *(ridebustang.com)* provides bus service to towns along the I-70 and I-25 corridors, as well as harder-to-reach destinations like Telluride and Crested Butte. To explore further, a car is essential. City roads and highways are paved and generally well maintained; smaller mountain towns often have dirt or gravel roads. A 4WD vehicle is helpful in winter, especially on icy roads. Some mountain passes close seasonally or when driving conditions are hazardous. Before heading out, check **Colorado Department of Transportation** *(codot.gov/travel)* for road closures and weather warnings.

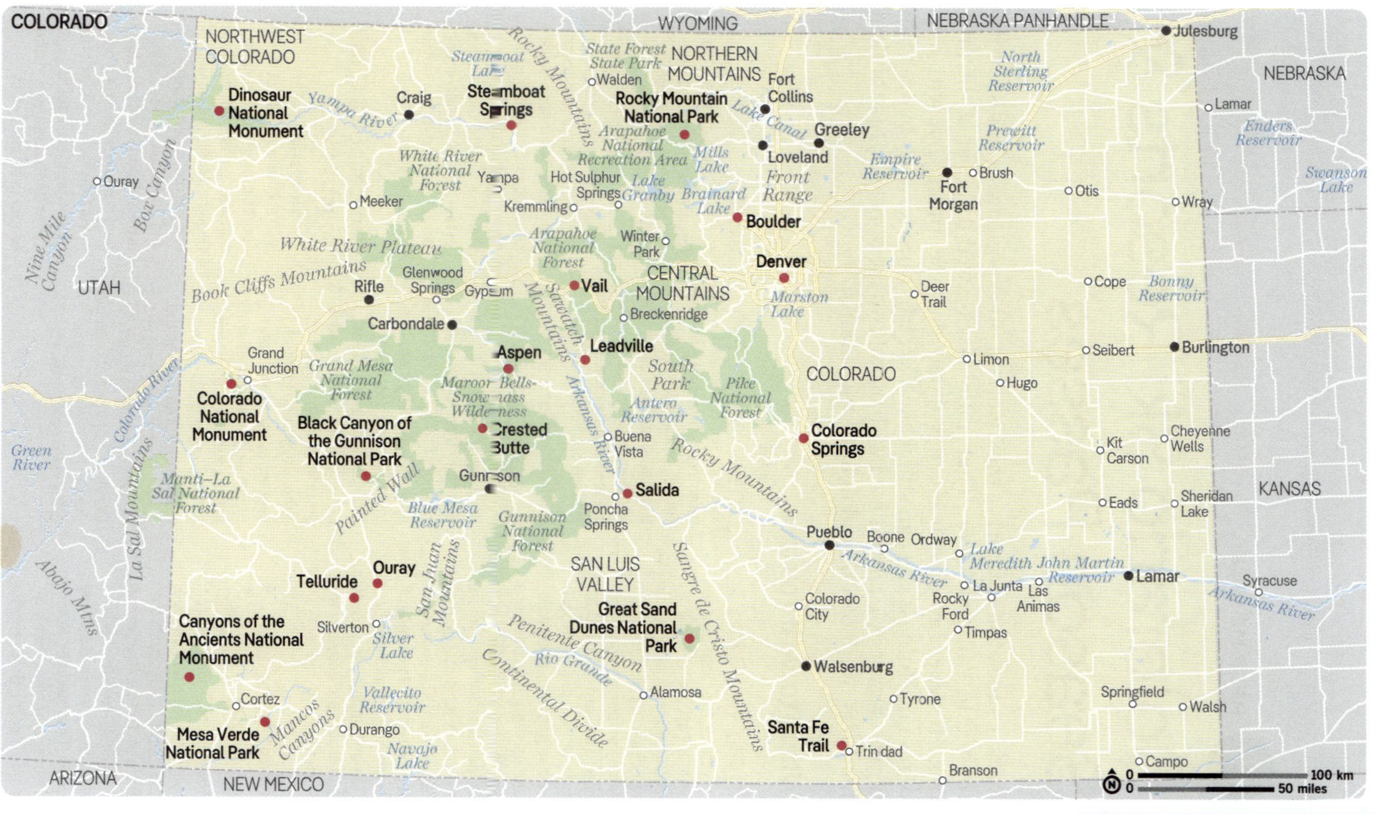
COLORADO
WYOMING
NEBRASKA PANHANDLE
NEBRASKA
KANSAS
UTAH
ARIZONA
NEW MEXICO
NORTHWEST COLORADO
NORTHERN MOUNTAINS
CENTRAL MOUNTAINS
SAN LUIS VALLEY
Dinosaur National Monument
Craig
Steamboat Springs
Rocky Mountain National Park
Fort Collins
Loveland
Greeley
Boulder
Denver
Vail
Leadville
Aspen
Crested Butte
Gunnison
Salida
Colorado Springs
Pueblo
Colorado National Monument
Black Canyon of the Gunnison National Park
Telluride
Ouray
Canyons of the Ancients National Monument
Mesa Verde National Park
Great Sand Dunes National Park
Walsenburg
Santa Fe Trail
Trinidad
Lamar
Burlington
Julesburg
Fort Morgan
Brush
Otis
Wray
Cope
Seibert
Limon
Hugo
Deer Trail
Kit Carson
Cheyenne Wells
Eads
Sheridan Lake
Boone
Ordway
La Junta
Las Animas
Rocky Ford
Timpas
Colorado City
Tyrone
Branson
Springfield
Walsh
Campo
Syracuse
Walden
Yampa
Meeker
Kremmling
Hot Sulphur Springs
Winter Park
Breckenridge
Rifle
Glenwood Springs
Gypsum
Carbondale
Grand Junction
Buena Vista
Poncha Springs
Alamosa
Silverton
Cortez
Durango
Ouray
Lamar
Rocky Mountains
Book Cliffs Mountains
White River Plateau
Sawatch Mountains
South Park
San Juan Mountains
Sangre de Cristo Mountains
Continental Divide
Penitente Canyon
Painted Wall
La Sal Mountains
Abajo Mtns
Nine Mile Canyon
Box Canyon
Mancos Canyons
Front Range
Yampa River
Arkansas River
Colorado River
Rio Grande
Green River
Steamboat Lake
State Forest State Park
Arapahoe National Recreation Area
Arapahoe National Forest
White River National Forest
Grand Mesa National Forest
Maroon Bells-Snowmass Wilderness
Gunnison National Forest
Pike National Forest
Manti–La Sal National Forest
Lake Canal
Mills Lake
Lake Granby
Brainard Lake
Marston Lake
Antero Reservoir
Blue Mesa Reservoir
Silver Lake
Vallecito Reservoir
Navajo Lake
Empire Reservoir
Prewitt Reservoir
North Sterling Reservoir
Bonny Reservoir
Lake Meredith
John Martin Reservoir
Enders Reservoir
Swanson Lake
0 100 km
0 50 miles

HELP ME PICK:

Colorado Ski Resorts & Season Passes

Sticker shock is a big part of the Colorado ski experience, and it's not just limited to Vail and Aspen. That initial slack-jawed disbelief at the price of a lift ticket can quickly change to outright resentment, but with a bit of resourcefulness you can still make a ski trip work for your budget. The biggest resorts are all affiliated with one of two mega-passes, Epic or Ikon, but don't overlook Colorado's indie mountains.

Where to ski if you love...

Family Vacations

Keystone, Breckenridge and Winter Park are all great destinations for kids, but they're not cheap for an out-of-state family of four: you can easily spend upwards of $10,000 for a week in high season. If you've got young kids who are still learning, consider a smaller resort like Ski Cooper, Monarch or Sunlight, where the prices for rental gear, lessons and accommodation are considerably cheaper. Howelsen Hill in Steamboat is free on Sundays, and Loveland and Eldora are easy day trips from the Front Range.

Great Skiing with Convenient Access

The resorts along I-70 are the largest in the state and are the easiest to access from Denver. You can't go wrong here: the peaks are high, the terrain is varied and the snow is featherlight. Summit County alone has four big-name resorts: Breckenridge, Keystone, Copper Mountain and A-Basin. Winter Park's turnoff is before the Eisenhower Tunnel, which sometimes translates into less traffic. Vail and Beaver Creek are the jewels in the interstate crown, but are located on the other side of Vail Pass.

Small Towns

If you want shorter lift lines and more throwback charm, consider basing yourself in an out-of-the-way mountain town. Crested Butte is a fabulous hideaway tucked behind Aspen. Steamboat is more upscale, but also has a remote enough location to keep away the crowds and preserve its Western charm. In the southwest, the steeps at Telluride and Silverton make experts go weak in the knees, but require flying into regional airports in Montrose or Durango. For more accessible terrain, head to Durango's offbeat Purgatory resort.

Aspen

And then there's Aspen. With its celebrity glitter, historic downtown and some of the best scenery in the state, Aspen is a terrific choice for those with an expense account. One lift ticket grants access to the Four Mountains: Aspen, Snowmass, Buttermilk and Aspen Highlands. There's plenty of upside-down-steep terrain here, X Games–level terrain parks, plus top-notch kids' amenities.

Backcountry & Cross-Country Skiing

If you love skiing but are less enthusiastic about the sport's corporate turn, then consider cross-country skiing. Groomed trails are found in most mountain towns, and day passes can cost as little as $30. Going into the backcountry, either on a day trip or via Colorado's backcountry hut system, is a magical opportunity, but training and proper gear are a must.

STEVE BOICE/SHUTTERSTOCK

Vail (p67)

HOW TO

Don't overlook independent resorts like Telluride, Silverton, Wolf Creek, Monarch and Loveland, which also offer incredible skiing and deep powder.

Save money by packing a picnic. It sounds obvious, but the number of people who pay outrageous prices for cafeteria food is astounding.

Want first tracks in backcountry glades after a big storm? Go snowcat skiing at Purgatory, Steamboat, Shrine Pass, Jones Pass, Aspen, Monarch or Loveland.

Got the itch for steep lines and an 'I can't believe this is real' backdrop? Fork out for heli skiing in Silverton or Telluride.

Ikon Pass Versus Epic Pass

There has been a tremendous amount of corporate consolidation in the US ski industry, and the biggest names are now all affiliated with one of two season passes: Ikon or Epic. Don't get confused by the word 'season' – these passes are fully customizable, from one day to unlimited, and from a handful of local hills to the whole hog, including destinations scattered around the world. If you're headed to a big resort, getting a pass in advance – the best deals are offered in spring for the following year – will save you money and allow you the luxury of skiing in more than one place. Passes also come with perks, like discounted tickets for friends and family.

Ikon *(ikonpass.com; four-day/base/full $479/969/1359)* offers access to Winter Park, Copper, Steamboat, Eldora, A-Basin and Aspen in Colorado. Other destinations range from Big Sky (Montana) to Alta and Snowbird (Utah), and Jackson Hole (Wyoming) to Chamonix (France). The Winter Park local passes *(midweek/full $559/749)* are a cheaper option.

Epic *(epicpass.com; four-day/local/full $423/762/1025)* offers access to Vail, Breckenridge, Keystone, Beaver Creek and Crested Butte in Colorado. Other destinations include Whistler (Canada), Park City (Utah), and Heavenly, Northstar and Kirkwood at Lake Tahoe. If you're looking for a more targeted pass, consider the Summit Value Pass *(Breckenridge and Keystone $615)* or Keystone Plus *(Keystone plus five days at Crested Butte $408)*.

THE MARADE

Denver's **Marade** – part march, part parade – is a huge, joyous, serious, welcoming, historic, and thoroughly Denver event. It's the largest Martin Luther King Jr Day celebration in the country, bringing together tens of thousands of Denverites to celebrate the life of Dr King and continue his fight for social justice. It's a massive outpouring of local people – students, elders, politicians, artists, workers, families with strollers, and activists with bullhorns – joining and chanting to manifest a better world. (Even when it's snowing, which it often does in January.) Marchers gather at the Dr King statue in City Park (p60) and march down Colfax Ave to **Civic Center Park** for rousing speeches.

Denver

Tony venues and train tickets

An iconic landmark, the Beaux-Art style **Union Station** *(denverunionstation.com; free)* opened its doors in 1914 and has served as Denver's transportation hub ever since. But it's way more than that. Wander through the Great Hall, with soaring ceilings, chandeliers and cozy leather couches; lively bars and cocktail lounges line the walls alongside ice-cream shops and bookstores. Or indulge yourself at one of the swanky restaurants – including **Mercantile** *(mercantiledenver.com)* and **Ultreia** *(ultreiadenver.com)*, brainchildren of James Beard Award–winning chefs. Or stay overnight at one of Denver's best hotels, **The Crawford** *(thecrawfordhotel.com)*. In summer, come for its outdoor plaza, where you can peruse its popular **Saturday farmers market**, while its **pop-up fountain** entices kids (and kids at heart) to play in the urban sprinklers.

World-class performances

Come to the **Denver Performing Arts Complex** *(artscomplex.com; prices vary)*, where you can score tickets almost nightly. Across four city blocks, you'll find 10 venues connected by a sky-high glass canopy, among them the historic **Ellie Caulkins Opera House** (aka 'the Ellie'), a luxe 2200-seat theater where Opera Colorado and Colorado Ballet perform. Or head to the magnificent **Boettcher Concert Hall**, the nation's first concert-hall-in-the-round, where the **Colorado Symphony** plays classics as well as modern-day crowd-pleasers. The Arts Complex's theater wing, the similarly named **Denver Center for the Performing Arts** (called 'The DCPA'), has eight venues staging everything from experimental productions to Broadway musicals. If you're a theater junkie, take a **behind-the-scenes theater tour** *(per person $12)* with stops in dressing rooms, design studios and costume shops. Purchase tickets online for big discounts, sometimes starting at just $10 per ticket for kids, students and seniors.

Have fun in Confluence Park

Named for the meeting of the South Platte River and Cherry Creek, **Confluence Park** is a pocket of outdoorsy activity in downtown Denver. Picnic on its terraced lawns, jog along the waterfront, or just sun and splash on the park's small sandy beach. In the summer, rent inner tubes and kayaks to ride on a fun human-made stretch of white water. Rentals available at **Confluence Kayaks** *(confluencekayaks.com; per day from $55)*.

Catch a ball (game)

Coors Field *(mlb.com/rockies/ballpark)* is one of the MLB's most home-run-friendly ballparks (apparently, it's the thin air), and catching a **Rockies** game *(mlb.com/rockies; adult/child from $4/1)* is easy with 80 home games and tickets starting at just $1 in the Rockpile (aka centerfield). Theme nights include freebies like trucker hats and commemorative cups; come decked out in your purple, black and silver best to fit right in. Die-hard fan? **Stadium tours** *(adult/child $27/10)* run 70 to 80 minutes and include the field, clubhouses and mile-high seats.

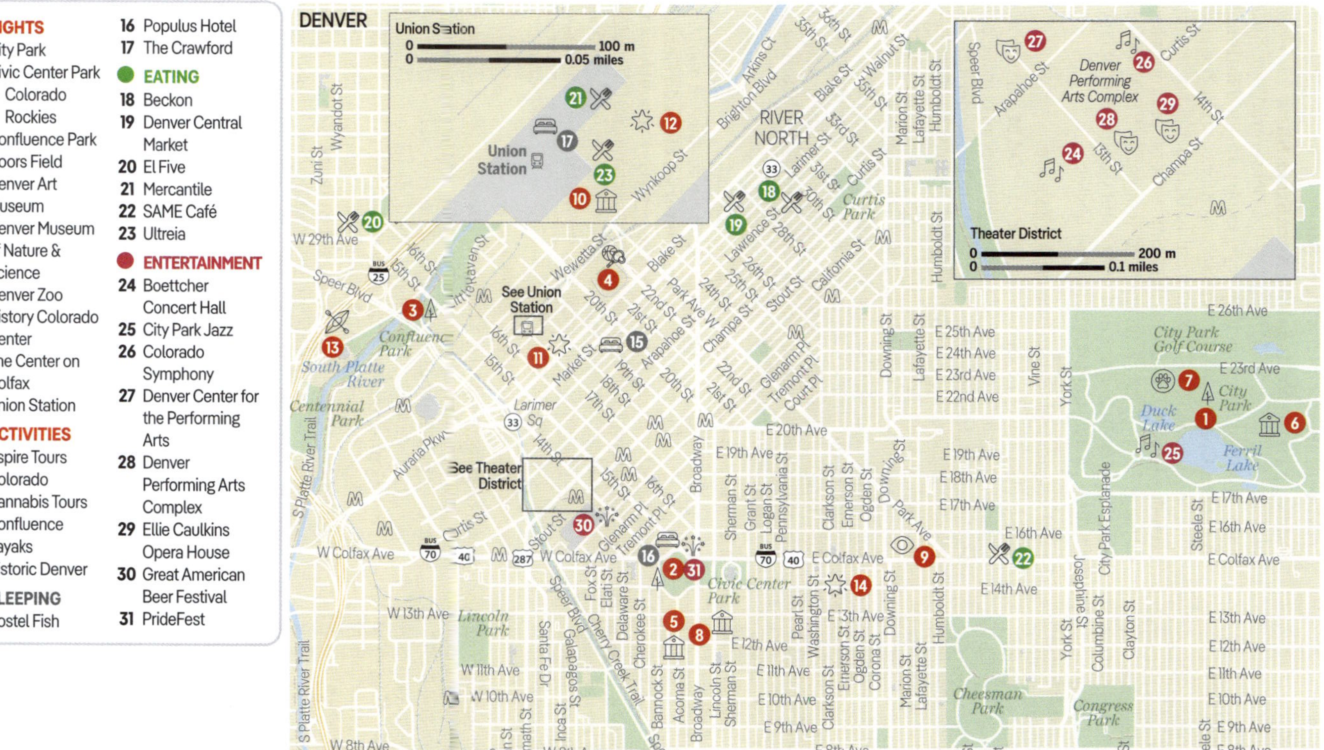

SIGHTS

1 City Park
2 Civic Center Park
see 4 Colorado Rockies
3 Confluence Park
4 Coors Field
5 Denver Art Museum
6 Denver Museum of Nature & Science
7 Denver Zoo
8 History Colorado Center
9 The Center on Colfax
10 Union Station

ACTIVITIES

11 Aspire Tours
12 Colorado Cannabis Tours
13 Confluence Kayaks
14 Historic Denver

SLEEPING

15 Hostel Fish
16 Populus Hotel
17 The Crawford

EATING

18 Beckon
19 Denver Central Market
20 El Five
21 Mercantile
22 SAME Café
23 Ultreia

ENTERTAINMENT

24 Boettcher Concert Hall
25 City Park Jazz
26 Colorado Symphony
27 Denver Center for the Performing Arts
28 Denver Performing Arts Complex
29 Ellie Caulkins Opera House
30 Great American Beer Festival
31 PrideFest

THE CENTER

Established in 1976, **The Center on Colfax** *(lgbtqcolorado.org)*, called simply 'the Center,' is the largest LGBTIQ+ community center in the Rocky Mountain region. A vital hub for support, advocacy and education, its support services span from youth (Rainbow Alley) to elder (Sage of the Rockies) and transgender programming. It's a good resource for LGBTIQ+ travelers too. Health services (including HIV testing and prevention), counseling and legal referrals are freely given. Or come for a drop-in event – watch parties, cooking classes and yoga are regularly offered. The Center also hosts the must-experience Denver's annual **PrideFest** *(denverpride.org)*, one of the largest and most festive LGBTIQ+ pride events in the US.

Sport your stetson at the Stock Show

Saddle up for the **National Western Stock Show** *(nationalwestern.com; adult/child from $17/4)*, a Denver tradition since 1906. A 16-day event held every January in the **National Western Center** *(nationalwesterncenter.com)*, it includes 20 or more rodeos, 15,000 farm animals, dancing horses and even dog shows. Don't miss the iconic kick-off parade, when dozens of Longhorn cattle are herded down 17th St in downtown Denver, high heels and power suits giving way to cowboy hats, chaps and impressive belt buckles.

Take in masterpieces at Denver Art Museum

The crown jewel of Denver's art scene, **DAM** *(denverartmuseum.org; adult/child $27-30/free)* houses an eclectic collection of art, from Old Master painters to the modern greats. It's also home to a stunningly rich collection of Native American art, one of the world's largest. Special exhibitions keep the museum buzzing year-round and interactive art stations keep kids engaged. Choose a few exhibits to see and wander the rest of the time – it's a massive museum spread between the Hamilton Building, a work of modern angular art, and the Martin Building, a fortress-like structure glittering in over a million reflective tiles.

All about the Centennial State

Learn all about the Centennial State, from ancient to modern times, at the state-of the-art **History Colorado Center** *(historycolorado.org; adult/child $15/free)*. Thoughtful and ever-changing exhibits present the spectrum of Coloradan voices. If time permits, fold some of the museum's excellent programming into your visit – a city walking tour, archaeological dig, a lecture and more.

Cornucopia of activity at City Park

City Park is the largest of Denver's open spaces, a 320-acre megapark just east of downtown. Stretch your legs on its leafy **trails** or **paddleboat** *(wheelfunrentals.com; adult/child per hour $12/7)* on its lakes. Or bring the kids to run wild on its sprawling **playgrounds** and **splash pads** or to check out the creatures at **Denver Zoo** *(denverzoo.org; adult/child $25/19)*. The **Denver Museum of Nature & Science** *(DMNS, dmns.org; adult/child $26/21)* is another family fave. From spring to fall, a weekly **farmers market** *(cityparkfarmersmarket.com)* brings a festival-like atmosphere, with live music, food

EATING IN DENVER: OUR PICKS

SAME Café: Pay-what-you-can, fair-exchange cafe serving ever-changing menu of healthy dishes, including vegetarian options. Walk-in volunteers welcome. *11am-2:30pm Mon-Fri* **$**

Denver Central Market: Warehouse turned gourmet marketplace, this food hall wows with its style and meal options. *8am-9pm Sun-Thu, to 11pm Fri & Sat* **$-$$**

El Five: Mediterranean-style tapas and floor-to-ceiling city views. Summer nights bring patio seating. *5-10pm Sun-Thu, to 11pm Fri & Sat* **$$**

Beckon: Intimate Michelin-starred restaurant with sumptuous, ever-changing Scandinavian-inspired menu. Prepayment required. *5-10pm Wed-Sat* **$$$**

JAY YUAN/SHUTTERSTOCK

Red Rocks Amphitheater

trucks and all manner of picnic fixin's. Summer nights also brings thousands for free **jazz concerts** *(cityparkjazz.org)*. And, that view! Skyscrapers with snowcapped mountains in the background…the icing on City Park's multilayered cake.

Experience a giant beer fest

Colorado takes its beer seriously, and with over 150 breweries in metro Denver, you certainly won't go thirsty. If you're visiting in late September/early October, try scoring tickets to the **Great American Beer Festival** *(greatamericanbeerfestival.com; from $85)*, the largest beer festival in the US. It draws over 2000 master brewers, with over 9000 beers vying for Best of Show medals in 263 categories. General admission includes unlimited 1oz tastings; pairings – small dishes created by lauded chefs – with a menu of beers are also offered. Best of all is the comradery of you and 40,000 beer buddies, all tasting outstanding brews one ounce at a time.

Be wowed by RiNo's murals

Unexpected and totally fabulous, the trendy RiNo neighborhood is draped in hundreds of murals. Bright, opinionated and ever-changing, the artwork stops you in your tracks, speaking to Denver's diversity, history and day-to-day musings. Wander the neighborhood to take them in, using **RiNo's website** *(rinoartdistrict.org/art/murals)* to find local faves. Or take a guided tour with **Denver Graffiti Tour** *(denvergraffititour.com; adult/child $30/15)*, known for its small groups and custom tours.

Catch a concert at Red Rocks Amphitheater

There's something almost primal about attending a concert at **Red Rocks Amphitheater** *(redrocksonline.com)* – the sounds of instruments enveloping you, the sight of people dancing under an umbrella of stars and the iconic 300ft-high red sandstone monoliths standing guard on either side. For many, it's reason enough for a trip to Colorado. Renowned for its natural acoustics and stunning beauty, Red Rocks is

BEST TOURS: DENVER & AROUND

Historic Denver: Denver's preservation society offers 90-minute docent-led tours *(historicdenver.org)* of the city's oldest neighborhoods.

Denver Microbrew Tours: Knowledgeable guides lead 2½-hour tours *(denvermicrobrewtour.com)* of award-winning breweries in LoDo and RiNo, tasting at least 10 brews.

Local Table Tours: Guided walking tours *(localtabletours.com)* cover some of Denver's top restaurants, integrating drink pairings and neighborhood history.

Colorado Cannabis Tours: Party-bus tours *(coloradocannabistours.com)* from two to 3½ hours, including grow operations and dispensaries.

Aspire Tours: Half- and full-day driving tours *(aspire-tours.com)* of Denver and surrounding areas, including sightseeing and hiking stops.

OPEN SPACE IS NO ACCIDENT

Boulder's unique and vast swathe of undeveloped land started back in 1898 when the city helped purchase the plot that became Chautauqua Park. In 1907 the government floated a public bond to buy Flagstaff Mountain, and in 1912 purchased 1200 more pristine mountain acres. Then, in 1967, Boulder voters legislated their love of the land by approving a sales tax specifically to buy, manage and maintain open space. This was historic. No other US city had ever voted to tax themselves specifically for open space and Boulder's Open Space and Mountain Parks *(osmp.org)* office was launched. In 1989 76% of voters increased the tax by nearly 100%; today the OSMP protects over 46,000 acres of land, criss-crossed with 155 miles of hiking trails.

synonymous with big-ticket concerts of all genres, even symphony orchestras. If a show isn't in the cards, the venue and its surrounding 816 acres are free to visit during the day. The amphitheater also regularly hosts events like early morning **yoga** *(per person $20)* and **movie nights** *(per person $20).*

The footprints of giants

The discovery site of the first stegosaur, **Dinosaur Ridge** *(dinoridge.org; free)* also has some of the world's best preserved dinosaur tracks and fossils. Sandwiched between Hwy 470 and Red Rocks Amphitheater, the exposed rock surfaces here reveal over 250 dinosaur footprints and sandstone-encased fossils dating to the Jurassic and Cretaceous periods. A steep, paved **interpretive trail** (2.2-mile round trip) leads through the site, signage providing insight into the behavior, movement and tropical environment of the dinosaurs that once roamed here. A **self-guided audio tour** *($8)* can be downloaded at the Visitors Center. Or take a 45-minute **bus tour** *(adult/child $20/14),* which includes three stops and a cheery guide.

Boulder

Shopping around Pearl St

Pearl Street Mall is the heart of downtown Boulder, a tree-shaded pedestrian zone filled with kids' climbing boulders and splash fountains, and lined with shops and galleries. People-watching aside, shopping is Pearl's raison d'être. Outdoor wear figures large with everybody from Italy's **La Sportiva** and Japan's **Montbell** to North American brands like **Patagonia**, **North Face** and **Black Diamond**. But it's not all ultralight puffies. Vintage shops like **Apocalypse** and **Heady Bauer** have a definite disco-hippie Boulder vibe, while trendy boutiques like **Bliss** and **Jones + Company** are a fun browse. Whatever you do, don't miss **Piece, Love & Chocolate** at the west end of Pearl St, a perfect place to relax with a decadent chocolate truffle.

Culture at Dairy Arts Center

The top cultural hub in town is the **Dairy Arts Center** *(thedairy.org),* a historic milk-processing factory turned arts center. It's a state-of-the-art facility with three stages, four gallery spaces and a 60-seat cinema. There's always something going on, from film screenings and plays to modern dance and art exhibits. The exhibits are always free.

EATING IN BOULDER: OUR PICKS

Mountain Sun: The town's favorite brewery is as Boulder as it gets. Great burgers, chili and brews, like Annapurna Amber. *noon-11pm Wed-Sun* $

Rosetta Hall: A sophisticated food hall, serving everything from falafel to green papaya salad to empanadas. Rooftop bar too. *8am-11pm* $$

Leaf: An ethical and elegant kitchen that serves meat-free gems, using ingredients grown at the restaurant's organic farm in nearby Lafayette. *11:30am-9pm* $$

Frasca: James Beard, Michelin and others have all named the northern Italian cuisine here as Boulder's finest. Prix-fixe menus only; reserve well ahead. *5-9pm* $$$

SIGHTS
1 Pearl Street Mall

SLEEPING
2 St Julien Hotel & Spa

EATING
3 Boulder County Farmers Market
4 Frasca
5 Leaf
6 Mountain Sun
7 Rosetta Hall

SHOPPING
8 Apocalypse
9 Black Diamond
10 Bliss
11 Heady Bauer
12 Jones + Company
13 La Sportiva
14 Montbell
15 North Face
16 Patagonia
17 Piece, Love & Chocolate

B-DUB IN KC/SHUTTERSTOCK

Lake of Glass

TOP EXPERIENCE

Rocky Mountain National Park

Colorado's crown jewel, Rocky Mountain National Park (RMNP) encompasses 415 sq miles of granite mountain top, alpine lake, wildflower-filled meadow, star-filled nights, and adventures large and small. Summer brings big-time crowds, but leave the main trailheads behind and you'll quickly find your own patch of solitude, so long as you're willing to share it with the wildlife that calls this place home.

DON'T MISS

- Trail Ridge Rd
- Kawuneeche Valley
- Lake of Glass hike
- Wild Basin Trailhead
- Moraine Park Discovery Center

Bear Lake Hiking

The **Bear Lake** and **Glacier Gorge Junction** trailheads are the most popular destinations in the park, and for good reason. From here you'll have a front-row vantage point of the dramatic glacial valleys and hulking granite summits that make Rocky Mountain such a singular landscape.

Hikes range from easy jaunts to **Alberta Falls** (1.6 miles) or **Dream Lake** (2.2 miles) and **Emerald Lake** (3.6 miles)

PRACTICALITIES

● nps.gov/romo ● per vehicle $30 ● 24hr

to more challenging excursions that follow the glacial valleys up to their origins. **Mills Lake** (5.6 miles) is a good choice, as is the **Loch** (6.2 miles), which can be extended to the exquisite **Lake of Glass** and **Sky Pond** (9.8 miles). And while **Flattop Mountain** (12,324ft, 8.8 miles) may not be the park's best summit, there's no denying its magnetic pull from down below. Note: in summer, the Bear Lake Corridor requires a special entry reservation between 5am and 6pm – buy early.

Wildlife Watching

RMNP is home to some 800 elk, 350 bighorn sheep, 60 moose, 20 to 30 bears, an unknown number of mountain lions and countless mule deer – and those are just the big guys. Smaller critters include beavers, marmots, pikas, porcupines, otters, foxes, coyotes and some 270 species of birds. While you probably won't spot the more elusive animals, if you pay attention, you'll likely see or hear traces of their passage. Good places to look for wildlife include **Moraine Park** (start with its excellent **Discovery Center**), **Beaver Meadows**, **Sheep Lakes**, **Trail Ridge Rd** and the marshy areas in the **Kawuneeche Valley**.

Driving Trail Ridge Road

The highest continuous paved highway in North America, Trail Ridge Rd is a remarkable 4000ft climb, offering visitors the chance to experience the Rockies' high-alpine tundra, complete with bighorn sheep, whistling marmots and eye-squinting panoramas in all directions. You can start in the east or west entrances of the park, make it a through trip or an out-and-back adventure, use it as a springboard for high-altitude hikes, or simply content yourself with a dozen superlative-worthy view points. In July, the lichen-covered boulders also light up with wildflowers. Among the can't-miss sights are the **Alpine Visitor Center** (11,796ft), which looks out over a hazy expanse of 400 sq miles, and the info-packed **Tundra Communities Trail**. Further west is the Continental Divide. Expect to spend a half-day exploring. Note: Trail Ridge Rd is only open from June through mid-October.

Rocky Mountain for Kids

The Park is an incredibly fun place for families to explore, though it may take some trial and error to find everyone's happy place. Budget time for special activities – horseback riding, a ropes course, ranger activities – to break up the monotony of driving around and posing for photos.

Don't miss the **Junior Ranger Headquarters** in Hidden Valley, which runs kids-themed programs throughout the day. A few family-friendly destinations in RMNP include Nymph and Dream Lakes (Bear Lake trailhead), Gem Lake (Lumpy Ridge Trailhead), MacGregor Ranch (adjacent to Lumpy Ridge), Eugenia Mine (Longs Peak Trailhead), Calypso Cascades (Wild Basin Trailhead), the Moraine Park Discovery Center (Bear Lake Rd), the Alpine Visitor Center (Trail Ridge Rd) and Lily Lake and Mountain (Hwy 7).

BEAR LAKE ALTERNATIVES

Couldn't score a coveted Bear Lake permit? Try these alternatives:

Fall River Area Hiking, bighorn-sheep spotting and a high-altitude drive.

Lumpy Ridge Trailhead Inspiring rambles among giant boulders and granite crags; Gem Lake (3.4 miles) is a favorite.

Wild Basin Trailhead Often overlooked, the southern corner of the park is chock-full of waterfalls.

Longs Peak Trailhead Variety of hikes from kid-friendly to the lung-busting peak.

TOP TIPS

- Timed entry tickets *(recreation.gov)* are required between late May and mid-October; buy your ticket on the first day of the month prior to your entry (ie May 1 for a June visit). Need a last-minute ticket? Reservations (40% of all available tickets) go on sale at 7pm for the following day.
- Most high-country trails are snowbound through late June; plan accordingly.
- Avoid encroaching on wildlife, for your safety and theirs. Stay at least 75ft away from elk and sheep, and 120ft away from moose and bears. And please, don't feed anything, no matter how cute it looks.

BOLDER BOULDER

Boulder's biggest party is, unsurprisingly, a 10km footrace held every Memorial Day, snow or shine. With more than 50,000 runners and pros mingling with costumed racers, live bands and sideline merrymakers, **Bolder Boulder** *(bolderboulder.com)* may be the most fun 10km run in the US. Course-side antics range from slip and slides and Elvis impersonators to red, white and blue paragliders spiraling down to the race's end at Folsom Field. Participants are divided into 100 waves, with wheelchairs going first, followed by the pros. Then come the walkers, elementary school kids and the costumed – eventually everyone makes it to the finish line. The latest addition to the race calendar is Colder Boulder, a 5km race in early December.

Hike in Chautauqua Park

Historic **Chautauqua Park** *(chautauqua.com)* is the gateway to Boulder's most magnificent swathe of open space: a wide-open prairie adjoining the iconic **Flatirons**, 1000ft red-rock slabs rising up out of the earth. It's a popular place for hikers, climbers and trail runners with 15 trails winding through the park.

No matter your destination, most people start on the **Chautauqua Trail** (1.5-mile loop), a relatively easy walk through a grassy meadow. If you're itching to go higher, the **Flatirons Loop Trail** (2.5 miles) leads you to the base of the First Flatiron, where climbers rope up for ascents; or do the full 700ft of elevation gain up to the top, following the trail as it zigzags up between the First and Second Flatirons. Want to go farther yet? The **Royal Arch Trail** (3.5 miles) has been a Boulder classic for over a century. This roughly 2½-hour trek leads you up to a natural arch past the Third Flatiron and has fantastic views. Expect to do some scrambling. The trails here connect to the rest of the city's open space via the long-distance **Mesa Trail**, giving you lots of options to customize your walk.

Founded in 1898 as part of the national Chautauqua Movement – an initiative aimed at adult education in rural settings – the park remains a cultural hub featuring historic cottages and dining hall as well as a 1300-seat auditorium that hosts world-class musicians, performers and speakers each summer. Plan ahead – events often sell out.

Parking is limited. On summer weekends and holidays, visitors are encouraged to take the free **Park-to-Park Shuttle** *(bouldercolorado.gov)*, which runs from downtown and satellite parking lots.

Farm fresh

The twice-weekly **Boulder County Farmers Market**, a block-long sprawl in front of the Dushanbe Teahouse, is a massive spring and summer bazaar of colorful, mostly organic 100% local food. Find flowers and herbs, as well as brain-sized mushrooms, delicate squash blossoms, crusty pretzels, vegan dips, grass-fed beef, raw granola and yogurt. Live music is as standard as the family picnics in the park along Boulder Creek. The Saturday market is a real community event, and it feels like the whole city comes out to socialize in the morning (8am-2pm). The Wednesday evening market (3:30-7:30pm) tends to be a little less busy, but it's still a notable midweek gathering place. In true Boulder style, all waste from the farmers market is recycled or composted. The market is closed in winter.

Steamboat Springs

Skiing Steamboat

Famous for its light and fluffy powder, **Steamboat Mountain Resort** *(steamboat.com; adult/child $285/230)* boasts stats that speak for themselves: 182 marked runs; 3668ft of vertical, and 3741 acres of terrain. While the summit tops out at 10,568ft, Steamboat makes up for its dearth of high-altitude steeps with super-fun tree slaloming runs. Serious skiers will also dig a number of mogul runs on the hill, and although

DAVID A LITMAN/SHUTTERSTOCK

Strawberry Park Hot Springs

these trails are a virtual factory of Olympic skiers and snowboarders, you don't have to be world class to enjoy them. Wide, well-groomed runs are ideal cruising for intermediate skiers, making this mountain among Colorado's best all-rounders, particularly for families. Throw in the cowboy-style charm and back-of-beyond location, and you have all the makings for a winter wonderland.

Steamboat's hot springs

Just 7 miles north of Steamboat, **Strawberry Park Hot Springs** *(strawberryhotsprings.com; $20)* is an idyllic spot: a handful of natural outdoor pools set beside a cool mountain stream and nothing but acres of wilderness surrounding you. Evening visits are particularly magical: whether you're treated to a meteor shower or a full moon rising through the pines, soaking in the steaming pools – with the occasional river plunge – is a marvelously restorative experience. Note that after dark, it's adults only. In winter, you'll need AWD and snow tires to get here; if your vehicle isn't equipped, or if it's a busy weekend, take the shuttle instead.

Vail

Ski the back bowls

Vail Mountain *(vail.com; adult/child lift ticket $319/220)* is hands-down one of the best ski resorts in the world, with 5317 skiable acres, 278 trails and, ahem, some of the highest

ANCIENT ASPENS

Come late September, Colorado's roads fill with leaf peepers, out in search of the glorious golden hues that wash across the mountainsides. Aspens, of course, are well known for their quaking leaves, but there's more to this tree than meets the eye. In fact, many aspen groves are not made up of individual trees, but are instead a single interconnected organism – the aspen's most common method of reproduction is cloning, where one plant sends out identical reproductions of itself via its root system. Because of this, aspens are not only considered the world's largest organism, but also the oldest: the Pando Grove in Utah (over 40,000 'stems' strong) is considered to be at least 10,000 years old.

EATING IN VAIL: OUR PICKS

Big Bear Bistro: An affordable fave in Vail Village, serving gourmet coffee, breakfast burritos and some damn good sandwiches at lunch. *8am-3pm* **$**

The Little Diner: The most popular place for a made-from-scratch breakfast is in Lionshead. No reservations. *7am-2pm* **$$**

Alpenrose: For the full alpine experience, get your pretzels, rösti and fondue at this Swiss German–themed restaurant. *11:30am-10pm* **$$$**

Sweet Basil: Vail's most celebrated restaurant: excellent seasonal, eclectic New American fare. *noon-3pm & 5-9pm Wed-Sun, 5-9pm Mon & Tue* **$$$**

THE VAIL DREAM

Tenth Mountain Division veteran Peter Seibert and his friend Earl Eaton climbed Vail Mountain in the winter of 1957. After one long look at those luscious back bowls, the pair knew they'd struck gold. At the time, the mountain was owned by the forest service and local ranchers. Seibert and Eaton recruited a series of investors and lawyers, eventually got a permit from the forest service and convinced nearly all of the local ranchers to sell. Much of the construction budget was raised by convincing investors to chip in $10,000 for a condo unit and a lifetime season pass. Finally, on December 15, 1962, the dream came alive. The cost of a lift ticket? $5 for nine runs.

lift-ticket prices on the continent. You can subdivide the mountain into three main zones: the front side (best for beginners and intermediate skiers), where most of the runs are groomed and the north-facing slopes offer good snow cover, even on sunny spring days; the back bowls (best for advanced skiers), with seven legendary bowls; and Blue Sky Basin (best for experts), with a more backcountry feel, including tree skiing, glades and cliffs. Distances are vast, and you'll spend a lot of time getting from one place to another, so if you have a specific destination in mind, plan carefully.

Summer adventures

All the usual suspects set up shop at Vail during the summer, from cycling to ziplining.

Bearcat Stables *(bearcatstables.com; from $80)* run one- to three-hour horseback rides, as well as longer trips like a four-day ride to Aspen. For wading and float-fishing trips, try **Gore Creek Fly Fishermen** *(gorecreekflyfisherman.com; from $345)*.

Zip Adventures *(zipadventures.com; $170)* runs six zipline tours over Alkali Canyon – followed by a cliff jump – with plenty of time to work on your primal scream.

Apex Mountain School *(apexmountainschool.com; $200-450)* offers guided climbing and mountaineering trips in both summer and winter, while **Bike Valet** *(bikevalet.com; rentals from $40)* rents cycles and runs a shuttle up to Vail Pass for the easy, scenic cruise back down.

Vail's summer amusement park, **Epic Discovery** *(vail.com; from $119)*, gets so-so reviews, though the **gondola ride** *(adult/child $59/39)* into the high country will always be impressive.

Leadville

Climb to the top of Colorado

Colorado's tallest peak and the second-highest in the continental US, **Mt Elbert** (14,433ft) is a relatively gentle giant. There are three established routes to the top, none of which are technical. The most common approach is via the northeast ridge; it's a 9-mile round trip hike with 4700ft of elevation gain, so expect to spend most of the day. The turnoff for the main trailhead is just south of Leadville on Rte 300. If you have 4WD, the South Mt Elbert Trailhead is accessed via Hwy 82, just east of Twin Lakes. It's a slightly shorter hike with only 4100ft of elevation gain.

Aspen

Skiing the four mountains

Aspen, for all its wealth, owes its current status to the surrounding slopes. Above all, this is a ski town and one of the best in America, with four mountains accessible from a **single lift ticket** *(aspensnowmass.com; adult/child lift ticket $244/164)* – each offering a different adventurous twist.

Aspen Mountain offers more than 3000ft of steep vertical right from the front door of the Little Nell. There's no

LANAG/SHUTTERSTOCK

Aspen

beginner terrain here, just 800 acres of bumps, trees and World Cup–worthy runs.

Snowmass is the biggest of the four, with over 3300 acres of ridable terrain and 150 miles of trails – this is the best all-around choice. At some point make your way to the Elk Camp chairlift, which has awesome views of the Maroon Bells from the top.

Buttermilk has lots of beginner-friendly cruisers, but it also has some gnarly terrain parks: this is where you can ride the same hits and 22ft superpipe as Chloe Kim and Shaun White.

Last but not least is **Aspen Highlands**. Although there are some beginner and intermediate runs, the Highlands is all about extreme skiing in the stunning hike-to Highland Bowl: expect chutes, vertiginous drop-offs, glades and super steep lines that plunge 3600 vertical feet.

Art galleries and museums

With a handful of outstanding art venues, Aspen is the state's most culturally happening spot west of Denver. Start with **Aspen Art Museum** *(aspenartmuseum.org; free)*, with three floors of gallery space enveloped in a striking exterior designed by Pritzker Prize–winner Shigeru Ban. Lesser known is Aspen Institute's **Resnick Center for Herbert Bayer Studies** *(thebayercenter.org; free)*, with rotating exhibits related to the Austrian artist and longtime Aspen resident – a Bauhaus treat. Smaller galleries, meanwhile, are everywhere – follow

BACKCOUNTRY HUT TRIPS

For some, backcountry skiing is what it's all about: pristine snow, all-pervading quiet and the magic of waking up in the wilderness on a winter's day. If you're keen, look into the **Summit Huts Association** *(summithuts.org)*, which operates five huts that are accessible by ski and snowshoe, and usually sleep around 20 people. All have amenities such as wood-burning stoves, full kitchens and solar-powered lights; in addition, three have wood-burning saunas. The most popular hut is Francie's Cabin, a great choice for first-timers (though all groups should have at least one experienced, avalanche-trained member). Note that you need to enter a lottery by February 15 to book a hut for the following year.

EATING IN ASPEN: OUR PICKS

Big Wrap: These vaguely healthy and definitely affordable wraps have won over legions of fans. Downstairs from the main sidewalk. *10am-6pm Mon-Sat* $

Spring Cafe: Vegetarian juice bar and cafe, with tofu scrambles, tempeh burgers, seitan fajitas and plenty of greens. *7am-5pm, from 8am Sat & Sun* $$

Bosq: Chef Barclay Dodge's playful, locally sourced menu (eg bison tartare) earned him Aspen's first Michelin star. Prix-fixe menu only. *5:30-10pm* $$$

Pine Creek Cookhouse: This log-cabin restaurant is past Ashcroft's ghost town and is accessible via sleigh, skis or horseback. *lunch & dinner Dec-Mar & mid-Jun–Sep* $$$

BEST ENTERTAINMENT IN ASPEN

Belly Up: The top nightspot in town, showcasing performers from John Legend to the Chainsmokers in intimate surrounds.

Silver City Aspen: This cowpoke-themed saloon in the basement of the historic Elks Building hosts live music performances as well as a weekly karaoke night.

Wheeler Opera House: A working theater since 1889, the Wheeler still stages opera, stand-up comedy, concerts and musicals.

Theatre Aspen: The gorgeous garden complex in Rio Grande Park is the summer home of the local theater, which puts on award-winning musicals and plays.

your curiosity, and you're sure to turn up something unique. Longstanding studios include **Galerie Maximillian**, **Christopher Martin Gallery** (a specialist in reverse glass painting) and **Baldwin Gallery**.

Hike the Maroon Bells

If you have but one day to enjoy a slice of pristine wilderness, spend it in the shadow of Colorado's most iconic mountains: the pyramid-shaped twins of **North Maroon Peak** (14,014ft) and **South Maroon Peak** (14,156ft). Eleven miles southwest of Aspen, it all starts at **Maroon Lake**, a stunning spot backed by the towering, striated summits. The surrounding wilderness area contains nine passes over 12,000ft and six fourteeners. Some jut into jagged granite towers, others are a more generous slope and curve. You can spend an hour here or several days: the choice is yours. **Crater Lake** is only 1.8 miles one-way, but if you're hungry for a little bit more, press on to **Buckskin Pass** (12,462ft; 4.8 miles one-way) – from the narrow ledge you can see mountains erupt in all directions. This is the start of the popular **Four Pass Loop** (28 miles), a stunning multiday backpacking trip that crosses three other 12,000ft passes. Parking is extremely limited at Maroon Bells. Instead, take a shuttle from **Aspen Highlands** (p69) *(aspenchamber.org; adult/child $16/10; late May-Oct);* advanced purchase required.

Salida

Rafting the Arkansas

The headwaters of the Arkansas are Colorado's best-known stretch of white water, with everything from extreme rapids to mellow ripples. Although most rafting companies cover the river from Leadville to the Royal Gorge, the most popular trips descend through **Browns Canyon National Monument**, a 16-mile stretch that includes class-III to -IV rapids, running between Buena Vista and Salida.

If you're with young kids, Bighorn Sheep Canyon is a good bet. Those after more of an adrenaline rush can head upstream to the Numbers or downstream to the Royal Gorge (Cañon City), both of which are class IV to V. If you'd like to go solo, outfitters also rent duckies (inflatable kayaks).

Most companies are based just south of Buena Vista, close to where Hwys 24 and 285 diverge, and typically offer full-day adventure packages including zipline tours, via ferrata or horseback riding. Established outfitters include **Rocky Mountain Outdoor Center** *(rmoc.com)*, **Independent Whitewater** *(raftsalida.com)* and **River Runners** *(riverrunnersltd.com)*. Expect to spend from $100 to 160 for a half to a full day of rafting.

Biking Monarch Crest Trail

If you've mountain biked before, then you know: **Monarch Crest Trail** awaits. One of the most famous rides in Colorado, this is an extreme 35-mile adventure, with fabulous high-altitude views. It starts off at Monarch Pass (11,312ft), follows

TASSANEE RIEBPADITH/SHUTTERSTOCK

Maroon Bells

the exposed ridge 12 miles to Marshall Pass and then either cuts down to Poncha Springs on an old railroad grade or hooks onto the Rainbow Trail. In Salida, rentals are available from **Sub-Culture Cyclery** *(subculturecyclery.com; half-day rental $70)*, and **Absolute Bikes** *(absolutebikes.com; $39)* runs shuttles to the trailhead on Fridays through Sundays at 8am. **High Valley Bike Shuttle** *(monarchcrest.com; $42)* also picks up cyclists in Poncha Springs and brings them up to the trailhead twice daily, at 8am and 10am.

Explore St Elmo ghost town

An old gold-mining ghost town tucked amid the Collegiate Peaks, **St Elmo** makes for a fun excursion. The drive is gorgeous, wending its way past stands of redolent ponderosa pine, a wildlife-viewing meadow and jagged peaks before petering out at what is Colorado's best-preserved ghost town. Over 40 buildings remain, most built around 1881: the schoolhouse, an old mercantile building and a miners' exchange are among the best kept, all providing a fascinating peek into Colorado's past, when gold and silver ruled these hills. St Elmo is located on County Rd 162, which becomes dirt about half-way up. It's no problem in summer, but in winter you'll want an AWD. Try to avoid weekends here, when ATV and snowmobile enthusiasts use St Elmo as a staging point – the revving of not-too-distant engines can take away some of the charm.

Crested Butte

Brave the Teocalli Bowls

One of Colorado's best, **Crested Butte Mountain Resort** *(skicb.com; adult/child lift ticket $195/127)* is known for its stomach-lurching steeps, with infamous runs like Rambo and Banana Chute bestowing bragging rights onto survivors. The Teocalli Bowls near the summit offer more extreme lines, including a backcountry-esque 20-minute hike out at the bottom. It's not all daredevil plunges, though – the town also has

RAFTING TIPS

Water flow varies by season, so time your visit for late May or early June for a wilder ride, when snowmelt has the river raging. If you've got young kids or are looking for a more relaxed experience, go in July or August when the water level is lower and warmer. Note that if you are rafting as a family, kids need to be at least six (sometimes older, depending on the trip) and weigh a minimum of 50lb. Early in the season, you'll need to wear a wetsuit (included) topped with a rain jacket, and whenever you go, take a wide-brimmed hat and sunglasses. Finally, bring a change of clothes for the end of the trip and don't forget to tip your guide.

FAT-TIRE REVOLUTIONARY

In April 1998, Neil Murdoch – local CB eccentric and the founder of mountain biking as the world knows it – slipped out town with just his clothes and a bike, hours before federal marshals closed in. Murdoch, aka Richard Barrister, had settled in little-known Crested Butte in 1974 after skipping bail on a cocaine-smuggling charge in New Mexico. A consummate tinkerer, Murdoch began outfitting old Schwinn bikes to be ridden off-road, including adding low gears and wide knobby tires – thus the 'Fat-Tire Revolution' was born. When he disappeared, Crested Butte rallied behind Murdoch in absentia, even establishing a fund for his legal defense. He was eventually caught in 2001 but is still revered as the godfather of mountain biking.

a terrific **Nordic Center** *(cbnordic.org; lift ticket $25)* with 50km of groomed trails and a special ski-in gourmet dinner at **Magic Meadows Yurt** (reserve). The **Adaptive Sports Center** *(adaptivesports.org)*, meanwhile, promotes mountain access for people of all abilities.

The birthplace of mountain biking

Crested Butte is one of the places that brought mountain biking to the world and it absolutely lives up to the hype. Take your pick between a fantastic **mountain bike park** *(skicb.com; lift tickets from $65)* or 450 miles of smooth-flowing singletrack crossing wildflower- and aspen-clad hills and meadows. The **Lupine Loop** is a great first trail, with outrageous views across the Slate River Valley. The 13-mile intermediate level ride has just enough climbing to keep you honest, interspersed with fun, flowing descents. **Big Al's Bicycle Heaven** *(bigalsbicycleheaven.com)* and **Alpineer** *(alpineer.com)* have rentals, maps and gear.

Wildflowers Everywhere

More than skiing, more than its mountain chic ethos, even more than mountain biking, Crested Butte is most famous for one thing: wildflowers. From vast hillsides of mule's ears to riverside pockets of elephant heads and shooting stars, and practically everywhere between, Crested Butte is saturated in wildflowers. Not surprisingly, the town hosts a popular **Wildflower Festival** *(crestedbuttewildflowerfestival.org)*, typically in the second week of July. The programming is almost as varied as the flowers, from guided hikes to painting and photography classes, and even guidance on how to identify medicinal and edible flowers. One unique option is a wildflower tour with the **Rocky Mountain Biological Laboratory**, a research and educational institute in the one-time ghost town Gothic, just north of town.

Canyon of the Ancients National Monument

Explore Ancestral Puebloan ruins

Visually stunning and imbued with ineffable spiritual energy, **Canyon of the Ancients National Monument** *(blm.gov/visit/canyons-ancient-national-monument; free)* is home to the largest known concentration of archaeological sites in the country – more than 6000 at last count. The ruins, accessible off rough roads and remote trails, are spread over 170,000 acres of public land and span 12,000 years of human

EATING IN CRESTED BUTTE: OUR PICKS

Frank's Deli: Local fave serving hearty sandwiches and breakfast burritos perfect for the trail. Ask about the specials. *9am-6pm Mon-Sat* $

Secret Stash: Award-winning pizzeria with a boho vibe, teahouse seating and tapestries included. Cocktails pack a serious punch. *11am-9pm* $$

Sunflower: Inventive, locally sourced dishes served in a homey cabin-like setting. Menu changes with seasonal ingredients. *6-10pm Wed-Sat* $$$

Breadery: Chewy sourdough flatbreads meet shared plates (pear ricotta ravioli), and soups and salads for a family style meal. Fresh bread to go. *5-9pm Wed-Sun* $$$

TRAVELLER70/SHUTTERSTOCK

Lowry Pueblo, Canyon of the Ancients National Monument

history. They range from singular hogans (traditional Navajo homes) to entire ancient pueblos – once-thriving population centers that persisted for thousands of years.

Canyon of the Ancients Visitor Center and Museum *(blm.gov/visit/canyons-ancients-national-monumentvisitor-center-and-museum; museum adult/child $6/free)* is an important first stop. A fascinating museum and research center, it has informative films and exhibits. Touch base with the rangers here; they can recommend specific sites and supply maps. A high-clearance vehicle is highly recommended. The **Southwest Colorado Canyons Alliance** *(swcocanyons.org; half/full day from $50/84)* also runs excellent tours.

The easiest ruin to visit is **Lowry Pueblo**, about 25 miles northwest of the visitors center on (mostly) paved roads. Dating to 1060 CE, the site has several stone structures and nine kivas (ceremonial enclosures), including the 47ft-wide Grand Kiva, believed to have been used for spiritual rites.

Alternatively, head to the southern entrance of Sand Canyon Trail, a relatively flat 6.5-mile (one way) trail through the breathtaking **McElmo Canyon**, with several cliff dwellings tucked into alcoves along the way. The largest, **Saddlehorn Pueblo**, is 1 mile from the trailhead.

Ouray & Around

Drive the Million Dollar Hwy

Deep in the San Juan Mountains, the **Million Dollar Hwy** connects the towns of Ouray and Silverton, and is a mind-blowingly scenic drive – one of Colorado's best. Twenty-five miles of hairpin turns and tight S-bends cut through the Uncompahgre Gorge, whose steep mountainsides loom large and close, rising into lofty, mist-shrouded peaks, while the valley floor lies far below, dotted with fir trees and wildflowers. Drive with caution – the road is formidable, even in good weather, and the lack of guardrails doesn't help. Be sure to take advantage of pullouts to see the dramatic **Bear Creek Falls** and 360-degree views from **Red Mountain Pass** (11,018ft).

WHY I LOVE CANYON OF THE ANCIENTS

Liza Prado, Lonely Planet writer.

Hiking solo through McElmo Canyon, the sky bright, the red earth dotted with yucca plants and sage brush, I can almost see them. The people who once called this red canyon home, carrying woven baskets filled with plants and berries, passing me on their way to their adobe brick homes that, remarkably, still stand in the alcoves. I can almost smell the smoke from their cooking fires and hear the sounds of their everyday life carried through the canyon – the chatter, the chopping of wood, the children playing. This place transports me, fills me with wonder and reminds me that, regardless of time or circumstance, we're all connected. For me, that's what travel is all about.

THOMAS TROMPETER/SHUTTERSTOCK

Cliff Palace

TOP EXPERIENCE

Mesa Verde National Park

Mesa Verde National Park spans 81 sq miles over two broad mesas, both rife with Ancestral Puebloan dwellings. Some are on the mesa tops, but the most compelling are built into high cliffs. While many are visible from overlooks, touring them means adventure at great heights, peering over edges, clambering up and down ladders and crawling through tunnels...all to experience these magnificent dwellings up close.

DON'T MISS

- Cliff Palace
- Balcony House
- Step House
- Petroglyph Point Trail
- Mesa Top Loop Rd
- Long House
- Cultural Performances

Ranger Tours

Taking a ranger-led tour is one of the most rewarding ways to experience Mesa Verde. You'll deep-dive into the history and lives of the Ancestral Puebloans and have access to otherwise restricted sites such as **Cliff Palace** and **Balcony House**, plus **Long House**, a sprawling dwelling in the park's rugged backcountry. They're not for the faint of heart! Most involve walking along cliff edges, climbing up and down wooden pole ladders and crawling through tight spaces. But they're so worth it. Plan on taking two tours if you have the time; buy tickets in advance – they sell out fast.

PRACTICALITIES

● nps.gov/meve ● per vehicle $20-30 ● 24hr

Cliff Palace

Cliff Palace is the largest known cliff dwelling in the American southwest, a grand engineering achievement with 151 rooms and 23 kivas (ceremonial enclosures) that once housed 25 families. It's remarkable for its fine construction and efficient design. Walk through it on a 45-minute tour, retracing the paths taken by the enclave's original inhabitants. If you can't join a tour, check out the site from afar from the Sun Temple overlook on Mesa Top Loop Rd.

Balcony House

The **Balcony House** tour requires you to descend a 100ft staircase, climb a 32ft ladder and crawl through a 12ft tunnel...and that's just to get there. There are more ladders and steps on the way out. It's well worth the effort: the 38-room village is built in a cliffside alcove with a long arching roof, and offers views of Soda Canyon, 600ft below.

Step House

Wetherill Mesa has the park's only self-guided cliff dwelling: **Step House**. A short but steep 0.8-mile trail leads to a two-in-one village, with 7th-century pit houses standing alongside 13th-century multistoried dwellings. Information booklets are available near the trailhead; a ranger is typically at the site to answer questions.

Mesa Top Loop Rd

A complement (or alternative) to scrambling through the cliff dwellings is a 6-mile driving tour along the **Mesa Top Loop Rd**. At various pull-offs, you can enjoy magnificent overlooks of Cliff Palace and other cliff dwellings, or take short paths to a dozen different surface sites (no teetering ladders on this route). A free **audio tour** *(nps.gov/podcasts/podcasts-mtl-audiotour.htm)* guides the way.

Petroglyph Point Trail

The 2.4-mile loop **Petroglyph Point Trail** follows a leafy footpath once used by the Ancestral Puebloans. Dropping below the canyon rim, it's occasionally steep and rocky before making a short scramble back to the top of the mesa. Look for the petroglyphs at the 1.4-mile mark – a 35ft-wide wall with almost three dozen human and animal figures, spirals and handprints. A gate at the trailhead is locked in the evenings. If you arrive in the early morning, begin the trail in reverse.

Dances & Demonstrations

In summer, the park hosts cultural dances and pottery demonstrations by Native peoples with ancestral connections to Mesa Verde. Fascinating and educational, the events are a way to learn about Mesa Verde's ancient inhabitants and their modern-day descendants. Events are in the Morefield Campground (p122) amphitheater or the main visitor center, typically in the evening.

STARGAZING IN MESA VERDE

An International Dark Sky Park, Mesa Verde's remote location, high elevation and arid climate make it one of the best places in the country to enjoy the night skies. Rangers offer regular nighttime programs, from lectures and star parties to astrophotography workshops, all for free. Alternatively, stop at an overlook (or step out of your tent) to take in the sky on your own.

TOP TIPS

- Visit mid-May to mid-October. Winter and spring bring closures to several areas and amenities, and tours are suspended.
- Tickets for ranger tours can only be purchased online *(recreation.gov)* or by phone, up to 14 days in advance. Tours often sell out, so reserve early.
- Information booklets are stocked in metal bins around the park.
- Fill your tank before you arrive – you'll be driving a lot. At a pinch, there's a gas station at Morefield Campground.
- Cellphone service is limited; download audio tours and maps ahead of time.
- Except for holiday weekends, Morefield Campground almost always has walk-up availability.

THE SUN DANCE

Ricky Hayes, Weeminuche Ute tribal member.

The Sun Dance is one of the most sacred ceremonies for my people, and one I've participated in several times over the course of my life. It's performed as a deep blessing for the tribe and the earth. It takes place the third week in June in a specially made lodge on Sleeping Ute Mountain, on the north side of the reservation. For four days, we pray, dance and fast – no food or water. The ceremony is sometimes called the Thirst Dance because of it. The fasting is especially difficult, given the physical effort and the heat. Many people collapse but eventually rise and continue.

KIT LEONG/SHUTTERSTOCK

Ouray Hot Springs

Hiking high above Ouray

Forming nearly a complete loop around Ouray, the 6-mile **Perimeter Trail** is one of the most scenic ways to experience the 'Switzerland of America.' Beginning across from the **visitor center** *(visitouray.com)*, the clockwise trail charts an up-and-down path through forests and aspen groves and across creeks and meadows. Highlights include the spectacular **Cascade Falls**, **Baby Bathtubs** (a series of smooth tub-like rock divots) plus the **Ouray Via Ferrata** *(ourayviaferrata.org)* and **Ice Park** *(ourayicepark.com)*, where you can spy people clambering along sheer rock faces or climbing frozen cascades. The pièce de résistance is **Box Cañon Falls** *(visitouray.com/box-canyon-falls; adult/child $7/5)*, a thundering 285ft waterfall that drops into a spectacular quartzite canyon.

Soak in historic springs

For a healing soak or kiddish fun, try **Ouray Hot Springs** *(visitouray.com/ourayhotspringspool; adult/child $26/16)*. The springs were used and considered sacred by the Ute people before they were pushed from the region; later, miners soaked in the same waters to help their tired bodies. Today, the springs are a year-round waterpark surrounded by 13,000ft peaks. Come for the eight-lane lap pool, waterslides, a climbing wall overhanging a splash pool and several adults-only soaking areas (74°F to 106°F; 23°C to 41°C). The geothermal water is crystal clear and free of sulfur smells – a major plus.

EATING IN OURAY: OUR PICKS

Maggie's Kitchen: Graffiti-bombed hole-in-the-wall known for deliciously sloppy burgers and onion rings. Seating on the deck. *11am-8pm Thu-Sat, to 6pm Sun* $

Kami's Samis: Bright, modern spot with decadent breakfasts, hearty burritos and gourmet sandwiches. Loads of vegan, gluten- and dairy-free options. *7am-2pm* $$

The Smokehouse: Finger-lickin' BBQ joint serving generous portions of goodness, smoked 'low and slow.' Perfect for a post-hike meal. *8am-2pm Mon-Wed, 8am-2pm & 5-9pm Thu-Sun* $$

Brickhouse 737: Cozy, upscale restaurant serving contemporary American cuisine with flair. Creative top-shelf cocktails. Reservations recommended. *5-9pm* $$$

Telluride

Telluride's past

A national historic landmark, Telluride is one of the country's most iconic Victorian-era towns, its streets lined with elegant buildings that once served as flophouses, saloons, schoolhouses and churches. Stop into the Smithsonian-affiliated **Telluride Historical Museum** *(telluridemuseum.org; adult/child $9/6)* to learn about Telluride's beginning as a Ute hunting ground, its mining past and its transformation into a world-class ski town. **Guided walking tours** *($15)* also offered on summer and fall afternoons.

Waterfalls, lakes and panoramic views

A network of trails branch out like arteries from the heart of Telluride, crisscrossing the town's box canyon, from easy strolls along the scenic **Telluride River Trail** (4.4 miles) to the strenuous, wildflower-filled **Sneffels Highline Trail** (12.5 miles). For something in between, hike to Colorado's tallest waterfall, the 365ft **Bridal Veil Falls** (2.5 miles to the bottom, 3.4 miles to the top), along rocky switchbacks through a thick aspen forest, passing two smaller waterfalls along the way. From there, extend your hike by continuing along a narrow mining road, passing through alpine meadows and forests to the otherworldly **Blue Lake** (5.7 miles, 12,400ft).

Ski and board in style

Known for plunging runs and deep powder, those gorgeous San Juan Mountain views and a certain high-society *je ne sais quoi*, **Telluride Ski Resort** *(tellurideskiresort.com; adult/child lift ticket $245/125)* is a special place. Decently sized in terms of lifts and acres – it has three distinct areas served by 19 lifts – Telluride has an outsize supply of advanced and expert terrain, from steeps to trees to wide open cirques, and even more if you are willing to hike for it, including iconic Palmyra Peak. There are also ample options for beginners and intermediate cruisers, including the playful, 4.6-mile Galloping Goose run.

Banjos, hula hoops and more

Telluride Bluegrass Festival *(bluegrass.com/telluride)* is the town's most famous fest, a summer solstice celebration of folk music and mountain life. It draws big-name bands and over 10,000 revelers daily – many donning hula hoops as dance partners. The main stage is set in the leafy town park

TELLURIDE TOURS

Telluride Offroad Adventures: Enjoy rugged passes and stunning scenery on a variety of deluxe 4WD tours, from two-hour jaunts to full-day adventures.

Telluride Wranglers: Authentic and adventurous trail rides of various lengths and skill levels, with small groups and expert guides.

Telluride Flyfishers: Memorable all-levels fly-fishing trips on the San Miguel and Dolores rivers, or hiking to alpine lakes and streams.

Telluride Outside: One-stop shop for excellent year-round adventuring, from snowmobiling to 4WD tours to stand-up paddleboarding.

Mountain Trip: Born out of an Alaska mountaineering school; trips include rock climbing, backcountry skiing and more.

EATING IN TELLURIDE: OUR PICKS

Brown Dog Pizza: Buzzing pizza joint known for its award-winning Detroit-style pizza. Come early or prepare to wait for a table. *11:30am-9pm* **$**

Butcher & Baker: Cute breakfast spot with generous to-go sandwiches and sides perfect for the trail. *7am-8pm Mon-Sat, 8am-2pm Sun* **$$**

Wood Ear: Ramen meets Texas smokehouse at this inventive underground spot. Creative cocktails available to go in reusable plastic flasks. *5-9pm* **$$$**

221 South Oak: New American cuisine by award-winning chef Eliza Gavin. Dine in the historic home or the leafy patio. *10am-1pm & 5-9:30pm Sun, from 5pm Mon-Sat* **$$$**

INTERNATIONAL DARK SKY PARK

Black Canyon of the Gunnison is an outstanding place for stargazing, thanks to its clear, dry weather and exceptionally dark skies. In 2015 the park became one of Colorado's first International Dark Sky Places (the state has 10), thanks to the park's work to limit light pollution and educate visitors on topics like astronomy and nocturnal ecosystems. Summer brings loads of **free astronomy programs** by park rangers and members of the Black Canyon Astronomical Society. In September, the park hosts **AstroFest**, with nightly telescope viewings, constellation tours, guest lectures by astronomers and info on the park's nocturnal animals.

with late-night concerts and free workshops held in smaller venues around town. Tickets sell out fast for the June event – buy early and consider a combo ticket-and-camping package for an all-in experience.

Telluride also hosts some two-dozen other festivals throughout the year. Faves include **Mountainfilm** *(mountainfilm.org)*, a documentary film festival held every Memorial Day Weekend (late May); **Telluride Mushroom Festival** *(tellurideinstitute.org/telluride-mushroom-festival)*, a celebration and education on all things fungi the third weekend in August (don't miss the parade); the internationally renowned **Telluride Film Festival** *(telluridefilmfestival.org)* over Labor Day Weekend (early September), and the season-ending **Blues & Brews Festival** *(tellurideblues.com)* in mid-September.

Black Canyon of the Gunnison National Park & Around

Views and climbing around a national park

With 2000ft-high canyon walls and colorful craggy spires, a drive along the spectacular south rim of the **Black Canyon of the Gunnison National Park** *(nps.gov/blca, per vehicle $30)* is the most popular way to experience it. For 7 miles, the flat, winding and paved **South Rim Rd** hugs the canyon's edge with a dozen overlooks offering heart-stopping views. Good pullouts include **Pulpit Rock Overlook**, a finger-like outcropping with expansive river views; **Chasm View**, the canyon's narrowest point, and **Painted Wall**, Colorado's tallest vertical cliff (2250ft), named after the magnificent pink pegmatite stripes that stretch half a mile across. Be aware there are few guardrails – keep small children close and watch your step, especially while taking selfies.

If you're an experienced climber, don't miss the lesser-traveled **North Rim**. An 80-mile drive from the South Rim (there's no bridge over the canyon), the area has 145 multipitch climbing routes rated between 5.9 and 5.13, including along the **North Chasm** and to the top of the **Painted Wall**. Wilderness permits are required, available for free at the **North Rim Ranger Station**. For guided climbing trips try **Mountain Trip** *(mountaintrip.com)* or **IRIS** *(irisalpine.com)*, an outdoors company catering to women, non-binary and trans people.

Note: in winter, South Rim Rd is only open to vehicles up to the visitor center; the remainder is open to cross-country skiers and snowshoers only. The North Rim roads are entirely closed.

Learn about the Ute

One of the few American museums dedicated to a single tribe, the **Ute Indian Museum** *(historycolorado.org/ute-indian-museum; adult/child $7/free)* in Montrose examines the many cultural and historical layers of Colorado's longest continuous residents. Artifacts, displays, videos and hands-on exhibits paint a powerful portrait of the Ute people, past and present. There are regular speaker series and film screenings, too. The museum sits on the homestead of legendary Ute Chief Ouray and his wife, Chipeta.

TOP EXPERIENCE

Dinosaur National Monument

At the end of desolate stretches of blacktop, Dinosaur National Monument is arguably Colorado's most remote destination. But for travelers fascinated by prehistoric life, it's worth every lonely mile. Spanning the Colorado–Utah border, it's one of the few places on earth where you can reach out and touch a dinosaur skeleton, snarling in its final pose, petrified eternally in rock and stone.

The Fossils

The park's indoor highlight is in Utah – the 150ft-long **Dinosaur Quarry Wall** with some 1500 dinosaur bones embedded in it. Part of an ancient riverbed where the remains of Jurassic-era dinosaurs were deposited and later fossilized, bones from allosaurus to stegosaurus can be seen.

Just outside, the **Fossil Discovery Trail** is one of the world's most spectacular open-air collections of fossils, with dinosaur bones, marine creatures and plants visible in the rocks. The moderate 1.2-mile trail has interpretive signs explaining the sights and distinct geological stages.

Panoramic Views

In Colorado, **Harpers Corner Trail** is a moderate 2-mile hike through juniper forests that eventually open to views of the park's winding canyons. At the trail's end, hikers are rewarded with spectacular views of the confluence of the Yampa and Green rivers at jutting **Steamboat Rock**. The trailhead is off Harpers Corner Rd, a scenic drive in itself.

Rafting

Rafting the Green and Yampa rivers is a popular way to experience the park. Expect class-III and -IV rapids, red-hued canyons, sandstone formations and petroglyphs. **Adrift** *(adrift.com; adult/child from $120/99)* and **OARS** *(oars.com; from $1049)* offer single and multiday trips, beginning in Utah.

TOP TIPS

- The Utah and Colorado entrances are 28 miles apart – about a 30-minute drive. Plan accordingly, especially to include a quarry visit.
- Services are few and far. Before heading out, fill your tank and be sure to carry drinks and snacks.

PRACTICALITIES

- nps.gov/dino
- per vehicle $25
- 24hr

TOP EXPERIENCE

Colorado National Monument

Colorado National Monument is a stunning natural area. Just 16 miles west of Grand Junction, it's a warren of canyons, their sheer walls painted a gorgeous cedar red and punctuated by long, rocky fins, dramatic sandstone spires and massive overhangs. It's an adventurer's (and photographer's) dream.

DON MAMMOSER/SHUTTERSTOCK

TOP TIPS

- Rim Rock Dr can close in winter or after storms – check the website for current conditions.
- Arrive in early morning for sightings of bighorn sheep, mule deer and golden eagles.
- Rim Rock Dr is popular with cyclists. Give them space on the narrow, curvy road.

Driving Past Red Rocks

The most popular way to experience the park is driving the paved 23-mile **Rim Rock Dr**, which weaves along the cliff edges, with 19 pull-outs offering vertiginous vistas of the red sandstone cliffs, monoliths and formations carved by millions of years of erosion. Pull-outs have interpretive signage explaining the park's history, geology, flora and fauna.

Hiking Through the Park

Forty-six miles of trails make for outstanding and varied hikes, allowing visitors to appreciate the landscape close-up. Popular trails include **Devil's Kitchen** (1.9 miles round trip), a short hike and scramble to a large stone outcrop; and **Monument Canyon Trail** (11.6 miles round trip), which passes many of the park's most interesting natural features, including **Kissing Couple**, **Independence Monument** and **Coke Ovens**.

PRACTICALITIES

- nps.gov/colm
- per vehicle $25
- 24hr

Climbing Sandstone

Colorado National Monument is a dream for experienced rock climbers, with towering sandstone spires of smooth rock interspersed with cracks, chimneys and ledges. Some favorites include **Otto's Route** on Independence Monument, the park's iconic 450ft sandstone monolith (5.9 rating); and **Sentinel Spire** with its beautiful crack routes such as West Face (5.11 rating), with steep, challenging terrain and breathtaking exposure. Head to **Gearhead Outfitters** *(gearheadoutfitters.com)* in Grand Junction for equipment, maps and route recommendations.

Colorado Springs

Olympic tour

The **Colorado Springs Olympic Training Center** *(usopc.org/training-centers; adult/child $16/12)* is one of just three such centers in the country. Tour the training facility (maybe spotting a few Olympic hopefuls in action), or check out the **US Olympic & Paralympic Museum** *(usopm.org; adult/child $30/17)* 2.5 miles away. The museum's spectacular and accessibly designed complex houses 12 galleries capturing Olympic history through memorabilia, athlete profiles and interactive training exhibits.

See the Garden of the Gods

This gorgeous vein of red sandstone (about 290 million years old) appears elsewhere along Colorado's Front Range, but the exquisitely thin cathedral spires and mountain backdrop of the **Garden of the Gods** *(gardenofgods.com; free)* are particularly striking. Gazing from the base of the highest rock formations on the **Perkins Central Garden Trail** inspires awe and humility. From there, numerous paved trails lead to central formations such as the **Kissing Camels**, **Three Graces** and **Montezuma's Tower**. Depending on your timing, you could easily spend an hour or two here. For more park information, stop in at the excellent visitors center. In summer, consider visiting **Rock Ledge Ranch** *(rockledgeranch.com; adult/child $8/4)*, a living history museum near the park entrance, that gives insight into the lives of the Utes and 19th-century homesteaders in the region.

Summit Pikes Peak

Pikes Peak *(coloradosprings.gov/drivepikespeak)* at 14,115ft may not be the tallest of Colorado's 54 fourteeners, but it's certainly the most popular – over 500,000 people summit it yearly. Called Mountain of the Sun by the Ute, it crowns the southern Front Range, majestically rising 7800ft from the plains. There are three ways to ascend it, all from Manitou Springs: Pikes Peak Hwy winding 19 miles to the top (three hours round trip; timed-entry reservations required late May to September); the 1891 cog railway (three hours round trip; reservations necessary), and **Barr Trail**, which most hikers split into a two-day trip due to the 7800ft elevation gain, camping at Barr Camp (10,200ft).

THE GREAT FRUITCAKE TOSS

Through the years it's been suggested that leftover fruitcakes (are there fruitcakes that are not leftover?) reincarnate as anything from doorstops to science experiments to an eco-friendly answer to street paving. Manitou has the answer: the **Great Fruitcake Toss** *(manitousprings.org)*, held each January in Memorial Park. Tosses are assessed for distance, balance, accuracy and aim, and fruitcakes are launched by mechanical devices. For staunch defenders of the edibility of fruitcakes, there's a bake-off for the best organic, non-GMO, natural fruitcake. The event supports the Manitou Springs Food Pantry and the tossed leftovers go to Jezebel the pig at Sun Mountain, so everyone is a winner.

EATING IN COLORADO SPRINGS: OUR PICKS

Birdtree Cafe: Fanciful and lively, with all-day breakfast and lunch. Veg/vegan options, rich coffee, gorgeous cocktails and a patio across from Acacia Park. *hours vary* **$$**

TAPAteria: Beautifully rendered, gluten-free Spanish tapas, with an extensive Spanish wine list. There's a 'secret' patio out back. *noon-10pm* **$$**

Uchenna: Expect homestyle cooking and a warm family atmosphere at chef Maya's Ethiopian restaurant, tucked in a shopping mall. *11:30am-2:30pm & 5-9pm Tue-Sat* **$$**

Westside Cantina: Vibrant and festive (the patio is lovely), offering cocktails and tacos with distinctive flavors and fresh ingredients. *hours vary* **$$**

THE SANTA FE TRAIL

The Santa Fe Trail linked Missouri with New Mexico (a Mexican province from 1821 to 1848), bringing manufactured goods west, and Mexican silver and Native American jewelry and blankets east. The 800-mile route took seven to eight weeks to cross in a covered wagon, and was defined by monotony and hardship. Near Dodge City in Kansas, the route divided: the southern road (Cimarron Route) cut down into New Mexico and was shorter but more dangerous, while the northern road (Mountain Route) continued through Bent's Fort and Trinidad, and was longer but safer. With the expansion of the railroad west, trade along the route eventually diminished, coming to a close in 1880.

SEAN XU/SHUTTERSTOCK

Great Sand Dunes National Park

Great Sand Dunes National Park

Experience a natural wonder

A standout even in a state with a tapestry of exceptional beauty, **Great Sand Dunes National Park** *(nps.gov/grsa; per vehicle $25)* appears like an undulating sea of sand bounded by jagged peaks and scrubby plains. Home to the tallest dunes in North America, including 750ft **Star Dune**, its hikes can be challenging on the shifting sand but the rewards are otherworldly views. For a thrill, try sandboarding down the sandy slopes on special wood planks; rentals are available at **Great Sand Dunes Oasis** *(greatdunes.com)* near the park entrance. If you time it right, you can even enjoy a beach day alongside the dunes – in late spring, **Medano Creek** is born from snowmelt that flows from the mountains, perfect for wading and water play, disappearing by mid-summer.

Santa Fe Trail

A drive through Colorado's complicated past

Drive Hwy 350 to experience the western reaches of the Great Plains and the Santa Fe Trail. Start at **Bent's Old Fort National Historic Site** *(nps.gov/beol)*. The beautifully restored adobe fort, used between 1833 and 1849, was once a cultural crossroads and the busiest settlement west of the Missouri.

Head northeast to Fort Lyon, where on November 29, 1864, US soldiers attacked a peaceful Cheyenne and Arapaho encampment. More than 150 people, mostly elders, women and children, were slaughtered, an event commemorated at nearby **Sand Creek Massacre National Historic Site** *(nps.gov/sand)*.

Drive through Granada to **Amache National Historic Site** *(nps.gov/amch)*. A WWII Japanese internment camp, it was the result of a racist response to the bombing of Pearl Harbor that forced the relocation and incarceration of people of Japanese descent, mostly US citizens. Amache once held 7567 prisoners, all brought from central California.

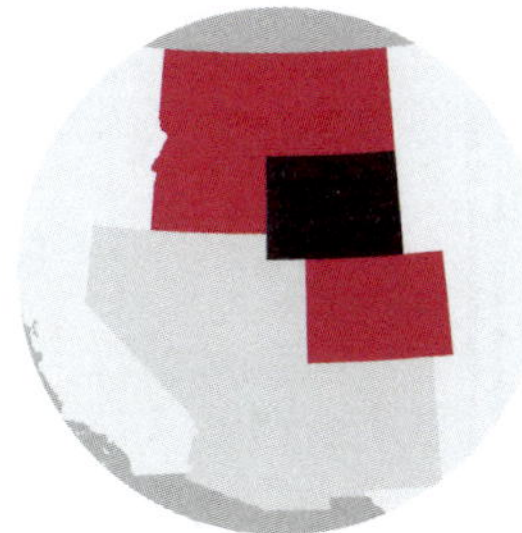

Wyoming

OTHERWORLDLY LANDSCAPES | COWBOY CULTURE | NATIVE HERITAGE

Wyoming is a land of extremes. Much of the state is a vast expanse of windswept plains and sagebrush hills, baking (or freezing) under brooding skies. Towns are infused with western grit and residents are content to keep this chunk of the West wild. But the country's least populated state (less than 600,000 inhabitants) is also home to one of the busiest and most recognizable natural destinations in the world, Yellowstone National Park, with its iconic geysers, unique geology and abundant wildlife. Add to that the glitzy ski destination of Jackson Hole and the truly grand Teton Range, and you'll forget Wyoming ever seemed so isolated. Wyoming also has a rich Native American history, including sites like Medicine Wheel and Devil's Tower National Monument. The Wind River Reservation hosts a remarkable regional powwow and is the final resting place of Sacajawea, the teenage mother who famously aided the Lewis and Clark expedition.

Places

GETTING AROUND

Wyoming has several airports, **Jackson Hole Airport** being the biggest and **Laramie Regional Airport** typically the cheapest. Once here, the long distances between destinations make having your own car much preferred – the **Greyhound** *(greyhound.com)* bus is mostly limited to small towns in the south and east. While 4WD may not be essential, a high-clearance vehicle will make navigating dirt roads easier. Wyoming is notorious for its winds and fierce gusts; take special care if you are driving a recreational vehicle (RV) or pulling a trailer. Gas stations are rare, even on major highways – don't miss a chance to gas up.

TOP TIP

The weather can change quickly throughout the entire state. Be sure to wear layers and check out **Wyoming Road Conditions** *(wyoroad.info)* before setting off. If the weather gets rough, highway patrol will shut an entire interstate until it clears.

WYOMING
MONTANA
0 100 km
0 50 miles
Cooke City
Yellowstone National Park
Absaroka Range
Shoshone National Forest
Powell
Lovell
Medicine Wheel National Historic Landmark
Sheridan
Devil's Tower National Monument
Black Hills National Forest
Yellowstone Lake
North Absaroka Wilderness
Cody
Greybull
Basin
Cloud Peak Wilderness
Devil's Tower National Monument
Sundance
Spearfish
SOUTH DAKOTA
Teton Range
John D Rockefeller Jr Memorial Parkway
Washakie Wilderness
Bighorn River
Buffalo
Gillette
Moorcroft
St Anthony
Teton Wilderness
Bighorn National Forest
Black Hills
Black Hills National Forest
Rapid City
Jedediah Smith Wilderness
Colter Bay Village
Worland
Ten Sleep
Snake River
Teton National Forest
Bighorn Mountains
Kaycee
Newcastle
Badlands National Park
Jackson
Dubois
Wind River Reservation
Thermopolis
Sussex
Thunder Basin National Grassland
Caribou National Forest
Gros Ventre Wilderness
Blackfoot
Fitzpatrick Wilderness
Midwest
Hot Springs
Snake River
Big Wind River
Shoshoni
Buffalo Gap National Grassland
Bridger Wilderness
Fort Washakie
IDAHO
Pinedale
Riverton
WYOMING
Soda Springs
Bridger National Forest
Lander
Casper
Chadron
Sinks Canyon State Park
Douglas
NEBRASKA
Wind River Range
Sweetwater River
Bear River
Medicine Bow National Forest
Fort Laramie
NEBRASKA PANHANDLE
UTAH
Green River
Laramie Range
Wheatland
Fort Laramie National Historic Site
Torrington
Alliance
Great Divide Basin
Cache National Forest
Rawlins
Green River
Yampa River
Rock Springs
Rocky Mountains
Medicine Bow Mountains
N Platte River
Great Salt Lake
Flaming Gorge National Recreation Area
Medicine Bow National Forest
Laramie
Encampment River Wilderness
Flaming Gorge National Recreation Area
Salt Lake City
Savage Run Wilderness
Cheyenne
Sidney
High Uintas Wilderness
Green River
NORTHWEST COLORADO
NORTHERN MOUNTAINS

Cheyenne

Experience Cheyenne Frontier Days

Every late July since 1897, **Cheyenne Frontier Days** *(cfdrodeo.com; prices vary)* – the country's largest rodeo and celebration of all things Wyoming – has been taking over the capital city. A 10-day showcase of cowboy culture, the heart of the action is in Frontier Park, where rodeo events like bronco and bull riding, barrel racing and team roping bring top contenders and big prize money. If the events are sold out or are just too pricey, free tickets to qualifying rounds, or 'slack' rodeos, are offered too. Or check out the wildly popular Frontier Town, recreating 19th-century life with costumed characters, making sure to stop in the Indian Village, where modern-day Native dance and storytelling traditions are showcased. Evenings bring big-name music acts to Frontier Park's arena too. In town, check out the seemingly nonstop lineup of concerts, parades, air shows, carnivals and chili cook-offs that transform the typically sleepy town.

A walk through the Old West

For a deep dive into Cheyenne's pioneer past and rodeo present, visit the **Old West Museum** *(cfdrodeo.com/event/old-west-museum; adult/child $15/10)* on the Cheyenne Frontier Days rodeo grounds. It's chock-full of rodeo memorabilia, from saddles to trophies. It also displays cowboy art and photography, houses a fine collection of horse-drawn buggies, and dispenses nuggets of history – such as the story of Steamboat, the unrideable bronco who likely isn't the one depicted on Wyoming's license plates (though many will tell you he is).

All about Wyoming's history

While in Cheyenne, stop in the **Wyoming State Museum** *(wyomuseum.wyo.gov; free)* a thoughtfully curated attraction focused exclusively on the state's natural and cultural history. Spread across two floors, exhibits showcase Wyoming's dinosaur findings and modern-day wildlife, mining and national parks, plus Native American peoples and pioneers. Three to four temporary exhibits keep the museum current. If you're traveling with little ones, don't miss the hands-on area with dress-up clothes, a pint-size tipi and a recreated chuck wagon.

MARDI GRAS OF THE WEST

Sam Masoudi, Chief Investment Officer, Wyoming Retirement System.

Frontier Days in Cheyenne is a really big deal. The city gets taken over with it! People dress up for it, and there are a lot of hardcore cowboys and a decent number of bikers too. If you're going to watch rodeo, it's extraordinary, with some of the best bull riders in the country and lots of other events like women's barrel racing and cattle drives. It also has one of the biggest country-music concerts in the country. There are chuck-wagon cook-offs, too, where people prep dishes only using ingredients and tools available during pioneer days. Plus, there's a US Air Force Thunderbirds flyover. It's all really interesting, so fun. It's like the Mardi Gras of Western culture!

EATING IN CHEYENNE: OUR PICKS

Luxury Diner: Go-to breakfast spot, set in a turn-of-the-20th-century trolley car. If in doubt, order anything with green chili. *7am-2pm Mon-Sat, to 1pm Sun* $

2 Doors Down: Popular burger joint specializing in offbeat toppings, from teriyaki to mac 'n' cheese. Bottomless fries too. *11am-9pm Mon-Sat* $

Napoli's: Upscale dinner spot with an art-deco ambiance. Expect mouthwatering Italian fare and attentive service. Don't miss the tiramisu. *4-9pm Tue-Sat* $$

Bunkhouse Bar & Grill: Honky-tonk serving steaks and Rocky Mountain oyster sandwiches. Live music on weekends. *11am-8pm Wed-Thu & Sun, 11am-11pm Fri & Sat* $$

SACAJAWEA

Sacajawea, the famed Shoshone interpreter on the Lewis and Clark expedition, has all but disappeared into popular myth. But this remarkable teenager embodied profound intelligence and resourcefulness. Born near Salmon, Idaho in 1788, she was kidnapped and enslaved by Hidatsa tribesmen at age 12. Two years later, a pregnant Sacajawea joined the expedition with her proclaimed husband, a French-Canadian fur trader who 'won' her gambling. Her presence proved invaluable; beyond her linguistic abilities, she helped secure horses and safe passage from the Shoshone. Though the details of her death are debated, Shoshone oral tradition holds she lived on the Wind River Reservation, dying in 1884. Her gravestone and statue sit on a quiet hillside cemetery in Fort Washakie.

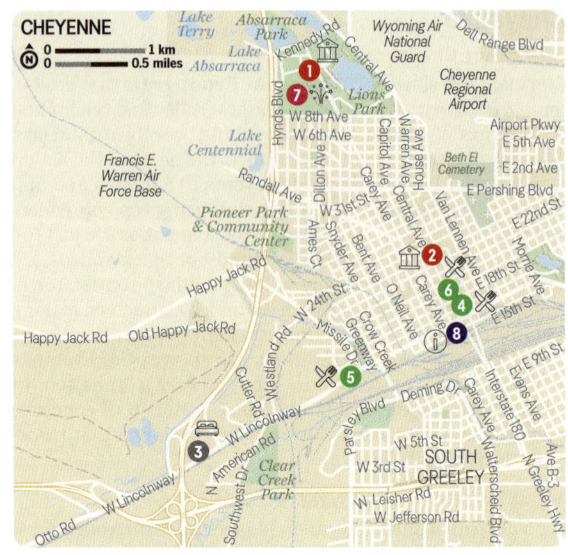

SIGHTS
1 Old West Museum
2 Wyoming State Museum

SLEEPING
3 Cheyenne Guest Inn

EATING
4 2 Doors Down
5 Luxury Diner
6 Napoli's

ENTERTAINMENT
7 Cheyenne Frontier Days

INFORMATION
8 Cheyenne Visitor Center

Touring Cheyenne's public art

Cowboy boots are about as Wyoming as Buffalo Bill, and sculptures of colorful, larger-than-life boots add quirky charm to downtown Cheyenne. Even better, these boots can talk. Stop by the **Cheyenne Visitor Center** *(cheyenne.org)* for the brochure *These Boots are made for Talking* (or download it from the website). With the brochure in hand, follow the map to any of the 35 boot-sculptures, dial 307-316-0067, then enter the number of the boot as shown on the brochure – you'll hear the story of the boot from the artist and, in the process, learn a whole new side to the city's history.

Laramie

Spend time in prison

Stop at the impressively restored **Wyoming Territorial Prison State Historic Site** *(wyoparks.wyo.gov; adult/child $9/4.50)* to learn all about the reality of prison life in the Wild West. It is also the only prison to have held Butch Cassidy, who was in for grand larceny from 1894 to '96, only to emerge a well-connected criminal who fast became one of history's greatest robbers. His life story is told in thrilling detail in a back room, while the faces of other 'malicious and desperate outlaws' – including several women – stare hauntingly at you as you explore the main cellblocks. Outside, tour the factory where convicts produced more than 700 brooms a day – one of the prison's short-lived revenue-generating schemes. Staff members are posted throughout the site, happily answering questions; free guided tours offered May to September.

Marvel at prehistoric finds

The Morrison Formation – a vast Jurassic-era sedimentary rock layer – stretches from New Mexico to Montana, with its fossil-rich center in Wyoming. This 150-million-year-old formation has produced some of the world's most significant dinosaur discoveries in paleontology, many of which are housed in the University of Wyoming's tiny, but well-worth-a-stop, **Geological Museum** *(uwyo.edu/geomuseum; free)*. Inside, marvel at a towering 75ft apatosaurus skeleton (formerly known as the brontosaurus) as well as a rare *Diatryma gigantea*, a 7ft-tall, flightless carnivorous bird that once roamed the region's prehistoric swamps. Be sure to linger at the 'Prep Lab' observation window, where researchers liberate brittle fossils from solid rock.

Sinks Canyon State Park

See a geological phenomenon

Six miles southwest of Lander lies **Sinks Canyon State Park** *(sinkscanyonstatepark.org; free)*, a beautiful forested park nestled deep in a glacial canyon. Popular for day hikes, it's best known for a geological phenomenon involving the Middle Fork of the Popo Agie River. Here, the fast-flowing river suddenly turns into a large limestone cavern, disappearing into cracks and fissures at its back wall, known as the Sinks. The river is not seen again for nearly a quarter-mile, until it reemerges in a tranquil pool called the Rise, which is filled with enormous trout. Despite the short distance between the two, dye tests indicate that in addition to taking over two hours for the river to make the subterranean journey, it also reemerges warmer and more voluminous. The reason continues to intrigue scientists. A paved trail between the two areas makes for a scenic walk, with interpretive signs along the way explaining more about the geology, ecology and history of the park.

Fort Washakie

Wyoming's largest powwow

In late June, head to Fort Washakie on the Wind River Reservation – home of the Eastern Shoshone and Northern Arapaho peoples – where **Eastern Shoshone Indian Days** *(windriver.org; free)* is hosted. The largest and longest-running powwow in Wyoming, the three-day event is a spectacular intertribal celebration of Native identity; expect all manner of competitive dancing, drumming groups and Grand Entry ceremonies, participants of all ages decked out in magnificent regalia. Beyond the arena, artisans and food vendors line the grounds, selling

MATTHEW SHEPARD

In October 1998, Matthew Shepard, a student at University of Wyoming in Laramie, was attacked and brutally beaten, tied to a roadside fence, and left to die – all because he was gay. Shepard's murder drew national attention to hate crimes against LGBTIQ+ people and spurred an outpouring of grief, outrage, activism and urgent creativity, including the critically acclaimed play *The Laramie Project*. Shepard's parents founded the **Matthew Shepard Foundation** *(matthewshepard.org)*, dedicated to promoting LGBTIQ+ rights, which helped to expand federal hate-crime legislation to include sexual orientation and gender identity. A memorial bench for Shephard now sits at University of Wyoming; it bears the quiet inscription 'He continues to make a difference.'

GREEN RIVER RENDEZVOUS

In mid-July, the town of Pinedale hosts the **Green River Rendezvous Festival** *(greenriverrendezvous.com)*, a four-day celebration of the region's mountain man heritage. The event commemorates the annual summer 'Rendezvous' of the early 1800s where fur trappers, Native Americans and traders would gather to buy supplies, trade goods and generally party. Today, the event includes a lively parade down Main Street, historical reenactments, shooting demonstrations, craft fairs and cultural performances by Shoshone and Arapaho people. Presentations by historians are also offered at the Museum of the Mountain Man, for those looking for a deeper dive into Wyoming's frontier history.

TERI VIRBICKIS/SHUTTERSTOCK

Devil's Tower National Monument

Native goods, art and eats. While the powwow is open to the public, be mindful when taking photographs – the arena is considered a sacred place. Keep an ear out for announcements limiting photography; if in doubt, ask before snapping a pic.

Visit the Shoshone Tribal Cultural Center

Inside Fort Washakie School, learn all about the history of Wind River Reservation and its people at the **Shoshone Tribal Cultural Center** *(easternshoshone.org/cultural-center; free)*. Exhibits highlight Eastern Shoshone history and contemporary tribal life as well as the legacy of Chief Washakie, renowned for his ability to navigate the changing physical and political landscapes of the West during the 1800s. There's also a display on the life of Sacajawea, Lewis and Clark's now-famous guide and interpreter. For a deeper dive in the Eastern Shoshone, ask about **guided tours of the reservation** *(by donation)*; led by staff member Robyn Rofkar, tours last a few hours to multiple days, providing unique insights into the tribe's history and enduring culture.

Pinesdale

Learn about the early pioneers

Make a pitstop in Pinedale for **Museum of the Mountain Man** *(museumofthemountainman.com, adult/child $10, free)*, a fascinating museum that deep-dives into the history of the

EATING NEAR FORT WASHAKIE & LANDER: OUR PICKS

Middle Fork: Welcoming breakfast place with local ingredients and homemade baked goods. The eggs Benedict with cottage bacon is tops. *7am-2pm* $

Lander Bake Shop: Family-owned from-scratch bakery and cafe. Sit down for brekkie and order a sandwich for the trail. *7am-4pm Mon-Fri, 8am-2pm Sat & Sun* $

Gannett Grill: Casual spot known for its local grass-fed beef burgers and stone-oven pizzas. In summer, nab a seat on the leafy patio. *11am-10pm* $

Cowfish: Upscale restaurant with surf-and-turf menu, perfect for date night. Order a flight of craft beer, delivered from the attached brewery. *5-10pm* $$$

fur trappers who came to the West during the 1820s in search of beaver pelts. An essential part of the region's development, exhibits cover everything from their food and clothing to trapping methods and marriage to Native American women.

Fort Laramie

Imagine life in a fort

In Wyoming's eastern plains, **Fort Laramie National Historic Site** *(nps.gov/fola; free)* is one of the most historically important sites in the state. Established as a fur trading post in 1834, it quickly became a place of rest and restocking for emigrants traveling on the Oregon, Mormon Pioneer and California Trails. By 1849, with surging numbers of Gold Rush fortune seekers – and increasing conflicts with Plains tribespeople – it transformed into one of the largest military forts in the West. Today, you can visit 22 original structures, including enlisted barracks, officers' quarters, a bakery and the post trader's store. Many are furnished with period artifacts. Interpretive signs provide historical context, while the visitor center has exhibits on the fort's complex role in westward expansion and the Indian Wars (don't miss the excellent film). During summer, you also can interact with staff in period dress, who talk about life in the fort and provide demonstrations in things like blacksmithing and military drills. Guided tours available from late May to early September.

Devil's Tower National Monument

Visit a sacred place

Devil's Tower National Monument *(nps.gov/deto; per car $25),* in northeastern Wyoming, is a dramatic, nearly vertical monolith, rising 1267ft above the Belle Fourche River. Designated the first US national monument in 1906, the tower consists of striking hexagonal columns, some 20ft wide, formed over 50 million years ago. For 20 Native American tribes, the tower – often called Bear Lodge or Bear's Tipi – is a deeply spiritual site. For rock climbers, it is considered one of the best crack climbing spots in the world. Except in June, when tribes request a voluntary climbing moratorium to hold sacred ceremonies, you'll see climbers tackling the tower on over 140 routes. If you'd like to join the crowd, **Sylvan Rocks** *(sylvanrocks.com)* and **Devils Tower Climbing Guides** *(devilstowerlodge.com/Climb)* are highly recommended guides, especially for newbies. Or keep both feet on the ground, and hike the 1.3-mile **Tower Trail** circling the base, with close-up views of the tower. Keep your eyes peeled for prairie dogs.

Medicine Wheel National Historic Landmark

An ancient place of prayer

Medicine Wheel National Historic Landmark *(fs.usda.gov; free)* sits atop Medicine Mountain in Wyoming's Bighorn Range at nearly 10,000ft. A remarkable 80-ft-wide limestone circle with 28 spokes radiating from its central cairn, it is a

INFINITE OUTDOORS ACCESS GRANTED

Accessing public lands in the West is often far more difficult than maps suggest. Though these lands are publicly owned, nearly 16 million acres across the West are considered 'landlocked' – surrounded by private property, with fences and 'No Trespassing' signs blocking entry. In Wyoming alone, over 4.25 million acres of Bureau of Land Management (BLM), state and national forest lands fall into this category. To address this problem, **Infinite Outdoors Access Granted** *(infiniteoutdoorsusa.com/access-granted)* launched an app in 2025 to help outdoor enthusiasts find free entry points to private lands bordering public lands. With an increasing demand for access to public land, this seems to be a viable solution. Time will tell.

GROWING FOOD IN CAPTIVITY

The first year was particularly difficult for the Japanese-American prisoners at Heart Mountain. Torn from their homes hundreds of miles away, they suffered amid the challenging climate and isolation of remote Wyoming. The bland canned food and poor-quality meat only made things worse. James Ito, who grew up on a farm in southern California and graduated from the Berkeley College of Agriculture, organized the Japanese-American farmers among the camp and set to work. Within a year, the camp was growing most of its own food, and by 1945, they were producing a surplus – a remarkable achievement given the growing conditions of the high Wyoming desert. Ito later held a position with the US Department of Agriculture.

sacred site for several Plains tribes. For centuries, it has been used for countless ceremonies, prayers and vision quests. Today, the wheel remains an active sacred site, where cloth bundles, eagle feathers and other offerings are tied to nearby fences. Visitors are welcome to visit from mid-June through September – a well-maintained 1.5-mile trail leads there. Be aware access is occasionally restricted for ceremonies; if one takes place while you're on-site, do not take photographs. And be sure not to touch the offerings.

Cody

A dark episode in US history

Following the Japanese bombing of Pearl Harbor, more than 110,000 Japanese Americans were sent to 10 detention camps across the US. **Heart Mountain Relocation Center** *(heartmountain.org; adult/child $14/10)* in northern Wyoming was among them. Approximately 14,000 Japanese Americans were forcibly relocated from their West Coast homes to live in the 450 flimsy tar-paper barracks that once stood here. Nevertheless, they made the best of their three years of confinement, setting up a newspaper, two theaters and a high school in what quickly became Wyoming's third-largest town. Though few original structures remain – a residential barrack, hospital and root cellar – a free app allows you to point your cellphone at 16 designated stops to see real-time scenes from the internment camp, making it easier to imagine what life was once like here. Be sure to set aside plenty of time to see the powerful exhibits in the interpretive center.

Explore everything Western

Do not miss Wyoming's most impressive human-made attraction: **Buffalo Bill Center of the West** *(centerofthewest.org; adult/child $23/16)*. This sprawling complex of museums showcases everything Western, from the spectacle of Buffalo Bill's world-famous Wild West shows and galleries featuring powerful frontier-oriented artwork in **Buffalo Bill Museum** to the **Cody Firearms Museum**, with over 7000 pieces. Meanwhile, the **Draper Museum of Natural History** brilliantly explores the Yellowstone region's ecosystem; look for Teddy Roosevelt's saddle and one of the world's last buffalo tipis. Be sure to spend time in the visually absorbing **Plains Indian Museum**, an exploration of the past and present of several tribes, as well as the **Whitney Western Art Museum**, home to a world-class collection of Western art plus the recreated

EATING IN CODY: OUR PICKS

Beta Coffeehouse: Locals' favorite boho coffee shop serving baked goods, breakfast fare, and all manner of coffee drinks. *7am-2pm Tue-Fri, 8am-1pm Sat* $

Fat Racks BBQ: Food truck turned diner serving smoky Texas-style BBQ with all the fixings. Eat at outdoor picnic tables or take to go. *11am-7pm Mon-Sat* $$

Pat's Brew House: Woman-owned and -operated brewery with an eclectic menu – steamed mussels to cheeseburgers – plus craft beers on tap. *11am-9pm Wed-Sun* $$

Cody Cattle Company: Popular Western-style buffet – grilled meats, beans, cornbread and more – paired with live country music. *5-7:30pm, summer only* $$$

studio of renowned artist Frederic Remington. Entry is valid for two consecutive days – and you'll need 'em.

Jackson

See elk herds up close

If you're here in winter, head to the **National Elk Refuge & Greater Yellowstone Visitor Center** *(fws.gov/refuge/national-elk; free)*, headquarters for the 24,700-acre reserve on the northeast edge of town. Established in 1912 to protect diminishing numbers of elk herds, it's home to one of North America's largest elk populations, with numbers reaching over 7000 in the colder months. (In summer, the herds migrate into the mountains.) From mid-December to early April, **guided tours on horse-drawn sleighs** *(nersleighrides.com; adult/child $40/25)* take you into the heart of the herd for close-up views, with the snow-covered peaks of the Grand Tetons in the distance. Alternatively, take a free **audio driving tour** through 3.5 miles of the reserve, available on the website; free binoculars, as well as educational exhibits, available at the visitor center.

Mushing in the backcountry

Experience Wyoming's wintry backcountry from a dog's point of view with five-time Iditarod veteran Billy Snodgrass' **Continental Divide Dogsled Adventures** *(dogsledadventures.com; from $190)*. Excursions leave from the Togwotee Mountain Lodge in the Bridger-Teton National Forest, with one or two passengers per sled and a guide driving the team. You'll learn dogsled lore and the sport's history while teams of eight to 14 Alaskan huskies whisk you through the wilderness. Want to mush? Most guides will teach you on a safe stretch of the trail. Round-trip transportation from Jackson available too.

Admire the wild indoors

Set aside a morning in Jackson to visit the nation's only museum dedicated exclusively to wildlife art: **National Museum of Wildlife Art** *(wildlifeart.org, adult/child $18/10)*, a two-story building housing over 5000 works by traditional wildlife masters like Carl Rungius and John Audubon, and modern icons like Pablo Picasso and Andy Warhol. Wander through the collection or take a tour using the museum's excellent app, available in Spanish and English. Kid-geared activities throughout the galleries keep little ones engaged too.

Continued on p94

JACKSON'S BEST OUTDOOR OUTFITTERS

Hole Hiking Experience: Excellent hiking and snowshoeing excursions with naturalists, from two hours to overnight.

Grand Fishing Adventures: Guided fly-fishing on the Snake, Green and Salt rivers, plus exclusive access to Fish Creek.

Dave Hansen Whitewater: Reputable outfit for white-water trips on the Snake River with class II and III rapids.

Jackson Hole EcoTour Operators: Wildlife-watching tours (in vehicles) plus half-day snowshoe and cross-country ski excursions.

Teton Backcountry Guides: Backcountry ski trips including a day of climbing followed by long (3000ft) descents.

Hoback Sports: Rent mountain bikes, road bikes, e-bikes, skis and snowboards.

EATING IN JACKSON: OUR PICKS

Persephone Café Jackson: French bakery-cafe featuring artisanal breads, pastries and breakfast masterpieces. In summer, patio seating is tops. *7am-6pm Mon-Sat, 7am-3pm Sun* $$

Café Genevieve: Log-cabin cafe serving homestyle breakfast and hearty salads and sandwiches. Breakfast s'mores are good anytime. *8am-2pm Mon-Fri, to 2:30pm Sat & Sun* $$

Gather in Jackson Hole: Upscale yet laid-back restaurant featuring modern American fare with Asian and Mediterranean twists. Elk, trout and bison feature prominently. *5-9pm* $$$

Gun Barrel Steak and Game House: Jackson's best steakhouse, offering all manner of game. Set in a one-time wildlife museum; taxidermy still features large. *5-9pm* $$$

BERZINA/SHUTTERSTOCK

Grand Prismatic Spring

TOP EXPERIENCE

Yellowstone National Park

Teeming with wildlife, America's first national park also contains some of its wildest lands. Yellowstone is home to over 60% of the world's geysers – hot springs that periodically erupt in towering explosions of water. And while these astounding phenomena, and their neighboring Technicolor hot springs and bubbling mud pots draw in over 4.5 million visitors yearly, the surrounding canyons, mountains and forests are no less impressive.

DON'T MISS

- Old Faithful
- Grand Prismatic Spring
- Artist Point
- Yellowstone Lake
- Tribal Heritage Center

Geyser Country

Yellowstone's **Geyser Country** holds the park's most spectacular geothermal features (over half the world's total) within the world's densest concentration of geysers (over 200 spouters in 1.5 sq miles). Many have boardwalks circling them, making it easy (and safe) to observe them up close. Don't miss **Old Faithful**, the park's poster child, spouting some 8000 gallons of water 180ft into the air every 90-ish minutes; **Black Sand Geyser Canyon** with its steaming vents and bubbling pools contrasted against rugged cliffs; and **Grand Prismatic Spring**, a 330-ft-wide shimmering hot spring, the largest in

PRACTICALITIES
● nps.gov/yell ● per vehicle $35 ● 24hr

the country. Most of Yellowstone's geysers line the Firehole River, whose tributaries feed 21 of the park's 110 waterfalls.

Mammoth Country

Mammoth Country is renowned for its geothermal terraces and the towering Gallatin Range to the northwest. **Mammoth Hot Springs** is the area's main attraction, a graceful collection of travertine terraces and cascading hot pools. Some terraces are bone dry; others sparkle with hundreds of minuscule pools, coral-like formations and a fabulous palette of colors. An hour's worth of boardwalks wind their way through a landscape so otherworldly it provided the backdrop for the planet Vulcan in *Star Trek* (1979).

Tower-Roosevelt Country

Ancient petrified forests, the wildlife-rich **Lamar Valley**, its tributary trout streams of Slough and Pebble Creeks, and the dramatic and craggy peaks of the Absaroka Range are the highlights in this remote, scenic and undeveloped region. Come to see one of the largest herds of bison and elk in North America.

Canyon Country

A series of scenic overlooks linked by hiking trails punctuate the cliffs, precipices and waterfalls of the **Grand Canyon of the Yellowstone**. Here the Yellowstone River continues to gouge out a fault line through an ancient geyser basin, most impressively at **Lower Falls**. South Rim Dr leads to the canyon's most spectacular overlook, at **Artist Point**, while North Rim Dr accesses the daring precipices of the Upper and Lower Falls.

Lake Country

Yellowstone Lake (7733ft) is Lake Country's shimmering centerpiece – one of the world's largest alpine lakes, with the biggest inland population of cutthroat trout in the US. Yellowstone River emerges from the north end of the lake and flows through Hayden Valley into the Grand Canyon of the Yellowstone. The lake's southern and eastern borders flank the steep Absaroka Range and the pristine Thorofare region, some of the wildest and remotest lands in the lower 48. This watery wilderness is best explored by boat; rentals available at **Bridge Bay Marina** *(yellowstonenationalparklodges.com; rowboat/motor boat from $53/76).*

Tribal Heritage Center

Located near **Old Faithful Visitor Education Center**, the **Tribal Heritage Center** pays homage to the region's 27 associated tribal nations. From mid-May through mid-October, Indigenous artists, historians and craft makers give presentations and demonstrations in everything from beadwork and moccasin-making to storytelling and dancing. It's a great place to learn from people with a deep connection to Yellowstone.

BISON PROWESS

Despite their docile, hulking appearance, bison are surprisingly agile. They become increasingly uneasy when approached. A raised tail indicates one of two possibilities: a charge or discharge. Statistically, bison are much more dangerous than bears. Every year visitors are gored and seriously injured, sometimes even killed, by bison. Keep your distance to avoid becoming an unwilling rodeo clown, especially in August when it's rutting season.

TOP TIPS

- Visit in May or October. Services may be limited, but there will be far fewer people.
- Hit the trail. Most (95%) of visitors never set foot on a backcountry trail; only 1% camp at a backcountry site (permit required).
- Bike the park. Most campgrounds have underutilized hiker/cyclist sites, and youcan slip through any traffic jam.
- Mimic the wildlife. Be active during the golden hours after dawn and before dusk.
- Pack a lunch. Eat at one of the park's many overlooked and often lovely scenic picnic areas.
- Wintertime means you'll likely have Old Faithful to yourself. Just bundle up.

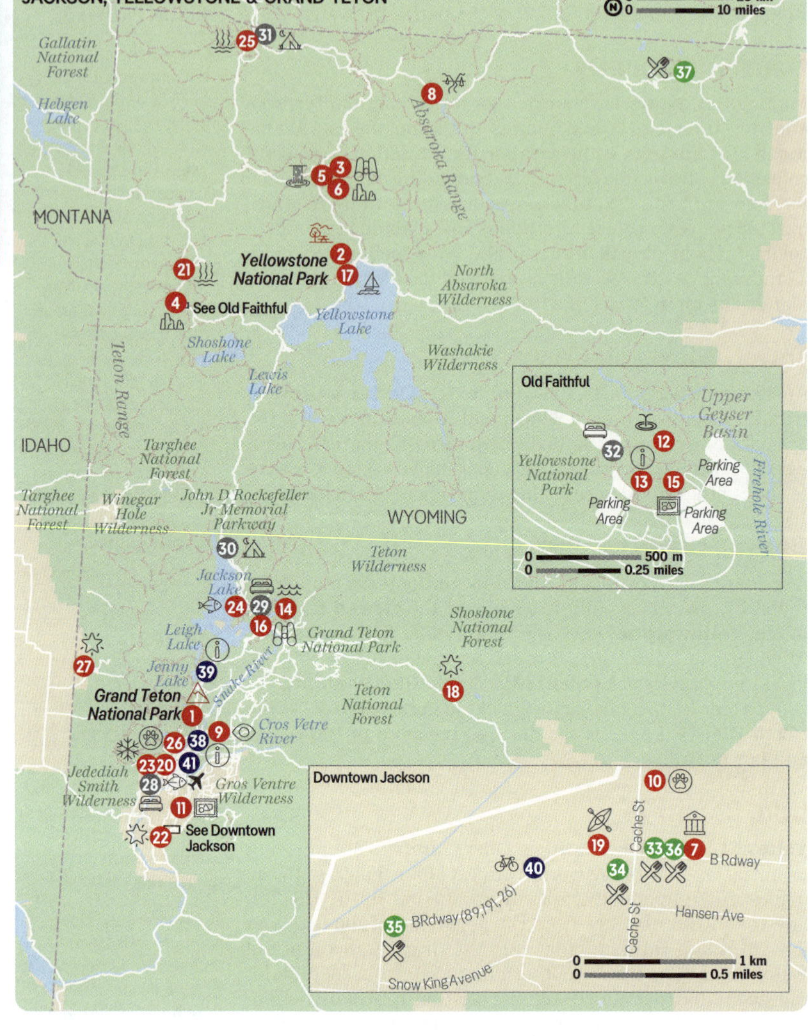

Continued from p91
Even if the museum is closed, the mile-long sculpture trail is worth visiting with works of art set into the rugged hillside, all with spectacular views over the National Elk Refuge (p91).

Examine Jackson's past

Stop at **History Jackson Hole** *(jacksonholehistory.org; adult/child $12/free)*, a state-of-the-art museum chronicling over 11,000 years of regional history through interactive displays and storytelling. Open artifact drawers and watch documentaries, peruse digital photo libraries, and step inside two preserved

HIGHLIGHTS
1 Grand Teton National Park
2 Yellowstone National Park

SIGHTS
3 Artist Point
4 Black Sand Geyser Canyon
5 Brink of the Lower Falls
6 Grand Canyon of the Yellowstone
7 History Jackson Hole
8 Lamar Valley
9 Mormon Row
10 National Elk Refuge & Greater Yellowstone Visitor Center
11 National Museum of Wildlife Art
12 Old Faithful
13 Old Faithful Visitor Education Center
14 Oxbow Bend
15 Tribal Heritage Center
16 Willow Flats Turnout

ACTIVITIES
17 Bridge Bay Marina
18 Continental Divide Dogsled Adventures
19 Dave Hansen Whitewater
20 Grand Fishing Adventures
21 Grand Prismatic Spring
22 Jackson Hole EcoTour Operators
23 Jackson Hole Mountain Resort
24 Jackson Lake
see 39 Jenny Lake Boating
25 Mammoth Hot Springs
26 Moose-Wilson Road
27 Teton Backcountry Guides

SLEEPING
28 Hostel
29 Jackson Lake Lodge
30 Lizard Creek Campground
31 Mammoth Campground
32 Old Faithful Inn

EATING
33 Cafe Genevieve
34 Gather in Jackson Hole
35 Gun Barrel Steak and Game House
36 Persephone Café Jackson
37 Top of the World Resort

INFORMATION
38 Craig Thomas Discovery & Visitor Center
39 Jenny Lake Visitor Center

TRANSPORT
40 Hoback Sports
41 Jackson Hole Airport

frontier-era cabins. Biographies dot the space in a loose timeline, introducing notable Native Americans, homesteaders, ranchers and skiers. Head upstairs to check out the community-curated gallery, which explores ever-changing themes.

Skiing a winter wonderland

Nestled in the Tetons just 12 miles from downtown Jackson, **Jackson Hole Mountain Resort** *(jacksonhole.com; lift tickets from $218)* is one of the country's top mountain destinations. Spread across two mountains – **Après Vous** and **Rendezvous** – the resort is renowned for its steep, dramatic terrain, stunning alpine views and deep, consistent snowfall (over 450in annually). It also has the steepest continuous vertical drop in North America – 4139ft – offering a challenge for intermediate and expert skiers and snowboarders. While there's no doubt the resort is world-class, Jackson Hole also provides rare open access to expansive wilderness skiing. If you have avalanche training, consider venturing into the 3000 acres of unpatrolled, backcountry terrain of the Bridger-Teton National Forest. Alternatively, hire one of the **resort's backcountry guides** *(jacksonhole.com/mountain-sports-school/backcountry; per person $393-1330)* to help navigate the rugged landscape, ensuring a safer powder adventure beyond the resort boundaries.

JACKON'S ANTLERS

Jackson's Town Square is famous for its four iconic arches made entirely of elk antlers. The arches weigh several tons, each made up of 2000 to 3000 antlers collected from the National Elk Refuge (p91) by local Boy Scouts, an annual spring tradition since the mid-1960s. No animals are harmed during the collecting – the antlers are naturally dropped by elk before being gathered. The arches attract thousands of visitors yearly, each posing next to and under the antlers, hoping for a classic Jackson photo op.

TOP EXPERIENCE

Grand Teton National Park

Awe-inspiring in their grandeur, the Tetons have captivated the imagination from the moment humans laid eyes on them: 12 glacier-carved summits framing the singular Grand Teton (13,775ft). While the view is breathtaking from the valley floor, it only gets more impressive on the trail or on the water. In winter, the Tetons make a magical setting for snowshoeing and cross-country skiing.

ROBNAW/SHUTTERSTOCK

Hidden Falls

TOP TIPS

- Stop in the **Craig Thomas Discovery & Visitor Center** for excellent exhibits and films as well as ranger help desks.
- Don't approach wildlife. Maintain at least 100yd from bears and wolves, 25yd from all others.
- Wear layers. The weather can change rapidly year-round.

PRACTICALITIES

- nps.gov/grte
- per vehicle $35
- 24hr

Scenic Drives

Cruise along **Hwy 191** and **Teton Park Rd**, stopping at staggeringly beautiful viewpoints, many with signage with interesting facts about the park. Make a slight detour to **Mormon Row**, home to the iconic Moulton Barns with the Tetons rising dramatically behind – possibly the most photographed site in the park. Or drive up **Signal Mountain Summit Rd** for sweeping mountain views.

Wildlife Watching

Head to **Oxbow Bend**, **Willow Flats** and **Moose–Wilson Rd** at dawn or dusk for your best chances of spotting moose, elk, grizzlies and bald eagles. Bring binoculars and be patient.

Hiking

Jenny Lake has a variety of breathtaking trail options. Consider hopping on a **shuttle boat** *(adult/child round trip $20/12)* to hike to **Hidden Falls** and **Inspiration Point** – a short hike with big-time views. For longer treks, head from there into **Forks of Cascade Canyon** (9.2-mile round trip) with alpine lakes and terrain.

On the Water

Rent **kayaks** *(from $35)* on **Jackson Lake** or **Jenny Lake** to experience the park from the water. Or take a **scenic rafting trip** *(adult/child from $126/74)* on the Snake River from **Jackson Lake Lodge** (p123).

Montana

MOUNTAIN ADVENTURE | COLLEGE VIBE | INDIGENOUS PRESENCE

Welcome to Big Sky Country, where the Great Plains hit the Rockies and just about anything seems possible. At Glacier National Park, known for its towering sculpted mountains and abundant grizzly bears, visitors can enjoy terrific vistas and guided boat rides in long finger-lakes formed by ancient glaciers. Montana's numerous rivers, including the Blackfoot and the Clark Fork, are famous for their rugged beauty and outstanding fishing (and for nearly stymying explorers Lewis and Clark near present-day Great Falls). Nearby, Missoula and Bozeman are lively college towns with urban energy and plenty to do, from fascinating museums to world-class skiing. And Montana's many Native American sites include a bison reserve near Flathead Lake and the Little Bighorn Battlefield National Monument, where Cheyenne, Sioux and Arapahoe warriors quashed an ill-fated attack by Lt Col George Custer. Come, explore and take in one of the most dramatically beautiful corners of the continent.

Places

GETTING AROUND

Montana's busiest airport is **Bozeman Yellowstone International Airport**, a good starting point both for trips deeper into the state and into Yellowstone National Park. Missoula and Billings also have well-connected airports.

Greyhound *(greyhound.com)* and **Jefferson Lines** *(jeffersonlines.com)* bus passengers around the state, while **Amtrak's Empire Builder** train *(amtrak.com/empire-builder-train)* can be an attractive option for accessing Glacier National Park and other parts of northern Montana.

A private car provides much more flexibility. Just remember it's a gigantic state, with deceptively long drives between popular sites; gas up when you can to avoid getting stranded.

TOP TIP

Snow can fall in Montana well into June, particularly at higher elevations and in northern regions like Glacier National Park (p106). Be sure to check forecasts and road conditions year-round. And pack layers.

MONTANA
CANADA
IDAHO
WYOMING
Rocky Mountains
Kootenai National Forest
Glacier National Park
Columbia Falls
West Glacier
Whitefish
Kalispell
Lake Pend Oreille
Pend Oreille River
Flathead Indian Reservation
Flathead Lake
Flathead National Forest
Polson
CSKT Bison Range
Flathead River
Condon
Lolo National Forest
Seeley Lake
Missoula
Bitterroot Valley
Hamilton
Selway-Bitterroot Wilderness
Blackfeet Indian Reservation
Browning
Cut Bank
Conrad
Lake Francis
Choteau
Augusta
Helena National Forest
Wolf Creek
Ovando
Lincoln
Helena
Deer Lodge
Boulder
Anaconda
Butte
Beaverhead National Forest
Dillon
Clark Canyon Reservoir
Lima Reservoir
West Yellowstone
Island Park Reservoir
Cascade Reservoir
Fresno Reservoir
Chester
Lake Elwell
Great Falls
Fort Benton
Belt
Missouri River
White Sulphur Springs
Canyon Ferry Lake
Toston
Madison River
Three Forks
Bozeman
Gallatin National Forest
Gardiner
Absaroka Range
Yellowstone Lake
Livingston
Springdale
Clyde Park
Big Timber
Melville
Martinsdale
Neihart
Stanford
Havre
Missouri River
Winifred
Hilger
Lewistown
Judith Gap
Harlowton
Grassrange
Lavina
Roundup
Billings
Yellowstone National Park
Beartooth Scenic Highway
Fort Belknap Indian Reservation
Nelson Reservoir
Malta
Glasgow
Fort Peck
Fort Peck Lake
Missouri River
Jordan
Hardin
Crow Agency
Crow (Apsaalooke) Indian Reservation
Big Horn Mountains
Bighorn River
Fort Peck Indian Reservation
Wolf Point
Plentywood
Medicine Lake
Culbertson
Missouri River
Williston
Sidney
Watford City
Circle
Yellowstone River
Glendive
Terry
Yellowstone River
Forsyth
Miles City
Baker
Yellowstone River
Colstrip
Northern Cheyenne Indian Reservation
Custer National Forest
0 100 km
0 50 miles

Bozeman & the Gallatin Valley

Montana's dinosaurs and peoples

One of Bozeman's most engaging museums, **Museum of the Rockies** *(museumoftherockies.org; adult/child $20/13)* focuses on the paleontological history of Montana with spectacular dinosaur exhibits that include an edmontosaurus jaw with its battery of teeth and the largest T-rex skull ever discovered. Multimedia displays include life-size dinosaur recreations that remind you that many dinosaurs were in fact clad in feathers and that sharks once swam the tropical seas covering current-day Montana. Once you've had your paleontological fill, a set of galleries focus on the cultural history of the state, including its Native American tribes, while **planetarium shows** ($5 extra) offer insight into the cosmos. In summer, don't miss the outdoor **Living History Farm**, an original 1889 homestead worked by staff in period clothing who happily engage with you, offering a glimpse into Montana's pioneer days.

The artsy side of Bozeman

A bulwark of the creative scene in Bozeman, the **Emerson Center for the Arts & Culture** *(theemerson.org; free)* is a nonprofit set in a 1918 public school building. Located a couple of blocks from Main St, here you can see – and buy – works by regional artists in the galleries and boutiques lining the 1st floor; come in the evening to take in the occasional indie film, musical performance, and open-mic night in the refurbished auditorium, the **Crawford Theater** *(prices vary)*. If you're visiting in summer, be sure to join locals for a taste of Bozeman at the free, ever-popular **Lunch on the Lawn** from 11am to 1pm on Wednesdays, with food trucks, live music and a general sense of revelry.

Hitting the trails

When it comes to hiking around Bozeman, the Gallatin Valley has a treasure trove of trails covering almost 2300 miles, much of it within **Custer Gallatin National Forest** *(fs.usda.gov/custergallatin)*. One standout is **Cinnamon Mountain Trail**, a moderately challenging 8.2-mile out-and-back trail that leads to the summit (9350ft), with spectacular 360-degree views of the surrounding peaks and valleys. For a slightly less demanding option, try **Lava Lake Trail** instead. A local favorite, the 6-mile round-trip trail winds through a

A GIANT OF PALEONTOLOGY

The former curator of the Museum of the Rockies is larger than life. Paleontologist Jack Horner is widely believed to have been the model for the character Dr Alan Grant in the book *Jurassic Park* and served as technical adviser to all the films. And yes, they did extract soft tissue from a Tyrannosaurus thigh bone, right here in Bozeman. Among scientists, Horner is perhaps best known for his discoveries related to the large herbivorous maiasaura, offering clear evidence that some dinosaurs cared for their young. Horner published over 100 research papers as well as a handful of books, including three titles about dinosaurs for children.

EATING IN BOZEMAN: OUR PICKS

Bozeman Coop Downtown: Community-owned grocery store with an array of prepared foods plus organic salad bar. *9am-8pm Mon-Sat, 11am-5pm Sun* $

Jam!: Breakfast fave, serving American classics plus offbeat international dishes. Puerco verde crêpe, anyone? Call ahead to get on the waitlist. *7am-3pm* $$

Montana Ale Works: Industrial-chic warehouse with award-winning craft brews and elevated pub grub, including wagyu, elk and bison burgers. *4-9:30pm* $$

Shan: James Beard finalist serving Chinese- and Thai-inspired dishes integrating locally sourced meats; set in a cozy *izakaya*-style dining room. *4:30-9pm Tue-Sat* $$

FLY-FISHING KNOW-HOW

Most of fly-fishing's etiquette boils down to not crowding other anglers or spooking the fish they're targeting. A few pointers:

Anglers working upstream (which will be most of them) generally have the right of way.

Avoid 'high holing' (stepping into the water directly upstream of an angler) or standing on the bank opposite someone – this can spook rising fish.

If someone is at a nice spot but not fishing, they may be 'resting the hole.' Ask if they plan to keep fishing there; if so, move on. By the same token, don't monopolize good spots. And be kind to folks who are still learning, especially kids – we've all been there once.

GOODLUZ/SHUTTERSTOCK

Fly fishing, Montana

forested canyon ending at a stunning alpine lake. Both hikes are especially beautiful in summer and early fall, when wildflowers are in bloom.

A river runs through It

Ever since Robert Redford and Brad Pitt made it look sexy in the 1992 classic *A River Runs Through It*, Montana has been closely tied to fly-fishing cool. Whether you are just learning or you're a world-class trout wrangler, the wide, fast rivers are always spectacularly beautiful and filled with fish. For DIY trout fishing, the **Gallatin River**, 8 miles southwest of Bozeman along Hwy 191, has the most accessible, consistent

DRINKING IN BOZEMAN: OUR PICKS

Bozeman Taproom: Popular sports bar with breezy rooftop seating. Order a flight from over 50 craft brews on tap. *11am-midnight Sun-Thu, to 1am Fri & Sat*

Plonk Bozeman: Stylish wine bar with an impressive selection of international bottles. Pair with a charcuterie board. *3pm-midnight Sun-Thu, to 1am Fri & Sat*

Treeline Coffee Roasters: Sit under shade trees sipping the best coffee in town, or head inside to the heady aroma of the roasting room. *6:30am-4pm*

Bridger Brewing: Friendly brewery offering a rotating selection of craft beers and mountain views. If in doubt, order the Lee Metcalfe Pale Ale. *11:30am-8:30pm*

angling spots, closely followed by the beautiful **Yellowstone River**, 25 miles east of Bozeman in Paradise Valley. If you'd like a hand, **Montana Angler** *(montanaangler.com)* and **Gallatin River Guides** *(montanaflyfishing.com)* offer guided fly-fishing trips and equipment rentals.

Year-round in Big Sky Resort

Big Sky *(bigskyresort.com; adult/child lift ticket $198/119)* is big skiing. Located between Bozeman and Yellowstone National Park, it's the fourth-largest ski hill in North America, covering 5800 acres of skiable terrain across four mountains. It's known for its steepness (4350ft vertical drop) and its surplus of advanced and expert trails; take the tram to **Lone Peak** (elevation 11,167ft) for 360-degree views and expert-only runs. Or come after the snow melts, when the resort transforms into a mountain-biking and hiking hub. You'll find over 40 miles of trails, accessible by two **scenic lifts** *(per person $25, with bicycle $40)*. Expect wildflower-filled meadows and high alpine ridges crisscrossed with all-level trails. Bike rentals available on site.

All about soul turns

Located just 16 miles north of Bozeman, **Bridger Bowl** *(bridgerbowl.com; adult/child lift ticket $84/39)* is the US' leading nonprofit ski resort. The 2000-acre, community-owned gem has a fiercely loyal following and is a true skier's mountain, with serious terrain and unpretentious mood (and affordable lift tickets to boot). Known for its 'cold smoke' – light, dry powder that blankets the slopes all winter – Bridger offers surprisingly good skiing and boarding for all levels. But its claim to fame is surely the Ridge – a massive ridgeline overlooking the entire resort, accessible only by hiking, with no official trails, and plenty of unmarked cliffs and chutes. Avalanche gear and training required.

West Yellowstone

Close encounters with apex predators

Near Yellowstone's west entrance, **Grizzly & Wolf Discovery Center** *(grizzlydiscoveryctr.org; adult/child $16.50/11.50)* is worth a stop to learn more about the region's creatures. A well-regarded refuge, it's home to grizzly bears and wolves – most removed from the wild after becoming habituated to humans and becoming a 'nuisance.' Several observation programs are offered. Among the most popular is watching one or two bears serve as 'product testers' while staffers share their backstories. Typically, they grapple with a cooler or trash can filled with treats; if they can't break in after an hour, the item earns a 'bear-proof' label. In the Naturalist Cabin, you can observe wolf packs – and even stare into the golden eyes of a wolf – through oversized windows. Staff is on hand to teach about their behavior and personality traits. If you have time, check out the sections dedicated to otters, reptiles, raptors and fish. The small on-site museum also provides fascinating and sometimes surprising insights.

BACKCOUNTRY IN BRIDGER

Wendy Bianchini, Montana State University, Instructor, Department of Health Development & Community Health.

Nothing feels better than doing a handful of Ridge hikes at Bridger Bowl. In a way, it feels more like ski mountaineering: traversing or boot packing with your skis on your back, and wearing an avalanche beacon. Hiking at Bridger opens access to some pretty spectacular mountain terrain – steep chutes, big bowls and rocky cliffs. The skiing is really fun and challenging! It's not necessarily something I'd recommend to somebody who doesn't know their way around, though. If people are passing through and want to check it out, they should talk to ski patrol and locals to get information so they can ski the Ridge...and do it safely.

POWWOW ETIQUETTE

Listen to the master of ceremonies for announcements related to protocol such as when to sit or stand, and when to refrain from taking photos or recording an event.

Do not call a Native person's outfit a 'costume'. Traditional clothing and adornments are called 'regalia,' and are often beloved family heirlooms and sources of deep pride.

Avoid touching anyone's clothing or headdress. If you're tempted, ask permission. (Prepare to be denied.)

Ask before taking photos. While it's typically acceptable to take photos of intertribal competitions, ask before taking candid photos of individuals.

Do not record drumming. Ask permission from the Head Singer if you want to record a song.

Beartooth Scenic Highway

Driving the Beartooth Scenic Hwy

Take a drive along the breathtaking **Beartooth Scenic Hwy**, one of the most beautiful routes in the country and a destination in its own right. Connecting the town of Red Lodge to Yellowstone's northeast entrance, the 68-mile-long road passes through Wyoming along a twisting, turning alpine route back into Montana. It's known for its vistas: alpine lakes and dramatic canyons plus sky-high peaks like the jagged **Bear's Tooth**, **Index Peak** and **Pilot Peak**. You'll even see skiers at **Beartooth Basin** *(beartoothbasin.com; half/full-day lift ticket $40/50)*, a high-altitude summer ski area. The road crests at **Beartooth Pass West Summit**, where **Top of the World Resort** *(topoftheworldresort.com)* makes a good pit stop for coffee before descending past **Beartooth Butte** to **Clarks Fork Trailhead**, a popular hiking area. The road is open May to October, taking around three hours to complete.

Billings

Crow Fair

Started as a harvest festival in 1904, **Crow Fair** *(crow-nsn.gov/crow-fair.html)* is a spectacular weeklong gathering of Plains tribes held every August in the town of Crow Agency. One of the largest Native American gatherings in the country, it draws tens of thousands to the banks of the Little Bighorn River, where attendees set up hundreds of tipis. Each day begins with a parade of families filing past tipis on horseback, in traditional regalia; afternoons bring powwows with competitive dancers in beaded dress and feathers, all-Native rodeos and death-defying relay races. Plenty of food vendors make it easy to fill up on classic Native treats (fry bread with powdered sugar, anyone?), while nearby artisans showcase handcrafted jewelry and goods. At heart a social event, the Crow Fair is a powerful expression of community, where all are welcome. Consider staying overnight in your own tipi, falling asleep to the sound of drums; **rentals available on site** *(ndnbattletours@gmail.com)*.

Helena

A walk through historic Helena

Helena's historic heart beats along **Last Chance Gulch**, a winding pedestrian mall that traces the path of a gold strike made by four down-and-out prospectors in 1864. That lucky

EATING IN HELENA: OUR PICKS

No Sweat Café: Wildly popular brunch spot with vegan and gluten-free options. Lunch menu integrates global flavors. *7am-2pm Tue-Fri, from 8am Sat & Sun* $

Bad Betty's BBQ: Simple spot serving award-winning Southern-style BBQ, from brisket and ribs to pulled pork. *11am-3pm & 4-8pm Wed-Fri, 11am-3pm Tue & Sat* $

Windbag Saloon & Grill: One-time brothel turned pub, serving hearty burgers and sandwiches. Twice-daily happy hour. *11am-midnight Mon-Fri, from 10am Sat & Sun* $$

Ristorante Bella Roma: Upscale restaurant with authentic Italian flavors, homemade pastas and local ingredients. Prix-fix menu and wine pairings. *5-10pm Tue-Sun* $$$

TOM OLSON/SHUTTERSTOCK

Pilot and Index Peaks

find – millions in placer gold – sparked a boom that transformed the gulch into Montana's lovely state capitol. Spend a morning on the mall strolling past the grand 19th-century buildings, many of them home to boutiques and cafes; interpretive signs and public art along the way bring the town's Wild West past to life. For more historic spots, head to nearby **Reeder's Alley**, Helena's oldest surviving neighborhood. Built in the 1870s, the narrow brick road is lined with log cabins and early city dwellings; while most are filled with small businesses, informational placards offer insight into the structures and people who first inhabited them. Want more info? Take a **guided walking tour** of Helena with **The Foundation for Montana History** *(mthistory.org; adult/child from $10/8)*.

Missoula

Wander into the past

Deep in the Garnet Range forest, **Garnet Ghost Town** *(garnetghosttown.org; adult/child $10/free)* is one of Montana's best-preserved mining towns. Over two dozen buildings in a state of 'arrested decay' are scattered along the mountainside – weathered cabins, saloons, general stores, a hotel from the

BRENNAN'S WAVE

Brennan's Wave is an artificial white-water feature on the Clark Fork River in downtown Missoula. On warm summer nights, crowds gather at Caras Park to watch surfers and kayakers shred and paddle in the surf, a treat in this mountain town. But the wave is more than just a playground. It's a living memorial to Brennan Guth, a Missoulian and world-class kayaker, who died while kayaking Chile's Río Palguín in 2001. It was his vision to transform the river's irrigation diversion into a training ground for white-water athletes. After his death, the community rallied around that vision, raising over $300,000 to transform the river. In 2006, Brennan's Wave debuted; it later hosted the 2010 US Freestyle Kayaking Championships. Brennan would be proud.

EATING IN MISSOULA: OUR PICKS

Bernice's Bakery: Beloved from-scratch bakery-cafe with delicious pastries and an ever-changing menu of sandwiches, soups and salads. *6am-6pm Mon-Sat, 8am-4pm Sun* $

Dinosaur Café: No-frills place with extraordinary Cajun food from jambalaya to po' boys. Located in Charley's Bar, a Missoula institution. *11am-9pm Mon-Fri, from noon Sat* $

Iron Horse Bar & Grill: Casual restaurant with an extensive international menu, from ahi tuna to BBQ. Set in a repurposed train depot. *11am-10pm* $$

Boxcar Bistro: Elegant European-style bistro – evocative of the dining cars of yesteryear – with a French-inspired menu. Perfect for a date night. *4-9pm Tue-Sat* $$$

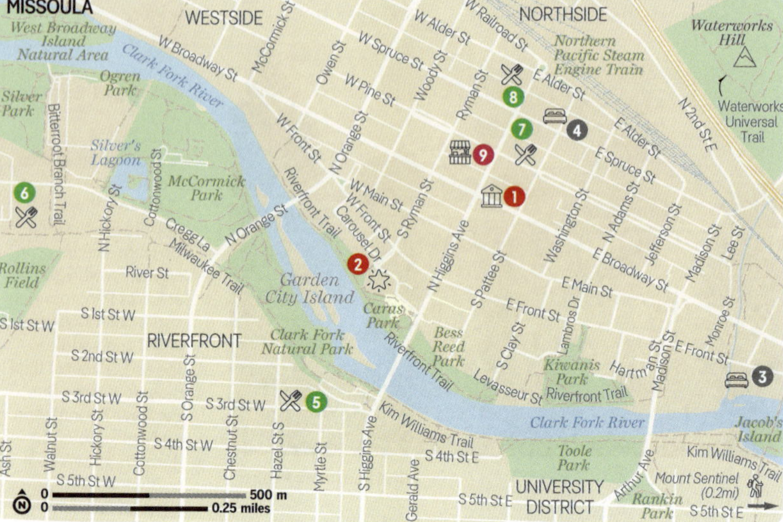

SIGHTS
1 Missoula Art Museum

ACTIVITIES
2 A Carousel for Missoula

SLEEPING
3 Goldsmith's Riverfront Inn
4 Shady Spruce Hostel

EATING
5 Bernice's Bakery
6 Boxcar Bistro
7 Dinosaur Café
8 Iron Horse Bar & Grill

SHOPPING
9 Missoula People's Market

late 1800s – transporting you to gold-rush days, when mining towns were built overnight and vanished almost as quickly. It's an evocative place, where you can wander around buildings that once bustled with over 1000 people, imagining what life was once like here. Informational placards lend more info and friendly forest rangers are often present and happy to answer questions. Several hiking and biking trails make it easy to spend the day here. Or stay overnight; in winter, two **primitive cabins** with no electricity or running water are available by lottery *(per night $50)*. The rub? From January to April, the site is only accessible by snowmobile or skis/snowshoe. Located about 40 miles east of Missoula, at the end of a 6-mile-long dirt road.

Take in regional art

All hail a city that encourages free-thinking art and then displays it free of charge! Set in a renovated public library, the sleek **Missoula Art Museum** *(artsmissoula.org; free)* is a small but powerful space, showcasing works by regional and local artists, with a focus on Native American works. Head to the top floor for special exhibits.

All about smokejumpers

When you're in town, don't miss the fascinating **Missoula Smokejumper Visitor Center** *(fs.usda.gov; by donation)*. Part of an active base for the heroic men and women who parachute into forests to combat wildfires, it's the starting point for an hour-long **tour** by a smokejumper, who guides you through the facilities to see where the crew lives and trains, including areas where they painstakingly sew, inspect and test their own parachuting gear. It's a humbling tour, offering a rare glimpse into the dangerous profession. Afterwards, check out the visitor center exhibits, which explore

KIRK FISHER/SHUTTERSTOCK

A Carousel for Missoula

the evolving nature of wildfire management in the face of warming climates. For deeper insight into the courage and cost of the job, pick up Norman Maclean's *Young Men and Fire* (1992), a tribute to Montana's Mann Gulch fire that took the lives of 12 smokejumpers.

Enjoy an artisanal fair

The highlight of summertime in Missoula is **Missoula People's Market** *(missoulapeoplesmarket.org; free)*, an artisanal fair held every Saturday morning from May through September. A popular community affair, the market transforms West Pine Street into a vibrant pedestrian zone filled with more than 80 stalls showcasing handmade goods by local artisans. Live music fills the air as you peruse stands filled with everything from pottery, jewelry and photography to leatherwork, wood carvings and organic skincare products. Food vendors make it that much easier to make a day of it.

Kiddie fun

If you're traveling with little ones, take a spin on **A Carousel for Missoula** *(carouselformissoula.com; adult/child $2/1)*, a beloved carousel with 40 hand-carved and individually painted horses and chariots. It was created by an army of volunteer artists who rallied around a local cabinet-maker's dream to restore a bit of whimsy to downtown. Afterwards, pop into **Dragon Hallow**, a fantastical playground next door, the product of another volunteer town effort.

Take on Mt Sentinel

The steep **Mt Sentinel** switchback trail (1.5-mile round trip) behind the University of Montana football stadium leads up to a concrete whitewashed 'M' (visible for miles around) on the 5158ft Mt Sentinel. Tackle it on a warm summer evening for glistening views of the city and its spectacular environs, including the Clark Fork River and mountains beyond. The trailhead is at Phyllis Washington Park on the eastern edge of campus.

FORT MISSOULA: ALIEN DETENTION CENTER

During WWII, Fort Missoula, originally an army post, was repurposed into an Alien Detention Center where around 1000 Japanese men were held. These lawful US residents, community leaders and successful professionals in West Coast towns were deemed 'enemy aliens' for no other reason than their Japanese heritage. Detainees lived in barracks behind barbed wire and under guard, undergoing hearings to determine whether they posed a threat to the US. None were charged with any crime. Eventually, they were transferred to Japanese internment camps like Amache (p82), Heart Mountain (p90) and Minidoka (p119). They remained unlawfully detained for the rest of the war, casualties of wartime hysteria and racial discrimination.

VACLAV SEBEK/SHUTTERSTOCK

TOP EXPERIENCE

Glacier National Park

Few places on earth are as magnificent and pristine as Glacier National Park. Protected in 1910, the glacially carved remnants of an ancient thrust fault left behind a brilliant landscape of snowcapped pinnacles, plunging waterfalls and glassy turquoise lakes. Its dense forests are home to an abundance of bears, while smart park management has kept the place accessible and authentically wild.

DON'T MISS

- Driving Going-to-the-Sun Rd
- Hiking Grinnell Glacier
- Wildlife-watching
- Paddling on Swiftcurrent Lake
- Blackfeet Nation exhibits and programming

Drive Going-to-the-Sun Road

Cutting through the center of Glacier National Park, **Going-to-the-Sun Rd** connects **West Glacier** with **St Mary** in the east. This epic rollercoaster ride over the Continental Divide, an engineering marvel chiseled out of raw mountainside, is considered one of the most spectacular roads in the US. Spanning 50 miles, it climbs up to Logan Pass (6646ft) and is bursting with soaring vistas, hiking opportunities, glacial melt spewing down the rocks and rushing waterfalls. Don't miss pullouts like **Bird Woman Falls Overlook**, with views

PRACTICALITIES

● nps.gov/glac ● summer/winter per vehicle $35/25 ● 24hr

of the highest waterfall (492ft) on the drive; and **Jackson Glacier Overlook**, to spy one of the remaining 25 glaciers in the park on the side of Mt Jackson (10,052ft). The entire road is usually open from late June to early October.

Hike Hidden Gems

Glacier is a hiker's paradise, with over 700 miles of trails. Near **Logan Pass**, the **Highline Trail** (11.6-mile round trip) hugs cliffs and wildflower meadows with sweeping mountain views, while the **Hidden Lake Overlook** (3-mile round trip) offers a shorter, family-friendly option. In **Many Glacier**, don't miss the hike to **Grinnell Glacier** (10.6-mile round trip), one of the most dramatic treks in the park, offering up-close views of a rapidly receding glacier (or shorten the hike to 7.6 miles by taking a boat shuttle across Swiftcurrent Lake). Other must-hikes include **Avalanche Lake** (4-mile round trip) via the **Trail of the Cedars** (0.9-mile round trip), an accessible raised-boardwalk loop through a cedar forest, and the moderate loop around **Iceberg Lake** (9.6-mile round trip), where floating ice dots a turquoise basin well into summer.

Wildlife Watching

Glacier is home to an incredible variety of wildlife. Head out early or stay out late for the best chances to see animals in motion. Search the rugged **Rising Wolf Mountain** slopes for sure-footed creatures like bighorn sheep and mountain goats. Meanwhile, moose are often seen at sunset along the road into **Two Medicine**. Look out for bear tracks in prairie environments and flower fields, plus **Dawson Pass** and **Scenic Point Trail**. Be sure to carry bear spray and follow park guidelines for a safe experience.

Experience the Water

Six **historic boats** *(glacierparkboats.com; adult/child $27/13.50)* – some dating back to the 1920s – ply four of Glacier's attractive mountain lakes, and some of them combine the float with a short **guided hike** led by interpretive, often witty, guides. For more solitude (and a bit of a workout), you also can rent **rowboats** ($32.50 per hour), **kayaks** ($32.50 per hour) and **paddleboards** ($24.20 per hour) at Lake McDonald, Swiftcurrent Lake and Two Medicine Lake.

Take a Century-Old Sightseeing Tour

Glacier's vintage buses, known as the 'Rubies of the Rockies,' are emblems of the park. Introduced in 1914, the elongated Model 706s have open tops for unobstructed views, but can be covered when it rains. A dozen **Red Bus Tours** *(glaciernationalparklodges.com; adult/child from $60/30)* whizz visitors around the park, hitting the big attractions and views – they range from a few hours to nine hours and run from mid-May to late September. Tours depart from several locations on both sides of the park.

BEAR ENCOUNTERS

Running Bad idea. Bears are faster, and running may elicit an attack from a non-aggressive bear.

Bear spray If a bear charges, spray a one- to two-second blast when the bear is 30ft away.

If the bear makes contact Drop, lie flat on your stomach and cover your neck with your hands. Don't move until the bear has left.

TOP TIPS

- Visit St Mary Visitor Center to learn about the Blackfeet Nation and its deep connections to the park land, from carefully curated exhibits and ranger talks to cultural programs.
- Park rangers will give tutorials on how to properly use bear spray – be sure to ask.
- Snow can fall year-round in the park; check weather conditions before heading out.
- A free hop-on, hop-off shuttle runs along Going-to-the-Sun Rd between Apgar and St Mary visitor centers. Buses leave every 15 to 30 minutes from Apgar (every 30 to 45 minutes from St Mary). The last trips down from Logan Pass leave at 7pm.

WARRIORS OF THE FOREST

The 3000-sq-mile **Blackfeet Indian Reservation** sits east of Glacier National Park and borders Canada, spanning an area twice the size of the park. It's home to 9500 tribal members, including those from the Northern Piegan (Blackfeet), Southern Piegan and Blood tribes, who lived in the Alberta area north of the border in the 1700s. The Blackfeet were best known for their horse and gun skills and had a reputation as exceptionally formidable warriors.

This spirit continues today, exemplified by the Chief Mountain Hotshots, an elite Blackfeet firefighting crew based in Browning. Known as the 'Warriors of the Forest,' this crew works in large-scale wildland firefighting, typically working 15 to 20 large fires and traveling between 10,000 and 20,000 miles each year.

CSKT Bison Range

Meet a living legacy

Home to over 350 bison, the **CSKT Bison Range** *(bison range.org; per vehicle $20)* spans 18,500 acres of grasslands, forests and rolling hills on the Flathead Indian Reservation. The bison are direct descendants of a small herd protected in the 1800s by tribal members at a time when bison were nearly extinct, making the herd biologically and culturally significant. Two dirt roads traverse the range: the 14-mile **Prairie Dr** and 19-mile **Red Sleep Mountain Dr** (open summer only), which climbs 2000ft for sweeping views of the Mission Mountains and surrounding valleys. Along the way, keep your eyes peeled for bison grazing, calves nursing and bulls wallowing in dust. You might also see elk, bighorn sheep, pronghorn and even black bears.

Whitefish

Family-friendly winter sports

Big mountain skiing at **Whitefish Mountain Resort** *(ski whitefish.com; lift ticket adult/child $110/55)* is a laid-back affair, great for families as well as expert skiers and snowboarders willing to hike up in order to rip up off-piste double-black-diamond glades. The mountain is known for its fog, but on bluebird days, views from the summit are unsurpassed. When there's fresh powder, join locals who ditch work to make fresh tracks.

Browning

Learn all about the Plains Indians

Don't be fooled by the drab exterior of the **Museum of the Plains Indians** *(doi.gov/iacb/ourmuseums; adult/child $7/3)* on the Blackfeet Reservation – inside, you'll find rich and meticulously curated exhibits on the history and cultures of the Northern Plains tribes, including the Crow, Cree, Sioux, Cheyenne and Blackfeet. Themes range from the arts and religion to hunting and warfare; expect detailed signage alongside all manner of ceremonial regalia, art, tools, toys and more. In summer, stop into the adjacent studio to watch local Native American artists at work, giving demonstrations and selling their works, too.

Great Falls

Step into the Lewis and Clark Expedition

As you're driving through Montana, make a pit stop in Great Falls to visit **Lewis and Clark National Historic Trail Interpretive Center** *(fs.usda.gov; adult/child $8/free)*. A labyrinthine museum, it tells the fascinating story of the 2½-year, 8000-mile trek of Meriwether Lewis and William Clark, American explorers commissioned by President Jefferson to map the newly acquired lands of the Louisiana Purchase,

RONNIE CHUA/SHUTTERSTOCK

Whitefish Mountain Resort

establish trade with Native American tribes and find a water route to the Pacific. The exhibits deep-dive into the journey with hands-on displays, films and even a two-story diorama depicting Lewis and Clark's men hauling canoes around the waterfalls of modern-day Great Falls. Keep your eyes peeled for Seaman, a volunteer therapy dog representing Lewis' beloved Newfoundland dog, the only four-legged member of the expedition.

Marvel at C.M. Russell's Art

Another excellent stop in Great Falls is the **C.M. Russell Museum** *(cmrussell.org; adult/child $20/7)*, a sprawling complex of buildings dedicated to the art and life of Charles M Russell (1864–1926), the iconic 'cowboy artist' of the American West. Begin in the museum, home to one of the largest Russell collections in the world – over 2000 oil paintings, watercolors, sculptures and illustrated letters – which rotates through its 16 different galleries and a sculpture garden. Afterwards, head next door to Russell's log studio, built of cedar telephone poles, and his Victorian-era home, both outfitted with period furnishings and Russell's personal effects; signage provides context on his life, family and friendships.

CASINOS EVERYWHERE

As you drive through Montana, one thing stands out: casinos – over 1300 of them. Their proliferation stems from a 1972 change to the state constitution granting the legislature authority to legalize gambling on a case-by-case basis. This paved the way for small-scale gaming across the state.

Most 'casinos' are tucked into in the corners of bars, restaurants, bowling alleys or gas stations. You won't find roulette wheels or blackjack dealers – just rows of video gambling machines offering poker, keno and line games. These machines are common in rural towns and larger cities, providing convenient entertainment for passersby. For business owners, they're a financial lifeline: a single machine can generate $28,000 annually.

TOP EXPERIENCE

Little Bighorn Battlefield National Monument

The Little Bighorn Battlefield National Monument, on the Crow (Apsáalooke) Reservation, 65 miles southeast of Billings, marks General George Custer's famous 'last stand.' Here, in 1876, Lakota Sioux and Cheyenne warriors led by Crazy Horse and Sitting Bull won a major victory – briefly boosting Native American resistance before US forces crushed it, forcing most Plains tribes onto reservations within five years.

DON MAMMOSER/SHUTTERSTOCK

TOP TIPS

- Battlefield Tour Rd closes 30 to 45 minutes before the official park closure; arrive early enough to assure you have time to drive through the site.
- In summer, visit in the early morning for cooler temperatures and fewer people.

PRACTICALITIES

- nps.gov/libi
- per vehicle $25
- 8am-6pm Fri-Sun Jun-Sep, to 4pm Oct-May

Self-Guided Tour

Battlefield Tour Rd runs through the site, a 4.5-mile road with frequent turnouts featuring free cellphone audio guides and informative panels that bring the conflict alive. Across the fields and valleys, and within sight of the road, white tombstones indicate where US soldiers are buried, while red granite markers symbolize where Native American warriors died. Crowning the battlefield is **Last Stand Hill**, where Custer fell, and nearby **Indian Memorial** is a fascinating tribute to the Sioux and Cheyenne stories.

Apsáalooke Tours

Learn more about the battle with **Apsáalooke Tours** *(adult/child $17/10)*. Led by Crow guides, these excellent one-hour bus tours give deeper insight into the conflict from a Plains tribespeople's perspective, from precognitive dreams to war traditions. Tours run every 1½ hours from 9am to 3pm Memorial Day to Labor Day, leaving from the parking lot.

Visitor Center

The visitor center offers deeper insight on the 1876 battle with well-conceived exhibits, a 20-minute film and artifacts including Native ledger art, weapons and uniforms – plus original soldiers' grave markers made from cartridges and handwritten name slips.

Idaho

OUTDOORSY | RUGGED BEAUTY | INDEPENDENT SPIRIT

Wedged between Montana and Oregon, Idaho is one of the most underrated destinations in the western US. The oddly shaped state has nearly 4 million acres of wilderness and some of the most scenic landscapes of the lower 48. The Sawtooth National Recreation Area and remote Bitterroot Mountains offer outstanding mountain escapes, from hiking trails and alpine lakes, to thrilling mountain biking. The Salmon River, aka the River of No Return, is arguably the country's premier white-water rafting destination. On the opposite extreme, Craters of the Moon National Monument has a dramatic (and vaguely apocalyptic) char-black volcanic landscape, nearly devoid of vegetation. Meanwhile, Boise, the state capital, is an appealing place to linger, whether museum hopping or strolling along the Boise River Greenbelt, which winds through town. And of course there's Sun Valley, ski resort of the stars, home of the world's first chairlift, and still swanky after all these years.

Places

GETTING AROUND

Small but busy **Boise Airport** is well connected, with nonstop flights to several domestic cities. Interstate bus lines like **Greyhound** *(greyhound.com)* and **Salt Lake Express** *(saltlakeexpress.com)* will get you to and from Boise, and a handful of other cities, but service within the state is fairly limited. For that, a private vehicle is essential. You won't need 4WD to get to Craters of the Moon National Monument (p120) and other major destinations, especially in the summer. But many remote areas are only reachable by dirt road, and having a high-clearance vehicle will make travel there easier and safer.

TOP TIP

Plan ahead when traveling through mountainous and rural areas: cell service can be spotty, so download offline maps. Keep your gas tank full and add cushion time between destinations – winding roads, mountain passes and unexpected gravel stretches can slow things down.

IDAHO
CANADA
MONTANA
IDAHO
NEVADA
UTAH
Cut Bank
Great Falls
Helena
Missoula
Anaconda
Butte
Salmon
Stanley
Sun Valley
Ketchum
Craters of the Moon National Monument & Reserve
Boise
Caldwell
Nampa
Mountain Home
Minidoka National Historic Site
Twin Falls
Pocatello
Blackfoot
Idaho Falls
Rexburg
Driggs
Preston
Idaho Panhandle
Coeur d'Alene
Post Falls
Sandpoint
Bonners Ferry
Libby
Whitefish
Kalispell
Polson
Thompson Falls
Wallace
Moscow
Lewiston
Clarkston
Lolo
Hamilton
Dillon
West Yellowstone
Challis
McCall
Weiser
Payette
Ontario
Idaho City
Riddle
Owyhee
Jackpot
Wells
Tremonton
Brigham City
0 50 km
0 25 miles

Boise

Museum-hopping in the park

In the heart of downtown Boise, the leafy **Julia Davis Park** is home to several museums, making it an easy place to spend a day – and to learn about the state – rain or shine. Start at the **Idaho State Museum** *(history.idaho.gov/museum; adult/child $10/5)*, a state-of-the-art building that uses Idaho's spectacularly diverse landscapes as the backdrop to its development, both in people and place. Exhibits are well conceived, integrating multimedia elements as well as kid-friendly installations. The Origins Gallery, with its Native American voices, is especially rewarding. Next door, the **Idaho Black History Museum** *(ibhm.org; free)* is housed in the historic St Paul Baptist Church building, the first Black church in Idaho. Simple exhibits line the one-room museum, outlining Black presence and achievement in the state. Nearby, don't be fooled by the nondescript building that houses **Boise Art Museum** *(boiseartmuseum.org; adult/child $9/5)*. Inside, the permanent collection includes masterpieces by heavy hitters like Ansel Adams and Deborah Butterfield while ever-changing temporary exhibits keep the space feeling current. Be sure to use the free cellphone audio and ASL guides.

Meandering on Boise River Greenbelt

Snaking its way through town, the **Boise River Greenbelt** is a lovely 29-mile-long riverside path with bridges, benches and shaded spots connecting a series of parks, many named after prominent Boise women. It originated as a plan in the 1960s to prevent development in the Boise River's floodplain in order to provide open space in the rapidly growing city. Today, the Greenbelt is just that: a path popular for its easy access to nature, especially known for the 150 types of birds seen year-round, from blue herons to bald eagles. Take an afternoon stroll along the river or explore further on an e-bike rental from **Sunrise Electric Bikes** *(sunrise-ebikes.com; from $40)*. To make a day of it, stop in at one of Julia Davis Park's museums, watch surfers at Boise Whitewater Park (p115) or enjoy a riverfront tasting at Telaya Wine Co (p115) or **Payette Brewing Co** *(payettebrewing.com)*.

Urban water play

There is no better way to spend a sunny summer day in Boise than floating down the river. Put in at **Barber Park**, where **Boise River Raft & Tube** *(boiseriverraftandtube.com)* rents

TREEFORT MUSIC FESTIVAL

One of Idaho's most popular events, **Treefort Music Fest** *(treefortmusicfest.com)* is a five-day indie music festival held every March in downtown Boise. Over 400 bands are featured at over 60 venues, from outdoor stages in Julia Davis Park to pop-ups in cafes, breweries and even shuttle buses. The fest draws tens of thousands of people showcasing Boise's vibrant, artsy spirit. Beyond music, the festival also features themed spaces or 'forts' around town like Foodfort, Filmfort, Comedyfort, Yogafort, Hackfort and Dragfort, which offer immersive experiences like food tastings, stand-up acts, wellness sessions, drag shows and more. Be sure to buy festival passes in advance – they often sell out.

EATING IN BOISE: OUR PICKS

The Warehouse: Cavernous food hall with 13 independent kitchens serving everything from burgers to fusion Vietnamese-Basque eats. *hours vary* $

Goldy's Breakfast Bistro: No-frills breakfast fave with hearty portions, scratch pancakes and hollandaise sauce. Arrive early or expect a wait. *7am-2pm* $$

Fork: Restaurant Row go-to serving a wide range of locally sourced dishes. Don't miss the asparagus fries. *hours vary* $$$

STIL: Small-batch ice-cream shop scooping creative flavors, which are paired with local beers and wines. *hours vary* $

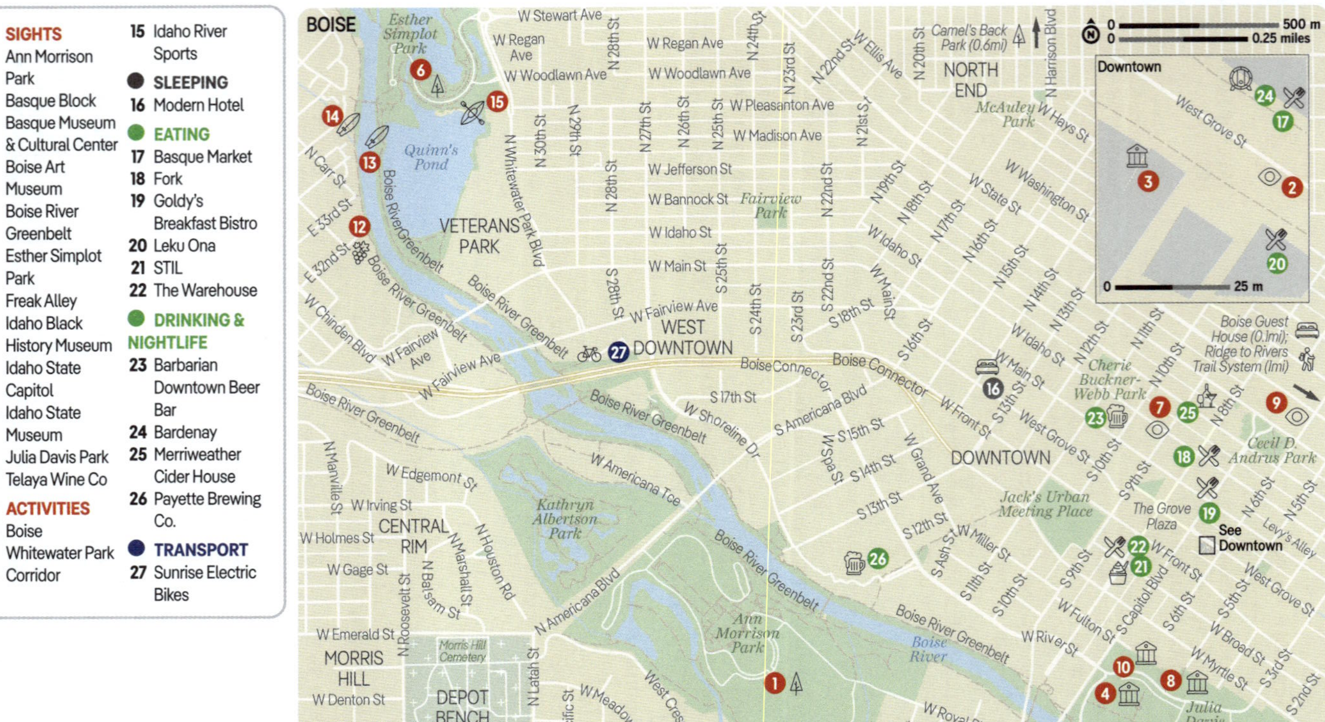

SIGHTS

1 Ann Morrison Park
2 Basque Block
3 Basque Museum & Cultural Center
4 Boise Art Museum
5 Boise River Greenbelt
6 Esther Simplot Park
7 Freak Alley
8 Idaho Black History Museum
9 Idaho State Capitol
10 Idaho State Museum
11 Julia Davis Park
12 Telaya Wine Co

ACTIVITIES

13 Boise Whitewater Park
14 Corridor
15 Idaho River Sports

SLEEPING

16 Modern Hotel

EATING

17 Basque Market
18 Fork
19 Goldy's Breakfast Bistro
20 Leku Ona
21 STIL
22 The Warehouse

DRINKING & NIGHTLIFE

23 Barbarian Downtown Beer Bar
24 Bardenay
25 Merriweather Cider House
26 Payette Brewing Co.

TRANSPORT

27 Sunrise Electric Bikes

tubes *(single/double $18/40)*, **rafts** *(four/six-person $75/85)* and **kayaks** *($50)* for self-guided 6-mile, 1½- to three-hour floats downstream to **Ann Morrison Park**. Return your watercraft there or take a shuttle bus back to Barber. Available June through August depending on river flows.

Or if you prefer a little more action, beeline to **Boise Whitewater Park**, where hydraulically controlled waves change daily, beckoning surfers, paddleboarders and kayakers year-round. There are no lifeguards, so know your limits – the rides can be rough! For rentals, steps away **Corridor** *(surfboise.com)* rents **surfboards** *(from $20)* and **wetsuits** *(from $15)* while in adjacent **Esther Simplot Park**, **Idaho River Sports** *(idahoriversports.com)* offers **kayak** and **paddleboards** *(from $25)*.

Take in street art

You don't have to wander far in Downtown Boise to stumble upon **Freak Alley** *(freakalleyboise.com)*, one of the largest open-air public art spaces in the West. Tucked between office buildings and trendy restaurants near Bannock and 9th streets, the gallery started in 2002 with just one painted door and has grown to become a two-block-long alley draped in vibrant murals created by over 200 artists. Every summer, more are added and existing works refreshed, providing a window into Boise's independent-minded artist community. Selfies encouraged.

A window into Basque Country

Boise is home to one of the largest Basque populations outside Spain, with approximately 16,000 residing here. The original émigrés arrived in the 1910s to work as shepherds when sheep outnumbered people seven to one. Few continue that work today, but many extended families have remained, and the rich elements of their distinct culture can be seen on a small stretch of Grove Street in downtown Boise known as **Basque Block** *(thebasqueblock.com)*. A leafy block, it's anchored by the **Basque Museum & Cultural Center** *(basquemuseum.eus; adult/child $7/5)*, a well-conceived space outlining the history of the Basque in Boise through detailed multimedia exhibits; the historic **Cyrus Jacobs-Uberuaga House**, a one-time Basque boardinghouse, also sits on-site. If the museum is closed, murals, sculptures, sidewalk etchings and interpretive signs provide insight into the Boise Basque community; the street itself incorporates the symbols and colors of the Basque flag. If hunger strikes, small businesses like

ARBORGLYPHS

The trees of the Wood River Valley and Boise National Forest bear a unique and picturesque record of alpine life about a century ago. Sheepherders, mostly Basque, carved pictures and messages into soft aspen and birch trunks as they drove their flocks between grazing lands.

Known today as 'arborglyphs,' the carvings date to the early and mid-1900s – the older ones are long gone as these smooth-barked trees are relatively short-lived (even more so with climate change).

Some of the pictures are remarkably detailed – boardinghouses, horses, birds, even the occasional naked woman – while poems about missing home capture the solitary lives of Idaho's early sheepherders.

DRINKING IN BOISE: OUR PICKS

Barbarian Downtown Beer Bar: Artisanal taproom known for its wide-ranging suds, from IPAs and sours to barrel-aged beers. *hours vary*

Merriweather Cider House: Family-owned cidery incorporating all manner of fruits. If in doubt, order the award-winning Plum Dandy. *hours vary*

Telaya Wine Co: Industrial-chic tasting room serving wines from Idaho and Washington. *noon-7:30pm Mon-Wed, to 8:30pm Thu-Sat, to 6:30pm Sun*

Bardenay: The country's first distillery-pub, pouring rum and whiskey made in-house. Located on Basque Block. *hours vary*

IDAHO'S SHAPE

Idaho owes its unusual shape to the warping effects of greed and politics. Originally, the Idaho Territory was massive (and roughly square), including most of today's Montana and Wyoming. When the Montana Territory was proposed in 1864, the border was to be set along the Continental Divide. But behind the scenes Idaho Supreme Court Justice Sidney Edgerton quietly convinced Congress to move the border west to the Bitterroot Mountains, lopping an extra 27,500 sq miles from Idaho, leaving just that narrow panhandle. It turns out Edgerton had been paid by Montana miners to lobby for the change. He went on to lay claim to the rich Bitterroot and Deer Lodge valleys and was named Montana's first governor.

ROBERT CROW/SHUTTERSTOCK

World Center for Birds of Prey

the **Basque Market** *(thebasquemarket.com)* and **Leku Ona** *(boisebasquefood.com)* offer traditional foods like braised chorizo or *croquetas*. In warmer months, their street-front patios are perfect for taking in the lineup of cultural events that are hosted outdoors, most integrating folk dancing and accordion beats.

Visiting the World Center for Birds of Prey

On Boise's south side, the **World Center for Birds of Prey** *(peregrinefund.org; adult/child $14/9)* is the headquarters of the Peregrine Fund, a nonprofit that has single-handedly brought back several species of raptors from the brink of extinction since the 1970s – from the peregrine falcon, the world's fastest bird, to the iconic California condor. Their method? A combination of captive breeding, habitat protection, local education and scientific research. Today, the center has several areas open to the public, including bird habitats, exhibit halls describing their work plus livestreams of on-site nesting areas. Knowledgeable staff members are ever-present and happy to talk raptors. Be sure to set aside time for a live raptor presentation – they are excellent!

Hiking Boise's Ridge to Rivers Trails

Easy access to some 210 miles of trails – hiking, mountain biking and horseback riding – is one of the best parts of visiting Boise. The **Ridge to Rivers** *(ridgetorivers.org)* trails meander across the city's foothills, eventually crossing grasslands, scrub slopes and tree-lined creeks on their way to the mountainous terrain of **Boise National Forest**. The options are almost endless: from short, leisurely strolls with skyscraper views to steep, challenging trails up mountainsides. For the most convenient access to the wilderness head to **Cottonwood Creek Trailhead** just east of the **capitol building**, or **Camel's Back Park** to the north. Check the Ridge to Rivers' website for detailed information about the trails, including interactive maps and current conditions.

Idaho Panhandle

Ride an epic trail

Take a ride through the spectacularly scenic Bitterroot Mountains on the **Route of the Hiawatha** *(ridethehiawatha.com; trail pass adult/child $20/16, shuttle adult/child $20/16)*. A 15-mile gravel trail near the Idaho-Montana border, the family-friendly route follows an old rail line, starting with the 1.66-mile St Paul Pass Tunnel - damp and completely dark - requiring a headlamp, a hoodie and some nerve. From there, the trail descends gradually through thick verdant forest, passing through eight rocky tunnels and crossing seven high trestle bridges, the highest 230-ft above the valley floor. Interpretative signs explain the route's railroad history, providing places to catch your breath and take some photos too. Shuttle buses save riders the uphill ride back. Bike rentals, including lamps, are available at the trailhead by reservation only. Book early. You also can save a few bucks by booking your trail passes and shuttle tickets online. Open late May to mid-September, weather-permitting.

Ketchum & Sun Valley

Hit historic slopes

Set in the stunning Sawtooth Mountains, **Sun Valley Resort** *(sunvalley.com; adult/child lift ticket $123/242)* began as the first purpose-built ski resort in the US, a venture by the Union Pacific Railroad to boost ridership. It opened in 1936 to much fanfare, thanks to both its luxury lodge and the world's first chairlift; the resort continued to gain cachet with the presence of celebrities like Ernest Hemingway, Ingrid Bergman and Gary Cooper, who received free trips as part of a marketing plan. It worked. Sun Valley and nearby Ketchum have been synonymous with luxury skiing and swanky Hollywood clientele ever since.

Today, join snow-sports lovers who flock here for the powder (and celebrity-spotting) on its two distinct mountains: **Dollar Mountain**, a treeless hill with mellow runs and extensive terrain parks; and **Bald Mountain** (aka Baldy), a favorite for its long cruisers, steep pitches and bowls. Both sit on opposite sides of Hwy 75; free shuttles from the resort village and Ketchum get you to either.

THE GEM STATE

Although long-running nickname, 'the Gem State,' was originally a reference to the state's rugged beauty. But miners searching for gold in Idaho's rivers would regularly stumble upon sparkling garnets, agates and jaspers in their pans. Gem mining began in earnest in the late 1800s, growing alongside Idaho's gold and silver booms, and expanding to include other stones. By 1967, over 70 different precious and semiprecious stones had been found in the state. The same year, the star garnet - a deep-red gemstone showing a four- or six-pointed star - was designated the state gem. Found only in India and Idaho, these garnets cemented Idaho's unique place in the gem world, as well as the appropriateness of its nickname.

DRINKING IN KETCHUM: OUR PICKS

TNT Taproom: Historic dynamite shed turned tap room with a rotating selection of local craft beers plus biodynamic wines. *2-9pm Mon-Thu, to 10pm Fri & Sat*

Warfield Distillery and Brewer:: Classy, laid-back gastropub with a rooftop bar and creative cocktails featuring award-winning organic spirits. *11:30am-9pm*

Grumpy's: Longtime local fave, this dive bar is known for its 32oz schooners of beer, chilled-out vibe, and beer-can wall décor. *11am-9pm*

Whiskey's on Main: Upscale sports bar with live music and dancing on weekends. *11am-10pm Sun-Tue, to midnight Wed-Thu, to 1am Sat & Sun*

THE ROUNDHOUSE

Kristine Bretall, Community Engagement Manager, Wood River Museum.

I love hiking in Sun Valley! And the smell when you're outdoors. In summertime, there's this scent of sage; it's this very lovely thing. In wintertime, it's this cold-snow, wood-smoke sort of a thing. And I love getting somewhere, anywhere, I can get up high. Like the **Roundhouse** on Bald Mountain. It's this octagonal structure built by Union Pacific Railroad engineers for skiers to stop and warm up. (It resembles one of those buildings used to turn around train engines.) It's an incredibly beautiful spot where you can really get a perspective on the landscape and see what it looks like all around.

Enjoy Sun Valley Music Festival

On summer evenings from late July to early August, join the crowd at the **Sun Valley Music Festival** *(svmusicfestival.org; free)*, the country's largest privately funded classical music event. For this free series, locals and visitors alike fill the open-air **Sun Valley Pavilion** (first-come-first-served seating) or spread blankets across its lawn to hear orchestral performances by some of the world's top musicians; expect everything from major symphonic works to modern pop. The atmosphere is informal – people come in hiking clothes, picnics are laid out and kids play nearby while the sound of the orchestra floats through mountain air. Come early for pre-concert talks.

Summer nights on ice

A summer showcase featured since 1937, **Sun Valley on Ice** *(sunvalley.com; grandstand adult/child from $104/58)* blends elite figure skating with panoramic mountain views. Held at the outdoor rink next to the **Sun Valley Lodge**, the Saturday night performances run from July through early September. Each show features Olympic and world-class skaters delivering solos, duets and ensemble pieces. Seating is up-close in the grandstands – a treat – or on the terrace, with buffet dinner included. Stay afterwards for autographs or meet-and-greets with the skaters.

Deep dive into the past

Learn all about the fascinating history of Sun Valley and Ketchum at the **Wood River Museum of History and Culture** *(comlib.org/museum; free)*. An arm of the Community Library, the engaging little museum traces the region's evolution from Shoshone and Bannock homelands to glitterati ski resort and town. Interactive exhibits include displays on sheep ranching, ski heritage and local oral histories though in true Sun Valley style, the exhibit on celebrity writer Ernest Hemingway kinda steals the show.

Stanley

Out in the Sawtooths

You'll find rivers to boat, mountains to climb, more than 300 lakes to fish, and over 700 miles of trails to hike or mountain bike in the dramatic **Sawtooth National Recreation Area** *(fs.usda.gov/sawtooth)*. It protects 1170 sq miles of public lands stretching between Ketchum and Stanley, offering almost endless opportunities for exploration and recreation.

EATING IN KETCHUM: OUR PICKS

Johnny G's Subshack: Sandwich shop serving up excellent 6in to 12in hoagies. Choose a specialty sub or build your own. *11am-4pm Mon-Fri, to 3pm Sat* $

Kneadery: Breakfast fave with a log-cabin vibe, including taxidermied creatures. Expect hearty egg dishes, French toast and freshly made pancakes. *8am-2pm* $$

Rickshaw: Cozy spot specializing in mouthwatering Southeast Asian street food. In summer, ask for a table on the leafy patio. *hours vary* $$

Fiamma: Upscale Italian with open kitchen concept highlighting its live-fire cooking. Its seasonal menu is mostly locally sourced. *4:30-10pm Wed-Sat, 10am-2pm Sun* $$$

There are several access points to the Sawtooths; among the most popular is **Galena Lodge** *(galenalodge.com)*. A community-owned spot that works in partnership with the National Forest Service, it serves as a hub to over 45 miles of well-maintained trails that crisscross the gorgeous Boulder Mountains. In the summer come for the hiking, mountain biking and wildflower-filled landscapes. In winter, it's all about cross-country skiing and snowshoeing, with groomed trails that wind through the snowy forest and alpine meadows. Friendly staffers provide trail recommendations though **snowshoeing tours** *(groups of minimum 3 people, per person $70)* and **guided mountain bike rides** *(from $175)* are a popular way to explore the area. Bike, ski and snowshoe rentals also available on-site as are hearty meals that will keep you fueled for the day.

Rafting the River of No Return

Rafting the **Middle Fork of the Salmon River** (aka River of No Return) is considered one of the greatest white-water trips in North America: a 104-mile route that winds its way through the heart of the River of No Return Wilderness Area, one of the most remote landscapes in the Lower 48. It's a clear, cold, fast-moving river – boats pass through deep canyons, alpine forest and granite gorges, and over 100 rapids, many class III and IV. Off the water, rafters can hike to waterfalls and soak in natural hot springs, spotting ancient pictographs and abandoned mining cabins along the way (not to mention bighorn sheep, bald eagles and black bear). Nights are spent camped on sandy riverbanks, eating around a campfire and sleeping under a blanket of stars.

Permits are required to ride the Middle Fork year-round; they are awarded by **lottery** *(recreation.gov)* but the competition is stiff – only about 2% of applicants receive one. Instead, most use river outfitters to access the river and to take care of all the details, from permits and shuttle service to meal prep and camp setup. Most are based in or near the sleepy towns of Salmon and Stanley, which come to life during the brief summer months. Recommended outfitters include **Solitude River Trips** *(rivertrips.com; six-day trip per person from $3250)* and **Idaho River Journeys** *(idahoriverjourneys.com; six-day trip per person from $3395)*.

Minidoka National Historic Site

Contemplate wrongful imprisonment

Located near the farming community of Jerome, **Minidoka National Historic Site** *(nps.gov/miin; free)* memorializes the incarceration of over 13,000 Japanese Americans who were forced to leave their homes by the US government to be unjustly imprisoned here during WWII. The internment camp, one of 10 in the country, was established under Executive Order 9066 as a racist reaction to the bombing of Pearl Harbor. Today, visitors can walk a 1.6-mile-long gravel **trail** past original structures like barracks, a mess hall, fire station and guard tower. Interpretive panels share personal stories

ERNEST HEMINGWAY

Ernest Hemingway's connection to Idaho ran deep, rooted in the wild, open landscapes that echoed his passion for the outdoors. He first visited Sun Valley in 1939, lured by Union Pacific's campaign to bring celebrities to the new ski resort. Captivated by the location, Hemingway returned almost yearly, hunting in the Sawtooth Mountains, fishing Silver Creek and writing prolifically. He eventually purchased a home in Ketchum, where he took his own life in 1961. Today, visitors can pay their respects at the **Hemingway Memorial** beside **Trail Creek** as well as his gravesite in **Ketchum Cemetery**. His final home, the **Hemingway House and Preserve**, is used for writer-in-residence programs, a lasting legacy.

TOP EXPERIENCE

Craters of the Moon National Monument & Reserve

This is a spectacularly vast, otherworldly place. Beginning some 15,000 years ago, a series of volcanic eruptions laid waste to the Snake River Plain, leaving a blistered land of lunar-like craters, lava-tube caves and fissures. The last eruption took place a mere 2000 years ago. The result is now a 750,000-acre national monument that's well worth a visit.

TOP TIPS

- The nearest gas station is in Cary, 25 miles away – be sure to gas up before arriving.
- From November to April, Loop Rd is closed to vehicular traffic; it's reserved for cross-country skiers and snowshoers. Plan accordingly.

PRACTICALITIES

- nps.gov/crmo
- per vehicle $20
- 24hrs

Drive Loop Road

A scenic **7-mile road** winds its way through the reserve, each turn revealing dramatic volcanic landscapes. Stop at pullouts for the views and signage, which give in-depth insight into the geology, flora, fauna and human history of the place.

Hike Volcanic Landscapes

Eight trails crisscross the reserve, offering a striking variety of features. If you're short on time, opt for the **North Crater Flow Trail** (0.3 miles), a breathtaking boardwalk suspended over young lava fields with snowcapped mountains in the distance; or take a short, steep climb to the summit of the jet-black **Inferno Cone** (0.4 miles), with 360-degree views of the reserve. For a longer hike, head to **Tree Molds Trail** (2 miles), an out-and-back trail with ancient trees preserved in hardened lava – subtle but haunting.

Enter Lava Tubes

Over **700 caves** exist in the reserve, most created by underground rivers of lava. **Indian Tunnel** is the largest and most accessible – an 800ft-long cave with a partially collapsed roof. Expect to scramble over jagged rock and uneven floors. **Cave permits** are required to enter, available for free at the visitor center.

and photographs that illuminate the harshness of life here – barbed wire, armed guards, extreme weather, minimal privacy...a memorial to Japanese-American resilience but also a reminder of the fragility of civil rights. The visitor center, open on weekends only, has further exhibits and a 30-minute film; ask about the excellent ranger led tours.

Blackfoot

Idaho Potato Museum

Driving through Blackfoot, you can't miss it – a statue of a gigantic baked potato (complete with sour cream and a pat of butter). It sits in front of the **Idaho Potato Museum** *(idahopotatomuseum.com; adult/child $7/3.50)*, a surprisingly engaging museum taking on the potato, from its global history and cultivation to its importance in Idaho. The exhibits are multilayered, including everything from films about McDonalds' fries to hands-on science experiments. There's also a bit of kitsch – animatronic displays, Mr. Potato Head stations, even the world's largest potato chip (25in by 14in). Don't miss the gift shop for quirky merch; and if you need a snack, the on-site cafe serves all manner of potato treats.

Driggs

Fly high at a hot-air balloon festival

For four days surrounding the July 4 holiday, the town of Driggs hosts the annual **Teton Valley Balloon Fest** *(tetonvalleyballoonrally.org; per vehicle $20)*, a quintessential Rocky Mountain festival, with colorful hot-air balloons soaring high above the verdant valley, the jagged, snowcapped Teton peaks in the background. It's a photographer's dream. Come at sunrise for tethered rides and the mass launch – over four dozen balloons ascending into bluebird skies. And return in the evening for the 'Rally Up and Get Down' party with live music, food-truck fare and giant balloons illuminating the Teton Valley Fairgrounds.

PERRING BRIDGE BASE JUMPERS

Standing 486ft above the Snake River, the **Perrine Bridge** in Twin Falls is the only human-made structure in the US where BASE jumping is allowed year-round without a permit. The extreme sport involves parachuting from a fixed object like a building, bridge or cliff and landing below – an especially dangerous endeavor due to low altitudes and short freefall times. At Perrine Bridge, BASE jumpers launch from platforms on the traffic-congested bridge, free-falling before deploying their parachutes to land in the canyon bottom. Nearly every day, you can see specially trained athletes from around the world preparing their parachutes in the parking lot and under nearby trees while captivated spectators line the bridge and the canyon rim.

EATING IN DRIGGS: OUR PICKS

Provisions Local Kitchen: Popular spot serving heaping plates of breakfast faves, sandwiches, salads and Mexican specialties like *choriqueso. 7am-3pm* $

Captain Ron's Smokehouse: Tiny shack serving finger-licking BBQ with all the fixin's. Eat at parking-lot picnic tables. *11am-4pm Tue-Sat* $

Citizen 33: Industrial-farmhouse style taproom serving tasty craft brews and elevated pub grub. If in doubt, get the mashed potatoes. *4-9pm* $$

Forage Bistro: High-end restaurant with casual vibe; the seasonal menu focuses on locally farmed meat and veggies. Happy-hour charcuterie boards. *noon-8pm* $$$

Places We Love to Stay

$ Budget $$ Midrange $$$ Top End

Denver p58

Hostel Fish $ Swanky hostel with plush dorms and cozy common areas. On-site bar plus neighborhood pub crawls bring a party feel.

Populus Hotel $$$ Luxurious carbon-forward hotel with nature-inspired features inside and out. Stunning city views. Rooms are a study in understated elegance.

Boulder p62

St Julien Hotel & Spa $$$ In the heart of downtown, Boulder's finest hotel is modern and refined with Flatiron views and a spa.

Rocky Mountain National Park p64

Glacier Basin Campground $ Ideally located in the Bear Lake corridor and surrounded by evergreens; 73 sites.

Murphy's Resort $$ Overlooking Lake Estes, this motor lodge has plenty of family-friendly activities. Six miles from the park.

Northern Colorado p66

Echo Park Campground (Dinosaur National Monument) $ Gorgeous, primitive Colorado-side campground at the confluence of the Yampa and Green rivers; 4WD highly recommended. First come, first served.

Vista Verde Guest Ranch (Steamboat Springs) $$$ The most luxurious of Colorado's top-end guest ranches. If you have the means, this is it.

Central Colorado p67

Crested Butte Hostel (Crested Butte) $ Luxurious hostel with restaurant-grade kitchen, crackling fireplace and a mix of dorms and private rooms.

Amigo Motor Lodge (Salida) $$ This cool motel is not only Southwestern stylish, it's got five retro trailers to sleep in.

Sebastian Hotel (Vail) $$$ Sophisticated hotel showcasing contemporary art and an impressive list of amenities, including a mountainside ski valet and luxury spa.

Mollie Aspen (Aspen) $$$ Make like Rihanna and book a room at Aspen's coolest new digs, with understated minimalist design and rooftop pool.

Western Colorado p72

Morefield Campground (Mesa Verde National Park) $ Full-service campground in a grassy canyon, 5 miles from the visitor center. General store sells basics.

South Rim Campground (Black Canyon of the Gunnison National Park) $ Large campground in a high-altitude scrub forest. Running water available summer only.

Saddlehorn Campground (Colorado National Monument) $ The park's only drive-up campground; potable water and flush toilets available. Open year-round.

Box Canyon Lodge & Hot Springs (Ouray) $$ Geothermically heated motel with modern pine-board rooms and 24/7 access to spring-fed hot tubs.

Telluride p77

Telluride Town Park Campground $ Creekside campground in the heart of Telluride, with showers, wi-fi, a pool and tennis.

Camel's Garden $$$ Ski-in, ski-out condo-hotel at the base of the gondola. Hit the 25ft hot tub at sunset.

Southeast Colorado p81

Pinyon Flats Campground (Great Sand Dunes National Park) $ Official park campground, with great location near the dune field. Reserve months ahead.

Cheyenne Mountain Resort (Colorado Springs) $$$ Overlooking Cheyenne Mountain, this woodsy resort has an air of indulgence with golf, a spa and lake activities.

Southeast Wyoming p85

Cheyenne Guest Inn (Cheyenne) $ Older, well-maintained inn with spick-and-span rooms and a tiny indoor pool. Continental breakfast included.

Mad Carpenter Inn (Laramie) $ Charming guesthouse with cozy, wood-trimmed rooms, a fully equipped cottage and a serious game room. Hot breakfast included.

Lander (Fort Washakie) p87

Mill House $$ Boutique hotel set in a beautifully renovated flour mill in downtown Lander; suites are modern with artful touches.

Northern Wyoming p89

The Cody (Cody) $$ New Western chic with green credentials; there's an indoor pool and hot tub, plus free breakfast.

Devil's Tower Lodge (Devil's Tower HS) $$ Unparalleled views and warm hospitality make this an excellent base, especially for climbers. Full breakfast included.

Yellowstone National Park p92

Mammoth Campground $ Yellowstone's only campground open year-round has 85 sites set amid scattered junipers and Douglas firs.

Old Faithful Inn $$$ Variety of rooms in a historic log-walled inn with a frenetic lobby that quietens by night.

Grand Teton National Park & Around p96

Lizard Creek Campground (Grand Teton NP) $ Small campground with pleasantly shaded sites set amid spruce-and-fir forest on the shores of Jackson Lake.

The Hostel (Jackson Hole) $$ Skiers' favorite for budget accommodations, including four-bed rooms, plus spacious lounge with pool table.

Jackson Lake Lodge (Grand Teton NP) $$$ Attractive hotel-style rooms and cottages, some with dramatic mountain views.

Bozeman & the Gallatin Valley p99

Howlers Inn (Bozeman) $$ Cozy log cabin-style B&B on a sanctuary for rescued captive-born wolves; profits support the cause.

RSVP Motel (Bozeman) $$$ Stylish upscale motel with colorful rooms and a great little on-site cafe and restaurant.

Rainbow Ranch Lodge (Big Sky) $$$ Rustic-chic lodge with stylish rooms, most with stone fireplaces and balconies. Located 5 miles from Big Sky turnoff.

Helena p102

Lamplighter Cabins & Suites $$ Cute, uniquely decorated cabins and contemporary suites, some with kitchenettes. Located steps from downtown.

Missoula p103

Shady Spruce Hostel $ Centrally located hostel in a renovated Victorian home; private rooms and dorms are clean, bright and spacious. Modern guest kitchen too.

Goldsmith's Riverfront Inn $$ Charming riverfront home converted into six cheery suites and fully equipped apartments.

Glacier National Park p106

Bowman Lake Campground $ Spacious sites in forested grounds, and beautiful Bowman Lake is only steps away.

Many Glacier Hotel $$$ A massive, Swiss-chalet-inspired lodge in a wondrous lakefront setting in the park.

Great Falls p108

Hotel Arvon $$ Boutique hotel set in a beautifully renovated historic building. Rooms are modern and spacious. Breakfast and parking included.

Boise p113

Modern Hotel $ Urban-chic motel with midcentury-modern rooms. A trendy on-site bar means creative cocktails by the firepit.

Boise Guest House $$ Historic home beautifully transformed into six tasteful suites with kitchenettes. There's a verdant backyard plus cruiser bikes.

Ketchum p117

Best Western Tyrolean Lodge $$ Chalet-themed motel with dated but comfortable rooms. Breakfast buffet included too. The best budget hotel in town.

Limelight Hotel $$$ Trendy downtown hotel with luxe rooms, many with mountain views. Outdoor pool, full breakfast and complimentary airport shuttle too.

Craters of the Moon National Park p120

Lava Flow Campground $ Small campsite set on volcanic landscape. Water and flush toilets available May to November only. First come, first served.

Driggs p121

Teton Valley Cabins $-$$ Pleasant log cabins on a forested lot, some with kitchenettes. In evenings, roast marshmallows around the communal fire pit.

Curated by
Anthony Ham

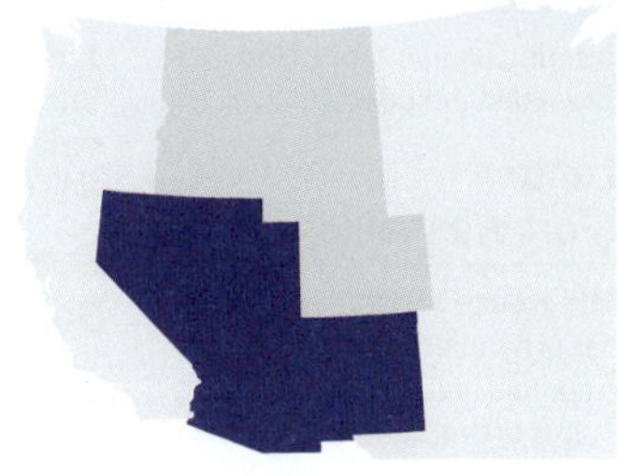

Southwest USA

ONE OF AMERICA'S GRAND EPICS

Soulful deserts and weirdly wonderful mountains. Frenetic cities and ancient stories. Las Vegas and the Grand Canyon. Welcome to America's fabulous west.

The Southwest could only happen in America. Take an astonishing landscape, the kind of place that is both cinematic in scope and part of a deeply American tradition of starring on the silver screen. Overlay that with a fascinating roll-call of civilizations, from the Ancestral Puebloans and Native American cultures like the Hopi, Navajo and Apache to the gunslingers and bandits (like Butch Cassidy or Billy the Kid) of the Wild West. And then, carrying all of this with you as you go – perhaps along Route 66 – rush headlong into the future toward places like Las Vegas or the space race of Las Cruces. Then let your mind consider the supernatural at Roswell and Area 51. And as you contemplate this remarkable collage that is America writ large, tuck into a meal laced with the green chiles of New Mexico in all their fiery manifestations.

But it's the backdrop to all of this – the landscapes that bring such gravitas to this corner of the country – that is the real star of the show. Yes, the Grand Canyon has no rivals. But the Mojave and Sonoran Deserts, the deep canyons and hallucinatory rock formations of Utah's national parks, or Monument Valley and the Petrified Forest, also combine to make a compelling case for calling the Southwest America's mostly wildly beautiful corner.

LHBLLC/SHUTTERSTOCK

THE MAIN AREAS

For places to stay in Southwest USA, see p212

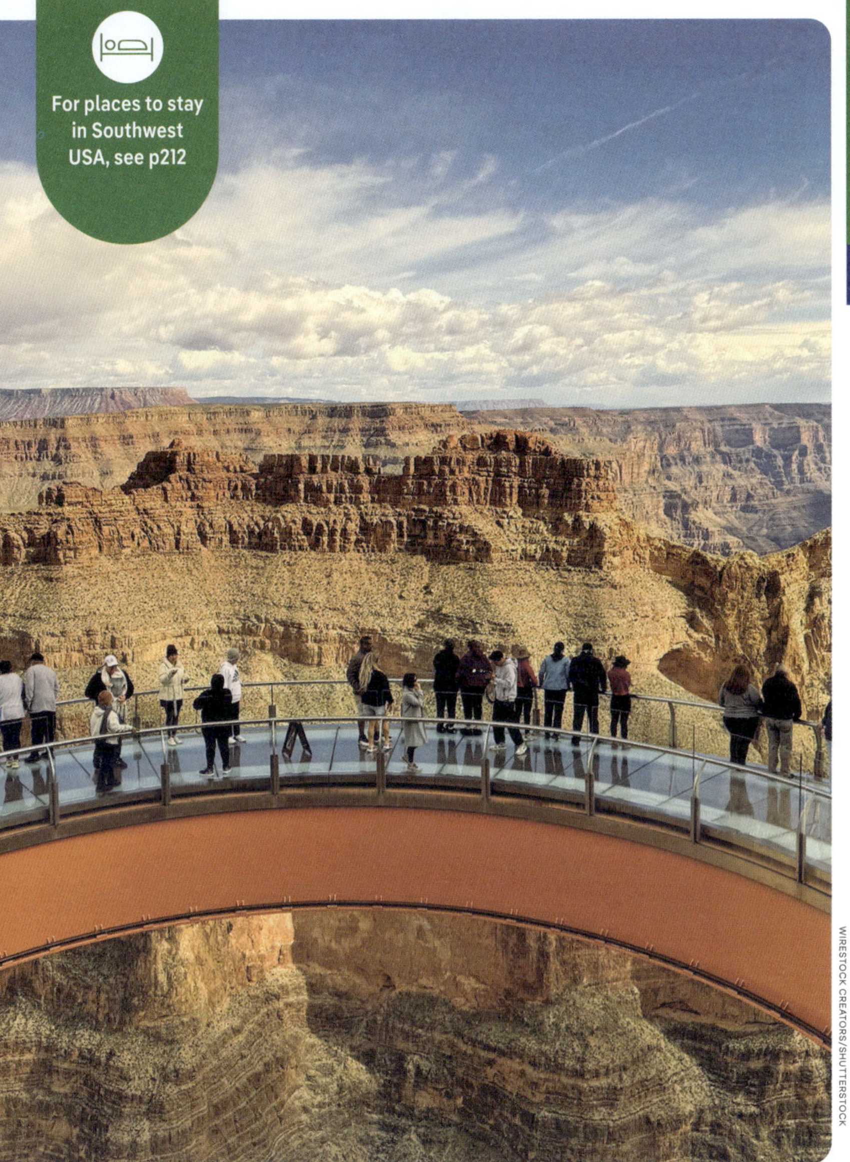

WIRESTOCK CREATORS/SHUTTERSTOCK

Skywalk (p153), Grand Canyon West

Find Your Way

Deserts, mountains and a very far horizon make for miraculous, big-sky road-making – no wonder Route 66 sends everyone a little crazy. Getting around is easy but requires careful map-plotting. Distances are huge. Plan accordingly.

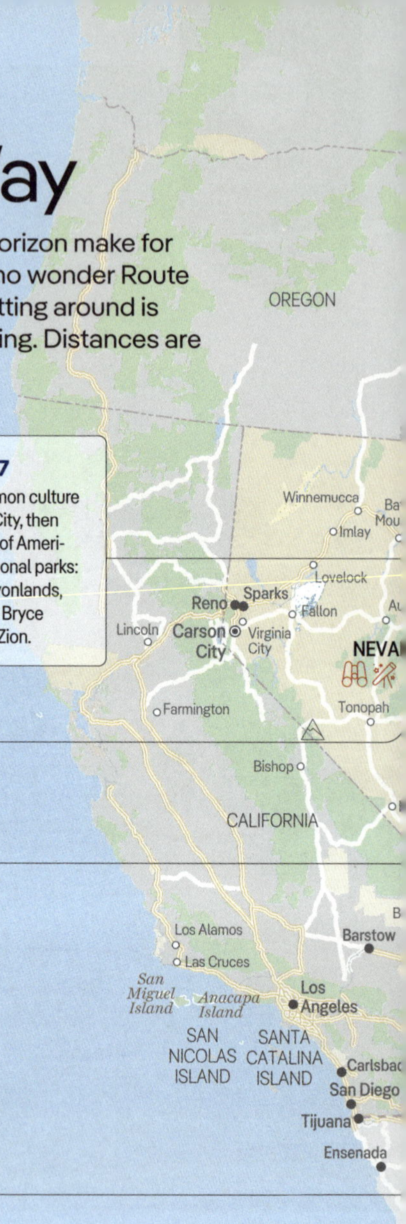

Utah, p177
Explore Mormon culture in Salt Lake City, then head for five of America's best national parks: Arches, Canyonlands, Capitol Reef, Bryce Canyon and Zion.

Nevada, p136
Reno, the Mojave Desert, Hoover Dam, Area 51... It's amazing how much Nevada packs into an area that's almost entirely (and beautifully) desert.

Las Vegas, p130
The Strip (Las Vegas Blvd) is among the most famous streets in the world. Fremont St and the Arts District are just as exciting.

Phoenix, p142
Arizona's capital, Phoenix is the epicenter of culture and cuisine in the Sonoran Desert, and luxurious resorts abound. Alfresco dining and sunsets are highlights.

Grand Canyon National Park, p147
This geologic wonder is worth the hype, with billion-year-old rocks, luminous sunsets and hiking trails that immerse you in its vast beauty.

TRAIN & BUS

Amtrak (trains) and Greyhound (buses) cross the Southwest. They're more useful for reaching the Southwest (or crossing it from one side to the other) than they are for traveling within the region.

CAR

Having your own vehicle means there are few places you can't go; consider renting a 4WD for following enticing dirt side roads. Most roads are in excellent condition, but plan for long stretches of tarmac between gas stations.

PLANE

To make the most of your time, flying a couple of legs is worth considering. Phoenix, Las Vegas, Reno, Salt Lake City, Santa Fe and Albuquerque receive flights from across the US, but you can also fly between them and other towns of the Southwest.

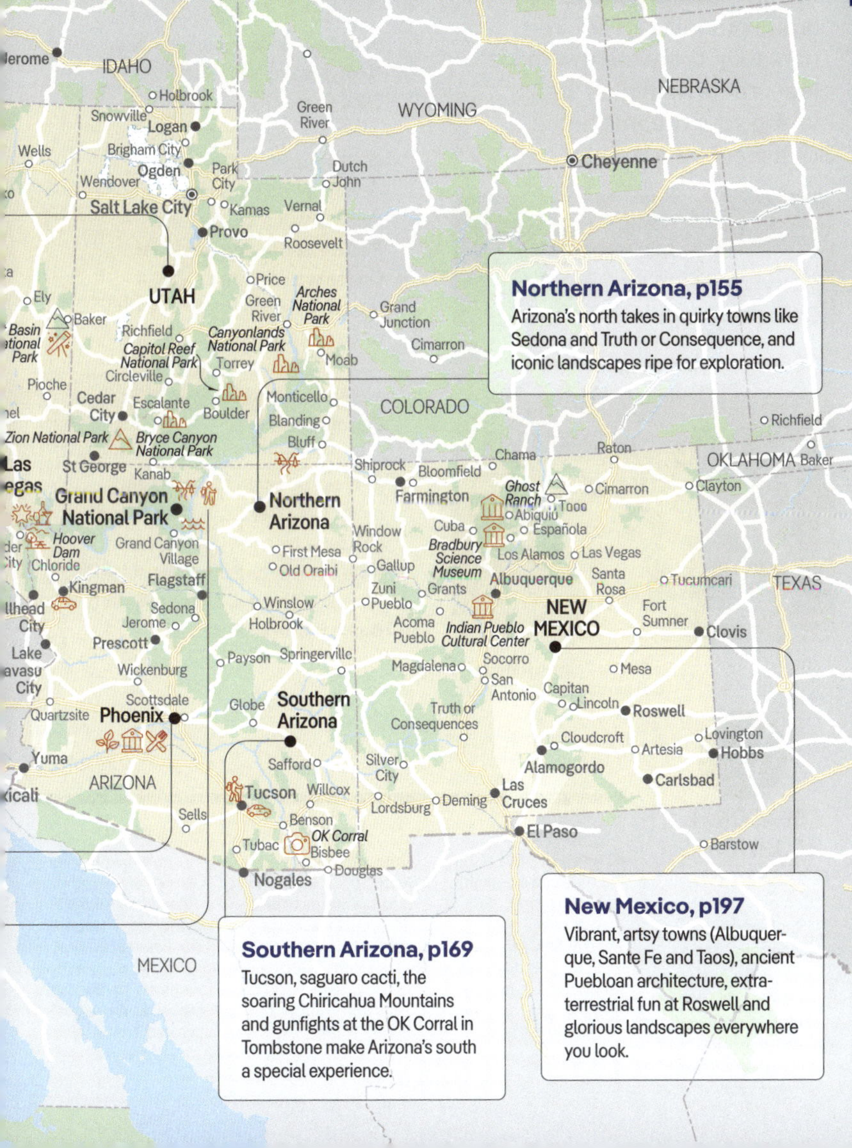

Northern Arizona, p155

Arizona's north takes in quirky towns like Sedona and Truth or Consequence, and iconic landscapes ripe for exploration.

Southern Arizona, p169

Tucson, saguaro cacti, the soaring Chiricahua Mountains and gunfights at the OK Corral in Tombstone make Arizona's south a special experience.

New Mexico, p197

Vibrant, artsy towns (Albuquerque, Sante Fe and Taos), ancient Puebloan architecture, extra-terrestrial fun at Roswell and glorious landscapes everywhere you look.

Plan Your Time

With so much ground to cover, careful planning is required. Thankfully, there are few more pleasurable pastimes than making your dreams of the Southwest take shape.

CAYCE CLIFFORD FOR LONELY PLANET

Red Rock Canyon National Conservation Area (p136)

Seven Nevada Days

- Begin two days in **Las Vegas** (p130) with a wander around the Strip, taking note of the Egyptian pyramid, summiting the Eiffel Tower and riding a gondola in a mock Venetian canal. Head downtown for people-watching along the Fremont Street Experience.
- Over the following two days, explore the surrounding desertscapes, such as the **Red Rock Canyon National Conservation Area** (p136) and the geologic wonderland **Valley of Fire State Park** (p137), and visit the **Hoover Dam** (p137) and the eerie ghost town of **St Thomas** (p138).
- Then, rather than driving 440 miles, fly to **Reno** (p138) and use it as a base for a day of exploration. With one day left, cross the state for the stirring magnificence of **Great Basin National Park** (p141).

SEASONAL HIGHLIGHTS

Summer can be fiercely hot in the Southwest, and its national parks overwhelmed by visitor numbers. Skiing is possible in places in winter, but fall and spring are lovely.

JANUARY

It can be bitterly cold at altitude and overnight in the desert. Ski centers like Park City, Reno or Santa Fe are at their busiest, although snow conditions vary significantly from one year to the next.

MARCH

Although June to early September is a popular time to visit the Grand Canyon, those same months are unbearably hot in southern Arizona. Instead, visit Phoenix and points south in spring.

APRIL

Late in April, Albuquerque is the backdrop for the **Gathering of Nations** *(gatheringofnations.com),* which brings together more than 500 tribes; it's the largest such gathering in North America.

Ten Arizona Days

- Head to the South Rim of the **Grand Canyon** (p150) for two days of exploring this utterly magnificent natural wonder, with at least another day around the low-key **Grand Canyon North Rim** (p152). Concentrate on following a small number of trails and seeing a handful of overlooks well, rather than racing around and trying to see everything. Allow an extra couple of days for Grand Canyon hikes.

- Loop around the crimson buttes of **Monument Valley** (p163), then start your **Route 66** (p167) retro drive in Kingman. Sip microbrews in **Flagstaff** (p161) and follow gorgeous **Oak Creek Canyon** (p159) to **Sedona** (p155) where you can try and locate your chakra. Swing through **Jerome** (p160) and **Prescott** (p160) for art and history.

Two Weeks in Utah & New Mexico

- Begin with a day spent exploring the Mormon story in multi-dimensional **Salt Lake City** (p179), followed by a couple of days each in two of Utah's best national parks where you're spoiled for choice: **Zion** (p194), **Bryce Canyon** (p192), **Arches** (p188), **Canyonlands** or **Capitol Reef** (p187). If you have the time, visit them all.

- Fly from Salt Lake City to **Albuquerque** (p199), which is worth a couple of days for its museums and opportunities to feast on feisty New Mexican dishes. **Taos** (p204) is another fun place to catch the magic of New Mexico.

- Reserve your final day for **White Sands National Park** (p211) or the little green men of **Roswell** (p208).

JUNE

Warmer temperatures in northern New Mexico are perfect for wildflower-laden hikes and rafting around Taos. Further afield, summer has yet to set the Southwest fully ablaze and summer crowds have yet to arrive en masse.

JULY

July 24 is **Pioneer Day** in Utah, a state holiday remembering the arrival of the first Mormon pioneers in 1847. Reenactors march through Salt Lake City, while non-Mormons prefer to mark it as 'Pie and Beer Day.'

OCTOBER

Neon aspen leaves, mild temperatures and so many festivals, including Albuquerque's **International Balloon Fiesta**. Apart from anything else, it's a beautiful time to be anywhere in the Southwest.

DECEMBER

Don your cowboy hat and spurs as **National Finals Rodeo** returns Las Vegas to its Western roots. On New Year's Eve, the Strip becomes a huge party as thousands turn out for headliner bands and fireworks.

Las Vegas

NON-STOP ENTERTAINMENT | SPECTATOR SPORTS | GREAT DINING

TOP TIP

If you're new to gambling, or on a budget, it makes sense to try your luck Downtown rather than on the Strip. Downtown casinos offer games with slightly better odds, and minimum bets are significantly lower.

The story of Las Vegas begins in Downtown, where the city was founded in 1905. That's right: this historic core and its casinos were thriving long before the glitz of Las Vegas Blvd took the spotlight, and in recent years, Vegas' Downtown has staged a comeback. The five-block Fremont Street Experience, beneath a canopy of millions of LED lights, debuted in the mid-1990s. Then in 2012, Zappos' CEO Tony Hsieh infused $350 million into revitalizing the neighborhood.

But Las Vegas is also the Strip – a 4-mile eruption of color and possibility also known as Las Vegas Blvd. This is what happens when unchecked indulgence reigns. Love it or loathe it, this over-the-top 'playground for grown-ups' taps into the hopes and dreams of the masses. They no longer come for just the gambling, either, but for the dazzling performances, intriguing art installations, world-class restaurants and ever-popular sporting events that relentlessly infuse the Strip with new energy.

Fremont Street

The beating heart of Downtown

Streaking down the center of Vegas' historic district, the **Fremont Street Experience** *(vegasexperience.com)* is a

GETTING AROUND

Downtown is mostly walkable. Most of the action is at the Fremont Street Experience, where you'll be on foot. If you prefer exploring on two wheels, the RTC bike-share program has stations Downtown. Taxis are widely available in front of hotels, and rideshares are popular (just be sure you're at the right pick-up area). The free Downtown Loop bus stops at all the big attractions. Walking the Strip is an adventure, often involving sidewalk performances, escalators and pedestrian bridges over the highway.

SEAN PAVONE/SHUTTERSTOCK

'Welcome to Fabulous Las Vegas' sign

five-block pedestrian mall lined with old-school casinos and topped by an arched steel canopy. Hourly from dusk until midnight, the 1400ft-long canopy turns on a six-minute light-and-sound show. The shows are cheesy, but mesmerizing if you're drunk. It's even more exhilarating if you happen to be zooming by on the zipline cables attached to the 12-story **SlotZilla** *(vegasexperience.com/slotzilla-zip-line; from $49)*, a slot-machine-themed platform at the mall's eastern end.

Welcome to Fabulous Las Vegas

Arriving on the Strip

The **'Welcome to Fabulous Las Vegas' sign**, in the center of bustling Las Vegas Blvd, makes for a great place to start your explorations. In a city famous for neon signs, this one reigns supreme, and is the unofficial beginning of the Strip.

Designed by Betty Willis at the end of the 1950s, this sign is a classic photo op and a reminder of Vegas' past. Get here by midmorning to avoid long lines of jovial, selfie-seeking tourists.

WEDDING CHAPELS

Driving along Las Vegas Blvd, it's impossible to miss the abundance of wedding chapels – a testament to how easy it is to get married here.

Near the iconic 'Welcome to Fabulous Las Vegas' sign, the **Little Church of the West** is one of the oldest of the dozens of wedding chapels in Las Vegas. Since 1941 this one has hosted the weddings of celebrities including Judy Garland and Mark Herron, Richard Gere and Cindy Crawford, and Billy Bob Thornton and Angelina Jolie. Hang around outdoors for a few minutes and you'll probably see some newlyweds posing for pictures.

EATING ON THE STRIP: BEST RESTAURANTS

Golden Steer: The Rat Pack, Marilyn Monroe and Elvis all dined at this fabulously retro steakhouse with steer's head out front. *4:30-9:45pm* **$$$**

Joël Robuchon: In the famous chef's art deco-inspired dining room, seasonal tasting menus deliver the meal of a lifetime. *5-9:30pm* **$$$**

Peppermill: This Vegas institution is famous for its campy atmosphere, firepit-fountains and massive portions. *hours vary* **$$**

Delilah: See and be seen in this modern supper club that drips with style and regularly attracts A-list celebs. No photos. *hours vary* **$$$**

HIGHLIGHTS
1 Fremont Street Experience
2 Strat
3 Welcome to Las Vegas Sign

SIGHTS
4 Eiffel Tower Experience
5 Graceland Wedding Chapel
6 High Roller
7 Little Church of the West
8 Mob Museum
9 Neon Museum

ACTIVITIES
10 SlotZilla

SLEEPING
11 Cosmopolitan
12 El Cortez
13 Luxor
14 Skylofts

EATING
15 Barry's Downtown Prime
16 Carson Kitchen
17 Delilah
18 Eiffel Tower Restaurant
19 Esther's Kitchen
20 Golden Steer
21 Joël Robuchon
22 Main St Provisions
23 Peppermill
24 Top of the World

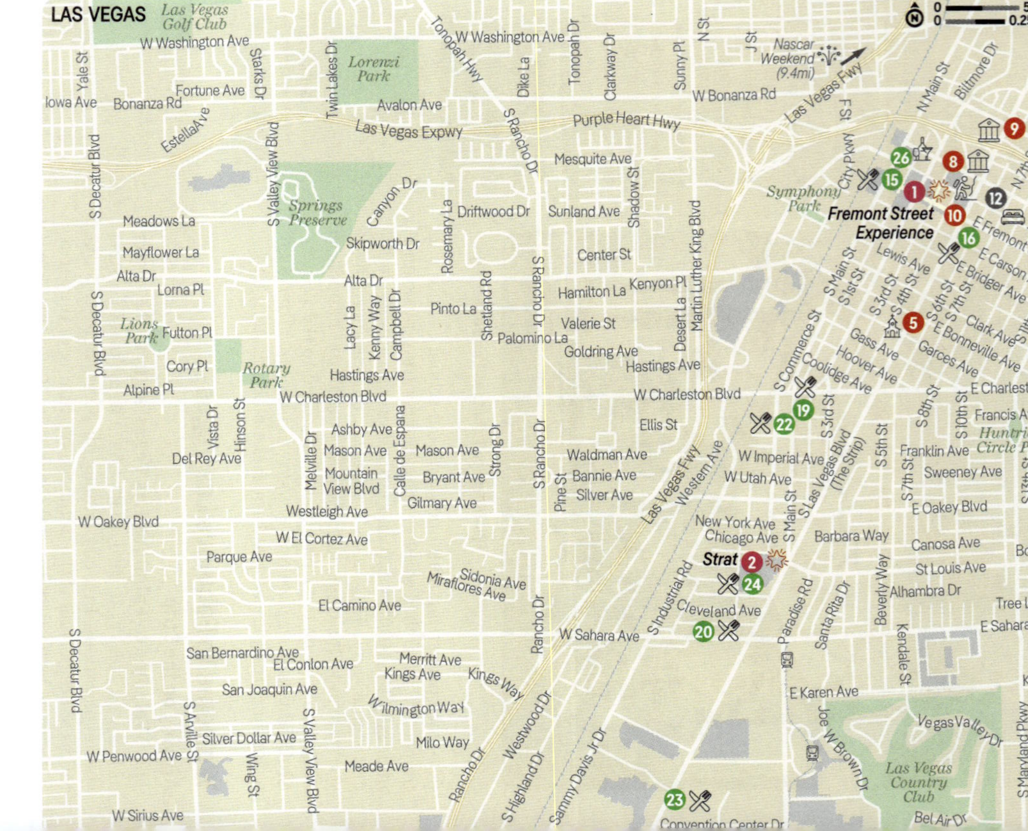

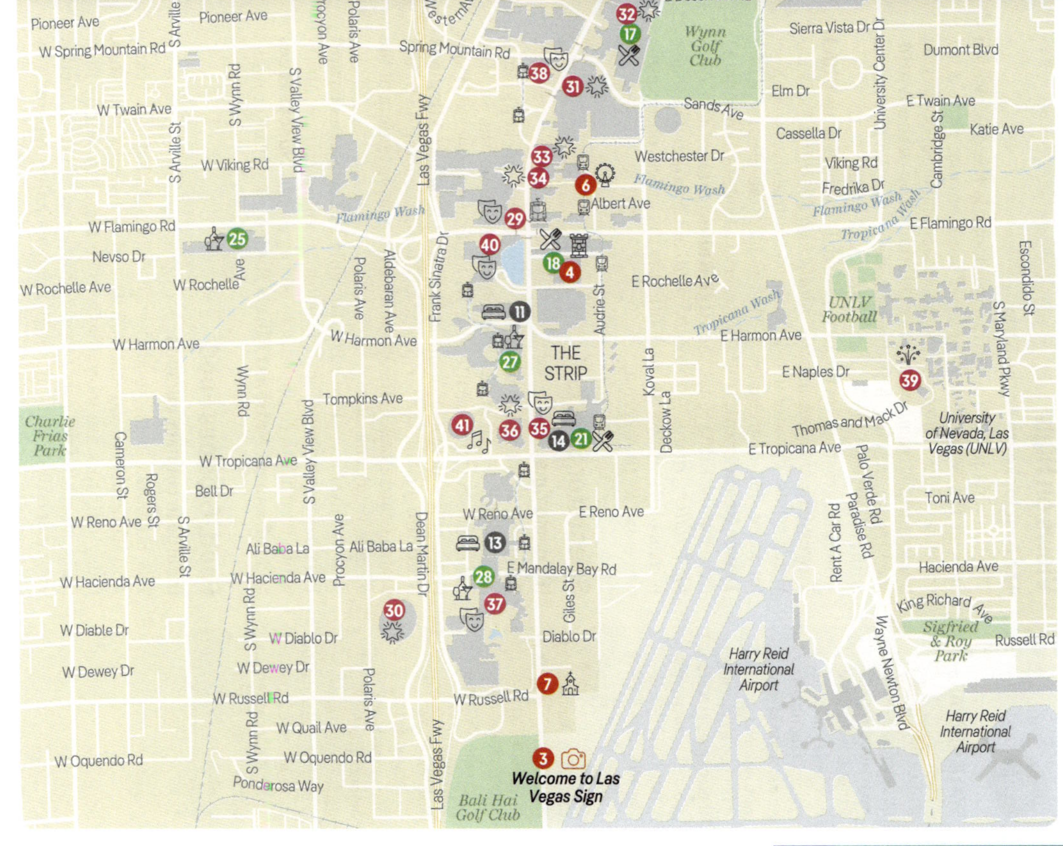

DRINKING & NIGHTLIFE

- **25** Ghostbar
- **26** Legacy Club
- **27** Skybar
- **28** Skyfall Lounge

ENTERTAINMENT

- **29** Absinthe
- **30** Allegiant Stadium
- **31** Atomic Saloon Show
- **32** Awakening
- **33** Big Elvis
- **34** DiscoShow
- **35** Kà
- **36** Mad Apple
- **37** Michael Jackson ONE
- **38** Mystère
- **39** National Finals Rodeo
- **40** O
- **41** T-Mobile Arena

WALK OF STARS

It's nowhere near as extensive as the Hollywood Walk of Fame, but the Strip has gotten into the game of recognizing some of the folks who helped to make it famous by putting their names in stars along the sidewalks.

You'll find Rat Packers Dean Martin and Frank Sinatra, plus siblings Donny and Marie Osmond, outside the Flamingo. In front of Paris, look for legendary performers Wayne Newton and Elvis Presley, as well as longtime drag performer Frank Marino. The full list includes more performers along with other notable folks such as composers, humanitarians and producers.

Views on High

The best lookouts on the Strip

The granddaddy of the Strip's overlooks is the observation deck at the **Strat** *(Stratosphere; thestrat.com; from $20)*, which provides visitors with both indoor and outdoor viewing opportunities from a whopping 1149ft up. **Top of the World**, the Strat's revolving, fine-dining restaurant, provides guests with magnificent views of the Las Vegas Valley.

Another great option for getting high is the half-scale **Eiffel Tower** *(caesars.com; elevator adult/child $25/19)* at Paris Las Vegas, whose elevator whisks visitors 540ft above street level for great 360-degree views. There's also the elegant **Eiffel Tower Restaurant**, 110ft up. Reserve a table by the window.

Over at the LINQ Hotel, the **High Roller** *(caesars.com/linq/high-roller; from $29/10 adult/child)* observation wheel also boasts bird's-eye views. At 550ft, it is the tallest observation wheel in North America.

Spectator Sports

It's game time

Want to catch a game in Vegas? Professional hockey's Golden Knights set up at the **T-Mobile Arena** on the Strip in 2017, and shortly thereafter, the NFL's Raiders relocated from Oakland to their new home at Vegas' $1.9 billion **Allegiant Stadium**, just off the Strip. The city is also gearing up to add Major League Baseball's Athletics with a new stadium at the former Tropicana site.

Each November since 2023, Formula 1's **Las Vegas Grand Prix** has transformed the Strip into a 3.8-mile racetrack. Meanwhile, UFC fights, championship boxing events, **Nascar races** and the annual **National Finals Rodeo** also draw crowds.

Food, Glorious Food

Indulge in culinary pursuits

The Strip has been studded with celebrity chefs for years. And while all-you-can-eat buffets and $10 steaks still exist, today's visitors are more likely to be found in trendy food halls or seeking out ever more sophisticated establishments, with meals designed – although not personally prepared – by famous taste-makers.

If food is your *raison d'être*, look no further than **Lip Smacking Foodie Tours** *(lipsmackingfoodietours.com)*.

DRINKING ON THE STRIP: BEST ROOFTOP BARS WITH STRIP VIEWS

GhostBar: Off the Strip at Palms, this 55th-floor club with outdoor deck is reached by a private lift. Fun vibe, great DJs. *7pm-2am Wed-Sat*

Skybar: Floor-to-ceiling windows enhance the vistas from this classy 23rd-floor bar at Waldorf Astoria. Great cocktails, too. *hours vary*

Skyfall Lounge: Sophistication, creative seasonal cocktails and killer views align on the 64th floor of Delano. *5pm-midnight*

Legacy Club: Downtown penthouse lounge on Circa's 60th floor with panoramic Strip views and killer weekend parties. *4pm-2am*

Showtime on the Strip

Are you not entertained?

Las Vegas is a hub for the world's top entertainers, and the nightly performances up and down the Strip reflect this remarkable consolidation of talent.

Cirque du Soleil captivates with its five productions: **O** at the Bellagio is a mesmerizing water-based show, featuring high-flying acrobatics and surreal aquatic stunts; **Kà** at MGM Grand tells a tale of familial love and conflict on a rotating, oftentimes vertical stage; **Michael Jackson ONE** at Mandalay Bay pays tribute to the King of Pop; **Mad Apple** is a homage to New York City in (where else) New York–New York; and **Mystère** at Treasure Island combines classic circus artistry with vibrant costumes and high-energy stunts.

Absinthe at Caesars Palace blends incredible acrobatic feats with edgy humor in an intimate setting beneath a Big Top. Meanwhile, **Atomic Saloon Show** at the Venetian is a mix of burlesque, comedy and acrobatics in a rowdy, Wild West–themed saloon. **DiscoShow**, in the LINQ Hotel, is a thrilling love letter to disco that invites the audience into the dance party.

The Wynn adds its own magic with **Awakening**, an extraordinary spectacle combining innovative stage design, elaborate costumes and mind-blowing special effects in a mythical adventure story.

Then there are, of course, the residencies. Superstars perform in resort theaters seating thousands for weeks, months and even years on end. And pop icons, comedians and magicians regularly perform at the Strip's many venues. Plan ahead and look into who you might be able to catch in residence.

FINDING ELVIS

Elvis has definitely left the building. In 1976 he ended a run of 636 shows at the International (later the Las Vegas Hilton). Now the Westgate, the hotel honors the King with a bronze statue in the lobby. Its International Theater remains, still attracting top-tier headliners.

Downtown's **Graceland Wedding Chapel** offers couples a package that includes an Elvis impersonator. And although Elvis-themed shows come and go, **Big Elvis** has been a hit in Strip lounges since 2002. Pete Vallee's voice is as rich as his jumpsuit is big. He once weighed an incredible 945lb but has since shed hundreds. He performs for free four afternoons a week at Harrah's.

The Mob & Neon Lights

Learn about gangsters and see vintage signs

The highly respected **Mob Museum** *(National Museum of Organized Crime & Law Enforcement; themobmuseum.org; from $34.95)* chronicles the era when gangsters controlled Las Vegas and got rich stealing casino profits. The museum shares gangster stories alongside those of the law enforcement officers whose job it was to nail the bad guys.

While not old itself, **Neon Museum** *(neonmuseum.org; adult/child $25/12.50 day, $35/17.50 evening)* is chock-full of vintage signs that once hung on long-gone properties such as Binion's Horseshoe, the Moulin Rouge and Stardust.

EATING DOWNTOWN: BEST BITES

Carson Kitchen: Tiny eatery with an industrial vibe, a rooftop patio and excellent shared plates of creative American classics. *hours vary* $$

Barry's Downtown Prime: Classy steakhouse; cuts are mouthwatering and lobster mac explodes from the shell. *hours vary* $$$

Esther's Kitchen: A cozy, popular restaurant with excellent Italian cuisine at commendable prices. *hours vary* $$

Main St Provisions: Delicious modern American place, it feels like a neighborhood staple while still offering foie gras add-ons. *hours vary* $$

Nevada

SCENIC LANDSCAPES | OUTDOOR ADVENTURE | URBAN CULTURE

Places

TOP TIP

The Mojave Desert is the driest desert in North America, and visitors often don't realize that just because they don't feel sweaty, they're still perspiring; it instantly evaporates in the hot and dry conditions. Dehydration can be deadly, so carry and consume lots of water.

Nevada has soul to go with the glitz and glamor of Las Vegas. Much of that comes from the Mojave Desert, which is a destination in itself, perhaps even the necessary counterpoint to the bright lights of Vegas. All across the Mojave, stunning natural wonders – the wind- and water-carved landscapes of Red Rock Canyon and the Valley of Fire, for example – rise from the desert floor. Even the human footprint can be seen on a grand scale, such as at the Hoover Dam, while the haunting ruins of St Thomas are a reminder of how fragile the human presence can be out here.

Ranging further afield, Reno, with its echoes of the Burning Man Festival, is like a more manageable Vegas but with history and art instead of nonstop show business. It's also an emerging adventure hub. In other words, there are good reasons why Nevada draws tens of millions of visitors each year.

Mojave Desert

Exploring the unspoiled desert

Drive just about any direction from Las Vegas and before long you'll be at one of Southern Nevada's wonderful natural resources that are light-years away from the neon of the Strip. Just 20 miles from the resorts, **Red Rock Canyon National Conservation Area** *(redrockcanyonlv.org; vehicle/bicycle $20/10; reservations required 8am-5pm Oct-May)* welcomes

GETTING AROUND

If you're short on time, tours out of Vegas can get you to highlights such as Hoover Dam, Red Rock Canyon and Valley of Fire, and coaches travel as far as the Grand Canyon. But given the state's great distances and the remoteness of popular destinations, to fully soak in the delights, a car – or better yet, a high-clearance SUV – is required. It's the only way you can reach off-the-beaten-path places. Rental cars are available at airports and some hotels. If you're sticking to the cities, several airlines (including Southwest and Spirit) connect Las Vegas and Reno.

more than two million visitors each year. There's a visitor center and a 13-mile paved road that winds through multicolored formations of sandstone. Visitors can hike or bike the paved road.

For a much less crowded desert park with great trails and petroglyphs, head south from Las Vegas to **Sloan Canyon National Conservation Area** *(blm.gov)*.

Travelers willing to venture further afield will relish their drive or hike through spectacular **Valley of Fire State Park** *(parks.nv.gov/parks/valley-of-fire; Nevada/non-Nevada vehicles $10/15)*. About an hour from Las Vegas, the park is home to mile after mile of awe-inspiring, otherworldly geologic curiosities, some with pastel hues and others rust-colored.

Hoover Dam

Hoover Dam and a Lake Mead ghost town

About 35 miles east of Las Vegas, Hoover Dam is an engineering marvel built in the 1930s to harness the Colorado River while providing a dependable water supply to Southern California and generating hydroelectric power. Although the dam's hydroelectric output has been significantly reduced due to drought in recent years, the towering 726ft structure still controls the

A CITY WITHOUT CASINOS

In all Nevada, there are only two communities where gambling remains illegal. The small Lincoln County town of Panaca is one and Boulder City is the other.

Built during the Great Depression to house dam builders, **Boulder City** was under control of the federal government, which saw gambling as a costly vice that should be discouraged. In 1931, after gambling had been legalized elsewhere in Nevada, the highway between Boulder City and Las Vegas became a busy thoroughfare as workers flocked to Downtown gambling halls in search of fortune – or at least an escape from the drudgery of their jobs. Now, there are casinos a few miles to the east and west of Boulder City.

RENO'S BEST EVENTS

Reno River Festival: The world's top freestyle kayakers compete in a mad paddling dash through Whitewater Park in mid-May.

Hot August Nights: Celebration of hot rods and rock 'n' roll in early August in various locations around Reno and beyond.

Great Reno Balloon Race: In one of Reno's most inspiring spectacles, more than 100 hot-air balloons race across the desert over three days every September.

Artown: Throughout July, this Riverwalk District celebration centers on art and culture, with hundreds of events, workshops and performances.

Reno Rodeo: Each June, roping and bull-riding action takes place at the Livestock Events Center, with a five-day cattle drive across the high desert.

flooding of the Colorado River, helps to irrigate more than 1.5 million acres of land and provides water to 25 million people.

Visit to learn about how 21,000 men built the dam during the height of the Great Depression – and how climate change threatens to diminish its functionality. First, though, you'll want to drive across the top of the dam into Arizona for the best views of the hulking construction. Another remarkable view can be found back in Nevada, where an accessible, albeit uphill, walkway leads to the sidewalk along the Mike O'Callaghan–Pat Tillman Memorial Bridge. Hold the railing when it's windy – this isn't for anyone with a fear of heights.

History buffs can delve deeper on a guided tour. They begin at the **Hoover Dam Parking Garage & Visitor Center** (which got a fancy new exhibition center in 2025). The one-hour dam tour ($30) explores historic tunnels, takes in the Colorado River through a ventilation shaft and rides an elevator to the top.

Hoover Dam created the enormous **Lake Mead**, which is actually a reservoir, in the 1930s. The lake is bisected by the Nevada–Arizona state line. The highlight of visiting Lake Mead is **St Thomas Ghost Town**. Navigate the deeply rutted road for roughly 3 miles to the end. From the history-filled kiosks, there's a 2.5-mile desert trail leading to the remains of the town flooded by the creation of Lake Mead following the construction of Hoover Dam. Submerged under 60ft of water for nearly eight decades, the foundations and walls of some of St Thomas' buildings have eerily re-emerged during the drought.

Reno

Learn Reno's historical story

Driving in beneath the downtown arch that proclaims Reno 'the Biggest Little City in the World,' and eyeballing its gaudy casinos and mid-century modern architecture, you may be tempted to label it a smaller Las Vegas. But once you've strolled through the Riverwalk District along the alpine-fed Truckee River, grabbed brunch and cocktails at a hip bistro in Midtown and been intrigued by public art at every turn, the truth becomes clear: Reno has a fascinating story and has come into its own.

The **Nevada Museum of Art** *(nevadaart.org; adult/child $15/3)* building was inspired by the geological formations of the Black Rock Desert to the north, and inside, a floating staircase leads to galleries showcasing its temporary exhibits and eclectic collection. Visitors are free to explore the Sky Room on the 4th floor, essentially a rooftop penthouse and patio with killer views, and a 50,000-sq-ft wing that opened in 2025.

EATING IN RENO: OUR PICKS

Beline Carniceria & Deli: Reno's best Mexican at this market counter and restaurant north of town. Don't miss the tortas. *9am-7pm* $

Perenn: Locals are obsessed with the boules and baguettes at this hip bakery. *7am-noon Midtown, to 2:30pm Village at Rancharrah* $

Brasserie Saint James: Eclectic menu, plus beers made using water from an aquifer underneath it. Great patio. *11am-9pm Tue-Sun* $$

Atlantis Steakhouse: Highly rated place serving premium Allen Brothers and Wagyu beef. Special-occasion vibes. *5-10pm Wed-Sun* $$$

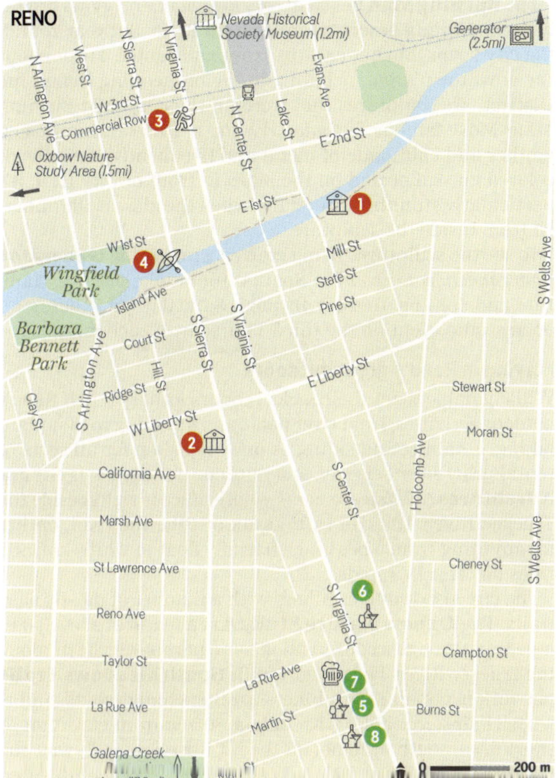

SIGHTS
1 National Automobile Museum
2 Nevada Museum of Art

ACTIVITIES
3 BaseCamp
4 Sierra Adventures

DRINKING & NIGHTLIFE
5 Craft Wine & Beer
6 Death & Taxes
7 Local Beer Works
8 Rum Sugar Lime

Get an understanding of the region's vibrant past with a visit to the **Nevada Historical Society Museum** *(nvculture.org/historicalsociety; adult/child $6/free)*. Opened in 1904, it's the state's oldest museum. Just beyond the entrance is its pride and joy: a collection of priceless, 19th-century baskets woven by Dat-So-La-Lee, a Washoe woman who lived in the area. Another exhibit explores the rich history of mining, and there's also a section devoted specifically to Reno's history.

The **National Automobile Museum** *(automuseum.org; adult/child $15/10)* has casino pioneer Bill Harrah to thank for its existence. While building resorts across the state, Harrah also amassed a mind-boggling collection of 1400 vintage cars, many of which used to be kept in warehouses in neighboring Sparks. The museum's gems include a 1907 Thomas Flyer 35, a 1937 Cord 812 and an original Batmobile from the 1960s.

Burning brightly year-round

Each August, 'Burners' from around the world descend on the Black Rock Desert to build Black Rock City, tear it down, and set fire to an effigy of 'the man,' with plenty of peace, love, music, art, nakedness, drugs, sex and frivolity thrown in.

RENO'S QUICKIE DIVORCES

Long before Las Vegas developed the moniker of 'Wedding Capital,' Reno's reputation focused on 'quickie' divorces. The process, also known as 'migratory divorce,' took six weeks, but that was quick compared to the long, drawn-out procedures elsewhere, which typically assigned marital property to husbands. In Reno, owners of everything from private homes to dude ranches to luxury hotels got in on the act of offering short-term rentals to women who, once they had lived in Nevada for six weeks, could get a divorce decree citing just about any circumstance. Thousands flocked to Reno from the 1930s to the '60s, but when divorce laws were relaxed in other states, the 'quickie divorce' industry fell into a steady decline.

AREA 51

After years of refusing to acknowledge that Area 51 existed, in 2013 the US government admitted that the desert site was used to develop specialized aircraft. Skeptics, however, believe that aliens from a UFO crash site near Roswell (p208), New Mexico, were brought to Area 51 in 1947. The unconfirmed legends continue to lure believers to the nearby Extraterrestrial Highway (NV375) and its alien-themed attractions.

From Ash Springs, it's a five-minute drive north on US 93 to the turnoff for NV 375, the road that runs tantalizingly close to Area 51. The junction is marked by the **ET Fresh Jerky** shop, which sells alien-themed merchandise and a wide variety of jerky flavors supposedly made from cows surrounding Area 51.

The **Burning Man Festival** *(burningman.org)* glows brightly in the Nevada desert 115 miles from Reno. But year-round, the city keeps 'Burner culture' front and center. Throughout the downtown area, including in the burgeoning Neon Line District, are sculptures that were first displayed at Burning Man. Most famous is *Space Whale,* a 40ft-tall humpback mother and calf made of metal and (frequently vandalized) colored glass. Located on the plaza in front of City Hall, it's particularly stunning after dark, when the glass is illuminated from inside the sculpture.

To see the sculptures being crafted, stop by the **Generator** *(therenogenerator.com)* in Sparks. Tours take place at 11am, 1pm and 5pm on Tuesday through Saturday, and there's an open studio event on the third Thursday of each month.

Playing in Reno's great outdoors

While gamblers get their kicks indoors, others relish Reno's outdoor activities, from river floats and kayaking to mountain biking, climbing and skiing. A one-stop shop for all sorts of rental gear, river services and outdoor excursions is **Sierra Adventures** *(wildsierra.com),* whose office is right beside the Truckee River. You can raft, kayak or tube the river, opting for anything from a beginner-friendly float to white-knuckle rides on class IV rapids.

The city also indulges hikers with a number of mostly easy trails. The **Oxbow Nature Study Area** features a level, 0.8-mile trail through a conservation park, part of which sits along the Truckee River. The paved, 5-mile **South Meadows Trails** network is popular with hikers, runners and cyclists, and is wheelchair-accessible, with only a 60ft gain in elevation. A short drive south of Reno, on the Mt Rose Scenic Byway, the **Galena Creek Recreation Area** *(galenacreekvisitorcenter.org)* has a great visitor center and a paved interpretive trail out back, plus a few longer trails. Two other recommended hikes just outside the city include **Hunter Creek Trail** (to a 30ft waterfall) and **Tom Cooke Trail** (along a scenic river).

A non-gaming property downtown, the Whitney Peak Hotel is known for **BaseCamp** *(basecampreno.com).* Along with a state-of-the-art indoor bouldering gym, BaseCamp includes outdoor climbing challenges on the hotel's east wall. The Big Wall, which holds a Guinness World Record as the planet's largest outdoor climbing wall, sends thrill-seekers on a 164ft ascent to the roof. BaseCamp also offers climbs and climbing classes for every skill level, from beginner to world-class professional athlete.

DRINKING IN RENO: OUR PICKS

Local Beer Works: Solid craft beers and fun seasonal specials. Don't miss the Irish Stout aged in Frey Ranch bourbon bottles. *hours vary*

Craft Wine & Beer: A bottle shop with products from small local brewers and growers, a cute little bar, a good crowd and tastings. *hours vary*

Death & Taxes: Perch on a Victorian barstool and sip delicious cocktails like works of art at this all-black, death-themed tavern. *hours vary*

Rum Sugar Lime: A bright and chic tropical cocktail bar in Midtown; killer rum drinks, strong list of non-alcoholic libations. *4pm-midnight Tue-Sun*

TOP EXPERIENCE

Great Basin National Park

One of the least-visited national parks, Great Basin National Park is a must for people in search of solitude and natural beauty. The free-to-visit park is lorded over by Wheeler Peak, a 13,063ft ice-sculpted horn, which shelters a shrinking but still-visible glacier. Hiking and camping opportunities abound, and the park is a designated International Dark Sky Park.

Wheeler Peak

Wheeler Peak Scenic Drive

Ascending 3000ft over 12 miles, this out-and-back scenic drive rises steeply through several distinct eco-regions. It winds first through low-lying sagebrush, then up past pinyon pines, a mountain mahogany wilderness, a mixed-conifer forest peppered with aspens and, finally, a zone of subalpine forest, at which point astonishing views of Wheeler come into sight.

Hitting the Trails

Great Basin is a hiker's wonderland, with over 60 miles of trails. The 26 trails traverse mountains studded with ancient forests and meander around glacier-fed lakes, and one even leads to Nevada's only glacier. Hikers of all levels will find plenty of options.

The **Glacier Trail** is one of the park's best. It culminates at the rock glacier ensconced beneath Wheeler Peak, and the 8.4-mile round trip also brings you to a grove of ancient bristlecone pines, the world's oldest non-cloned organisms.

Lehman Caves

A colossal marble cavern, Lehman Caves has a staggering collection of formations including stalactites, stalagmites, helictites, flowstone, popcorn and rare shields. They are a fragile resource, accessible only by guided tour.

TOP TIPS

- Baker (population 36), less than 5 miles from the park, has lodgings and food.
- The park has five developed campgrounds ($20 per night).
- Book your Lehman Caves tour two weeks in advance; spots fill quickly.
- Don't miss the evening astronomy ranger program – it's excellent.

PRACTICALITIES

- nps.gov/grba

Phoenix

ENDLESS SUNSHINE | SOUTHWEST CULTURE | OUTDOOR ADVENTURES

TOP TIP

Consider the weather before booking. From January to March, warm desert temps make Phoenix a popular winter retreat for snowbirds. June to August is scorching hot, but you can score incredible deals on upscale resorts. Temps are nearly perfect in October and November, before winter's peak rates arrive.

A thriving desert metropolis, Phoenix is the cultural and economic heart of Arizona. The city is also a convenient base for desert and red-rock wanderings. Southwestern and Mexican restaurants abound and swanky resorts stand ready to pamper. With more than 300 days of sunshine a year, exploring, eating and relaxing should be on your agenda – except in the searing heat from June to August.

The city offers an opera, ballet, several theaters and three of the state's finest museums – the Heard, Phoenix Art and Musical Instrument museums – while the Desert Botanical Garden is a stunning introduction to the region's ecology. There are plenty of options to hike, mountain bike and climb in the regional parks, all easily accessible. Golf may as well be the official sport of the area, with nearly 200 courses covering Greater Phoenix. So slather on the sunscreen and get outside.

Visit the Heard Museum

Native American art and culture

A 30ft-long fence of blown-glass cactus ribs and small sculptures of desert animals is an evocative portal into the Home

GETTING AROUND

To hop around Greater Phoenix, a car is a must in this colossal urban sprawl. Rent one on arrival at Sky Harbor International, Phoenix's major airport. The much smaller Phoenix-Mesa Gateway Airport on the easternmost edge of the Valley of the Sun only serves Allegiant Air and Sun Country Airlines. Phoenix public transportation is not as expansive as other major US cities, but the reliable Valley Metro light rail covers Phoenix proper, Tempe and Mesa. If you stay in one general part of town, Uber and Lyft rideshare will be sufficient for your stay.

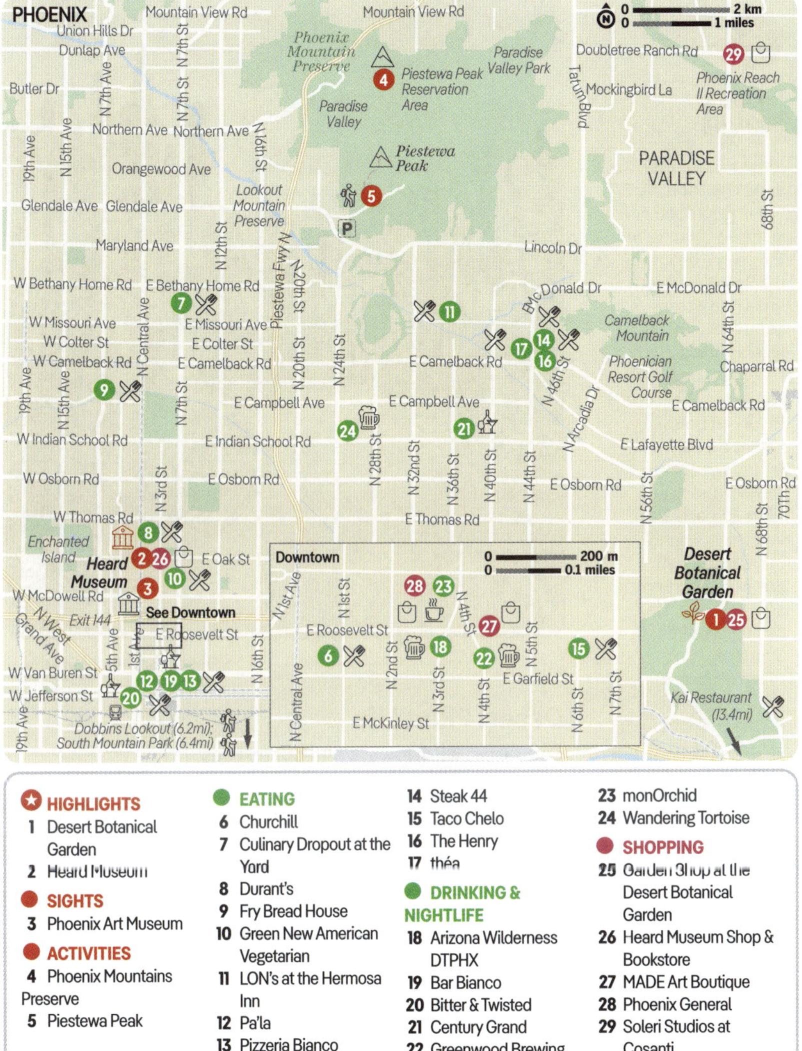

Gallery, the heart of the **Heard Museum** *(heard.org; adult/child $26/10)* and a showcase for the art and culture of the 22 sovereign tribes in Arizona. Poems, quotes and videos supplement the baskets, ceramics, jewelry, textiles and Hopi kachinas (spirit dolls) on display.

The Heard is one of the best museums of its kind in the US. Annual events enliven the grounds, including competitions of mesmerizing hoop dancing in February and the Indian Fair & Market in March.

HIKING IN PHOENIX

It's actually pretty easy to escape the urban jungle and immerse yourself in the unique beauty of the Sonoran Desert. When the weather's right, enthusiastic hikers flood the trails on **Camelback Mountain**, **Piestewa Peak** and **South Mountain Park** for the sweeping views of the Valley, while Pinnacle Peak and Tom's Thumb in the **McDowell Sonoran Preserve** are challenging but can't-miss climbs in Scottsdale.

Find maps and trail descriptions for the above from *@arizonahikers guide* on Instagram or at *phoenix.gov*. Remember to carry lots of water as you'll be hiking in the harsh Arizona sun. If you want a more remote experience, try the East Valley's Superstition Mountains.

CHRIS CURTIS/SHUTTERSTOCK

Desert Botanical Garden

Desert Plant Life

Saguaros, wildflowers and butterflies

Reconnect with nature and learn about desert plant life at the 55-acre **Desert Botanical Garden** *(dbg.org; adult/child $32.95/14.95)*. There are 2 miles' worth of looping trails arranged by theme, including a Sonoran Desert nature loop and an edible desert garden. The showstopping Desert Wildflower Loop trail showcases bluebells and Mexican gold poppies blooming from March to May. It's stunning year-round, but busiest and most colorful in the flowering spring season.

Ramble Down Roosevelt Row

Downtown arts and beer gardens

The *Welcome to Roosevelt Row* mural on the corner of Roosevelt and N 7th Sts is a launchpad for downtown's most vibrant neighborhood.

First, for a good craft beer, pop into the stylish indoor-outdoor digs at **Greenwood Brewing** *(greenwoodbrews.com)* or snag a table in the beer garden at the welcoming **Arizona Wilderness DTPHX** (p146; *azwbeer.com*). Snack on the tacos, duck-fat fries and churro bites. Dinner options range from tacos and tortas at trendy **Taco Chelo** *(instagram.com/tacochelo)* to elite burgers and pizza at the **Churchill** *(thechurchillphx.com)*, a shaded courtyard housing multiple food stands, bars and locally owned shops. The **monOrchid** *(monorchid.com)* is a coffee shop, gallery, gift shop, brewery and event space rolled into one. On the first Friday of the month, 70 or so galleries open for mingling and art viewing (6pm to 10pm).

Sample Native American Tastes

Award-winning indigenous menus

For a rewarding culinary tour through locally sourced native dishes, drive to **Kai Restaurant** *(kairestaurant.com)*. Here, Native American cuisine – based on traditional crops grown along the Gila River – includes creations such as grilled buffalo tenderloin with smoked corn puree and cholla buds, or wild scallops with beef tongue pastrami and tepary-bean crackling. Kai is located at the **Sheraton Grand at Wild Horse Pass** *(wildhorsepass.com)* on the Gila River Indian Reservation in Chandler. Book ahead and dress nicely.

Back in Phoenix, try the **Fry Bread House** *(frybreadhouseaz.com)*. Known as an elephant ear or Navajo taco, frybread is a flat piece of fried dough topped with meat, beans and veggies, or, for dessert, smeared with honey.

Hiking Piestewa Peak & Phoenix Mountains Preserve

Steep hike to city views

Covered in saguaros, ocotillos and teddy-bear cholla, the picturesque summit of **Piestewa Peak** *(phoenix.gov/parks)* was previously known as Squaw Peak. It was renamed for a local soldier, Lori Piestewa, who was killed in Iraq in 2003. Be warned: the 1.2-mile trek to the 2608ft peak is difficult but hugely popular for the south-facing views of downtown Phoenix. The surrounding **Phoenix Mountains Preserve** *(phoenix.gov/parks)* has nearly 70 trails and typically gets jammed on winter weekends.

For an easier hike, follow the Freedom Trail around the base of the peak. Look for parking lots along Piestewa Peak Dr within the park.

ORIENTATION

The Valley of the Sun is ringed by mountains that encompass a hot pancake, otherwise known as Greater Phoenix. A few important east-west roads cut across town: beginning in the south, these are Washington St, Van Buren St, Roosevelt St, McDowell Rd, Indian School Rd and Camelback Rd.

Phoenix is Arizona's largest city and houses the state capitol, the oldest buildings, several important museums and pro sports facilities. Scottsdale starts at around 56th St, east of Phoenix. The main drag, Scottsdale Rd, is technically 72nd St. Southeast of Phoenix is Tempe ('tem-*pee*'), home of Arizona State University, which is anchored around Mill Ave and University Rd.

EATING IN PHOENIX: OUR PICKS

théa: Order pasta, seafood and skewers for the table at the Global Ambassador hotel rooftop. *4-10pm Mon-Fri, from noon Sat & Sun* $$$

Steak 44: Top-tier steaks and seafood in a stunning setting. Check online for the dress code. *4-10pm Sun-Thu, to 11pm Fri & Sat* $$$

Pa'la: Seasonal veg and sustainably sourced seafood served hot off the grill. Two locations. *5-10pm Tue-Sat, to 9pm Sun* $$

The Henry: A cozy, elegant stop. Short rib, seafood and salad options and a deep wine list. *7am-9pm Sun-Thu, to 10pm Fri & Sat* $$$

Durant's: A gloriously old-school steakhouse with cozy red-velvet booths, juicy steaks and effortless cool. *4-8:30pm Wed-Sun* $$$

Culinary Dropout at the Yard: Next-level pub food between games of cornhole and ping-pong in this open-air space. *hours vary* $$

Green New American Vegetarian: Mock meats as good as, if not better than, their carnivorous counterparts. *11am-9pm Mon-Sat* $

LON's at the Hermosa Inn: Quaint hacienda where Phoenicians bring guests for fine dining and glorious sunsets. *7am-9pm* $$$

BEST PLACES TO SHOP IN PHOENIX

Soleri Studios at Cosanti: Studio of Frank Lloyd Wright student Paolo Soleri, whose signature bronze and ceramic bells are crafted and sold here.

MADE Art Boutique: Jewelry, ceramics, art prints, candles and more from mostly local artists. On Roosevelt Row in downtown Phoenix.

Garden Shop at the Desert Botanical Garden: Plant your own desert garden with a starter cactus kit, plus Southwestern cards and cactus jellies.

Phoenix General: Bring the smell of desert rain to your shower with one of the sustainably harvested creosote bundles.

Heard Museum Shop & Bookstore: Top-notch collection of American Indian original arts and crafts.

Chris Bianco: 35+ Years of Pizza Wizardry

Wood-fired pizzas and gourmet sandwiches

Awarded the Outstanding Restaurateur award by the James Beard Foundation in 2022, Chris Bianco has been crafting thin-crusted wood-fired pizzas in Phoenix since 1988. In the process, he pioneered an 'artisanal pizza revolution' nationwide and expanded from his downtown mothership to a half-dozen successful ventures. The tiny **Pizzeria Bianco** *(pizzeriabianco.com)* is the original restaurant – a convenient stop for travelers exploring Heritage Square. Pro tip: there is almost always a wait, so put your name on the list before exploring the square, or pop next door to **Bar Bianco** for a glass of waiting wine.

Get Inspired at the Phoenix Art Museum

Western, contemporary and totally immersive art

Make a beeline for the **Phoenix Art Museum** *(phxart.org; adult/child $28/18)* to see how the Arizona landscape has inspired everyone from early pioneers to modernists. From here, Arizona's premier repository of fine art only gets more interesting, with works by Claude Monet, Frida Kahlo, Georgia O'Keeffe and Kehinde Wiley. Navigate to the far-back reaches of the museum for a trippy moment inside Yayoi Kusama's infinity mirror room, *You Who Are Getting Obliterated in the Dancing Swarm of Fireflies.*

Explore South Mountain Park

Morning hikes and petroglyphs

Pima Canyon is just one of many hiking destinations at the enormous **South Mountain Park** *(phoenix.gov/parks)*, where a 51-mile network of trails (leashed dogs allowed) dips through canyons, over cacti-studded hills and past granite walls. Hike or drive to **Dobbins Lookout** for valley views at sunset.

The main entrance is at 10211 S Central Ave; the Pima Canyon entrance is at 4771 E Pima Canyon Rd.

DRINKING IN PHOENIX: OUR PICKS

Wandering Tortoise: Unpretentious hangout with 20+ draft beers and a fridge full of cans. Food truck on-site, with outside food welcome. Dog-friendly. *hours vary*

Arizona Wilderness DTPHX: Environmentally conscious beers with some of the best brewery food around. Duck-fat fries are a must. *11am-11pm Mon-Thu, to midnight Fri & Sat, to 10pm Sun*

Century Grand: With three different bar concepts under one roof, this place consistently lands on lists for the best cocktail bars in the US. *4pm-midnight Tue-Thu, from 2:30pm Fri-Sun*

Bitter & Twisted: Sip a playful Bear Witness out of a honey bear bottle, or let the expert bar staff surprise you. *4pm-midnight Tue-Thu, to 1am Fri & Sat*

Grand Canyon National Park

SPECTACULAR SCENERY | MEMORABLE TRAILS | FASCINATING GEOLOGY

The Grand Canyon lives up to the hype: its immensity, its grandeur, its beauty and its very age all scream for superlatives. At about two billion years old, the layer of Vishnu schist at the bottom of the canyon is some of the oldest exposed rock on the planet. It was exposed by the Colorado River, which continues to carve its way 277 miles through the canyon – as it has for the past six million years.

At Grand Canyon National Park, you can descend into the canyon depths, stroll the rim or relax at an outcrop at either the North or South Rims. Though views from both rims are equally stunning, the South Rim boasts many more official and dramatic overlooks. One of the most beautiful, however, was the view that whispered from the Grand Canyon Lodge's patio on the canyon's quieter north side; the lodge burned to the ground in mid-2025, but there are other views nearby.

A 215-mile drive, or a strenuous day hike, connects the two rims.

Rock Out at the Geology Museum

Rock layers and the Trail of Time

Take a moment to find the Colorado River while gazing through the large windows that overlook the canyon from the small **Yavapai Geology Museum** *(nps.gov/grca; free)*, where interpretive panels explain the formations below. Behind you, a topographic relief map highlights the canyon's multilayered geologic history. From here, walk west along the Trail of Time about 1.5 miles to the **Grand Canyon Village Historic District**. The trail traces the history of the canyon's formation – each meter equals one million years of geologic history. Stop by for a ranger geology talk at the museum at 11am daily.

GETTING AROUND

The South Rim is an easy 60-mile drive north of I-40 at Williams. Hwy 67 is the only road to the North Rim, closed December 1 to mid-May. Although the North Rim is only 11 miles from the South as the crow flies, it's a 215-mile, four- to five-hour drive.

Grand Canyon Village is congested March to September. Park at one of the four visitor center lots and catch a free shuttle bus. There are smaller lots at Shrine of the Ages, Market Plaza, Yavapai Geology Museum and Backcountry Information Center.

TOP TIP

The park is an International Dark Sky Park, so evening light pollution is minimal and stargazing is superb. Bring a flashlight to dinner at the North Rim – the walk to your room is dark!

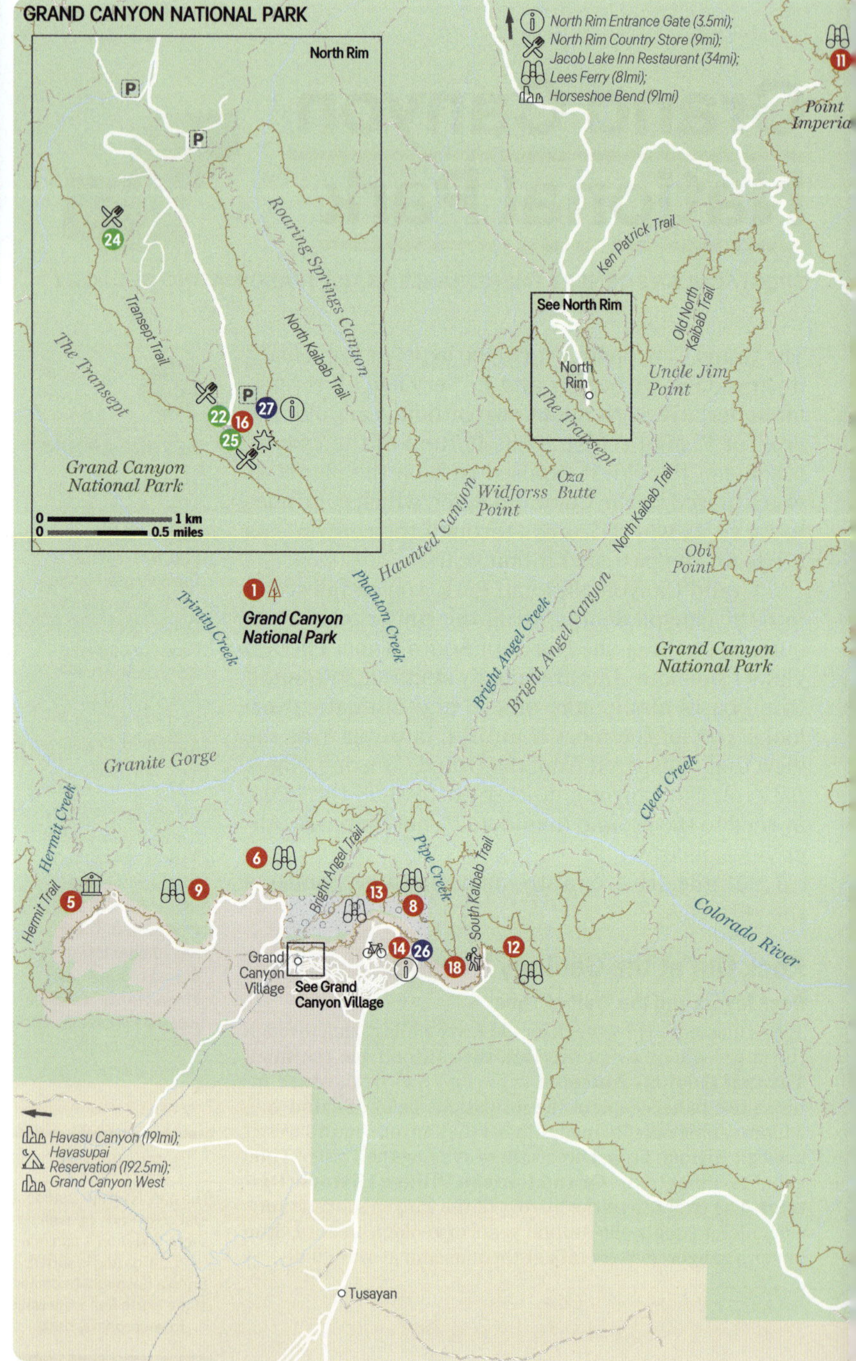
GRAND CANYON NATIONAL PARK
North Rim Entrance Gate (3.5mi);
North Rim Country Store (9mi);
Jacob Lake Inn Restaurant (34mi);
Lees Ferry (81mi);
Horseshoe Bend (91mi)
North Rim
Roaring Springs Canyon
Transept Trail
The Transept
North Kaibab Trail
Grand Canyon National Park
0 1 km
0 0.5 miles
Point Imperial
Ken Patrick Trail
See North Rim
North Rim
Old North Kaibab Trail
Uncle Jim Point
The Transept
Widforss Point
Oza Butte
Haunted Canyon
North Kaibab Trail
Obi Point
Grand Canyon National Park
Trinity Creek
Phantom Creek
Bright Angel Creek
Bright Angel Canyon
Grand Canyon National Park
Granite Gorge
Clear Creek
Hermit Creek
Hermit Trail
Bright Angel Trail
Pipe Creek
South Kaibab Trail
Colorado River
Grand Canyon Village
See Grand Canyon Village
Havasu Canyon (191mi);
Havasupai Reservation (192.5mi);
Grand Canyon West
Tusayan

HIGHLIGHTS
1 Grand Canyon National Park

SIGHTS
2 Angels Window
3 Cape Royal Point
4 Grand Canyon Village Historic District
5 Hermits Rest
6 Hopi Point
7 Lipan Point
8 Mather Point
9 Mohave Point
10 Moran Point
11 Point Imperial
12 Yaki Point
13 Yavapai Geology Museum

ACTIVITIES
14 Bright Angel Bicycles
15 Bright Angel Trail
16 Canyon Trail Rides
17 Grand Canyon Mule Rides
18 South Kaibab Trail

SLEEPING
19 Bright Angel Lodge
20 El Tovar

EATING
21 Arizona Steakhouse
22 Deli in the Pines
see 20 El Tovar Dining Room
23 Harvey House Cafe
24 North Rim General Store
25 Rough Rider Saloon

INFORMATION
26 Grand Canyon Visitor Center
27 Old North Rim Visitor Center site

FELA SANU/SHUTTERSTOCK

South Rim

TOP EXPERIENCE

Grand Canyon

Welcome to one of the greatest natural shows on earth. Whatever you've heard about the Grand Canyon, it never disappoints, as beloved by veterans of this remarkable place as by first-time visitors. If you are among the latter, we envy you: nothing can compare with the first time you lay eyes on this beauty, and you've so much to look forward to.

DON'T MISS

- Mather Point
- Grand Canyon Visitor Center
- Bright Angel Trail
- South Kaibab Trail
- Rafting the Colorado River

Big View

If you're a first-time visitor, there's one requirement after entering from the South Rim: park your car at the **Grand Canyon Visitor Center** *(nps.gov/grca)* then dash to **Mather Point** to gaze upon the canyon in all its glory. It's a time-honored tradition and one you'll likely never forget.

PRACTICALITIES

● nps.gov/grca ● Admission to Grand Canyon National Park is $35/30 per vehicle/motorcycle and $20 per individual (under-15 free) arriving by foot, bicycle, bus, trail or raft, and is valid for seven days at both rims.

After that first mad glimpse, however, it's worth spending time at the visitor center itself. On the visitor-center plaza, bulletin boards and kiosks display information about ranger programs, the weather and tours. You'll also find helpful trail summaries. Inside is a ranger-staffed information desk, a lecture hall and a theater screening *Grand Canyon: A Journey of Wonder* – an introduction to the park's geology, history, and plant and animal life – and *We Are Grand Canyon,* a welcome from the 11 regional tribal communities. Each film is 24 minutes. The visitor center is also a stop on several shuttle routes.

Hike into the Canyon

As you'll quickly discover, the **Bright Angel Trail** is spectacularly scenic as it makes a 7.8-mile descent to the Colorado River. Though steep, long stretches near the start of this trail are not overly precarious, making this an excellent choice for families. Day hikers should turn around at one of the two rest houses (3- or 6-mile round trip) or hit the trail at dawn for longer hikes to Indian Garden and Plateau Point (9.2- and 12.2-mile round trip).

The **South Kaibab Trail** combines stunning scenery and unobstructed 360-degree views. Steep, rough and wholly exposed, this ridgeline descent plummets 4470ft along 6.4 miles to the Colorado River. You'll twist down tight switchbacks – flanked by a wall of Kaibab Limestone – before reaching Ooh Aah Point, a popular marked turnaround, at 0.9 miles. If you have more time, continue to Cedar Ridge at 1.4 miles. In addition to expansive views of the canyon, you'll find pit toilets here and a large, red-dirt overlook – mostly without shade – for a picnic.

Rafting the Grand Canyon

As you push off from **Lees Ferry** and float toward the soaring red walls of Marble Canyon, the sense of anticipation is something you won't soon forget. To come? More than 160 sets of rapids, camping under the stars, a float down the turquoise waters of the Little Colorado, hikes into mysterious slot canyons and a sense of camaraderie born from shared adventure – and no outside communications. Yep, a weeklong rafting trip on the Colorado River is a worthy bucket-list adventure, and one that is totally doable by the average traveler.

Consider the following before booking a trip: the number of days you want to be on the river, where you want to begin and end, and the type of boat – dory, oar-powered raft, paddle-steered raft or a motorized pontoon raft. The latter are the only ones that can travel the canyon's 277-mile course in a week. The national park *(nps.gov/grca)* has approved 15 commercial outfitters, listed on its website.

GAS & GARAGES AT THE GRAND CANYON

The **Desert View Chevron Service Station** is the only gas station on the South Rim, but gas stations in Tusayan are about 7 miles south of Grand Canyon Village. There is one gas station in the park on the North Rim, near the campground. You can also fill up in Jacob Lake or on Rte 67 at the **North Rim Country Store**.

TOP TIPS

- No cash is accepted at either the South or North entrance gates – credit/debit cards only.
- From the South Entrance it's 5 miles to the Grand Canyon Visitor Center, the primary informational hub.
- Transportation desks at Bright Angel, Maswik and Yavapai Lodges book bus tours.
- The Bright Angel desk also assists with Phantom Ranch and mule-ride reservations.
- The Backcountry Information Center supplies maps and backcountry permits.
- Cars are not allowed on the road to the South Kaibab Trailhead and Yaki Point nor, from March through November, on Hermit Rd.

BEST OVERLOOKS

Mohave Point: For a look at the river and three rapids. With multiple viewing spots, Mohave is particularly good for sunrise and sunset in high season.

Hopi Point: Magnificent east-west views, making it an excellent choice for dawn and dusk.

Lipan Point: Geology buffs: you can clearly see the tilting layered rocks of the Grand Canyon Supergroup here.

Moran Point: River views and excellent panorama of the canyon's geologic history. Named after Thomas Moran, the landscape painter who spent many winters at the canyon from 1899 to 1920.

Yaki Point: A favorite spot to watch the sunrise warm the canyon's features.

DUSTY ROADS/SHUTTERSTOCK

Angels Window

Shake the Crowds along Hermit Road

Hike, bike or ride the shuttle

Dotted with nine incredible canyon overlooks and roughly paralleling the rim, the 7-mile Hermit Rd stretches west from Grand Canyon Village Historic District to **Hermits Rest**. Designed by Mary Colter in 1913, the low-slung stone building at Hermits Rest is the South Rim's westernmost scenic overlook. The road is accessible year-round by bike, bus tour and by hiking the Rim Trail. Private vehicles can drive it December through February only. From March 1 through November 30, a park shuttle services all overlooks.

One of the best ways to experience Hermit Rd is by bike; rent one at **Bright Angel Bicycles**. You can also hike between shuttle stops via the Rim Trail.

Ride a Mule on the North or South Rim

Epic views and private cabins

If you take a mule ride, you're going to be sore – even if the ride lasts just an hour or two. But weary muscles have not scared away riders – they've been clip-clopping to the bottom

EATING ON THE SOUTH RIM: OUR PICKS

Harvey House Cafe: Savor a double-bacon cheeseburger and other American fare with canyon views. *6:30-10:30am, 11am-3pm & 4-9:30pm* $$

Arizona Steakhouse: Not just steaks – salads, sandwiches and burgers are on the menu, steps from South Rim. *11:30am-3pm & 4:30-9pm* $$

El Tovar Dining Room: Park dining at its best; windows frame the Rim Trail and canyon. Reserve. *6-10am, 11am-2:30pm & 4:30-9:30pm* $$$

of the Grand Canyon for more than 100 years. On the South Rim, **mule rides** *(grandcanyonlodges.com; from $1231)* follow the Bright Angel Trail – a bumpy, 10-mile trip with big views – to Phantom Ranch, which sits just north of the Colorado River. After one or two nights, they saddle up for an 8-mile ascent on the South Kaibab Trail. All meals are included in the ticket price. Make your reservation 15 months in advance.

Family-run **Canyon Trail Rides** *(canyonriders.com; 1/3hr $60/120)* offers one- and three-hour trips on the North Rim-from mid-May through mid-October.

Drive the Scenic Cape Royal Road

North Rim ponderosas and canyon views

Cape Royal Rd is a scenic must-do for any North Rim visitor. And your payoff after driving it is the chance to stand upon **Angels Window**, a natural arch that juts into the canyon, dropping dramatically on three sides. A place for awe and plenty of photos.

Descending gradually from the trailhead at 8200ft to 7865ft at Cape Royal, Cape Royal Rd ribbons scenically for 15 miles through evergreens and ponderosas. Along the way you can take the spur road to 8803ft-tall **Point Imperial**, the highest viewpoint in the park, for a look at Marble Canyon.

At the end of the drive, a 0.6-mile paved path, lined with pinyon, cliffrose and interpretive signs, leads to the arch and to **Cape Royal Point**, arguably the best view from this side of the canyon.

Peer Through a Glass Skywalk

A transparent overlook

The glass-bottomed **Skywalk**, perched 4000ft above the floor of the Grand Canyon, is not for the faint of heart. But it is pretty darn cool. The Skywalk is one of several attractions at **Grand Canyon West** *(grandcanyonwest.com; general admission & Skywalk $68)*, a commercial venture managed by the Hualapai Nation.

Also be aware that Grand Canyon West is not part of the Grand Canyon National Park, which is 240 miles east. But it is a convenient, if pricey, place to see the canyon if you're staying in Las Vegas.

TIPS FOR THE GRAND CANYON

Avoid the temptation to run from overlook to overlook, snapping photos, looking for that perfect view and determined to see them all. A few hours sitting on a rock, the sun on your face and miles of layered canyon expanding in panorama around you, may just be the perfect canyon experience.

The canyon is best appreciated slowly, with patience, humility and respect.

Never hike to the river and back in one day.

Bring a cooler and snacks. Park food is notoriously bad and expensive.

Stay hydrated; dehydration and altitude sickness can ruin a canyon visit.

Spend at least three nights in the park, and let the park reveal itself slowly.

EATING ON THE NORTH RIM: OUR PICKS

North Rim General Store: Beside the campground, this market sells basic grocery items, plus snacks and ice cream. *7am-9pm* $

Deli in the Pines: Takeaway salads and sandwiches for a picnic, plus pizza, soft-serve ice cream. Elk chili is the winner. *10am-8pm* $

Rough Rider Saloon: Grab morning pastries and breakfast burritos at the counter; slices of pizza in the evening. *11am-11pm* $

Jacob Lake Inn Restaurant: Welcoming spot for breakfast, lunch or dinner 45 miles north of the North Rim. Great cookies! *7am-9pm* $$

GETTING STARTED AT THE NORTH RIM

The **North Rim Entrance Gate**, 31 miles south of Jacob Lake, does not accept cash; only credit and debit cards. The entrance is open 24 hours; a pass is valid for seven days.

From here, it's another 13 miles to where the visitor center and **Grand Canyon Lodge** were located, until a fire in 2025 destroyed them. Check the National Park Service website *(nps.gov)* for updates. Without the Grand Canyon Lodge, which was the only lodging inside the park on the North Rim, the nearest accommodations are in Jacobs Lake.

Full services are available on the North Rim from mid-May through mid-October. From December 1 to May 14, North Rim roads are closed to all vehicles.

RONNYBAS/SHUTTERSTOCK

Havasu Falls

Swimming Holes & Blue-Green Waterfalls

Get in the water

The blue-green waterfalls of **Havasu Canyon** are among the Grand Canyon region's greatest treasures. Tucked away in a hidden valley, the five stunning, spring-fed waterfalls – and their inviting azure swimming holes – sit in the heart of the 185,000-acre **Havasupai Reservation** *(havasupai reservations.com)*, which can only be accessed by trail.

The Havasupai Reservation is located south of the Colorado River and four hours west of Grand Canyon National Park's South Rim, off Route 66.

Hike or Paddle at Horseshoe Bend

Views and kayaks

Calling the view dramatic at **Horseshoe Bend** *(horseshoe bend.co; car/motorcycle parking $10/5)* is a wild understatement. The scenic overlook here sits on sheer cliffs that drop 1000ft to the river below, which carves a perfect horseshoe through the Navajo sandstone. And guardrails are few.

The trailhead is south of Page off Hwy 89, just past Mile 545. It's a 1.2-mile round-trip walk from the parking lot.

You can also **kayak** *(kayakhorsehoebend.com or kayakthe colorado.com; from $115)* the Colorado River through Horseshoe Bend and admire its soaring grandeur from below. **Horseshoe Bend Slot Canyon Tours** takes you to views from the south.

Northern Arizona

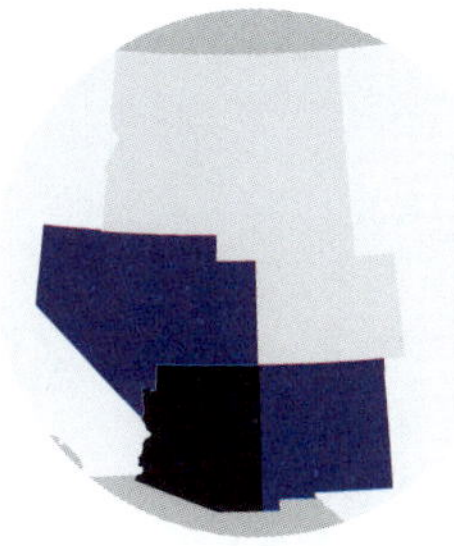

ANCIENT CULTURES | SPIRITUAL JOURNEYS | DESERT LANDSCAPES

If you broaden your horizons beyond Phoenix and the Grand Canyon, you'll move through the heartland of the American West. This is a world where crimson buttes, saguaros and ponderosa pines are the backdrop for outdoor adventures. Elsewhere, mountain towns and cliff dwellings offer introductions to a fascinating past.

Grand Canyon National Park may be Arizona's biggest draw, but it's also a launchpad for visits to nearby sites that delve into the culture and history of 11 tribal nations. Much of the area in the north and center of the state lies on, or just below, the Colorado Plateau, a high-desert playground that is cool, wooded and mountainous. Anchored by Flagstaff, this region is blessed with the state's most diverse and scenic sites. As a starting point, you can explore a vortex in Sedona, camp beside Oak Creek Canyon, or admire the 1000-year-old dwellings of the Ancestral Puebloans. Stargazing is amazing everywhere.

Places

TOP TIP

A Red Rock Pass ($5/15 day/week) covers everything from parking to spending time exploring National Forest land around Sedona, Oak Creek Canyon, Flagstaff and surrounds. It's available at ranger stations, visitor centers, most trailheads and *recreation.gov*.

Sedona & Around

Good vibes and vortexes

It's hard to have a bad day in Sedona. Red rock buttes, forested canyons and lush creek sides – it's a spectacular backdrop that has long attracted spiritual seekers, artists and healers. Over

GETTING AROUND

The sixth-largest state in the US, Arizona rewards those who explore by car; rentals are available from airports, but you'll find a better deal closer to your hotel. The main airports are at Phoenix, Flagstaff and, in the south, Tucson, with regular flights between the three. And if you prefer to ride the rails, Amtrak connects Los Angeles with Kingman, Flagstaff and Winslow on the daily *Southwest Chief*, which continues east to Albuquerque, NM. The daily scenic Grand Canyon Railway runs between Williams and Grand Canyon Village.

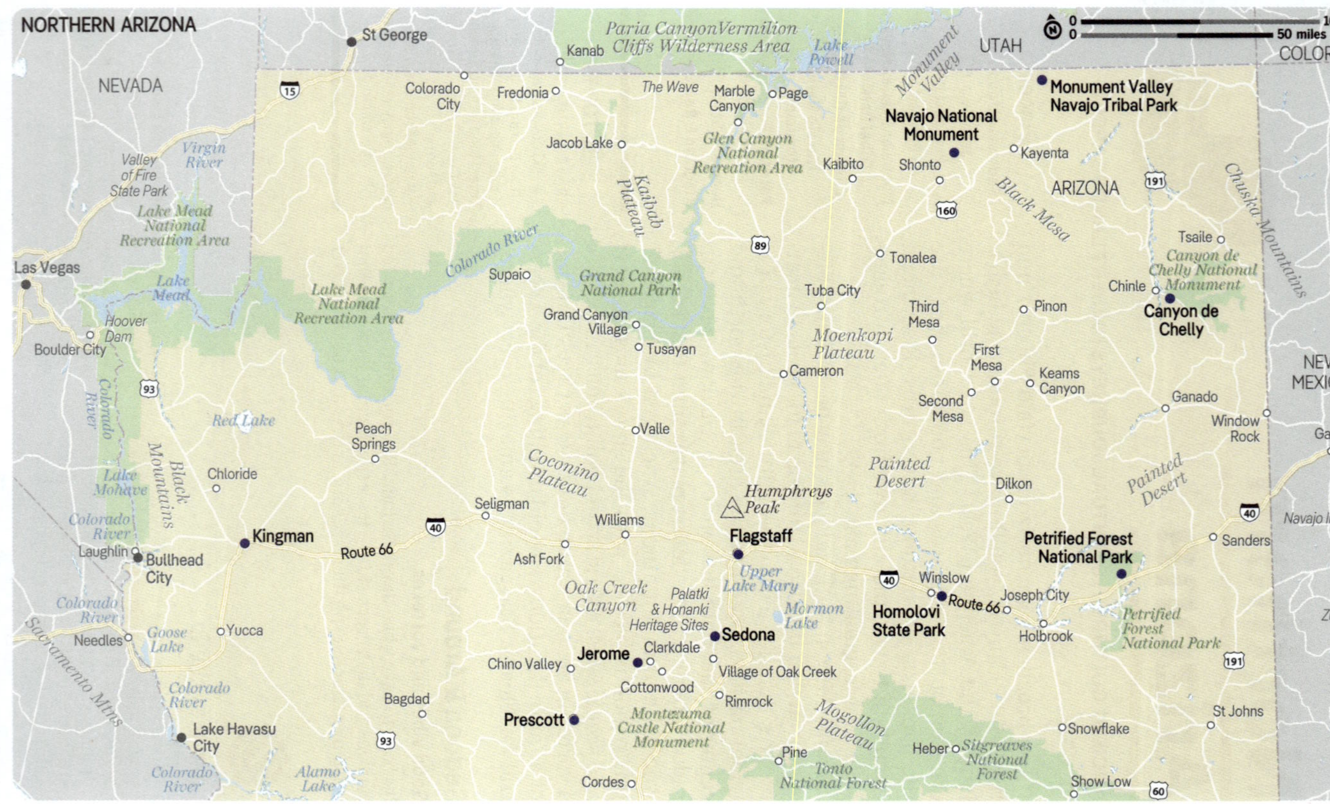
NORTHERN ARIZONA
0 100 km
0 50 miles
NEVADA
UTAH
ARIZONA
COLORADO
NEW MEXICO
St George
Kanab
Paria Canyon Vermilion Cliffs Wilderness Area
Lake Powell
Monument Valley
Monument Valley Navajo Tribal Park
Colorado City
Fredonia
The Wave
Marble Canyon
Page
Navajo National Monument
Kayenta
Jacob Lake
Glen Canyon National Recreation Area
Kaibito
Shonto
Valley of Fire State Park
Virgin River
Lake Mead National Recreation Area
Kaibab Plateau
Black Mesa
Chuska Mountains
Chaco River
Tsaile
Canyon de Chelly National Monument
Chinle
Canyon de Chelly
Las Vegas
Lake Mead
Colorado River
Supaio
Grand Canyon National Park
Tonalea
Tuba City
Third Mesa
Pinon
Hoover Dam
Boulder City
Grand Canyon Village
Tusayan
Moenkopi Plateau
Cameron
First Mesa
Keams Canyon
Second Mesa
Ganado
Window Rock
Gallup
Red Lake
Peach Springs
Valle
Painted Desert
Chloride
Black Mountains
Lake Mohave
Coconino Plateau
Seligman
Williams
Humphreys Peak
Dilkon
Navajo IR
Kingman
Route 66
Ash Fork
Flagstaff
Petrified Forest National Park
Sanders
Laughlin
Bullhead City
Oak Creek Canyon
Palatki & Honanki Heritage Sites
Upper Lake Mary
Mormon Lake
Winslow
Homolovi State Park
Joseph City
Holbrook
Petrified Forest National Park
Zuni IR
Needles
Goose Lake
Yucca
Sedona
Chino Valley
Jerome
Clarkdale
Cottonwood
Village of Oak Creek
Rimrock
Sacramento Mtns
Bagdad
Prescott
Montezuma Castle National Monument
Mogollon Plateau
St Johns
Snowflake
Lake Havasu City
Pine
Heber
Sitgreaves National Forest
Tonto National Forest
Alamo Lake
Cordes
Show Low
15
93
89
160
191
40
60

the years Sedona has developed into an extremely popular New Age destination. The reason? Spiritual-minded folks believe that the sandstone formations here hold vortexes, which vibrate to the frequencies of the deepest earth energies. Many believe this energy encourages healing and spiritual well-being.

To learn more, step inside the **Center for the New Age** *(sedonanewagestore.com)*, the big purple building on Hwy 179 south of Uptown. Shelves of this metaphysical superstore are crammed with crystals, spirituality books and vortex guides. Similar shops are scattered across town. The best-known vortexes are **Bell Rock** (near the Village of Oak Creek), **Cathedral Rock** (near Red Rock Crossing), **Airport Mesa** (Airport Rd) and **Boynton Canyon**.

Airport Mesa is the closest to town, and the drive up Airport Rd opens up to panoramic views of the valley. It's a half-mile walk from the mesa-top parking lot ($3) to the best viewpoint: a red rock hilltop with astounding 360-degree views.

Red rocks encourage deep thoughts at two beloved spots in Sedona. The better known of the two is the **Chapel of the Holy Cross** *(chapeloftheholycross.com; free)*, a small 1956 Roman Catholic chapel that soars from the surrounding rock like a slice of the majestic land itself.

A consecrated Buddhist shrine is set quite stunningly amid pinyon and juniper pine and the ubiquitous rocks at the low-key **Amitabha Stupa & Peace Park** *(tara.org/amitabha-stupa; free)* in West Sedona. Trails meander past colorful prayer flags, leading to a labyrinth and more red rock views.

Petroglyphs and cliff dwellings

The more than 1000 images (deer, turtles, birds, an embracing couple) carved into the sandstone panels at **Crane Petroglyph Heritage Site** *(fs.usda.gov; 9:30am-3pm Fri-Mon)* were created by the Sinagua people between 1150 and 1400 CE.

Seven miles of dirt road in northwestern Sedona lead to 1000-year-old Sinaguan cliff dwellings and rock art at the **Palatki Heritage Site** *(fs.usda.gov; reservations required)*, which is perched enchantingly on the edge of the wilderness. You can view more Sinaguan ruins 3 miles north at sister site **Honanki**. Both are open from 9:30am to 3pm Thursday to Tuesday and to noon Wednesday.

Red Rock ($5 per vehicle) and National Park passes (price varies) grant admission to all three sites, which are located in the Coconino National Forest.

BEST HIKES IN SEDONA & OAK CREEK CANYON

Bell Rock & Courthouse Butte: Easy 4-mile loop; follows multiuse Bell Rock Pathway around the immense Bell Rock then circles Courthouse Butte.

Boynton Canyon: Pretty 6-mile round-trip hike with shaded stretches, petroglyphs and Sinaguan ruins. Look for the side trail to Kachina Woman rock formation.

Devil's Bridge: Crowded, but the namesake arch is a photogenic prize on this 4-mile round-trip hike from Mescal Trailhead.

West Fork Trail: A 6½-mile round-trip Oak Creek Canyon hike with 13 creek crossings; red rock walls soar more than 200ft in some places. Gorgeous October foliage.

EATING IN SEDONA & AROUND: OUR PICKS

Sedonuts: Apple fritter is the top seller, but we dig the Red Rock Oreo at this decadent West Sedona doughnut shop. *6am-noon* $

Indian Gardens Cafe & Market: The breakfast sandwich is a delicious mess of eggs, chimichurri, cheddar; in Oak Creek Canyon. *8am-4pm Sat-Thu, to 8pm Fri* $$

Hudson: Prickly pear ribs, smoked-salmon bruschetta and fireball chicken wings infuse Sedona with urban cool. Great red-rock views. *11:30am-9pm* $$$

Mariposa: Stunning red-rock views and divine Latin-inspired food from the grill are the hallmarks of this upmarket option. *11am-2pm & 4-9pm* $$$

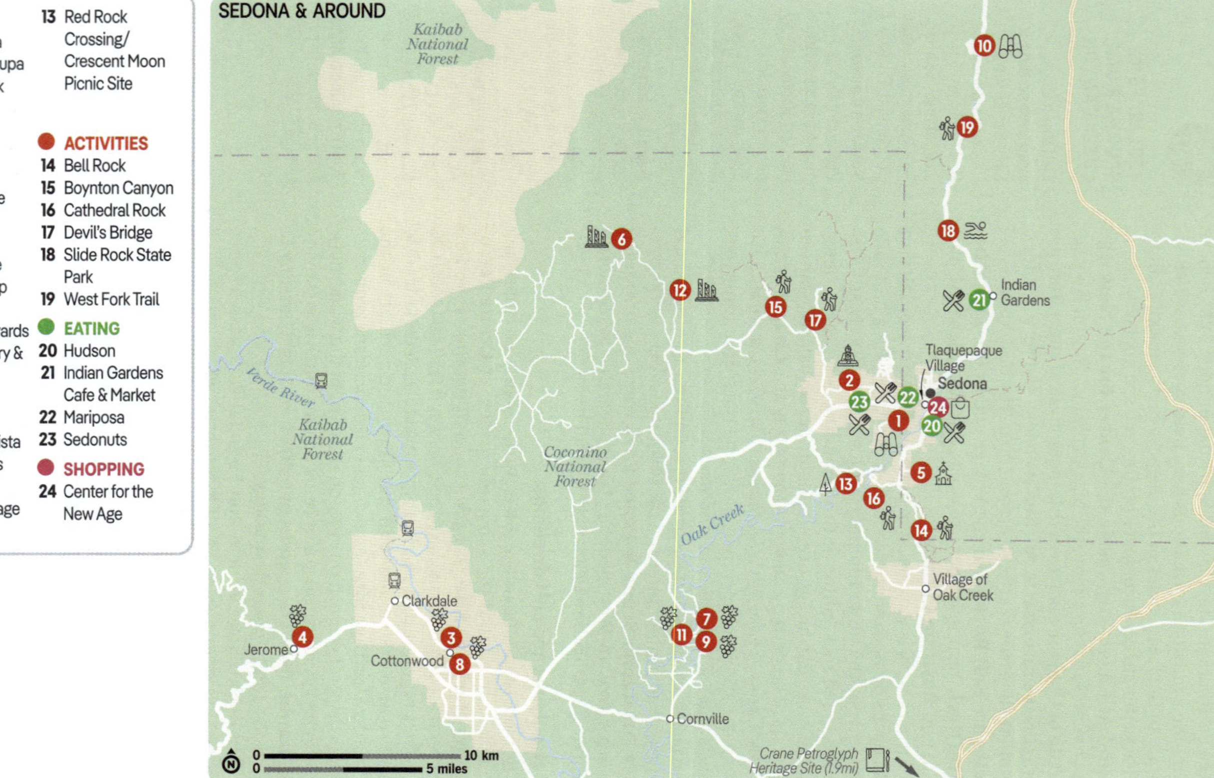

SIGHTS
1 Airport Mesa
2 Amitabha Stupa & Peace Park
3 Arizona Stronghold
4 Caduceus Cellars
5 Chapel of the Holy Cross
6 Honanki Heritage Site
7 Javelina Leap Vineyard
8 Merkin Vineyards Hilltop Winery & Trattoria
9 Oak Creek Vineyards
10 Oak Creek Vista
11 Page Springs Cellars
12 Palatki Heritage Site
13 Red Rock Crossing/ Crescent Moon Picnic Site

ACTIVITIES
14 Bell Rock
15 Boynton Canyon
16 Cathedral Rock
17 Devil's Bridge
18 Slide Rock State Park
19 West Fork Trail

EATING
20 Hudson
21 Indian Gardens Cafe & Market
22 Mariposa
23 Sedonuts

SHOPPING
24 Center for the New Age

Hike Oak Creek Canyon

From the soaring overlook at **Oak Creek Vista**, 14 miles south of Flagstaff, the pine-draped glory of Oak Creek Canyon swoops south to the horizon like an unruly child just released from Nature's time-out. From the overlook, you'll corkscrew down Hwy 89A into the 13-mile canyon, where russet and vermilion cliffs soar above the creek and the highway. Giant cottonwoods clump along the waterway, providing a scenic, shady backdrop for trout fishing and swimming. If hiking is on your agenda, pull over for the popular **West Fork Trail**, which crosses Oak Creek 13 times as it winds through the canyon. Its imposing walls can soar more than 200ft.

A few miles south, an 80ft sandstone chute whisks swimmers through Oak Creek at **Slide Rock State Park** *(azstateparks.com; $10-30 per vehicle)*. The chute and the rock slides here are a blast but they can get oppressively crowded in summer, particularly between 10am and 3pm.

Drive the Red Rock scenic routes

The easiest scenic drive is also one of the best: the **Red Rock Scenic Byway** *(redrockscenicbyway.org)*. This National Scenic Byway and All-American Road tracks Hwy 179 from I-17 (exit 298) north of Phoenix for 7.5 miles, passing red hills and the Red Rock Ranger District Visitor Center before ending just north of the Village of Oak Creek in a pull-over, grab-your-camera explosion of red-rock impressiveness that includes Bell Rock and Courthouse Butte.

Any time is a good time to drive the winding 7-mile **Red Rock Loop Road**, which can be accessed via Upper Red Rock Loop Rd off Hwy 89A, 4 miles west of the Y intersection in Sedona. First up is the **Crescent Moon Picnic Site** *(vehicle/pedestrian $12/3)*, where a small army of photographers usually gathers at sunset at Red Rock Crossing to record the dramatic light show unfolding on iconic **Cathedral Rock**, a vortex.

Taste Verde Valley wines

The **Merkin Vineyards Hilltop Winery & Trattoria** *(merkintrattoria.com)* in Old Town Cottonwood – a 25-minute drive from Sedona – has a grand patio with sweeping views of the Verde Valley, where you can sip some darn good wines while nibbling on bruschetta and lasagna 'cupcakes.'

Merkin is one of two dozen or so vineyards, wineries and tasting rooms in the well-watered valley of the Verde River. Bringing star power to the **wine trail** *(vvwinetrail.com)* is Maynard James Keenan, lead singer of the band Tool and owner of Merkin Vineyards and **Caduceus Cellars** (*caduceus.org*). His 2010 documentary *Blood into Vine* takes a no-holds-barred look at the northern Arizona wine industry.

Another good stop in Old Town Cottonwood is the tasting room at **Arizona Stronghold** (*azstronghold.com*). Three wineries with tasting rooms hug a scrubby stretch of Page Springs Rd between Sedona and Cottonwood, near Cornville: bistro-housing **Page Springs Cellars** *(pagespringscelllars.com)*, the welcoming **Oak Creek Vineyards** *(oakcreekvineyards,net)* and the mellow-rock-playing **Javelina Leap Vineyard & Winery** *(javelinaleapwinery.com)*.

SEDONA SHUTTLES

Several helpful **shuttles** *(sedonashuttle.com)* crisscross the city.

Free **hiker shuttles** run to the most popular trailheads Thursday to Sunday, 7am to 5:30pm, with extra days when it's busy. These shuttles pick up passengers from three park-and-ride lots and run to Cathedral Rock/Little Horse, Dry Creek Vista/Mescal and Soldier Pass. Be aware that the Cathedral Rock and Soldier Pass Trailhead lots are closed to cars on the days the shuttle is running.

The new **Sedona Shuttle Connect** *(6:30am-6pm Thu-Sun, one way $2)* is an on-demand, app-driven service with stops in a defined area. **Verde Shuttle** *(6am-10pm; one way $2)* connects Sedona with Cottonwood, with stops along the way.

ARIZONA TIME ZONES

Arizona is on Mountain Time (seven hours behind GMT). It is the only Western state not to observe daylight saving time from spring to fall. The exception is the Navajo Reservation, which – in keeping with those parts of the reservation located in Utah and New Mexico – does observe daylight saving time. Confusingly, the small Hopi Reservation, which it surrounds, follows Arizona. The varying time zones come into play in Page and Monument Valley, which straddle the Arizona/Utah state line, during daylight saving time. Many hotels have two clocks on the wall, so you'll know what the times are. Keep the discrepancy in mind when scheduling tours in the region or your hotel check-in.

Jerome

Galleries, saloons and old hotels

Jerome can really mess with your mind: it can be hard to tell whether the buildings are winning or losing their battle with gravity. The **Sliding Jail**, lodged in the dirt southeast of the **Chamber of Commerce** visitor center, has moved 225ft from its original 1927 location. It isn't surprising, considering that there are 88 miles of tunnels, many of which were frequently dynamited and cut into steep hills, under your feet.

Main St is home to the engaging **Mine Museum** *(jeromehistoricalsociety.com; $2),* which spotlights local characters and stories. Just north, the allegedly haunted 1898 **Connor Hotel** (p212; *connorhotel.com)* was the town's first solid-stone lodging – don't miss the **Spirit Room**, the fun in-house saloon with murals sporting bordello scenes. From here, a climb leads to **Jerome Grand Hotel** (p212; *jeromegrandhotel.com),* the one-time home of the United Verde Hospital. Known for its ghosts and the venerable **Asylum Restaurant** *(asylumrestaurant.com),* it's a cool place to enjoy expansive views of the crimson-gold rocks of Sedona and the Verde Valley.

Prescott

Have a beer on Whiskey Row

Montezuma St, west of the plaza, was the infamous **Whiskey Row**, where 40 drinking establishments supplied suds to rough-hewn cowboys and miners. In 1900 a devastating fire destroyed 25 saloons, five hotels and the red-light district, although several early buildings remain. Many are still bars to this day, mixed with boutiques, galleries and restaurants.

Push through the swinging doors to enter the historic **Palace Saloon** *(whiskeyrowpalace.com).* It can be hard to tell if the men in cowboy hats are costumed waiters or actual cowboys. But no mind. This bar was once frequented by Wyatt Earp and Doc Holliday, so Old West duds come with the territory. Rebuilt in 1901 after the fire, it displays a museum's worth of Old West photos and artifacts. A scene from the 1972 Steve McQueen movie *Junior Bonner* was filmed here, and a mural honoring the film covers an inside wall.

Art, history, booze and good eats collide in the saloon and other century-old buildings surrounding **Yavapai County Courthouse**, which anchors an elm-shaded plaza in the heart of Prescott. Pause for breakfast or lunch at the cafe inside historic Hotel St Michael (p212).

EATING IN JEROME & PRESCOTT: OUR PICKS

Haunted Hamburger: Perched high on a Jerome hill, this beloved hamburger joint also serves big views and tasty margaritas. *11am-9pm* $

Clinkscale: Hot new kid in Jerome serving New American fare in stylish digs. *8:30am-8:30pm* $$

Farm Provisions: Farm-to-table Prescott favorite with gourmet options like deep-fried deviled eggs or kicky tacos with cilantro aioli. *11am-9pm Wed-Sun* $$

El Gato Azul: Creative Southwest and Spanish dishes that all sound good, including green-chile mac and cheese in Prescott. *11am-8pm most days* $$

KALIREY27/SHUTTERSTOCK

Mt Elden

Buildings east and south of the plaza escaped the fire. The three-story Burmister Building houses a snazzy gift shop as well as **Superstition Meadery** *(superstitionmeadery.com)* and the **County Seat** *(countyseataz.com)* restaurant.

The **Chamber of Commerce Visitor Center** leads free guided walking tours (10am, Friday to Sunday from May to October).

Flagstaff

Flagstaff at all hours

Begin your Flagstaff day with chilaquiles and banana-split French toast at the now-legendary downtown **MartAnne's bistro** *(martannes.com)*. Come hungry for this one. Red walls, black booths and a bevy of oil paintings convey a unique, salon-like feel, and this Day of the Dead vibe is part of the quirky charm. And it ultimately plays well with the wonderfully messy creations on the menu. Of these, the Jerry el Mujeriego (Jerry the Womanizer; a green-chile pork enchilada topped with cheese, sour cream and two eggs) takes the top honors. Just don't plan on doing anything too strenuous immediately afterward. It's open 8:30am to 8pm most days.

Once you've recovered, it's time for a museum. Housed in an arts-and-crafts-style stone building, the small but excellent **Museum of Northern Arizona** *(musnaz.org; adult/Native American/child $15/10/10)* spotlights regional Native American archaeology, history and culture, as well as geology, biology and the arts. Representatives from 10 regional tribes worked with museum curators to select items displayed in the 'Native Peoples of the Colorado Plateau' ethnological exhibit, where you'll see baskets, pottery, jewelry and even a skateboard. Video messages from tribal members enhance the experience. On the way to the Grand Canyon, the museum makes a wonderful introduction to the human and natural history of the region.

TOP HIKES IN FLAGSTAFF

Fatman's Loop: Moderate 2-mile loop with volcanic rock formations, city views, varied trees and one tight squeeze. Begins 5 miles northeast of downtown.

Elden Lookout: Six-mile round-trip hike with a steep 2300ft climb to the summit of Mt Elden, a lava dome. End at a historic fire tower with views of Flagstaff, Sunset Crater and the San Francisco Peaks.

Aspen Nature Loop Trail: On the slopes of Mt Humphreys, this 2.5-mile trail loops past wildflowers, meadows and a forest thick with aspen, spruce and pine.

Kachina Trail: Aspens glow a luminous yellow in fall on this moderate forest-and-meadows trail on Mt Humphreys. It's a 10-mile round trip.

DISCOVER ROUTE 66 & HISTORIC HOTELS

Enjoy a mix of culture and history on this easy downtown walk that takes in public art, a gallery and Old West hotels.

START	END	LENGTH
Flagstaff Visitor Center	Flagstaff Visitor Center	0.5 miles; 30 minutes

Exploring downtown Flagstaff is an agreeable experience – just don't get hit by a passing train. Daily, more than 100 of them whizz past the 1 **Flagstaff Visitor Center**, which shares space with Amtrak inside a Tudor Revival station house. For details about the city's 40 murals, pick up the Flagstaff Public Art Map. Across San Francisco St, the bronze 2 **Gandy Dancer** statue depicts a hardworking railroad man. Cross Route 66 and stroll into downtown, where Old West heritage looms large. Pop into the 3 **Artists' Gallery** for locally made art, jewelry and ceramics. A neon sign towers over the 4 **Hotel Monte Vista**, which opened in 1927. Past guests include John Wayne, Clark Gable and Humphrey Bogart.

Built in 1888 by the Babbitt family on the northwest corner of Aspen Ave and San Francisco St, the sandstone 5 **Babbitt Building** was the first two-story structure in town. A long-running department store, it now houses an outdoor gear and apparel shop. In summer, 6 **Heritage Square** is a hub for festivals, movies and live music. Home to three separate bars, the 1900 7 **Weatherford Hotel** (p212) is the coolest building in town. Two icons of the west, artist Thomas Moran and author Zane Grey, are former guests. Open since 1917, the 8 **Orpheum** hosts live music, films and community events. Cross Route 66 again and return to the visitor center.

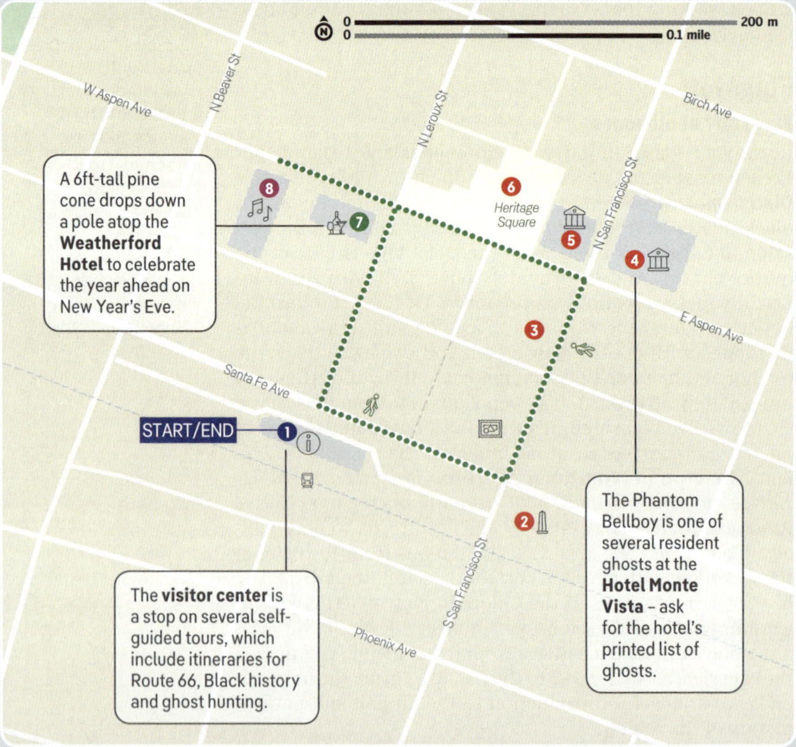

As darkness falls, the **Museum Club** *(museumclub.net)*, an enormous log cabin perched right beside Route 66, comes into its own. To appreciate fully the kitschy appeal of this country-music roadhouse, sometimes called the Zoo, step inside to the large wooden dance floor, animal mounts and a sumptuous elixir-filled mahogany bar. Stick around for the band to fully immerse in the fun. Check its website for the live-music schedule and free line-dancing lessons.

Then when it's *really* dark, it's time for some stargazing. Flagstaff became an official Dark Sky City in 2001 – the very first community in the world to earn this designation from the International Dark-Sky Association. Cherished by astronomers for its dark and cloud-free night skies, Flagstaff is home to **Lowell Observatory** *(lowell.edu; adult/child/senior $35/20/30)* where you can check the marquee for details about daily talks and tours. At night, the Giovale building slides back to expose its telescopes – and budding astronomers – to a jaw-dropping view of the night sky. Evening constellation tours start nearby. For information about star parties and celebrations visit flagstaffdarkskies.org.

Monument Valley Navajo Tribal Park

Explore Monument Valley and Navajo history

If you drive south from Utah on Hwy 163, the rugged sandstone formations of **Monument Valley Navajo Tribal Park** *(navajonationparks.org; $8 per person)* initially rise into view like the ramparts of a prehistoric fortress, a huddled collection of red and gold defenses protecting ancient secrets.

Up close they're hypnotic, an alluring mix of familiar and elusive. Yes, we've seen them in the John Ford Westerns, but the big screen doesn't capture the changing patterns of light, the imposing height, or the strangeness of the angles and forms. You'll see the most striking formations from the rough **17-mile dirt road** *(7am-7pm; shorter hours in winter)* that loops through the park.

The **Wildcat Trail** is a 3.8-mile loop trail around the West Mitten formation that begins at the entrance to the 17-mile drive.

Rounding out your experience (and understanding) of these Navajo lands, it's time to listen to revisit the past. The Navajo Nation became the new owners of **Goulding's Lodge** *(gouldings.com)*, a storied trading post and hotel near the tribal park, in 2023. Harry Goulding and his wife Leone (better known as 'Mike') established the trading post in 1925. In

GUIDED TOURS

Tour guides at Monument Valley shower you with details about the reservation, movie trivia and whatever else comes to mind. They can also take you into the backcountry.

Navajo guides set up kiosks in the parking lot at the visitor center. They are pretty easygoing, so don't worry about high-pressure sales. Tours leave frequently in summer, less so in winter.

Outfits in Kayenta and at Goulding's Lodge also offer tours. To reserve in advance, check out the list of guides on the tribal park's website *(navajo nationparks.org)*. Rates start at about $70 for a 2½-hour motorized trip, and may require a two-person minimum. You do not need a guide to hike the Wildcat Trail.

EATING IN FLAGSTAFF: OUR PICKS

Karma Sushi Bar: Delicious sushi, but the tonkotsu ramen is legendary. On Route 66. *11am-9pm Sun-Thu, to 10pm Fri & Sat* **$**

Pizzicletta: Come here for gourmet toppings heaped on wood-fired pizzas. *noon-9pm Fri-Mon, 5-9pm Tue-Thu* **$$**

Josephine's: New American fare in a 1911 arts-and-crafts bungalow. Good for Saturday breakfast. *5-8:30pm Mon-Sat, 9am-2pm Sat* **$$**

Tinderbox Kitchen: Casual sophistication, chef-driven fare. Annex Cocktail Lounge for drinks. *3-10pm Mon-Thu, to midnight Fri & Sat* **$$$**

GHOST TOWNS

The discovery of gold, silver and copper brought fortune seekers to Arizona from the 1860s. New towns mushroomed overnight near the richest mines, and they were notoriously wild and dangerous places. Abandoned mining towns are scattered across the state's scrub-covered mountains and deserts. Typically there is not much to see at these sites unless you're into rusty equipment and weathered wooden shacks, but they can be cool for photos and for understanding the harshness of mining-town life.

For a list of sites across Arizona and the Southwest, visit americansouthwest.net/ghost-towns.html. For an atmospheric introduction, visit **Vulture City & Mine** *(vulturecityghosttown.com; adult/child $18/10)*, 12 miles west of Wickenburg.

KOJIHIRANO/ISTOCKPHOTO/GETTY IMAGES

the ensuing years, Goulding convinced director John Ford to film his Westerns in the butte-dotted valley. Today Goulding's is home to the lodge as well as a restaurant, a campground and a free museum inside the old trading post. Step inside the museum to see a replica of the store, a room dedicated to the movies shot here, the couple's upstairs living quarters and a collection of black-and-white photos of Navajos and the surrounding landscape.

Canyon de Chelly

Embrace the silence at Spider Rock

If you drive to the **Spider Rock Overlook** at Canyon de Chelly in the late afternoon, you might just have the place to yourself. And the empty silence is strangely invigorating as you gaze down at **Spider Rock**, a 800ft bifurcated sandstone spire guarding the place where **Canyon de Chelly National Monument** *(nps.gov/cach; free)* meets Monument Canyon. The overlook is the fifth and final stop on the 16-mile **South Rim Drive**, which runs along the main canyon and shares dramatic vistas.

EATING IN MONUMENT VALLEY & KAYENTA: OUR PICKS

Blue Coffee Pot: So this is where everybody is. This busy spot in Kayenta serves Navajo tacos and diner fare. *7am-9pm Mon-Fri* $

Amigo Cafe & Coffee Bar: Huevos rancheros, burgers with chipotle aioli, mutton tostadas on this tasty menu in Kayenta. *8am-8pm Tue-Sat* $

Stagecoach Restaurant: Impressive views in Goulding's Lodge. So-so American and Navajo fare and can swarm with tourists. *7am-9pm* $$

View Restaurant: The Navajo food doesn't always shine, but whoa, that view of the monuments is sublime. *7-11am & 5-9:30pm* $$

Spider Rock, Canyon de Chelly

For the most part, **North Rim Drive** follows a side canyon called Canyon del Muerto, which has four overlooks. At the first, **Antelope House Overlook**, a short walk ends at stunning cliff-top views of a natural rock fortress and cliff dwellings. To see the latter, walk to your right from the walled **Navajo Fortress Viewpoint** to a second walled overlook.

If you have a 4WD, you could go a little further. Past the mouth of Canyon de Chelly, heading deeper into the valley, the canyon's sandstone walls soar ever higher, narrowing your views of the sky. But the view ahead? It grows lush, filling with crops, livestock and cottonwood trees, all hugging a growing stream. Petroglyphs and cliff dwellings here are portals to the past, while hogans (homes) and fences give a nod to the vibrant present.

Check the **Navajo Nation Parks & Recreation** website *(navajonationsparks.org)* or stop by the national monument visitor center for a list of tour guides. Guided trips with **Beauty Way Jeep Tours** *(beautywaytours.com; 3hr tour $95.40)* travel all the way to White House Ruin deep in the canyon.

Navajo Code Talkers

WWII prompted the first large exodus of Native Americans from the reservations, when they joined the US war effort. The most famous were the Navajo code talkers – 420 US marines who used a code based on their language for vital messages in the Pacific Theater. Navajo is a notoriously complex Athabascan language, and Japan never broke the code. Code talkers were considered essential to US victory. You'll find code-talker exhibits at the Burger King in Kayenta and the **Explore Navajo Interactive Museum** in Tuba City. The work of the code talkers was kept classified until 1968, and they were granted Congressional Gold Medals in 2001.

STANDING ON THE CORNER IN WINSLOW

Thanks to the lyrics of the Eagles' catchy '70s tune 'Take It Easy,' tiny Winslow is now a popular roadside spot. At the small **Standin' on the Corner Park** on Route 66 you can pose with a life-size bronze statue of a hitchhiker backed by a charmingly hokey trompe l'oeil mural of that famous girl – my Lord! – in the song's famous flatbed Ford. Above, a painted eagle keeps an eye on the action.

For information about Winslow and historic exhibits, stop by the town **visitor center**, which is tucked inside the renovated Lorenzo Hubbell Trading Post five blocks west of the park.

WHAT IS A PETRIFIED LOG?

The Painted Desert at Petrified Forest National Park is strewn with fossilized logs predating the dinosaurs. The 'trees' are fragmented, fossilized 225-million-year-old logs scattered over a vast area of semidesert grassland. Many are huge – up to 6ft in diameter – and at least one spans a ravine to form a natural bridge. The trees arrived via major floods, only to be buried beneath silica-rich volcanic ash before they could decompose. Groundwater dissolved the silica, carried it through the logs and crystallized it into solid, sparkly quartz mashed up with iron, carbon, manganese and other minerals. Uplift and erosion eventually exposed the logs.

Navajo National Monument

Solitude and cliff dwellings

Hikers who love history, beauty and a bit of a challenge should detour to the serene **Navajo National Monument** *(nps.gov/nava; free)*, which is anchored by two sublimely well-preserved cliff dwellings. But plan ahead. The monument sits in a remote corner of the Navajo Reservation between Monument Valley and Tuba City, and the guided cliff-dwelling hikes are only offered on certain days.

You'll reach **Betatakin**, which translates as 'ledge house,' on a strenuous, ranger-led, 5-mile round-trip hike (late May to early September) that leaves the visitor center early on Saturdays and Sundays. This hike is first come, first served. For a distant glimpse of Betatakin, follow the easy **Sandal Trail** about half a mile from the visitor center.

The trail to the astonishingly beautiful **Keet Seel**, the largest Ancestral Puebloan structure in Arizona, is a challenging two-day guided hike (17 miles round trip; May to September) with one night of backcountry camping – and possibly quicksand! This trip is capped at 20 people. Register and confirm dates in March.

Petrified Forest National Park

Crystallized logs, petroglyphs and badlands

The 28-mile scenic drive through the **Petrified Forest National Park** *(nps.gov/pefo; car/motorcycle/bicycle/pedestrian $25/20/15/15)* has more than a dozen pullouts with interpretive signs and short trails. Several trails near the southern entrance provide the best access for close-ups of the petrified logs: the 0.4-mile **Giant Logs Trail** (with the park's largest log behind the Rainbow Forest Museum), the 1.6-mile **Long Logs Trail**, the 0.75-mile **Crystal Forest Loop** and the **Jasper Forest lookout**.

A highlight in the center section is a 3-mile loop drive to **Blue Mesa**, where you'll be treated to 360-degree views of spectacular badlands, log falls and logs balancing atop hills with the leathery texture of elephant skin. The 0.9-mile **Blue Mesa Trail** drops scenically into the badlands. Nearby, at the bottom of a ravine, hundreds of petroglyphs are splashed across **Newspaper Rock** like some prehistoric bulletin board. You'll find more petroglyphs and Ancestral Puebloan ruins at **Puerco Pueblo**.

North of I-40 lies a Route 66 interpretive marker and an especially brilliant section of the **Painted Desert**. Nature puts on a kaleidoscopic show here at sunset: the most mesmerizing views are from **Kachina Point** behind the historic **Painted Desert Inn**. The Painted Desert is a beautiful place to camp. A free permit is required. Pick one up at the **Painted Desert Visitor Center** at the north entrance before 4:30pm.

Videos describing how the logs were fossilized run regularly at Painted Desert Visitor Center and the visitor center at **Rainbow Forest Museum** near the south entrance. Both visitor centers have park exhibits, maps and gift shops.

STEVEN GROUP/SHUTTERSTOCK

Petrified Forest National Park

Homolovi State Park

Petroglyphs and ancient pueblos

A grasslands park beside the Little Colorado River, **Homolovi State Park** *(azstateparks.com; vehicle/pedestrian/bicycle $7/3/3)* protects artifacts and archaeological sites within the sacred Hopi homeland. Short hikes lead to petroglyphs and partly excavated pueblos, most likely built by the Ancestral Hopi. The trail to the **Homolovi II ruins** is paved and wheelchair accessible. Before the area was converted into a park in 1993, bold thieves used backhoes to remove artifacts.

There's a **campground** with electric hookups, water and showers near the excavated pueblos. The park is 3 miles northeast of Winslow via Hwy 87.

Kingman & Route 66

Celebrate Route 66 – and some new stuff!

The best attractions along Route 66 are eye-catching and enormous, and the drive-thru Route 66 sign at the **Kingman Visitor Center** *(explorekingman.com)* is no exception. Park your ride beneath the sign, then, if you're alone, ask a kind-hearted stranger to take your photo. The visitor center, tucked inside the 1907 Powerhouse, stocks the requisite free brochures, but the big draw is the engaging **Route 66 Museum** *(mohavemusuem.org; adult/child $10/free)*, which shares an informative historical overview of travel along the Mother Road.

From here, it's a short drive to Beale St, the axis of the historic downtown. After sunset, cruise Route 66 and immerse yourself in its neon glory. The next morning, breakfast is served with a side of kitsch at **Mr D'z Route 66 Diner**, a roadside vision in turquoise and 1950s nostalgia.

PETRIFIED FOREST ORIENTATION

Straddling I-40, Petrified Forest National Park has an entrance at exit 311 off I-40 in the north, and another off Hwy 180 in the south. These are the only two entrances, and a 28-mile paved scenic road within the park links them. Note that the south entrance has the highest concentration of petrified wood and so is the most interesting part of this park.

To reach the south entrance from I-40, without following the park scenic road, you will need to leave the interstate at exit 285 and follow signs to Hwy 180 and the national park. The south entrance is 18 miles from I-40, so you can't simply pull over for a quick look if you're on I-40.

ROUTE 66, UNINTERRUPTED

North of Kingman, Route 66 arcs north away from I-40 for 115 dusty miles through the high desert. It merges with I-40 near Seligman then reappears briefly as Main St in Williams. Cell service is unreliable and gas stations are rare, so make sure you have enough fuel. The road is not heavily traveled, and you'll likely find that your car is the only vehicle on the road for miles at a time. The total distance to Williams is 130 miles.

Nicknamed the 'Mother Road' by novelist John Steinbeck and completed in 1926, Route 66 travels through eight states, linking a series of small towns between Chicago and Los Angeles.

MAGIC ALBERTO/SHUTTERSTOCK

Kingman (p167)

Leaving Kingman, 9 miles east of Peach Springs, a plaster dinosaur marks your arrival at **Grand Canyon Caverns** *(gccaverns.com; per person $69.95)*. Tours of this fascinating cave complex deep underground run regularly. Above ground, you'll find a campground, motel and restaurant. The complex is now owned by the Havasupai Tribe, and the motel doubles as the check-in point for tours.

Further along, look for red-and-white Burma Shave signs on the 23 miles of road slicing through the rolling hills to **Seligman**, the inspiration for Radiator Springs in Pixar's *Cars*. Angel Delgadillo retired from **Angel's Barbershop** *(route66giftshop.com; 9am-5pm)* in roadside Seligman in 2022 at age 95 – but his barber's chair is still there. Today the barbershop is a museum and souvenir store. Angel's madcap brother Juan, who died in 2004, ruled prankishly supreme over the nearby **Delgadillo's Snow Cap** – a Route 66 institution still serving burgers and ice cream. Beware the fake mustard bottle! For a full-service meal, try the German and American dishes at **Westside Lilo's Cafe** *(westsidelilos.com)*.

From Seligman, one of the last sets of **Burma Shave signs** reads: 'Passing cars... When you can't see... May get you a glimpse... Of eternity.'

DRINKING IN KINGMAN: OUR PICKS

Cellar Door: Downtown wine bar with more than 120 wines and dozens of beers, live music and trivia nights. *varies 3-9pm Wed-Sat*

Rickety Cricket: Creative beer selections – we're looking at you Snoszberry – plus pizza, nachos and tiramisu. *varies 11am-9pm*

Liquid Bistro & Coffee Shop: Low-key coffee shop with mid-century cool, but no kitsch. Distinctive turquoise-and-white digs. *7am-3pm*

Desert Diamond Distillery: Sample whiskey and rum at this small distillery near Kingman airport. *10am-5pm Sun-Thu, to 6pm Fri & Sat*

Southern Arizona

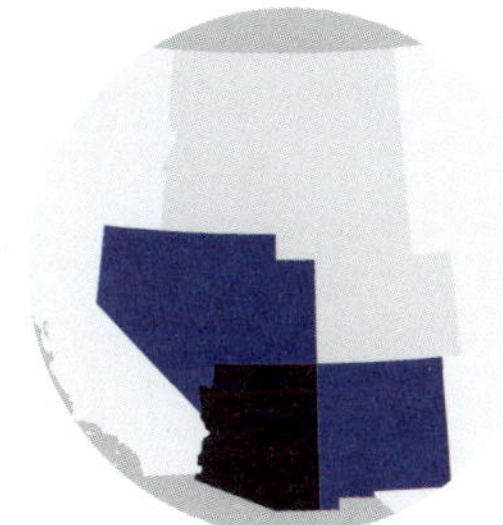

VIBRANT CITY | OLD WEST | SCENIC DRIVES

Arizona's deep south concentrates some of the state's most rewarding attractions. Tucson is one of the most engaging towns in the entire West, a cultural powerhouse, not to mention an emerging culinary superstar. It has so much to offer, both as an underrated destination in its own right and as gateway to a region that can seem like a stereotype of the Old West. You barely need to leave Tucson before Saguaro National Park and the Sonoran Desert offer up classic landscapes and the world's most recognizable cactus. A little further afield, it's the old mining town of Bisbee and gunfights at the OK Corral in Tombstone; the latter is one of the must-see places if you're eager to immerse yourself in the legends of the storied West. Crowning this beautiful region are the Santa Catalina Mountains, which are the perfect place to explore on a series of scenic drives.

Places

TOP TIP

Don't be fooled by how close the attractions of southern Arizona can appear: it's only by comparison to the rest of the state. Plan to spend longer than you expect, and add a day or two to your plans to allow you to follow curiosity down quiet back roads.

Tucson

Explore an Arizona desert city

Set in a flat valley hemmed in by snaggle-toothed mountains and swaths of saguaro, Arizona's second-largest city smoothly blends Native American, Spanish, Mexican and Anglo traditions. Distinct neighborhoods and 19th-century buildings

GETTING AROUND

As ever out here in the West, having your own vehicle will greatly enhance your experience: many attractions in these parts can only be reached in your own SUV or 4WD. Rental is easy (book ahead to ensure the best rates) at Tucson airport or downtown. Tucson International Airport serves southern Arizona, with regular flights around the Southwest. Part of the mix for getting to Tucson from beyond the region includes train: Amtrak's thrice-weekly *Sunset Limited* links Tucson with LA, Houston and New Orleans.

SOUTHERN ARIZONA
Danby Lake
CALIFORNIA
Palen Dry Lake
Colorado River
Alamo Lake
Parker
Blythe
Quartzsite
Colorado River
Colorado River
Yuma
San Luis
Laguna Salada
Gulf of California
MEXICO
Sonoyta
Organ Pipe Cactus National Monument
Ajo
Dateland
Gila River
Gila Bend
Wenden
Wickenburg
Congress
Cordes
Black Canyon City
Pleasant Lake
Cave Creek
Wintersburg
Buckeye
Phoenix
Scottsdale
Mesa
Apache Junction
East Valley
Saguaro Lake
Maricopa
Casa Grande
Eloy
Red Rock
Santa Cruz River
Tucson
Saguaro National Park - West (Tucson Mountain District)
Saguaro National Park
Saguaro National Park - East (Rincon Mountain District)
Sierrita Mountains
Sells
Pisinimo
Arivaca
Sasabe
Tubac
Nogales
Nogales
Patagonia
Sierra Vista
Bisbee
Tombstone
Naco
Douglas
Benson
Willcox
Chiricahua National Monument
Animas Mountains
Lordsburg
Gila River
Duncan
Safford
Pima
Gila River
Clifton
Mogollon Mountains
Gila River
NEW MEXICO
Alpine
White Mountain Reservoir
Springerville
Show Low
Whiteriver
Black River
Cibecue
Mogollon Plateau
Pine
Payson
Roosevelt Dam
Salt River
Globe
Superior
Peridot
San Carlos Lake
Hayden
Florence
Oracle
Mammoth
San Pedro River
93
10
8
10
60
60
70
191
191
60
10
19
0 100 km
0 50 miles

give a rich sense of community and history not found in more modern, sprawling Phoenix. The eclectic shopping, affordable restaurants, whimsical murals and fun-loving dive bars don't let you forget Tucson is a college town at heart, home turf to the 50,000-strong University of Arizona (U of A).

The **Tucson Museum of Art** *(tucsonmuseumofart.org; adult/child $15/free)* is part of the low-key **Presidio Historic District** and embraces the site of the community's original Spanish fort and upmarket 'Snob Hollow.' This is one of the oldest continually inhabited places in North America: the **Spanish Presidio de San Augustín del Tucson** *(tucson presidio.com; adult/child $9/6)* dates back to 1775, but the fort itself was built over a Hohokam site that has been dated to between 700 and 900 CE. The district teems with adobe townhouses and restored 19th-century mansions. **Old Town Artisans** *(oldtownartisanstucson.com)* is the place for Mexican and Southwestern art and crafts.

When it's time to eat, tucked in a rambling downtown hacienda, the buzzing **El Charro Café** (p173; *elcharrocafe.com)* celebrated its centennial in 2022. Overseen by chef-owner Carlotta Flores, it's famous for its *carne seca,* sundried lean beef that's been reconstituted, shredded and grilled with green chile and onions. The fabulous margaritas also pack a serious punch. The restaurant's original matriarch, Monica Flin, is said to have invented the chimichanga after accidentally dropping a burrito into a deep fryer.

Elsewhere, Tucson's signature dish is the Sonoran dog, a bacon-wrapped hot dog layered with tomatillo salsa, pinto beans, shredded cheese, mayo ketchup, mustard, chopped tomatoes and onions. Dig into one at one of two **BK Carne Asada & Hot Dogs** *(bktacos.com)* locations.

And as the day draws to a close, you have a couple of great options for watching the sunset in west Tucson. The **Brown Mountain Trail** *(pima.gov)* climbs past saguaros, cholla and other desert vegetation to sweeping ridgeline views of the Tucson Mountains, the Tohono O'odham Reservation, the Santa Rosa Mountains and the Aguirre Valley. This view is awash in luminous color at sunset. If you don't want to hike, drive to the **Gates Pass Scenic Lookout** *(nps.gov)* on West Gates Pass Rd for a splendid, expansive sunset view of the saguaro-dotted mountain pass.

Drive the Mt Lemmon Scenic Byway

Generations of Tucsonans have escaped the summer heat by driving up Mt Lemmon in the Santa Catalina Mountains. You

BEST UNIQUE TUCSON MUSEUMS

Ignite Sign Art Museum: More than 900 old neon signs, primarily from Tucson, light up the museum. Watch a neon bending demo or take a class.

Mini Time Machine Museum of Miniatures: Delightful museum with intriguing dioramas that are fantastical and historical.

Pima Air & Space Museum: An SR-71 Blackbird spy plane and B-52 bomber are among the stars of this extraordinary private aircraft museum.

Center for Creative Photography: Ever-changing, high-caliber exhibits. Administers the archives of Ansel Adams.

Coit Museum (formerly the History of Pharmacy Museum): Old-timey tinctures and a full-size pharmacy replica once found on Disneyland's Main Street, USA.

EATING IN TUCSON: OUR PICKS

Charro Steak & Del Rey: Scrumptious steaks, seafood and libations in a modern rustic space. *3-9pm* $$$

Beyond Bread: Daily breads and a mouthwatering array of sandwiches. Several locations. *7am-7pm* $

HUB Restaurant & Ice Creamery: Upscale comfort food in exposed-brick digs on Congress St. Save room for ice cream. *11am-9pm Sun-Thu, to 11pm Fri & Sat* $$

Maynards: Regionally sourced and seasonal American fare in the Historic Depot downtown. *5-9pm Wed-Sun* $$

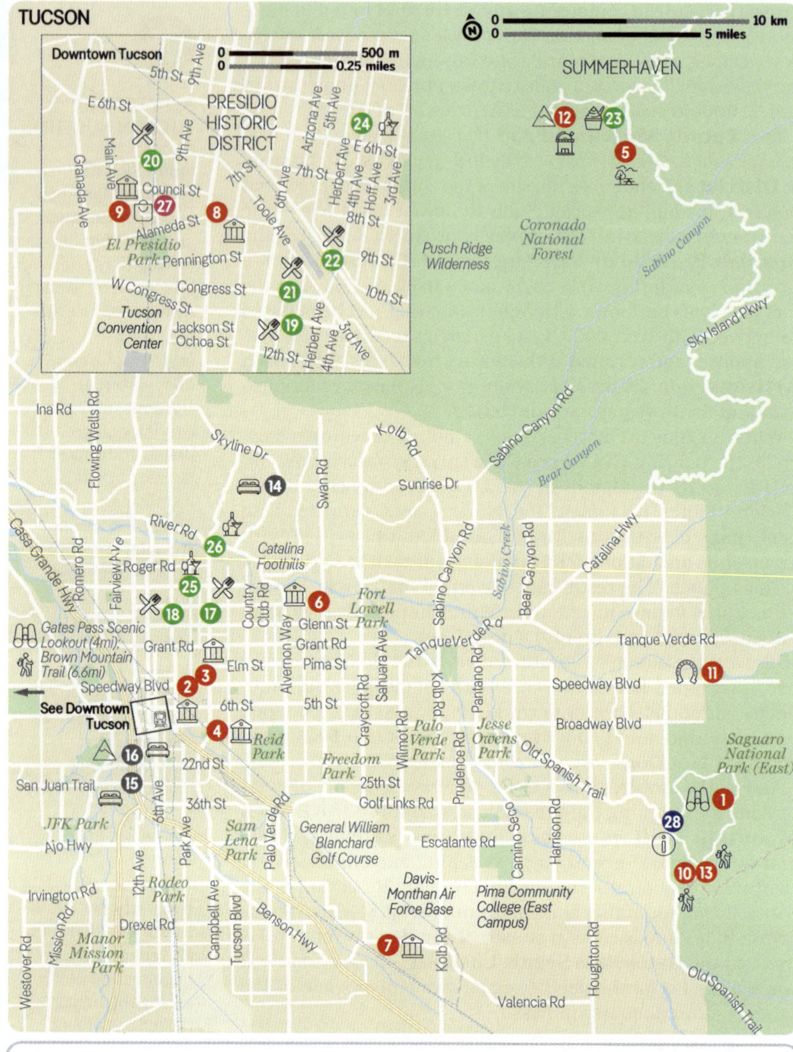

SIGHTS

1 Cactus Forest Loop Drive
2 Center for Creative Photography
3 Coit Museum
4 Ignite Sign Art Museum
5 Marshall Gulch Picnic Area
6 Mini Time Machine Museum of Miniatures
7 Pima Air & Space Museum
8 Spanish Presidio de San Augustín del Tucson
9 Tucson Museum of Art

ACTIVITIES

10 Freeman Homestead Trailhead
11 Houston's Horseback Riding
12 Mt Lemmon SkyCenter Observatory
13 Tanque Verde Ridge

SLEEPING

14 Hacienda del Sol Guest Ranch Resort
15 Hotel McCoy
16 Tuxon

EATING

17 Beyond Bread
18 BK Carne Asada & Hot Dogs
19 Charro Steak & Del Rey
20 El Charro Café
21 HUB Restaurant & Ice Creamery
22 Maynards
23 Mt Lemmon Cookie Cabin

DRINKING & NIGHTLIFE

24 BOCA by Chef Maria Mazon
25 Guadalajara Original Grill
26 Reforma Modern Mexican

SHOPPING

27 Old Town Artisans

INFORMATION

28 Rincon Mountain Visitor Center

can follow their tracks on the very picturesque **Mt Lemmon Scenic Byway** (also called the Catalina Hwy Scenic Drive), which meanders 27 miles from saguaro-dappled desert to pine-covered forest near the summit (9157ft). Allow at least three hours for the round trip and watch for cyclists.

Of the vista points, Babad Do'ag, Windy Point and Aspen are the most rewarding. In lofty Summerhaven, everybody stops for ice cream and cookies the size of your face at the **Mt Lemmon Cookie Cabin** *(thecookiecabin.org)*. Nearby, the loop connecting the **Marshall Gulch Trail & Aspen Trail** *(fs.usda.gov; day pass per vehicle $8)* is a recommended 4-mile hike through ponderosas, aspens and firs.

You can attend an evening SkyNights StarGazing Program at the **Mt Lemmon SkyCenter Observatory** *(skycenter.arizona.edu; adult/child $85/60)*. Reserve a spot at least one week in advance.

MT LEMMON: NEED TO KNOW

There is no cost for the drive or for stopping at the vista points, but to explore the forest you must get the **Coronado Recreation Pass** *(fs.usda.gov; per day/week $8/10)*. Buy it online, at trailside kiosks or at the Palisades Visitor Center (Mile 19.6).

For an audio tour explaining the science behind the sights you'll see along the 27-mile drive, download the free Mt Lemmon Audio Tour app on your smartphone (see visittucson.org).

Several campsites line the drive, with overnight rates ranging from $20 to $28. Call the Pima County Sheriff's Road Conditions hotline at 520-547-7510 for road conditions.

Bisbee

Mining museum and mine tour

Bisbee built its fortune on ore discovered in the surrounding Mule Mountains. In their 19th- and 20th-century heyday, the underground and open-pit mines here coughed up copper worth more than $6 billion.

Start your day with huevos rancheros at the **Bisbee Breakfast Club**, followed by a stroll along adjacent Erie St. Lined with vintage cars and pickup trucks, as well as storefronts from an earlier era, the street is an eerily accurate model of a mid-century downtown.

Now it's time to go underground. You'll don a hard hat and a safety vest during the pre-trip orientation at the **Queen Mine** *(copperqueenmine.com; adult/child $16/8)* south of downtown. Today, visitors ride 1500ft into the mountain on a subterranean mine train, often guided by the mountain's last miners or their offspring.

In the 1897 former headquarters of the Copper Queen Consolidated Mining Company, the **Bisbee Mining & Historical Museum** *(bisbeemuseum.org; adult/child $10/free)* traces the town's past.

Echoes of Bisbee ripple out across the surrounding countryside. A former mining community southeast of Bisbee, Lowell was mostly consumed by the adjacent Lavender Pit mine. Today, this short strip of Americana – mostly abandoned

DRINKING IN TUCSON: WHERE TO GET A MARGARITA

El Charro Café: There are 18 delicious margaritas on the menu, and all of them pack a punch. *11am-9pm Wed-Sat, to 8pm Sun*

Guadalajara Original Grill: The frozen Bandera margarita is stacked with three colorful layers – green, white and red – to resemble the Mexican flag. *11am-10pm Sun-Thu, to 11pm Fri & Sat*

BOCA by Chef Maria Mazon: They serve them by the carafe, and at happy hour the house margaritas are $8. *noon-9pm Mon & Tue, to 10pm Fri & Sat, to 8pm Sun*

Reforma Modern Mexican: Mango habanero, blueberry basil, blood orange, prickly pear are among Reforma's elevated options. Kick back and sip away on its beautiful patio. *hours vary*

TOP EXPERIENCE

Saguaro National Park

Saguaros are icons of the American Southwest, and an entire cactus army of these majestic, ribbed sentinels is protected in Saguaro National Park. Exploring these strange life forms - they can really mess with your mind on a moonlit night - is the main reason to visit this beautiful park.

HIGH FLIERS/SHUTTERSTOCK

Go for a Drive or Ride

The 8-mile **Cactus Forest Loop Drive** *(nps.gov/sagu)* in the Rincon Mountain District is special, and its beauty is open to drivers and cyclists alike. The scrubby desert scenery here also evokes the Old West. To embrace the John Wayne vibe, saddle up for a horseback ride with family-run **Houston's Horseback Riding** *(tucsonhorsebackriding.com)*.

Hike Saguaro Trails

Hikers pressed for time can follow the 1-mile round-trip **Freeman Homestead Trail** *(nps.gov/sagu)* to a grove of massive saguaros. For a full-fledged desert adventure with high-elevation views, head out on the steep and rocky **Tanque Verde Ridge Trail** *(nps.gov/sagu)*, which climbs to the summit of Tanque Verde Peak and back in 18 miles. An $8 backcountry camping permit is required for overnight use. The **Rincon Mountain Visitor Center** *(nps.gov/sagu)* has information about day hikes, horseback riding and backcountry camping. Seven-day passes per vehicle/motorcycle/bicycle cost $25/20/15. Cash is not accepted.

Learn about Saguaros

Saguaros (suh-*wah*-ros) only grow in the Sonoran Desert and they do so slowly, taking about 15 years to reach a foot in height, 50 years to reach 7ft and almost a century before they begin to take on their typical many-armed appearance. In April each year, the cacti begin blossoming with lovely white blooms – Arizona's state flower. By June and July the flowers give way to ripe red fruit that local Native Americans use for food. It is illegal to damage or remove saguaros.

TOP TIPS

- The national park is divided into east and west, separated by 30 miles and Tucson itself.
- Each section distributes its own hiking guide with maps and trail summaries.
- The busy season runs November through March; temperatures range from the high 50°Fs to mid-70°Fs (around 14°C to 24°C).

– gives a nostalgic nod to the 1950s. Just north on Hwy 80, look for the not-so-truthful 'Scenic View' sign. It's pointing toward the Lavender Pit, an immense stair-stepped gash in the ground that produced about 600,000 tons of copper between 1950 and 1974.

Tombstone

OK Corral and Old West museums

If you were to visit one town to capture the essence of the Wild West, we'd make it Tombstone.

Like death and taxes, the daily reenactment of the gunfight at the **OK Corral** *(ok-corral.com)* is a sure thing. Before the show, you'll see Doc Holliday and the Earp brothers silently stroll down dusty Allen St. The thrice-daily performance ($10) takes place inside the corral, which is the heart of both historic and touristic Tombstone.

From here, plank sidewalks and dirt roads are portals to the Old West, with wooden storefronts and a horse-drawn stagecoach setting the scene. It's hokey, but also fun, and it's easy to imagine cowboys, gunslingers and miners roaming the streets.

The **Bird Cage Theatre** *(tombstonebirdcage.com)* was a one-stop sin-o-rama, with onstage shows as well as a saloon, dance hall, gambling parlor and a home for 'negotiable affections.' Today, with its dusty knickknacks, illicit history and ghost tours, it's ground zero for kitschy deliciousness – a place for which road trips are made.

And the epitaphs at **Boothill Graveyard** *(discoverboothill.com; $6)* tell you everything you need to know about living – and dying – in Tombstone in the late 1800s. 'Murdered.' 'Shot.' 'Suicide.' They spotlight the violence of the place, where life was hard and often short. The graves of Billy Clanton and Tom and Frank McLaury, all killed at the shoot-out at the OK Corral, are in Row 2. Some headstones are twistedly poetic: the oft-quoted epitaph for Lester Moore, a Wells Fargo agent, may be the most famous: 'Here lies Lester Moore, Four slugs from a .44, No Les, no More.'

GUNFIGHT AT THE OK CORRAL

Tombstone is the location of the infamous 1881 gunfight at the OK Corral, when Wyatt Earp, his brothers Virgil and Morgan, and their friend Doc Holliday gunned down outlaws Billy Clanton and Tom and Frank McLaury, who belonged to a loose association of rustlers and thieves called the Cowboys. On the day of the shoot-out, the Cowboys had come to Tombstone and were in apparent violation of the law, requiring them to check their weapons. The ensuing gunfight only lasted about 30 seconds but so caught people's imaginations that it not only made it into the history books, but also onto the silver screen – many times – including the 1993 flick *Tombstone*, starring Kurt Russell and Val Kilmer.

Chiricahua National Monument

Volcanic rocks and Apache history

From the viewing area at Massai Point, the rhyolite rock pinnacles at the remote **Chiricahua National Monument** *(nps.gov/chir)* resemble a goblin army, a vast force ready to march down the mountain and do battle for their goblin king. This rugged yet whimsical wonderland, covering nearly 19 sq miles across a desert sky island in the Chiricahua Mountains, is one of Arizona's most evocative landscapes, a wind-chiseled volcanic landscape of fluted pinnacles, natural bridges, balancing boulders and soaring spires. The remoteness made Chiricahua (cheery-*cow*-wha) a favorite hiding place of Apache warrior Cochise and his men in the 1800s. The park is a two-hour drive from Tucson.

APACHE CONFLICTS

For decades, US forces pushed west across the continent, killing or forcibly moving tribes of Native Americans who were in their way. The last serious conflicts were between US troops and the Apache, partly because raiding was the essential path to manhood for the tribe. US forces and settlers moving into Apache land became obvious targets for the raids that were part of the Apache way of life. This continued under the leadership of Mangas Coloradas, Cochise, Victorio and Geronimo.

Geronimo surrendered in 1886 after being promised that he and the Apache would be imprisoned for two years, then allowed to return to their homeland. As with many promises made during those years, this one was broken.

AZCAT/SHUTTERSTOCK

Chiricahua National Monument (p175)

Past the entrance, the paved **Bonita Canyon Scenic Drive** climbs 8 miles to **Massai Point** at 6870ft, passing several scenic pullouts and trailheads. If you're short on time, hit the **Massai Point Nature Trail** (0.5 miles round trip), the most common stop for photos, or hike the **Echo Canyon Trail** at least half a mile to the **Grottoes**, an amazing 'cathedral' of giant boulders where you can lie still and enjoy the wind-brushed silence. The most striking formations cluster in the **Heart of Rocks**, reached via several linking trails on a 7.3-mile round-trip hike. A free hiker shuttle runs from Faraway Ranch and Bonita Campground to the Echo Canyon and Massai Point trailheads from September to May. Reserve ahead.

Chiricahua is one of 127 designated Dark Sky Parks worldwide, making it an increasingly popular destination for astrophotography. Depending on the time of year, you'll have clear views of the Milky Way, Orion, Big Dipper and comets at night. There is no cell-phone service in the park and very limited service in the surrounding area. Water is available only at the visitor center. The closest gas station is 27 miles away in Sunizona. The nearest community, Willcox, is 37 miles away.

Utah

STIRRING LANDSCAPES | NATIONAL PARKS | MORMON HEARTLAND

Before Native people and Mormon pioneers, dinosaurs once roamed this land, and remnants of all three collide in the 45th state. Utah's incredible diversity of geological formations were shaped by millions of years of erosion, despite there being so little water in sight. Utah boasts five national parks – the densest concentration of any state, with Arches, Canyonlands, Capitol Reef, Bryce Canyon and Zion – that rank among the big hitters of the American wild. And with dozens more national monuments, recreation areas and state parks, everything in this state feels ready-made for big adventures. Towns like Moab and Park City can seem like they're set up for getting you out and into nature on a mountain bike, skis or a white-water raft. In the midst of it all, Salt Lake City, the heartbeat of Mormon belief and governance, is one of the most intriguing urban experiences anywhere in the US.

Places

TOP TIP

Distances in Utah are longer than they look and each national park is worth exploring in depth. You'd need *at least* a couple of weeks to do them all well. If you're here for a shorter period, plan to see one or two parks well, rather than trying to do too much.

GETTING AROUND

As is so often true out in the West, unless your itinerary is limited to a few locations, having your own set of wheels is essential for getting around Utah. Rent a car in Salt Lake City or even Las Vegas, Nevada. If you're staying in a town like Salt Lake City, Moab or Park City, shuttle and other buses sometimes connect you with nearby ski stations or hiking trailheads. Amtrak has five stations in Utah on the *California Zephyr* line, but the daily departures mean the train is not a viable option for most travelers.

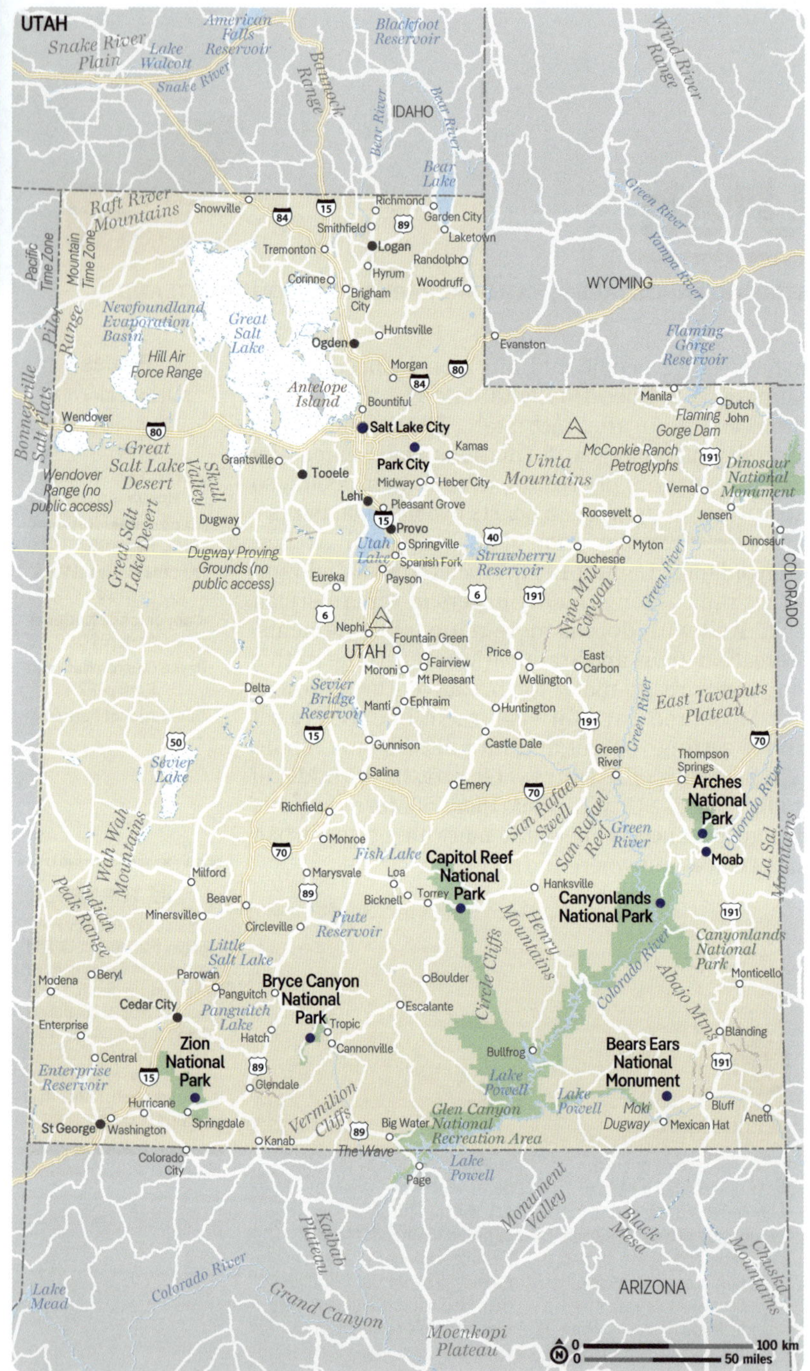
UTAH
IDAHO
WYOMING
COLORADO
ARIZONA
Snake River Plain
Lake Walcott
American Falls Reservoir
Snake River
Bannock Range
Bear River
Blackfoot Reservoir
Bear River
Bear Lake
Wind River Range
Green River
Yampa River
Flaming Gorge Reservoir
Raft River Mountains
Snowville
Richmond
Garden City
Smithfield
Laketown
Tremonton
Logan
Randolph
Hyrum
Corinne
Woodruff
Brigham City
Pacific Time Zone
Mountain Time Zone
Pilot Range
Newfoundland Evaporation Basin
Great Salt Lake
Hill Air Force Range
Huntsville
Ogden
Evanston
Morgan
Antelope Island
Bountiful
Manila
Dutch John
Flaming Gorge Dam
Bonneville Salt Flats
Wendover
Salt Lake City
Great Salt Lake Desert
Grantsville
Tooele
Park City
Kamas
McConkie Ranch Petroglyphs
Uinta Mountains
Dinosaur National Monument
Wendover Range (no public access)
Skull Valley
Midway
Heber City
Vernal
Lehi
Pleasant Grove
Jensen
Roosevelt
Dugway
Provo
Springville
Myton
Dinosaur
Great Salt Lake Desert
Dugway Proving Grounds (no public access)
Utah Lake
Spanish Fork
Strawberry Reservoir
Duchesne
Eureka
Payson
Nine Mile Canyon
Green River
Nephi
Fountain Green
UTAH
Price
East Carbon
Moroni
Fairview
Mt Pleasant
Wellington
Delta
Sevier Bridge Reservoir
Manti
Ephraim
Huntington
East Tavaputs Plateau
Green River
Gunnison
Castle Dale
Sevier Lake
Salina
Green River
Thompson Springs
Arches National Park
Emery
San Rafael Swell
San Rafael Reef
Richfield
Green River
Colorado River
Wah Wah Mountains
Monroe
Moab
Fish Lake
Capitol Reef National Park
La Sal Mountains
Milford
Marysvale
Loa
Hanksville
Indian Peak Range
Beaver
Bicknell
Torrey
Canyonlands National Park
Minersville
Circleville
Piute Reservoir
Henry Mountains
Circle Cliffs
Canyonlands National Park
Little Salt Lake
Colorado River
Abajo Mtns
Modena
Beryl
Parowan
Bryce Canyon National Park
Boulder
Monticello
Panguitch
Cedar City
Escalante
Panguitch Lake
Enterprise
Tropic
Hatch
Blanding
Zion National Park
Cannonville
Central
Bullfrog
Bears Ears National Monument
Enterprise Reservoir
Lake Powell
Glendale
Hurricane
Lake Powell
Glen Canyon National Recreation Area
Vermilion Cliffs
Bluff
Moki Dugway
Aneth
St George
Washington
Springdale
Big Water
Mexican Hat
Kanab
The Wave
Colorado City
Lake Powell
Page
Monument Valley
Kaibab Plateau
Black Mesa
Chuska Mountains
Lake Mead
Colorado River
Grand Canyon
Moenkopi Plateau
0 100 km
0 50 miles
15
84
89
80
191
40
6
50
70

Salt Lake City

Explore Mormon SLC

Founded in 1847 by Mormon pioneers in what was then Mexican territory outside the boundaries of the US, Salt Lake City (SLC) remains the headquarters of the Church of Jesus Christ of Latter-day Saints; it's the Mormon equivalent of Vatican City for Catholics.

The epicenter of the Church of Jesus Christ of Latter-day Saints (LDS) is **Temple Square** *(churchofjesuschrist.org; free)* in the heart of downtown Salt Lake City. Members of the church, wearing name badges and modest clothing, happily assist with questions and directions. (Don't worry, they won't try to convert you unless you express interest.)

Start your visit at the **Conference Center**, which is serving as a visitor center during ongoing renovations. Join a tour or poke around the grand 21,000-seat auditorium yourself. Don't miss the rooftop garden with expansive views of the Salt Lake Valley.

Lording over Temple Square is the impressive **Salt Lake Temple**, the largest LDS temple in the world, completed in 1893 after more than 40 years of construction. The interior is open only to church members in good standing. Six spires, the tallest measuring 210ft, reach into the heavens. Home to the world-famous Tabernacle Choir, the **Salt Lake Tabernacle** is a domed 1867 auditorium with an 11,623-pipe organ and incredible acoustics – wait for the demonstration of a pin being dropped, which can be heard almost 200ft away.

Time your visit for noon Monday to Saturday or 2pm Sunday for a free organ recital (without the choir). The choir rehearses on Thursday evenings (7:30pm to 9:30pm) and Sunday mornings (8:15am to 9:30am) but is sometimes on tour elsewhere; check *thetabernaclechoir.org/upcoming-events*.

West of Temple Square, the **Church History Museum** gets into the nitty-gritty of the church's foundations. About a 5-mile drive east of Temple Square, the 450-acre **This Is The Place Heritage Park** *(thisistheplace.org; adult/child $18.95/14.95)* is dedicated to the 1847 arrival of the Mormons in Utah. Buy tickets at the Pioneer Center and then head into the living history village, which has several streets of original and replica pioneer buildings. Inside, costumed docents recount mid-19th-century life.

HIP 'HOODS

Get under the skin of Salt Lake by exploring the neighborhoods beyond downtown.

9th & 9th (900 South & 900 East): Several spots fly Pride flags in this mini 'gayborhood.' In 2016, 900 South was renamed Harvey Milk Blvd in honor of the gay-rights activist.

Sugar House: Walkable neighborhood with restaurants, coffee shops, breweries and a beloved urban park.

15th & 15th (1500 South & 1500 East): Enclave of excellent international restaurants and an indie bookstore.

Marmalade: This historic district west of the capitol is ideal for architecture lovers, so called because it was an orchard for early Mormon settlers.

EATING IN SALT LAKE CITY: OUR PICKS

Copper Onion: Elevated American food served brasserie style: think ricotta dumplings and Wagyu stroganoff. *11:30am-10pm or later Mon-Fri, from 10:30am Sat & Sun* $$

Lucky 13: Divey bar with the best burgers in the capital. The Nutter Butter Burger with peanut butter is a divine, delicious mess. *10am-2am* $

Red Iguana: Mexican food that's worth the inevitable wait. Get the mole sampler to try all its famous sauces. *11am-9pm or later* $$

Pago: Beautifully plated farm-to-table New American dishes pair perfectly with the acclaimed wine list. *5-9pm* $$$

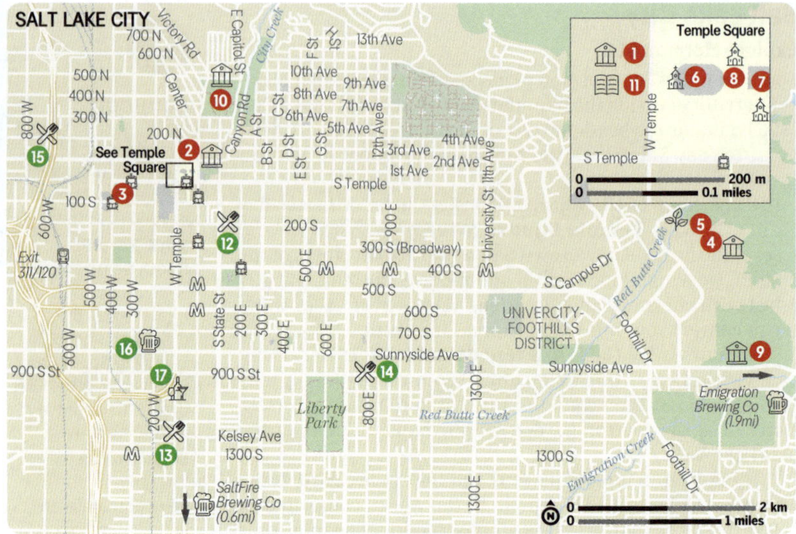

- **SIGHTS**
  1. Church History Museum
  2. Conference Center
  3. Delta Center
  4. Natural History Museum of Utah
  5. Red Butte Garden
  6. Salt Lake Tabernacle
  7. Salt Lake Temple
  8. Temple Square
  9. This Is the Place Heritage Park
  10. Utah State Capitol
- **ACTIVITIES**
  11. FamilySearch Library
- **EATING**
  12. Copper Onion
  13. Lucky 13
  14. Pago
  15. Red Iguana
- **DRINKING & NIGHTLIFE**
  16. Fisher Brewing Company
  17. Water Witch

Trace your family tree

Mormons believe that families can be united in heaven for eternity, and since 1894 the church has collected genealogical records. Open to all, the church-sponsored **FamilySearch Library** *(familysearch.org/en/library; free)* houses the largest repository of family history on the planet, with information on more than three billion deceased people from around the world.

Friendly researchers can help you track down records of your family and will even print out a free 3ft-by-2ft full-color poster of the lineage documented during your visit for you to take home.

Tour the Utah State Capitol

Completed in 1916, the neoclassical-style **Utah State Capitol** *(utahstatecapitol.utah.gov; free)* is where state laws have been made for more than a century. You're free to wander around

DRINKING IN SALT LAKE CITY: OUR PICKS

Fisher Brewing Company: Known for its experimental brews made in a former auto shop. *11am-10pm or later*

Emigration Brewing Co: 'Mountain minimalist' brewery in a scenic canyon setting. *5-9pm Mon-Fri, from 10am Sat, 10am-2pm Sun*

SaltFire Brewing Co: Sociable taproom with friendly bartenders. Don't miss the chai stout. *3-9pm Mon-Thu, to 11pm Fri, noon-11pm Sat, to 8pm Sun*

Water Witch: Go 'roulette' and allow the mixologists to pour perfection from the cocktail shaker. *3pm-1am Mon-Wed, from noon Thu-Sun*

the five floors yourself or join a guided tour, which run on the hour between 10am and 3pm Monday to Friday. Guided tours give access to the basement, where you can see the base isolators that can move up to 2ft to protect the building from earthquakes. The capitol's interior dome, which reaches 165ft above the rotunda floor, steals the show.

Culture on campus

Established in 1850, the University of Utah, often shortened to 'the U,' provides lessons in history, botany and art for all, no matter your enrollment status.

The **Natural History Museum of Utah** *(nhmu.utah.edu; adult/child $22.95/17.95)* is housed in the sleek, modern Rio Tinto Center in the foothills of the Wasatch Mountains. The five-floor building showcases a dozen permanent exhibits, including displays on Utah's Native tribes, the Great Salt Lake and dinosaurs. Put on your hiking shoes before you head next door to **Red Butte Garden** *(redbuttegarden.org; adult/child $16/8)*, which has 5 miles of trails in addition to 21 acres of beautifully tended display gardens, originally cultivated by a botany professor.

Park City

Activities for all seasons

From boarder dudes to families with tots, everyone is on the slopes at **Park City Mountain Resort** *(parkcitymountain.com; day lift ticket adult/child from $140/73)*. The awesome terrain – 7300 acres of skiable slopes rising above the Old Town – couldn't be more family friendly or more accessible, with ski-in-ski-out access to Park City's Main St via the **Town Lift**. This area offers 344 runs (8% beginner, 44% intermediate, 48% advanced) and is a particular favorite for snowboarders – it hosted snowboarding and skiing half-pipe events in the 2002 Winter Games and is putting them on again in 2034. The first ski area you reach when visiting Park City from Salt Lake City, **Canyons Village** is part of Park City Mountain Resort and is known for having the first heated-seat chairlift in North America, the Orange Bubble Express.

On Park City's southern side, **Deer Valley** *(deervalley.com; day lift ticket adult/child from $229/142)* is a skiers-only resort of superlatives: superb dining, a complimentary ski valet so you can drop them off like a coat check and even tissue boxes at the base of the slopes. Deer Valley has 123 runs (25% beginner, 43% intermediate, 32% advanced) and a vertical

SALT LAKE CITY PRACTICALITIES

SLC is a car-centric city, but TRAX, the light-rail system, is a great way to get around. Buy tickets (one way/24hr $2.50/5) from machines at station platforms or on the **Transit app** *(transitapp.com)*. Cycle lanes abound. Grab a set of wheels from **Greenbike** *(greenbikeutah.org)*, SLC's bike-share system. For parking, download the **Park SLC app** *(parkslc.com)*. Spaces are often limited to two hours on weekdays ($2.25 per hour).

Attraction costs add up quickly, so check whether buying the **Salt Lake Connect Pass** *(visitsaltlake.com)* makes sense. It's valid for one, two or 365 days and also includes places in Park City and Snowbird.

EATING IN PARK CITY: OUR PICKS

Davanza's: Crowd into the small space to carb load for another day on the slopes with burgers, sandwiches and pizzas. *11am-9pm* $

Farm: Slope-side bistro-style dining room in Park City that uses seasonal local ingredients. *11:30am-10pm Dec-Apr* $$$

Five5eeds: Australian cafe serving strong coffee and all-day breakfasts of smashed avo toast and pulled pork Benedict. *7:30am-3pm* $$

Top of Main Brew Pub: Utah's first craft brewery still serves pints and pub grub. *11:30am-9pm Mon-Fri, from 10:30am Sat & Sun* $$

BEST MOAB BIKE SHOPS

Moab Cyclery: High-performance bike shop offering tours and rentals. Offers shuttles and good half-day, full-day, multiday and multisport tours.

Bike Fiend: Specialists in desert bikepacking, with everything you need for your overnight trip, including bags.

Poison Spider Bicycles: Shuttles to Bar M, Whole Enchilada and more, allowing you to have more riding time and fun.

Chile Pepper Bike Shop: Rent, service or buy a bike to explore the nearby desert at this friendly shop.

E-Bike Moab: The place to pick up bikes to cover longer distances quickly.

Rim Cyclery: Moab's longest-running family-owned bike shop offers tours, rentals and repairs.

drop of 3000ft. Its East Village expansion will nearly triple Deer Valley in size.

Fun in Park City doesn't stop when the snow melts. More than 300 miles of hiking and mountain-biking trails criss-cross the mountains, and you'll feel on top of the world in the peaks over the town. Pick up summer trail maps at the resorts or the **Park City Visitors Center** *(visitparkcity.com)*. The ski resorts and outdoor outfitters around town rent mountain bikes.

Watch Olympians

Built for the 2002 Winter Games, **Utah Olympic Park** *(utah olympiclegacy.org)* was the site of the Games' ski jumping, bobsleigh, skeleton and luge events, and it will host many events again for the 2034 Games. The US Ski Team practices here year-round, and when there's no snow on the slopes, you can watch freestyle jumpers land in a bubble-filled jetted pool.

Not content to sit on the sidelines? Pretend to be an Olympian for the day by taking a 60mph **bobsleigh ride** *(per person winter/summer $225/100)* with up to 5Gs of centrifugal force. **Guided tours of the park** *(adult/child $20/15)* are available at 11am, 1pm and 3pm daily – even just peering over the edge of the ski jump is an adrenaline rush.

Moab

Scenic off-road drives

Moab's hundreds of miles of primitive back roads are coveted by 4WD enthusiasts. **Hell's Revenge** *(blm.gov/visit/hells-revenge-trailhead)* is the best-known 4WD road in Moab, but the extreme terrain mandates solid driving experience. It's in the BLM-administered area east of town and follows an 8.2-mile route up and down shockingly steep slickrock.

The 33-mile **Hurrah Pass** offers jaw-dropping vistas of the Colorado River, Dead Horse Point and **Grand View Point** in Canyonlands National Park, while on the other side of the Colorado River, the 15-mile scenic desert drive on **Potash Road** passes mining remnants on the way into dry country with soaring rock walls and solitude.

Outfitters such as **Cliffhanger Jeep Rental** *(cliffhanger jeeprental.com)* and **Twisted Jeeps** *(twistedjeeps.com)* rent Rubicons and Wranglers. If you'd rather someone else does the driving, join a group 4WD tour, dubbed 'land safaris,' in modified six- to eight-person Humvee-like vehicles. **Dan Mick's Jeep Tours** *(danmick.com)* is a highly regarded local operation that visits some 25 trails, including Hell's Revenge.

DRINKING IN MOAB: OUR PICKS

Proper Burger & Brewing Co: Southerly outpost of the SLC brewery; heaven for hopheads. *11:30am-9pm or later Wed-Mon*

Moab Brewery: The hometown brewery makes nearly a dozen beers in the vats just behind the bar area. *11:30am-8pm*

Woody's Tavern: 'World famous' neighborhood bar open for 60-plus years; live music on Fridays and Saturdays. *2pm-1am*

Moab Coffee Roasters: Low-key downtown spot to kick back with coffee, gelato and affogato. *7am-7pm Mar-Oct, to 5pm Nov-Feb*

Utah Olympic Park

The country's mountain-biking capital

Moab's mountain biking is world famous. Challenging trails ascend steep slickrock and wind through woods and up 4WD roads outside of town in every direction. Bike-shop websites and **Discover Moab** *(discovermoab.com/mountainbiking)* are good trail resources.

East of town in the Sand Flats Recreation Area, Moab's legendary **Slickrock Trail** *(blm.gov/visit/slickrock-national-recreation-trail; 1-/7-/365-day pass $5/10/20)* will kick your butt. The physically and technically difficult 12-mile round-trip route is for experts only, as is the practice loop. Plan on half a day.

Beat the heat on the **Moonlight Meadow Trail**, a 10.8-mile loop among aspens and pines that reaches a 10,500ft altitude in the La Sal Mountains south of Moab. The nearby **Whole Enchilada** trail system combines six routes that offer everything from high-mountain descents to slickrock. It's a full-day affair for advanced riders, with 7500ft of vertical drop and 34 miles of trails.

White waters of the Colorado and canyons

Rafting might be the highlight of your visit to Moab. Choose from full-day floats, white-water trips, multiday excursions and jet-boat trips.

Half- and full-day trips stick to the Colorado River, northeast of Moab. With class I to II rapids, the most popular stretch of

MOAB'S MOVIE HISTORY

Even if you haven't been to the countryside around Moab before, you've almost certainly seen it. This stunning scenery has starred as the background of major movies for nearly a century. The **Moab Museum of Film & Western Heritage** (*redcliffslodge.com/the-lodge/moab-museum-of-film-and-western-heritage; free*), based at Red Cliffs Lodge on Hwy 128, has memorabilia from locally shot movies, and the ranch itself was the filming location for many of the first films set around Moab, such as *Wagon Master* and *Rio Grande*.

Movies as diverse as *Austin Powers*, *Thelma & Louise* and *Mission Impossible II* have been filmed here. Actor and director Kevin Costner premiered his locally shot passion project *Horizon: An American Saga* in 2024.

EATING IN MOAB: OUR PICKS

Desert Bistro: Southeastern Utah's top restaurant, serving perfectly plated game and seafood in an 1892 dance hall. *5-9pm* **$$$**

Moab Food Truck Park: A dozen-plus trucks dishing up crowd-pleasing Chinese dishes, pizza, hot dogs, sushi and more. *11am-9pm* **$**

Milt's Stop & Eat: Moab's oldest restaurant (established 1954), with classic diner grub: burgers, fries and milkshakes. *11am-8pm* **$**

Birdy's Finer Diner: Elevated comfort food in an Insta-worthy former Denny's covered in bold wallpaper and mod furnishings. *5:30-9:30pm Wed-Sun* **$$$**

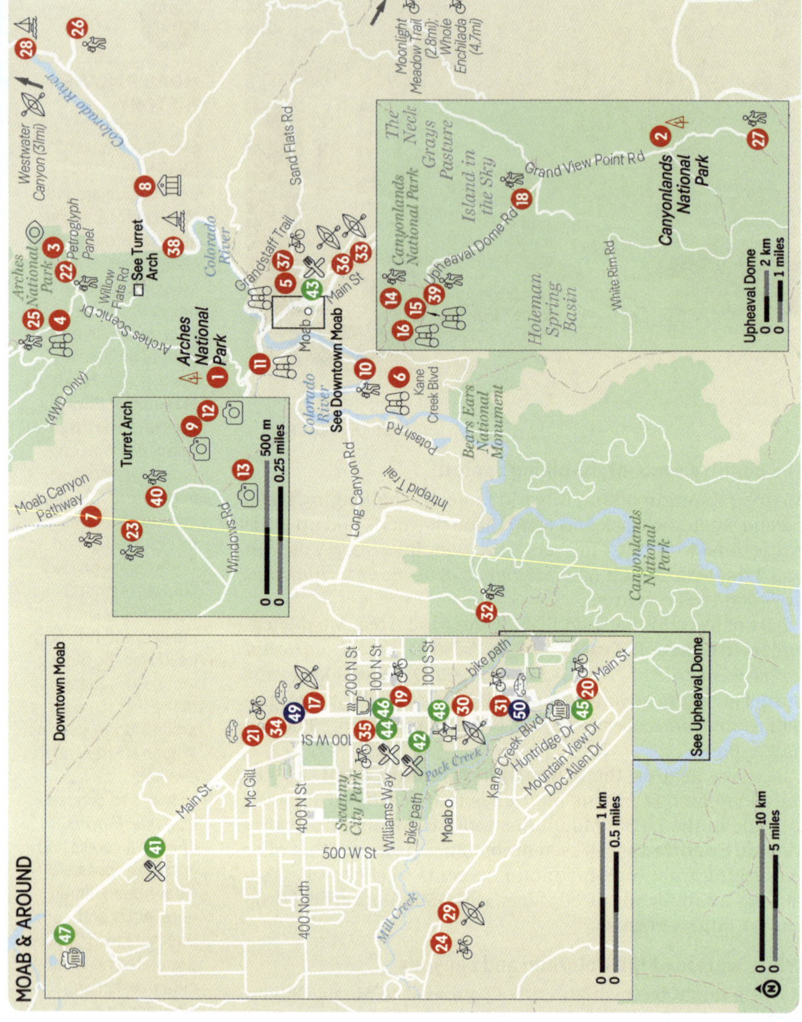

river near Moab is from **Hittle Bottom** to **Takeout Beach**, perfect for first-timers.

Longer multiday expeditions head to Cataract Canyon, Westwater Canyon and Desolation Canyon. The legendary class V rapids of **Cataract Canyon** are Utah's most intense stretch of white water. Outfitters run excursions lasting two to six days.

Find serious white water at **Westwater Canyon**, which boasts class III and IV rapids squeezed by 1200ft rock walls. Over on the Green River, **Desolation Canyon** is an epic four- to six-day adventure that starts with a scenic flight from Moab to the launch point.

HIGHLIGHTS
1 Arches National Park
2 Canyonlands National Park

SIGHTS
3 Delicate Arch
4 Fiery Furnace Viewpoint
5 Hell's Revenge
6 Hurrah Pass
7 Mill Canyon Dinosaur Tracksite
8 Moab Museum of Film & Western Heritage
9 North Window
10 Poison Spider Trailhead
11 Potash Road
12 South Window
13 Turret Arch
14 Upheaval Dome
15 Upheaval Dome First Overlook
16 Upheaval Dome Second Overlook

ACTIVITIES
17 Adrift Adventures
18 Aztec Butte Trail
19 Bike Fiend
20 Chile Pepper Bike Shop
21 Dan Mick's Jeep Tours
22 Delicate Arch Trailhead
23 Double Arch Trail
24 E-Bike Moab
25 Fiery Furnace
26 Fisher Towers Trail
27 Grand View Point Trail
28 Hittle Bottom
29 Mild to Wild
30 Moab Adventure Center
31 Moab Cyclery
32 Neck Spring Trail
33 OARS
34 Poison Spider Bicycles
35 Rim Cyclery
36 Sheri Griffith River Expeditions
37 Slickrock Trail
38 Takeout Beach
39 Upheaval Dome Trailhead
40 Windows Trailhead

EATING
41 Birdy's Finer Diner
42 Desert Bistro
43 Milt's Stop & Eat
44 Moab Food Truck Park

DRINKING & NIGHTLIFE
45 Moab Brewery
46 Moab Coffee Roasters
47 Proper Burger & Brewing Co
48 Woody's Tavern

TRANSPORT
49 Cliffhanger Jeep Rental
50 Twisted Jeeps

Rafting season runs from April to September; the jet-boating season lasts longer. Water levels crest in May and June.

Discover dinosaur tracks near Moab

The first fossils found in the western US were discovered near Moab in 1859. Just off Potash Rd (Hwy 279), the **Poison Spider Dinosaur Tracksite** *(free)* has prints from at least 10 three-toed meat-eating theropods walking along the edge of a lake.

At the **Mill Canyon Dinosaur Tracksite** *(blm.gov/visit/mill-canyon-dinosaur-trailhead-interpretive-site; free)* north of Moab, a raised boardwalk leads travelers above prints from at least 10 species of dinosaur. They include sickle-clawed raptors and long-necked herbivores as well as crocodile ancestors, giving it the most diversity of any site in North America, with 200 individual tracks.

Copper Ridge Dinosaur Tracksite *(blm.gov/visit/copper-ridge-dinosaur-tracks-interpretive-site; free)* is the first place in Utah where the prints of a Jurassic-period sauropod (a herbivore with a long neck) were discovered.

Bears Ears National Monument

Hike through ancient landscapes and cultures

The first national monument created at the request of Native tribes, **Bears Ears** *(blm.gov/visit/bears-ears-national-monument)* covers more than 2100 sq miles and is named for a pair of reddish, nearly symmetrical buttes. The huge area protects sites of cultural significance to Native people, with ancient rock art, cliff dwellings, ceremonial sites and granaries. Bears Ears has been the focus of political ping-pong

BEST RAFTING COMPANIES

Mild to Wild: Excellent rafting trips for any amount of time, including half-day sessions. *(mild2wildrafting.com)*

Adrift Adventures: Combine a trip on the river with a Jeep tour. *(adrift.net)*

OARS: Has a permit for Canyonlands and runs epic weeklong expeditions that raft and hike to tough-to-reach parts of the national park. *(oars.com)*

Sheri Griffith River Expeditions: Operating since 1971, this rafting specialist offers a great selection of activities, from family floats to rapids. *(griffithexp.com)*

Moab Adventure Center: Tons of boat tours for every level of adrenaline, including thrilling jet boats. *(moabadventurecenter.com)*

VISIT WITH RESPECT

Bears Ears is a delicate environment, in terms of both the environment and archaeology. Keep the impact of your visit to a minimum by following these guidelines.

Leave fossils and cultural artifacts undisturbed: This includes pieces of pottery, corn cobs, animal tracks and bones.

Steer clear of ancient structures: Do not touch, climb or stand on historic buildings or lean on their walls.

Stay on established trails and roads: Protect cryptobiotic soil by walking and driving on durable surfaces.

Use rubber-tipped hiking poles: Sharp tips scratch the rocks.

Pay your fees: This money ensures that sites are monitored and facilities are maintained.

for several years. In one of his final acts as president, Barack Obama designated the land as a national monument in 2016, but when Donald Trump took over the White House, he cut the monument's size by 85%. Biden later issued a proclamation that restored Bears Ears to its original size.

Given its recent establishment and back-and-forth status, Bears Ears can be confusing to visit. The monument doesn't have clear entrances, and signage on the ground is minimal, so you might not even know when you're in it. Start your visit at the **Kane Gulch Ranger Station** *(blm.gov/visit/kane-gulch-ranger-station; open spring & fall only)* on Hwy 261 or the **Bears Ears Education Center** *(bearsearspartnership.org/education-center)* in Bluff, a community-run information center with interpretative displays. At either spot, pick up maps and ask for advice on exploring the area.

Bears Ears is divided into three sections: Indian Creek, Cedar Mesa and the San Juan River. Cedar Mesa is the most easily accessible area, mostly along Hwy 95. Some sites, such as the 700-year-old **Mule Canyon Kiva**, are short and easy roadside stops. The 1-mile round-trip **Butler Wash Trail** crosses slickrock to reach a viewpoint looking toward a cliff dwelling across the chasm. An easy 2-mile hike along the South Fork creek of Mule Canyon leads to small Ancestral Puebloan granaries known as **House on Fire**, so named because one of the small dwellings appears to be engulfed in flames due to an unusual gold-orange sandstone overhang.

One of the largest and most evocative archaeological sites is **Moon House**, which has 49 rooms across three well-preserved dwellings. Its name comes from pictographs that show the lunar phases. Access to Moon House is limited to 20 people per day, doled out by permit on recreation.gov for $5 per person, plus a $6 reservation fee. Permits often sell out several days in advance, and in spring and fall they must be validated in person at the Kane Gulch Ranger Station or the **BLM Monticello Field Office** *(blm.gov/office/monticello-field-office)*, a 1½-hour drive from the trail. The road to the trailhead requires a high-clearance 4WD vehicle.

Hiking in the canyons of Cedar Mesa, including to House on Fire, requires day-use permits (per person per day/week $5/10), which you can purchase on recreation.gov (cell signal is poor, so do this in advance) or by using the fee envelopes at trailheads. Backpackers also need permits to camp overnight.

The land protected by Bears Ears National Monument remains sacred to five Native tribes – the Hopi, Navajo, Ute Mountain Ute, Zuni and Ute – who formed a coalition in 2015 to appeal for its preservation. Louis Williams, a member of Diné Bikéyah (the Navajo Nation), founded tour company **Ancient Wayves** *(tourancientwayves.com)* to enrich visitors' experience of hiking in Shash Jaa' (Bears Ears in Diné) with a Native perspective. Hikes head to trailheads around Cedar Mesa, Butler Wash and other locations for half-day, full-day and multiday excursions.

In addition to hikes, Williams, a longtime river runner, also operates rafting trips on the San Juan, the northern boundary of Diné Bikéyah.

TOP EXPERIENCE

Capitol Reef National Park

In a forgotten fold of the Colorado Plateau, slot canyons appear as cathedrals cut from the earth, and giant cream-colored domes arc into perfectly blue skies. Capitol Reef National Park doesn't always make it onto travelers' itineraries. Discover petroglyphs and early Mormon settlements, sandstone streaks and hidden arches, as you hike a labyrinth of canyons stretching back millions of years.

Cassidy Arch

Grand Wash

Grand Wash, Capitol Reef's most captivating canyon off Scenic Dr, is worth visiting just to walk between the Narrows' sheer walls. This flat, easy hike with just 200ft of elevation change is sandwiched between the sides of a Navajo sandstone canyon that at one point tower 80 stories high but are only 15ft apart.

Cassidy Arch

A 3.3-mile round-trip side trail from Grand Wash leads to Cassidy Arch, a natural red-rock formation. With 670ft of elevation change, this hike is more difficult than Grand Wash, switchbacking up the cliffside and traversing some sheer drops, but the views en route are worth it. The arch is named after Utah-born Butch Cassidy, who, according to legend, hid from the law high on these cliffs.

Hickman Bridge Trail

Hickman Bridge Trail, Capitol Reef's most popular trail, is diverse, offering a canyon and desert-wash walk to a natural bridge, plus big-sky views and spring wildflowers. This hike is easy enough for anyone to enjoy. Because the route is largely exposed, it's best to hike in the early morning.

TOP TIPS

- Capitol Reef's gateway town is tiny Torrey, population 257, 11 miles west, where you'll find restaurants, gas stations and accommodations.
- Torrey doesn't have a full-sized grocery store; if you need specific items, Loa lies 17 miles west.

PRACTICALITIES

- nps.gov/care
- 7-day pass per vehicle $20
- national parks pass accepted

ADAM SPRINGER/SHUTTERSTOCK

Delicate Arch

TOP EXPERIENCE

Arches National Park

Giant sandstone arcs frame snowy peaks and desert landscapes at Arches National Park, home to 2000 rock arches, the highest density of them anywhere on earth. You'll lose all perspective on size at some, and a scenic drive through the park makes the spectacular arches accessible to all. Arches has many short trails, with most of the main sights close to paved roads.

DON'T MISS

- Windows Trail
- Turret Arch
- Double Arch Trail
- Delicate Arch
- Fiery Furnace
- Fiery Furnace Viewpoint
- Baby Arch

The Windows Trail

The Windows Trail is an easy 1-mile loop trail that gently climbs to three massive photogenic arches: North Window, South Window and Turret Arch. It's hard to grasp the immensity of these gigantic marvels until you're beside them. This hike is one of the busiest in the park, but you can leave some of the crowds behind by returning on the longer **Windows Primitive Loop**, with a beautiful back view of the two

PRACTICALITIES

- nps.gov/arch
- 7-day pass per vehicle $30
- national parks pass accepted

windows. The primitive trail is less obvious and doesn't have as many trail markers.

The trail forks about 500ft from the parking lot. Take the left fork and head to the **North Window**, which measures 51ft high and 93ft wide and frames the distant desert. A spur trail (part of the Windows Primitive Loop) heads to the **South Window**, sitting higher from the ground than the North Window. The main Windows Loop trail then circles to the castle-like **Turret Arch**.

For a bonus arch, head back to the parking lot and set off on the 0.6-mile **Double Arch Trail**. Double Arch is the tallest in the park at 112ft, and you're allowed to walk and scramble underneath it (but not on the arch itself).

Delicate Arch

You've seen Delicate Arch before: it's the unofficial state symbol, stamping nearly every Utah tourist brochure and gracing license plates. While two viewpoints provide perspective (and an easier hike) from below, the best way to experience the arch is close up.

The trail to Delicate Arch may seem interminable on the way up, but the rewards are so great that you'll quickly forget the toil, provided you wear rubber-soled hiking shoes and drink a quart of water along the way – there is zero shade. This hike is best tackled early in the day when you'll feel less like an ant under a magnifying glass.

Fiery Furnace

So named because of its spectacular rock formations that glow red and orange in the sunset, the narrow sandstone maze of Fiery Furnace has no marked trails and provides an extra level of adventure for hikers. Because of the extreme nature of wayfinding here (online maps and GPS do not work well because of the high canyon walls), as well as sections that require jumping across ledges and shimmying through crevices, permits are required – the only hike in Arches where they are mandatory.

Permits come in two flavors: ranger-led ($16 per person) or self-guided ($10 per person). Purchase them on recreation.gov a week in advance.

The National Park Service recommends that people hiking Fiery Furnace for the first time go on a ranger-guided tour. Permits must be picked up the day before or the day of the hike at the Arches National Park Visitor Center, which opens at 7:30am.

If you don't manage to snag a hiking permit, still survey the scene from the **Fiery Furnace viewpoint**.

OUTSTANDING ARCHES

Karen Henker has worked at the national park for more than a decade.

Double Arch
More than 100ft high, this arch in the Windows section is the park's tallest.

Baby Arch
Not marked on the park map, this one near the Courthouse Towers is a hidden treasure.

Delicate Arch
I recommend the easy Lower Viewpoint walk; the long hike up is like climbing 50 flights of stairs.

TOP TIPS

- If you're planning to visit between 7am and 4pm from April through October, you must reserve an hour-long entry window on recreation.gov, which costs $2 and doesn't include the park entry fee.
- Driving is the best way to get around. There's no shuttle or public transportation. Some companies in Moab run bus tours through the park.
- Cyclists beware: it's a steep climb right after the visitor center and about 17 miles one way to the end of the scenic drive.
- The park has no non-camping accommodations or anywhere to buy food.
- Usually no cell-phone service. Download maps and apps before you arrive.

COLIN D. YOUNG/SHUTTERSTOCK

Aztec Butte

TOP EXPERIENCE

Canyonlands National Park

A 527-sq-mile vision of ancient earth, Canyonlands National Park is Utah's largest – and least-visited – national park. Vast serpentine canyons tipped with white cliffs loom 1000ft over the Colorado and Green Rivers. Skyward-reaching needles and spires, deep craters, swirling tie-dye mesas and majestic buttes dot the landscape. The 6000ft-high Island in the Sky promises some of the most enthralling vistas in Utah.

DON'T MISS

- Island in the Sky
- Neck Spring
- Aztec Butte
- Upheaval Dome Trail
- Needles District
- Slickrock Trail
- Chesler Park Loop

Neck Spring

One of Canyonlands' few loop trails, Neck Spring (5.6 miles, moderately challenging) is good for solitude seekers. Despite its proximity to the visitor center, this trail attracts few hikers, perhaps because it doesn't take in the panoramic vistas that are the signature of **Island in the Sky**, but this stream canyon is a magnet for wildlife and fills with wildflowers in springtime as one of the plateau's rare water sources.

PRACTICALITIES

- nps.gov/cany
- 7-day pass per vehicle $30
- national parks pass accepted

Aztec Butte

Shortly after the turnoff on Upheaval Dome Rd, the moderately challenging 1.4-mile round-trip Aztec Butte Trail climbs to the only archaeological site at Island in the Sky. The short ascent of a Navajo sandstone dome yields stellar views; it's a steep hike over slickrock to the top.

A little more than a quarter mile from the parking area, a spur trail leads to a granary built around 1200 to 1300 CE, tucked below an overhang on the butte's northern side. (Despite the name, the structure was built by Ancestral Puebloans, not the Aztecs.) Use the cairns and switchbacks to follow the route up to the butte, which levels off at the top, revealing panoramic views and endless sky.

Upheaval Dome

Was Upheaval Dome created by salt or something from outer space? Scientists disagree over how the feature formed. Some suggest it's a collapsed salt dome, while more recent research posits that it was the site of a meteorite strike some 60 million years ago. Scope out the geological drama on the moderately challenging **Upheaval Dome Trail**, which leads to two overlooks that gaze out at the 3-mile-wide crater.

It's an easy 0.3 miles one way to the **first overlook**. To reach the **second overlook**, return to the fork in the trail and bear right, descending over slickrock before clambering to a final steep ascent. From here, you have a broader panorama of the surrounding landscape. The afternoon light is magnificent, and this viewpoint adds only 1 mile to the trip.

Slickrock Trail

Over in the Canyonlands' Needles District, the ridgeline Slickrock Trail (2.4 miles, easy) is high above the canyons with views below, almost entirely on its namesake type of stone. Keep an eye out during your hike – bighorn sheep are occasionally seen here.

If you're short on time, at least visit **Viewpoint 1** for a panorama where giant red cliffs hang like curtains below high buttes and mesas, the district's namesake needles touch the sky, and the La Sal and Abajo Mountains lord over the whole scene.

Chesler Park Loop

Get among the namesake 'needles' formations on the Chesler Park Loop, an awesome 11-mile route across desert grasslands, past towering red-and-white-striped pinnacles, and between deep, narrow slot canyons, some only 2ft across. Elevation changes are mild, but the distance makes it a challenging day hike. Make sure you plan your route and download maps in advance, as this area has a number of intersecting circular trails.

WHO WERE THE ANCESTRAL PUEBLOANS?

The Ancestral Puebloans were a Native people who lived across the Four Corners region (modern-day Utah, Colorado, New Mexico and Arizona) from as far back as the 12th century BCE. Prime examples of their impressive architecture can be found at Mesa Verde National Park (p200) in southwestern Colorado. Their modern descendants include the Pueblo, Hopi and Zuni.

TOP TIPS

- The park's two rivers form a Y that divides the park into four separate districts, inaccessible to one another from within the park.
- Cradled atop the Y, Island in the Sky is the most developed and visited district because of its proximity to Moab and Arches National Park's entrance, both about 30 miles from the visitor center.
- The easiest way to visit Canyonlands' Island in the Sky district is by car. There is no shuttle system or public transportation.
- Some companies in Moab run bus tours through the park.
- From Island in the Sky, it's a two-hour drive south to the Needles.

RICHARD WESTLUND/SHUTTERSTOCK

Fairyland Loop

TOP EXPERIENCE

Bryce Canyon National Park

You never forget your first sight of otherworldly Bryce Canyon National Park. Yes, you're still in the desert, but it's the wonderful power of water that sculpted this soft sandstone and limestone into alien formations that tickle the imagination. Though it's the smallest of Utah's national parks, Bryce Canyon stands among the most prized. In Utah, that's quite a claim.

DON'T MISS

- Rim Trail
- Silent City
- Thor's Hammer
- Fairyland Loop
- Tower Bridge
- Peekaboo Loop Trail

Rim Trail

The easiest hike in the national park, the 0.5- to 5.5-mile (one-way) Rim Trail outlines Bryce Amphitheater from Fairyland Point to Bryce Point, promising a journey of incredible views. From Bryce Point to **Inspiration Point**, the trail skirts the canyon rim atop white cliffs, revealing gorgeous formations, including the Wall of Windows. After passing briefly through trees, it continues along the ridge top to the uppermost level of Inspiration Point, 1.3 miles from Bryce Point. The leg to

PRACTICALITIES

- nps.gov/brca
- 7-day pass per vehicle $35
- national parks pass accepted

Sunset Point drops 200ft in 0.75 miles, winding its way along limestone-capped cliffs. Below the rim, **Silent City** rises in all its hoodoo glory.

Stay the course and look for **Thor's Hammer** as you continue the 0.5-mile stroll along a paved path to **Sunrise Point**, the most crowded stretch of trail in the entire park. The views are worth it. Past Sunrise Point the crowds thin as the trail climbs 150ft toward North Campground. Topping out near North Campground, the path ambles across gently rolling hills on the forested plateau before rejoining the canyon rim at Fairyland Point, 2.5 miles from Sunrise Point.

Fairyland Loop

Fairyland Loop is a great 8-mile day hike and a good workout, with 1900ft of elevation gain. Unlike Bryce Amphitheater, Fairyland is spared the crowds. This trail is difficult primarily because it meanders in and out of the hoodoos, down into washes, and up and over saddles.

This trail begins at **Fairyland Point** and circles the majestic cliffs of flat-topped, 8076ft Boat Mesa, emerging on the rim near Sunrise Point. The last 2.5 miles of the loop follow the Rim Trail back to the trailhead.

From Fairyland Point, the trail dips gradually below the rim. At Fairyland Canyon, 600ft below your starting point, towers of deep-orange stone stand like giant totem poles. Zigzagging up and down, the trail eventually reaches a seasonal wash on the floor of Campbell Canyon. Keep an eye out for **Tower Bridge**, which connects three spires to two windows. To reach the base of the formation, take the clearly marked dead-end spur from the wash. From Tower Bridge it's a 950ft climb over 1.5 miles to the Rim Trail.

Peekaboo Loop Trail

An ideal half-day hike, the Peekaboo Loop Trail sees the most variety of terrain and scenery in Bryce, with 1560ft of elevation change.

From Bryce Point, follow signs to the Peekaboo Connecting Trail east of the parking area. Just over a mile down the trail, past where hoodoo columns take on a bright orange hue, work your way down the switchbacks, watching for the **Wall of Windows**, which juts above the hoodoos atop a sheer vertical cliff face perpendicular to the canyon rim.

As you continue, you'll pass ancient bristlecone pines, some of whose roots are over 1000 years old; an inch of these trees' trunks represents a century of growth. Other highlights include the cluster of delicate red spires at Fairy Castle, spectacular views of Silent City, and the Cathedral, a majestic wall of buttress-like hoodoos.

SEEING STARS IN BRYCE CANYON

Amateur astronomers are in for a treat at Bryce Canyon. The National Park Service puts on some 100 astronomy programs a year, including an **Astronomy Festival** in June, full-moon hikes and regular ranger talks. Check the park's calendar online (nps.gov/brca/planyourvisit/calendar.htm) and stop by the visitor center when you arrive to see what's happening while you're here.

TOP TIPS

- When the free park shuttle is running, you can take it to any one point and return from another, instead of backtracking to your car.
- You can join the Rim Trail anywhere along its 5.5-mile route. Note that shuttle buses don't stop at Fairyland.
- If you time your visit for the new moon, when the skies are darkest, watch as the Milky Way shimmers all the way to the horizon.
- At full moon, see the hoodoos take on spooky personalities when rangers lead 1- to 2-mile walks (taking about two hours) among the formations in the moonlight. Reserve a spot ($1) on *recreation.gov*.

GALYNA ANDRUSHKO/SHUTTERSTOCK

The Narrows

TOP EXPERIENCE

Zion National Park

Visiting heavenly Zion National Park can feel like a religious experience. The park's soaring red and white cliffs, one of Utah's most dramatic natural wonders, rise high over the Virgin River. From the canyon floor to Zion's highest peak there is nearly 5000ft of elevation change, resulting in a fabulous range of ecozones and experiences.

DON'T MISS

- Riverside Walk
- The Narrows
- Emerald Pools Trails
- Canyon Overlook Trail
- Observation Point

Riverside Walk

The easy 2-mile out-and-back Riverside Walk is the dry and paved part of the experience, for those who like an easy adventure. Shadowed from the sun by lofty canyon walls, this fun path parallels the Virgin River's slippery cobblestones and rambles by seeps, hanging gardens and wading spots. Points along the way give access to the riverbank and water, making it a family favorite.

The Narrows: Zion's Classic Hike

At the end of the Riverside Walk, stairs descend to the water and the adventure begins. Hiking through a rocky river in

PRACTICALITIES

- nps.gov/zion
- 7-day pass per vehicle $35
- national parks pass accepted

ankle- to chest-deep water as the canyon walls rise up to 1000ft tall and press in to just 20ft wide: the Narrows is quintessential Zion.

The best part about hiking the Narrows is that you can walk for as little or as long as you'd like and still have a great time; the further you go, the smaller the crowds. This out-and-back route is not about reaching a specific spot, but simply soaking up the scene. Day hikers are allowed to go as far as **Big Spring**. Don't underestimate the difficulty or distance (9.4 miles return, about eight hours).

You'll want a sturdy hiking stick to avoid falling in the water, plus quick-drying fabrics, layers and proper footwear. In cooler months, bring waterproof bags and warm, waterproof gear, which you can rent from outfitters near the park entrance like **Zion Outfitter** *(zionoutfitter.com/narrows-rentals)*.

Emerald Pools

Short and sweet, the Emerald Pools trails are a superb introduction to Zion's unique ecology and microhabitats. The paved **Lower Emerald Pool Trail**, the easiest of the three, gradually rises and falls for 0.6 miles before reaching the first pool. Waterfalls cascade down a multicolored, mineral-stained overhang, misting the trail (and you) as you pass beneath. A dirt trail ascends 150ft to the less dramatic **Middle Emerald Pool** feeding the waterfalls below. From here a steep 0.5-mile spur leads to the **Upper Emerald Pool**. It's the loveliest grotto of all, surrounded by Lady Mountain's sheer-walled skirts.

Canyon Overlook Trail

A convenient stop off Hwy 9, the 1-mile out-and-back Canyon Overlook Trail is a relatively quick hike with a much photographed panoramic vista. Although it's not a particularly strenuous hike, the slickrock terrain is somewhat rugged. The final sweeping Canyon Overlook has lower Zion Canyon views. The hike's most challenging part might be finding somewhere to park. If the small lot near the trailhead is full or if you're coming from Mt Carmel, park in the overflow lots 300ft east of the **Zion–Mt Carmel Tunnel**.

Observation Point

It feels deliciously like cheating to wander along a mostly flat woodland path and then descend to Observation Point, which towers more than 700ft above **Angels Landing** – you get all of the rewards with hardly any of the work. If you're planning to hike Angels Landing, know that you can't just show up and hike it; you have to apply for a permit.

The **trailhead** is at the end of a small parking area off a 4WD road in East Zion. The parking lot fills early, and the road is often too rough for standard sedans. Instead, book a spot on a shuttle run by **East Zion Adventures** *(eastzion adventures.com; round trip per person $7)*, which leaves from nearby Zion Ponderosa Ranch Resort (p213).

CAUTION

Preparation and timing are the keys to a successful Narrows adventure. *Always* check conditions and the flash-flood forecast with rangers before setting off. A sudden rainstorm miles away can send down a surge of rock- and log-filled water that sweeps away everything in its path. Some years there's little change in water levels, but the Narrows could be closed in April, May or June.

TOP TIPS

- Avoid visiting in summer if you can: this is the third most-visited national park in the country and summers can feel claustrophobic.
- For most of the year, private vehicles are not allowed on Zion Canyon Scenic Drive. Instead, you must ride the Zion Park Shuttle, which makes nine stops between the visitor center and the Temple of Sinawava.
- Limited free parking is available inside the park; arrive as early as possible.

DRIVING THE COLORADO RIVER SCENIC BYWAY

The curvy Colorado River Scenic Byway (Hwy 128) follows the winding waters through gorgeous red-rock country of high cliffs, alfalfa fields and sagebrush.

START	END	LENGTH
Matrimony Spring	Dewey Bridge	30 miles; 1½ hours

The Colorado River forms Arches National Park's southern boundary for the first 15 miles of this journey. Near the start of the 'river road' just east of Hwy 191, ❶ **Matrimony Spring** is said to have magical properties, and couples who drink from it might soon hear wedding bells. After the first major bend is the ❷ **Grandstaff Canyon Trailhead**, which leads to a beautiful arch.

At the head of the next bend (6 miles from Hwy 191), spot boulderers on the rocks at ❸ **Big Bend Recreation Site**, where you can picnic by the river. As you round the mesa near Red Cliffs Lodge, look on the right for ❹ **Castleton Tower**, a narrow 400ft sandstone spire that rises above Castle Valley and is one of the area's most iconic rock climbs. In the 1960s and '70s, Chevrolet filmed TV commercials here, helicoptering a car to the summit. Carry on to the turnoff for ❺ **Fisher Towers**. The 900ft-high Titan, standing solemnly at the end of the formation, is the country's tallest freestanding natural tower.

The road finally crosses the river at ❻ **Dewey Bridge**, where you might spot rafters drifting by. The scenic byway soon ends at a three-way intersection. Return to Moab or double back to the La Sal Mountain Loop Rd. You're also less than 10 miles from I-70.

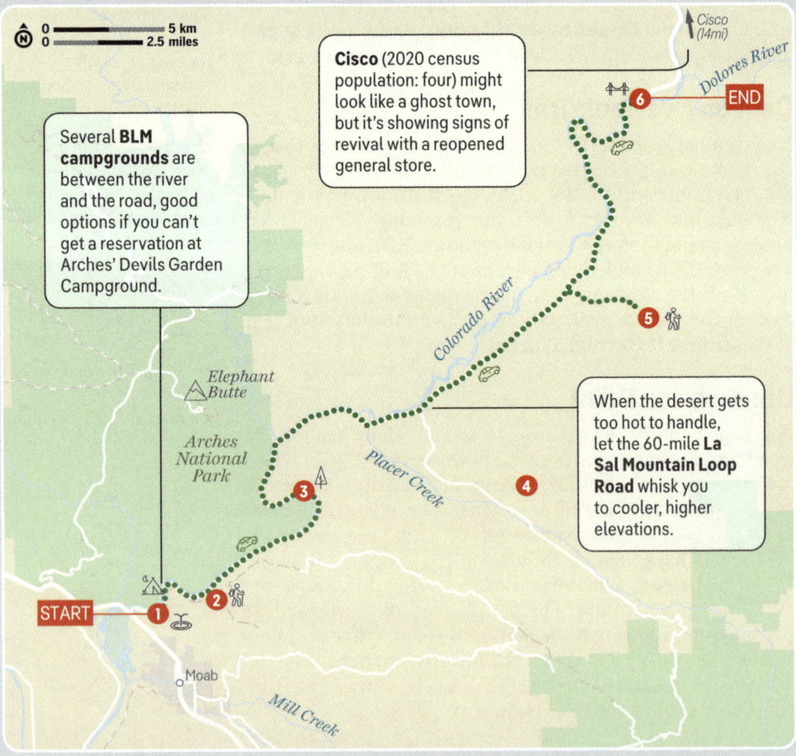

0 5 km
0 2.5 miles

Cisco (14mi)

Cisco (2020 census population: four) might look like a ghost town, but it's showing signs of revival with a reopened general store.

Dolores River

END

Several **BLM campgrounds** are between the river and the road, good options if you can't get a reservation at Arches' Devils Garden Campground.

Colorado River

Elephant Butte

Arches National Park

Placer Creek

When the desert gets too hot to handle, let the 60-mile **La Sal Mountain Loop Road** whisk you to cooler, higher elevations.

START

Moab

Mill Creek

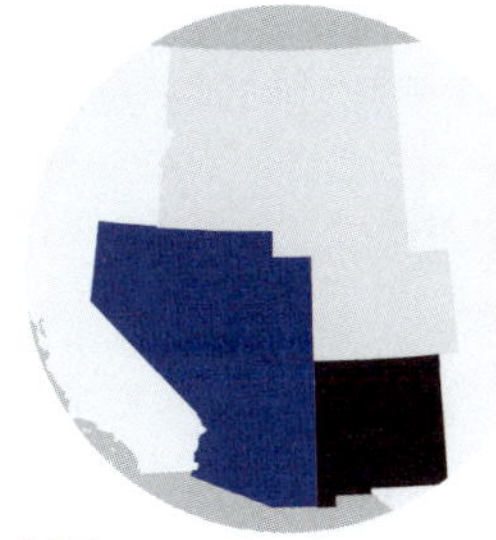

New Mexico

FASCINATING HISTORY | UFO MYSTERIES | SPACE RACE

Traveling in New Mexico is a journey through time and space. It's one big living museum, home to 1000-year-old Indigenous dwellings and some of the longest continuously inhabited communities in the US. It's also the setting for the most famous alleged UFO sighting, it's where the Space Race began, and the state now has the first airport serving trips beyond earth's orbit.

New Mexico doesn't have a single standout city or site – Santa Fe, Taos, Albuquerque and its phenomenal national parks all top the list. The best way to visit is with a road trip along one of many scenic byways or retro Route 66, where neon signs and dry shrubs transform into ghost towns and high-mountain forests.

The best way to fuel any New Mexico adventure? With chili (or chile, as it's spelled here) – practically everything is smothered with the delicious spicy fruit and the chance to explore New Mexico's unique culinary culture is yet another very good reason to visit.

GETTING AROUND

Renting a car is your best bet if you want to travel beyond Albuquerque and Santa Fe. Both cities have plenty of rental offices. A 4WD drive is desirable, especially in the Four Corners Region, but most cars with high clearance should do. Between cities, you can take the Rail Runner Express commuter train from Albuquerque to Santa Fe. Albuquerque and Santa Fe have internal bus services. Greyhound serves some cities and towns, though they're usually best for getting to and from New Mexico rather than around the state.

Places

TOP TIP

Don't make too many UFO jokes around New Mexicans. There's a good chance they've seen something in the sky that they can't explain. Despite its small population, New Mexico often ranks near the top when it comes to UFO sightings compared to other states.

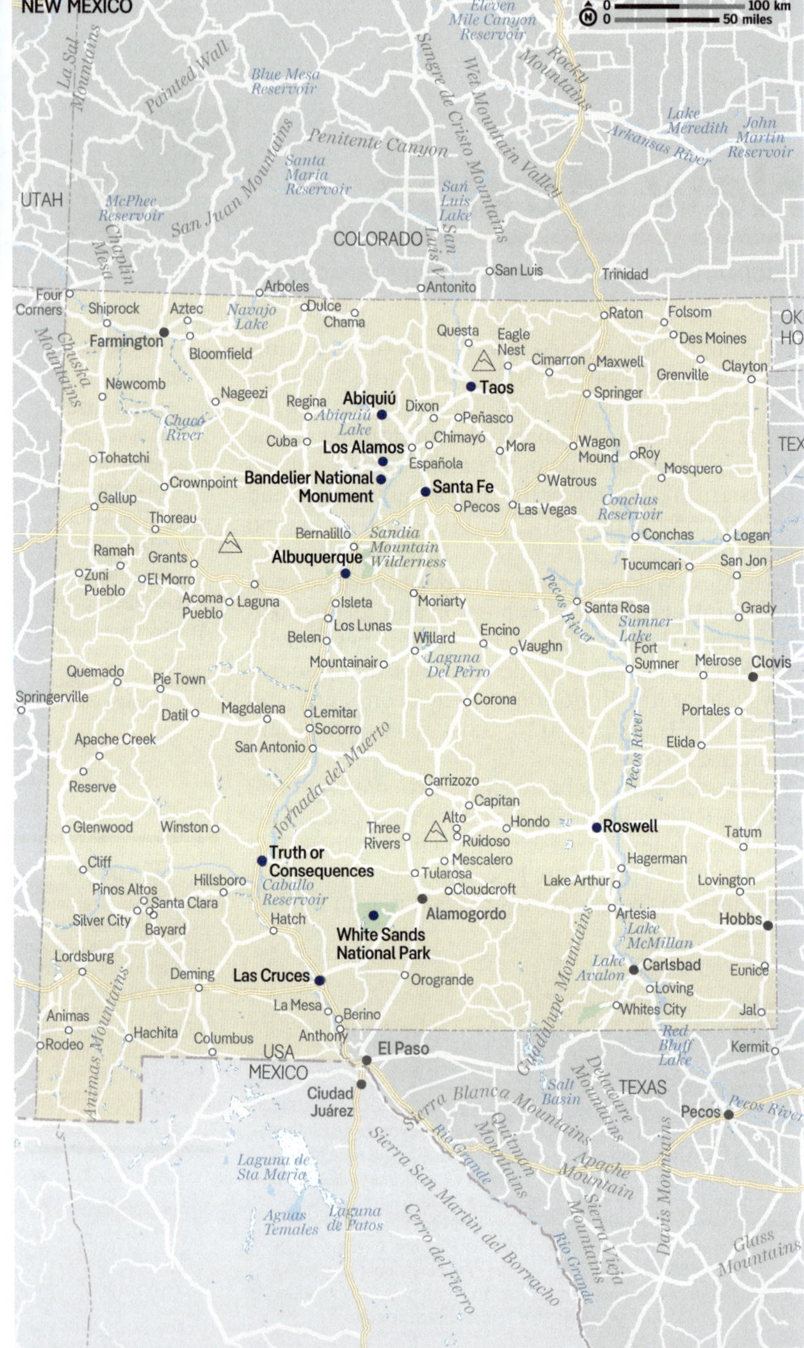
NEW MEXICO
0 100 km
0 50 miles
UTAH
COLORADO
TEXAS
USA
MEXICO
Farmington
Abiquiú
Taos
Los Alamos
Bandelier National Monument
Santa Fe
Albuquerque
Clovis
Roswell
Truth or Consequences
Alamogordo
White Sands National Park
Las Cruces
Carlsbad
Hobbs
El Paso
Ciudad Juárez
Pecos
Four Corners
Shiprock
Aztec
Bloomfield
Arboles
Dulce
Chama
Antonito
San Luis
Trinidad
Raton
Folsom
Des Moines
Questa
Eagle Nest
Cimarron
Maxwell
Clayton
Grenville
Springer
Newcomb
Nageezi
Regina
Dixon
Peñasco
Cuba
Chimayó
Mora
Wagon Mound
Roy
Mosquero
Española
Tohatchi
Crownpoint
Watrous
Gallup
Pecos
Las Vegas
Thoreau
Bernalillo
Concha
Logan
Ramah
Grants
Tucumcari
San Jon
Zuni Pueblo
El Morro
Acoma Pueblo
Laguna
Isleta
Moriarty
Santa Rosa
Grady
Los Lunas
Belen
Willard
Encino
Vaughn
Fort Sumner
Melrose
Mountainair
Quemado
Pie Town
Springerville
Datil
Magdalena
Lemitar
Socorro
Corona
Portales
Apache Creek
San Antonio
Elida
Reserve
Carrizozo
Capitan
Alto
Hondo
Ruidoso
Three Rivers
Glenwood
Winston
Tatum
Cliff
Mescalero
Hagerman
Tularosa
Lake Arthur
Lovington
Hillsboro
Cloudcroft
Pinos Altos
Santa Clara
Silver City
Bayard
Hatch
Artesia
Lordsburg
Deming
Orogrande
Eunice
Loving
Animas
Whites City
Jalo
La Mesa
Berino
Rodeo
Hachita
Columbus
Anthony
Kermit
La Sal Mountains
Painted Wall
Blue Mesa Reservoir
Eleven Mile Canyon Reservoir
Rocky Mountains
Sangre de Cristo Mountains
Wet Mountain Valley
Lake Meredith
John Martin Reservoir
Arkansas River
Penitente Canyon
Santa Maria Reservoir
San Juan Mountains
San Luis Lake
McPhee Reservoir
Chaplin Mesa
Navajo Lake
Chuska Mountains
Chaco River
Abiquiú Lake
Conchas Reservoir
Sandia Mountain Wilderness
Pecos River
Sumner Lake
Laguna Del Perro
Jornada del Muerto
Caballo Reservoir
Lake McMillan
Lake Avalon
Guadalupe Mountains
Animas Mountains
Red Bluff Lake
Salt Basin
Delaware Mountains
Sierra Blanca Mountains
Quitman Mountains
Apache Mountain
Rio Grande
Sierra San Martin del Borracho
Cerro del Fierro
Sierra Vieja Mountains
Davis Mountains
Glass Mountains
Laguna de Sta Maria
Aguas Temales
Laguna de Patos

Albuquerque

Wander the century-old adobe houses

Once a homeland for the Tiwa people, starting around 1250, 'Alburquerque' was taken over by Spain in the 1680 Pueblo Revolt, and in 1706, 15 Spanish families settled here in Old Town. The neighborhood's plaza and **San Felipe de Neri Church** *(sanfelipedeneri.org; free entry)* – look out for the Virgen de Guadalupe carved inside a tree trunk outside the church – were the hub of daily life and a major rest stop for those passing through. Outlaw Billy the Kid allegedly frequented a brothel or two here in the 1870s.

The plaza graciously remains, and Old Town is starting to evolve, especially since the COVID-19 pandemic, with quality shops and galleries promoting New Mexican artisans hoping to revamp the historic core.

When your feet get tired, have a Southwestern lunch at **Church Street Cafe** *(churchstreetcafe.com)*, before tasting chile wine at **Noisy Water Winery** *(noisywaterwinery.com)* and pondering the cool art in the adjacent **Lapis Room** *(lapisroom.com)*.

The world's largest balloon festival

What started at a shopping mall in 1972 has ballooned, quite literally, into one of America's largest festivals, attracting nearly one million people every year to **Balloon Fiesta Park** *(balloonfiesta.com; free park entry; Balloon Fiesta tickets $15)* on the northern edge of Albuquerque city limits for nine days in early October. Standing beneath so many balloons is a surreal experience; the 2022 fest reported a record 648.

You arrive at the grounds before sunrise and are ushered into parking lots (shuttles can get you to the grounds and an app tracks where you parked). Then you're greeted by dozens of vendors offering everything from loaded ribbon fries to hot coffee and, of course, breakfast burritos. At dawn, referees in striped uniforms clear the hordes as balloons are laid out flat before being launched one by one. Besides sunrise flights, events throughout the day include drone shows, chainsaw exhibitions, a sunset flight and fireworks.

Riding in a balloon is typically reserved for local crews, though **Rainbow Ryders** *(rainbowryders.com; prices vary)* offers a handful of visitor spots. You'll have a better chance of booking sunrise flights throughout the year.

Balloon Fiesta Park is also home to the **Anderson-Abruzzo Albuquerque International Balloon Museum**

GREEN OR RED CHILE?

New Mexico is not the same as south of the border or even Texas. It has its own distinct flavors, influenced by Pueblo and other Indigenous groups, Spain, Mexico and Hispanic or Mexican Americans.

The dominant ingredient in New Mexican food is chile (spelled like the country, not the meat stew), a spicy bell pepper infused into everything from chocolate to wine, though you'll find it most often as a sauce. Red or green? That's a question you'll hear in New Mexico, asking you to choose your type of chile sauce. Green chiles ripen first and tend to be spicier. Undecided? Ask for Christmas, which means half and half.

Vegetarians beware that chile sauces are usually made with pork.

EATING IN ALBUQUERQUE: BEST NEW MEXICAN FOOD

Sadie's: Gigantic portions of New Mexican food. Seriously, do not tackle the large nachos alone. *10:30am-10pm* $

El Pinto: Delicious plates in a Southwestern-themed dining room in an old hacienda. Try red-chile ribs. *11am-9pm Sun-Thu, to 10pm Fri & Sat* $

Los Cuates: Our favorite branch on Lomas Blvd has a low-key retro dining room and good red- or green-chile rellenos. Try the cucumber jalapeño margaritas. *11am-9pm* $

Los Compadres: Route 66 spot with a huge menu (and lineup) and classics like saucy carne adovada. *9am-8pm Tue-Sat, to 2pm Sun* $

SIGHTS
1 Anderson-Abruzzo Albuquerque International Balloon Museum
2 Indian Pueblo Cultural Center
3 Lapis Room
4 San Felipe de Neri Church

ACTIVITIES
5 Rainbow Ryders

SLEEPING
6 Hotel Chaco
7 Monterey Motel
8 Painted Lady

EATING
9 Church Street Cafe
10 El Pinto
11 Indian Pueblo Kitchen
12 Los Compadres
13 Los Cuates
14 Sadie's

DRINKING & NIGHTLIFE
15 High Noon Saloon
16 Noisy Water Winery

ENTERTAINMENT
17 Gathering of Nations Powwow
18 International Balloon Fiesta

(balloonmuseum.com; adult/child/under 5 $6/3/free), which details the history of hot-air balloon flights dating to 1783 with interactive exhibits and games for kids.

Find out about Pueblo culture

North of I-40 on 12th St was the site of one of America's first 'Indian' schools, where Indigenous children were forcibly assimilated and punished for speaking their language or practicing their culture. The land has since been reclaimed by 19 of New Mexico's Pueblo tribes and transformed into the fascinating **Indian Pueblo Cultural Center** *(indianpueblo.org; adult/child/under 5 $12/8/free)*. Learn about the knowledge of agriculture and the stars that allowed thousands of Indigenous groups to thrive in the Southwest through artifacts, interactive videos and exhibits. Guided tours are offered at noon on Thursdays and Fridays.

The center is also home to one of Albuquerque's best places to try New Mexican cuisine, **Indian Pueblo Kitchen** *(indianpueblokitchen.org)*, which serves fry-bread tacos, housemade stews served with Pueblo oven bread and red- or green-chile-smothered enchiladas alongside the Three Sisters (corn, beans and squash).

At the end of April, Albuquerque hosts North America's biggest powwow, **Gathering of Nations** *(gatheringofnations.*

EATING IN SANTA FE: BEST NEW MEXICAN FOOD

Tia Sophia's: The first to put breakfast burritos on a menu and to offer Christmas sauces. *7am-2pm Mon-Sat, 8am-1pm Sun* $

La Choza: Local favorite, often with a line; blue-corn versions of the specialties and cocktails. *11am-2:30pm & 4:30-9pm Mon-Sat* $$

Cafe Pasqual's: Cozy space with New Mexico classics and dishes that lean south of the border. *8am-9:30pm Wed-Mon* $$

Coyote Cafe: Credited with putting upscale Southwest cuisine on the culinary map. *11:30am-9pm Sun-Thu, to 9:30pm Fri & Sat* $$$

com; entry from $25 per person), which attracts more than 500 tribes from across the Americas and beyond.

Santa Fe

Roam the historic city center

New Mexico's state capital feels culturally, aesthetically and geographically different to others in the US. There are many reasons for this. One of the biggest reasons is that, founded in 1607, it's the oldest capital in the nation and was one of the earliest European settlements – this is reflected in Santa Fe's distinctive architecture. Pueblo Revival style dominates the landscape with low-slung, earth-colored adobe houses inspired by pueblos – built with mud, earth and straw – plus striking old churches, chapels and missions.

Santa Fe is easily walkable and peppered with memorable sites. Start from the **Plaza**, which has stood as the heart of the city for 400 years. The close-by **St Francis Cathedral** *(cbsfa.org; free)* with its dramatic facade in Romanesque Revival style looks more suited to Europe than the Wild West, but inside it's New Mexican in appearance with a Hispanic altarpiece and folk art.

Two minutes by foot south is the **Loretto Chapel** *(lorettochapel.com; adult/child/under 5 $5/3/free)*, the first Gothic-style building west of the Mississippi. The chapel was built by French and Italian architects in 1878, but its unsupported wooden staircase, St Joseph's Miraculous Staircase, is what draws the crowds, spiraling upward without center or side supports.

Up Old Santa Fe Trail, **San Miguel Mission** *(sanmiguelchapel.org; free)* is considered the oldest Catholic Church in the US. Next to the mission, the blue-doored **Casa Vieja** (1646) is considered the oldest house in the US.

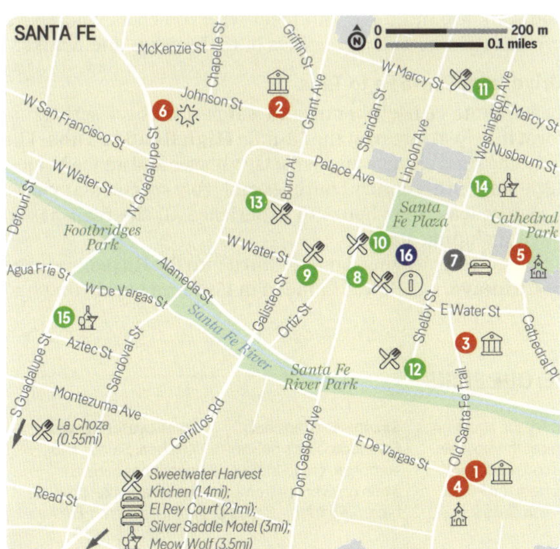

NEW MEXICO CULTURAL FESTIVALS

San Ildefenso Feast Day: Traditional dances and Taos Pueblo's famous pottery; January 23.

Taos Fall Arts Festival: Celebrating the creativity of the area; October.

1680 Pueblo Revolt Anniversary: Picuris Pueblo, 20 miles south of Taos, celebrates with a ceremonial foot race, pole climb, dances; August 10.

Fiestas de Taos: Dance and music pours onto the streets in this celebration of Spanish culture; July.

SIGHTS
1 Casa Vieja
2 Georgia O'Keeffe Museum
3 Loretto Chapel
4 San Miguel Mission
5 St Francis Cathedral

ACTIVITIES
6 Santa Fe School of Cooking

SLEEPING
7 La Fonda

EATING
8 Cafe Pasqual's
9 Coyote Cafe
10 Five & Dime
11 Horno
12 Sazón
13 Tia Sophia's

DRINKING & NIGHTLIFE
14 Anasazi
15 Cowgirl

INFORMATION
16 Santa Fe Plaza Visitor Center

MARGARITA TRAIL

Get a Margarita Trail booklet at the **Santa Fe Visitor Center** or download the app ($2.99) for the ultimate Santa Fe booze crawl. More than 50 restaurants and bars offer jazzed-up margaritas that are $1 off with the booklet or app. Drinks include the **Meow Wolf** Meowgarita (reposado tequila, Cointreau, agave, fresh lime juice, butterfly-pea-flower tea topped with a puffy colorful cloud); the **Cowgirl** Cadillac Margarita (Dulce Vida tequila, Grand Marnier, sweet and sour mix, lime and orange juice); and the **Anasazi** Sandia y Pepino Margarita (Mi Campo tequila, agave, watermelon and cucumber juice, tajin-lime salt rim). Get a stamp at each bar to win prizes, including a T-shirt. You can only earn two stamps per 12 hours.

Ski, hike and bike

Sitting at more than 7000ft above sea level, Santa Fe is the USA's highest state capital, bordered by the imposing Sangre de Cristo Mountains (part of the Rocky Mountains). It never feels claustrophobic, thanks to easy access to nature and outdoor pursuits like hikes and skiing.

Just 16 miles from town, **Ski Santa Fe** *(skisantafe.com; ski passes $48-90 depending on ability)* in the Sangre de Cristo Mountains offers dry powder like its more famous cousin, Taos Ski Valley, with a higher base elevation (10,350ft). It includes seven lifts and 86 runs. **North Central Regional District** *(ncrtd.org/ski-bus)* offers free buses to the top, stopping along trailheads on the way up the mountain.

Trails here range from all-day adventures to short strolls. From the ski basin parking lot, the challenging 10.8-mile **Raven's Ridge** loop cuts east along the **Upper Winsor Trail** after the first steep mile of switchbacks to follow the Pecos Wilderness boundary high above the tree line to the top of **Lake Peak** (12,409ft).

Aspen Vista, the premier path for immersing yourself in the magical bright-yellow fall foliage, lives up to its name. The first mile of the 11.5-mile full-day trail is easy, gaining little elevation and following an old dirt road.

Learn to cook like a New Mexican

Once you've eaten plenty of breakfast burritos, enchiladas and gallons of green chile, you can learn how to make New Mexican food at home with a specialty cooking class. Family-run **Santa Fe School of Cooking** *(santafeschoolofcooking.com; 3hr class from $100)* has been teaching New Mexican cuisine for more than three decades and offers a number of different kinds of classes in a beautiful space west of the Plaza.

On Fridays, the cooking school leads restaurant tours where you walk around town and meet with top chefs who give a presentation as well as tastings of their dishes and drinks.

Drive from Santa Fe to Taos

Leave Santa Fe northbound and watch shrubby desert transform into lush forest on the 58-mile **High Road to Taos**. The winding road zigzags up past artsy villages and adobe homes, 18th- and 19th- century churches and truly spectacular views. Leave at least four hours to experience all the road has to offer, including stops.

Shortly after leaving Santa Fe, turn into the Hispanic village of **Chimayó**, which was founded in 1598 on a pueblo that had

EATING IN SANTA FE: OUR PICKS

Five & Dime General Store: Try a Frito Pie – chile, beans, beef, onions and cheese in a bag of Fritos. *9am-9pm* $

Horno: Try the squid-ink capellini at this upscale street-food restaurant a block from the Plaza. *5-9pm Mon-Sat* $$

Sazón: Mexican chef Fernando Olea's delicious, surprising creations put a grin on every patron's face. *5-9pm Mon-Sat* $$$

Sweetwater Harvest Kitchen: Salads and smoothies here use farmers market produce. *10am-3pm Mon-Fri, 9am-3pm Sat & Sun* $$

AMBER WALKER/SHUTTERSTOCK

El Santuario de Chimayó

been abandoned 200 years prior and holds major significance for Catholics. **El Santuario de Chimayó** *(holychimayo.us; free)* was built in 1816 atop a spot of 'holy dirt' said to be miraculous and to hold curative powers. During Holy Week (mid-April) some 30,000 pilgrims walk to Chimayó from Santa Fe in the largest Catholic pilgrimage in the US.

Up the road, turn off into **Truchas**, an 18th-century Spanish town with century-old adobe buildings and a couple of galleries. In **Peñasco**, the **Peñasco Theatre** *(facebook.com/penascotheatre; prices vary)* bills itself as the area's only solar-powered hand-built adobe theatre. Continue northbound by making a U-turn at Hwy 518 to the most forested part of the road to Taos (p204).

Abiquiú

Hike in Georgia O'Keeffe's footsteps

Iconic artist Georgia O'Keeffe spent summers on mesmerizing **Ghost Ranch** *(ghostranch.org; adult/child $10/free)* with its multicolored bluffs, gorgeous canyons, plains and grasslands filled with spectacular trails. O'Keeffe painted more than 100 paintings on these grounds.

Many visit to do the 3-mile climb up to **Chimney Rock**, an enormous pillar that breaks off from the mesa top with breathtaking views.

O'Keeffe's main **home** and studio, where she lived from 1949 to 1984, sits 12 miles south of Ghost Ranch in Abiquiú. It has Native American and Spanish Colonial building styles, and some rooms date to 1744. It was given National Historic Landmark status in 1998 and is now part of Santa Fe's **Georgia O'Keeffe Museum** *(okeeffemuseum.org; adult/child/under 5 $22/12/free)*. There's also a nearby **O'Keeffe Welcome Center** next to the Abiquiu Inn, with a gift shop and some of her personal effects.

CONTINENTAL DIVIDE TRAIL

Hundreds of thru-hikers brave the 3100-mile Continental Divide Trail each year, which crosses into New Mexico's **San Pedro Parks Wilderness** northwest of Santa Fe. The trail is less popular but no less extraordinary than some of the US' 11 other National Scenic Trails, including the Appalachian and Pacific Crest trails. Many begin the trail on the US border with Chihuahua in Mexico and wind all the way to Alberta, Canada. It takes six months if you hike 17 miles a day.

In New Mexico, the trail stretches 820 miles from the Southwestern desert through Silver City and Gila National Forest to Grants, Jemez Mountains and the Chama Wilderness before hitting the Colorado Rockies. It can also be hiked in shorter segments.

OPPENHEIMER'S DOWNFALL

J Robert Oppenheimer was born in New York in 1904, visited New Mexico as a teen, then studied at Harvard, Cambridge and Göttingen in Germany before being selected as the physicist in charge of the Manhattan Project. After the bombs were dropped on Japan in 1945, Oppenheimer opposed continued development of nuclear weapons. FBI Director J Edgar Hoover began to investigate Oppenheimer for Communist Party links and while none were found, he was stripped of his security clearance in 1954 during the Red Scare, and dismissed for opposing the arms race.

The US went on to do more than 1000 nuclear tests until 1992. *Oppenheimer,* a film directed by Christopher Nolan, was released in 2023.

Bandelier National Monument

Ancient Indigenous caves and petroglyphs

Ancestors of Navajo and current Pueblo people lived in this 33,000-acre area now run by the National Park Service. Some 3000 settlements have been discovered in **Bandelier National Monument** *(nps.gov/band; $25 per vehicle).*

You can visit some of the cave dwellings, just 400yd from the visitor center, by climbing ladders on the 1.4-mile **Pueblo Loop Trail**. There are also remains of adobe-brick buildings and petroglyphs on the cliff face. If you're up for a bigger day of hiking, Bandelier is 70% wilderness with 70 miles of backcountry trails. Get a backcountry permit at the visitor center.

Los Alamos

Where the atomic bomb was born

Los Alamos occupies a special place in US history as one of the creation places of the atomic bomb, and its excellent **Bradbury Science Museum** *(lanl.gov/engage/bradbury; free)* is worth making a trip for. Learn about the history and people behind the Manhattan Project, see a replica of the bomb dropped on Nagasaki and learn about the government research that continues today, including nanoscience, sustainable technology and preventing infectious diseases.

The story here doesn't flinch from the truth. It was here, in 1942 at the height of WWII, that Franklin D Roosevelt called on Lieutenant General Leslie Richard Groves Jr and physicist J Robert Oppenheimer to assemble a secret lab to develop a weapon unlike anything the world had ever seen. The result was the world's first atomic bomb detonation, on July 16, 1945, at the Trinity Site in southern New Mexico. The nuclear bombs designed by the Manhattan Project killed an estimated 135,000 to 215,000 people.

Taos

See where Pueblo culture thrives

A magical spot even by the standards of this Land of Enchantment, Taos is a beautiful town in northern New Mexico surrounded by 12,300ft snowcapped peaks that hit a sage-speckled plateau before plummeting 800ft into the Rio Grande Gorge.

One of the oldest continuously inhabited communities in the US and both a UNESCO World Heritage Site and US National Historic Landmark, **Taos Pueblo** *(taospueblo.com; adult/child under 10 $25/free)* is an extraordinary place to

EATING IN TAOS: OUR PICKS

La Cueva Cafe: Probably Taos' most popular restaurant. New Mexican classics from breakfast to close. *10am-8pm Mon-Fri, to 5pm Sat* $

ACEQ: Pronounced 'ah-sec,' this popular Arroyo Seco spot has great food and is Guy Fieri–approved. *5-10pm* $$

Love Apple: Romantic candlelit restaurant in a 19th-century chapel serving seasonal fare and funky wines. Cash only. *5-9pm Wed-Sun* $$

Chokola: Fair-trade and organic bean-to-bar chocolate tasting room in the Plaza for six kinds of mousse, ice cream, cakes and bars. *11am-6pm* $

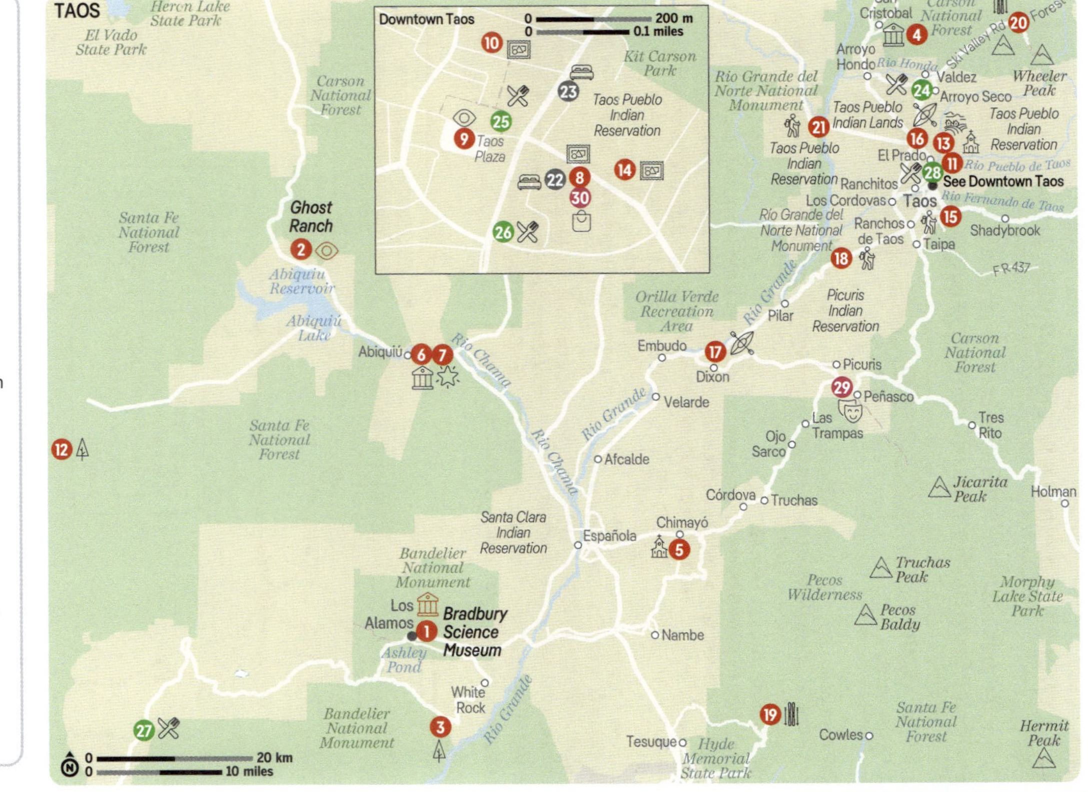

HIGHLIGHTS

1 Bradbury Science Museum

2 Ghost Ranch

SIGHTS

3 Bandelier National Monument

4 DH Lawrence Ranch & Memorial

5 El Santuario de Chimayó

6 Georgia O'Keeffe Home

7 O'Keeffe Welcome Center

8 Parsons Gallery of the West

9 Plaza

10 Robert L Parsons Fine Art Gallery

11 San Geronimo Church

12 San Pedro Parks Wilderness

13 Taos Pueblo

14 Wilder Nightingale Fine Art

ACTIVITIES

15 Devisadero Loop Trail

16 Far Flung Adventures

17 New Mexico River Adventures

18 Rift Valley

19 Ski Santa Fe

see 15 South Boundary

20 Taos Ski Valley

21 West Rim

SLEEPING

22 Doña Luz Inn

23 Historic Taos Inn

EATING

24 ACEQ

25 Chokola

26 La Cueva Cafe

27 Los Ojos Restaurant & Saloon

28 Love Apple

ENTERTAINMENT

29 Peñasco Theatre

SHOPPING

30 El Rincón Trading Post

ENCHANTED CIRCLE SCENIC DRIVE

One of the prettiest drives in this Land of Enchantment, along the aptly named Enchanted Circle Scenic Byway, circling Wheeler Peak.

START	END	LENGTH
Taos	Taos	90 miles; 3–6 hours

This drive along Hwys 522, 38 and 64 passes crystalline lakes, pine forests draped with feldspar, alpine highlands, windswept meadows and old-timey ski towns. From ❶ **Taos** head north to Hispanic town ❷ **Questa**, whose name is a typo – it was originally called 'cuesta,' Spanish for cliff or large hill. Questa's adobe St Anthony's Church was built in 1842 but collapsed in 2008. Fortunately, locals volunteered 49,000 hours to revive it, and it was reconsecrated in 2016. Northeast of town, ❸ **Latir Peak Wilderness** has sweet but intense multiday backpacking trails that ascend 12,708ft up the mountain.

A gold-mining boomtown in the 19th and 20th centuries with saloons and brothels, ❹ **Red River** is now a family-friendly ski town. The main drag is lined with shops, with German-style wooden lodges mixed with an Old West theme. On summer Saturdays at 4pm outside ❺ **Frye's Trading Post**, catch the cowboy shoot-out reenactment, a Red River tradition since 1950.

The western part of the trail flattens out and mountain runoff accumulates in 2400-acre ❻ **Eagle Nest Lake State Park**, filled with pike and motorboats in summer. ❼ **Angel Fire** looks like time-share condo land, but it's a popular ski hill with mostly blue and green runs and plenty of lodges. Loop around the remainder of Rte 64 for 18 miles through farmland and Carson forest, then back to Taos.

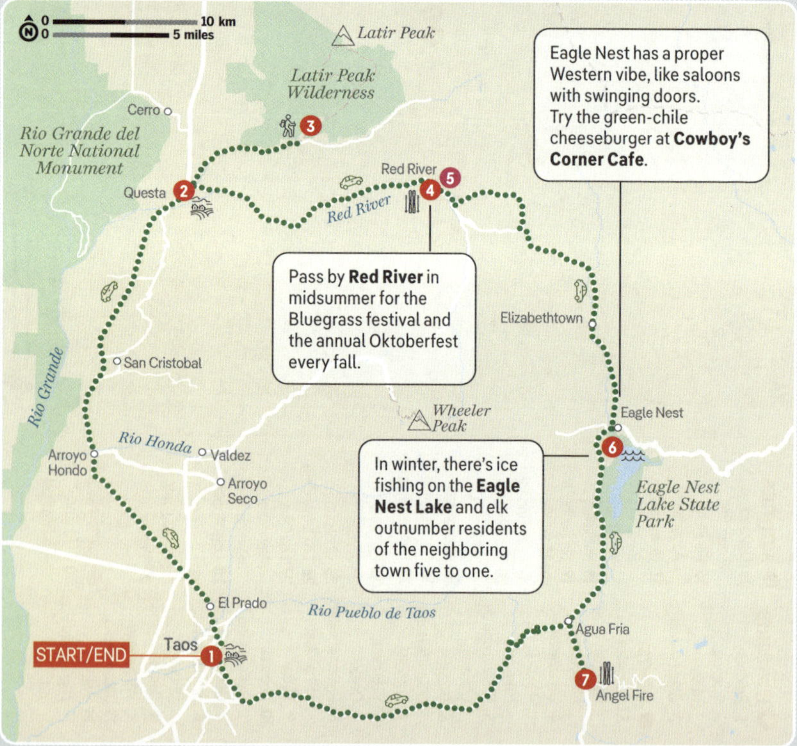

Eagle Nest has a proper Western vibe, like saloons with swinging doors. Try the green-chile cheeseburger at **Cowboy's Corner Cafe**.

Pass by **Red River** in midsummer for the Bluegrass festival and the annual Oktoberfest every fall.

In winter, there's ice fishing on the **Eagle Nest Lake** and elk outnumber residents of the neighboring town five to one.

START/END

KWAN TSE/SHUTTERSTOCK

Eagle Nest Lake State Park

see New Mexican Pueblo culture thriving in the present day. Three miles northeast of Taos Plaza, the Pueblo's multistory mud-and-straw adobe apartments stand tall and proud under the backdrop of the Sangre de Cristo Mountains, as they've done for 1000 years.

Taos Pueblo welcomes visitors for guided tours. Visitors are taught about Pueblo ways of life, adobe architecture and history, including the 1680 Pueblo Revolt that tossed out the Spanish. You can also visit Taos Pueblo's unique **San Geronimo Church** *(ologtaos.com; free)*, which highlights Mary rather than Jesus at the pulpit.

Taos Pueblo is closed from late winter (usually end of January) to the third week of March.

The art of Taos

Taos went on to become a trading post on the Santa Fe Trail and later an attraction for early-20th-century artist transplants from New York and California, who came to visit and couldn't leave after witnessing the sapphire-blue skies and paint-stroke sunsets.

Taos centers on its atmospheric **Plaza**, with a green park and benches in the middle of a square of adobe homes, the old courthouse and Taos jail on the north side of the Plaza, and buildings dating to 1796. The nearby **Robert L Parsons Fine Art Gallery** *(parsonsart.com)* on Bent St sells works from Taos Society of Artists painters. Its sister, **Parsons Gallery of the West** *(parsonsart.com/parsonswest)* on Kit Carson Rd, features 20 different artists, mostly from Taos, in a beautiful hacienda built in 1803. Across the road, **Wilder Nightingale Fine Art** *(wnightingale.com)* has been selling an eclectic collection of contemporary Taos art for more than 30 years from its huge gallery. For Indigenous art and jewelry, pop into the dusty museum-like **El Rincón Trading Post** *(instagram.com/elrincontradingpost)*, which has been open since 1909 and hasn't changed much.

BEST MOUNTAIN-BIKING TRAILS AROUND TAOS

Taos Ski Valley & Angel Fire: Ride the lifts and zoom down the mountain.

Rift Valley: Mostly flat, winding single-track trail suitable for intermediate cyclists and fun for advanced riders.

South Boundary: Twenty-eight-mile ride considered one of the nation's best mountain-bike trails. Experienced cyclists only.

West Rim: Easy 9-mile trail in Rio Grande del Norte with great views of the Rio Grande Gorge.

Devisadero: Steep and difficult trail with plenty of rocks. Watch out for rattlesnakes.

BEST SALOONS IN NEW MEXICO

Melody Groves, author of *Hoist a Cold One! Historic Bars of the Southwest*, shares New Mexico's best Old West saloons.

No Scum Allowed: Funky White Oaks bar in an 1884 building – the best part is the name.

Double Eagle: During the Civil War, Confederate officers used the back room of this Mesilla bar as a ballroom.

High Noon Saloon: Albuquerque Old Town saloon bar dating to 1785. It's now a steakhouse and apparently haunted.

Buckhorn Saloon: This Pinos Altos saloon north of Silver City is old, as is the bar itself.

Los Ojos: This Jemez Springs place is 100 years old and cool, too. Stop for beer or food.

Tackle the rivers

From April through October, sections of the Rio Grande near Taos are the best places in New Mexico to go white-water rafting. Guides lead trips into the turbulent **Taos Box** north of town, which has lots of class IV and sometimes class V rapids. Boats do tend to flip, and the remoteness of this area makes it extra scary – and thrilling. If Taos Box intimidates you, the **Racecourse** and **Lower Gorge** downriver near Pilar are popular family-friendly spots with gentler waves.

You can book half-, full- or multiday rafting trips with the reputable and knowledgeable **New Mexico River Adventures** *(newmexicoriveradventures.com; rafting $40-450)* and **Far Flung Adventures** *(farflung.com; rafting $54-400)*, which has been in the business since 1976 and has permits from the Forest Service and local tribes. Rock climbing, horseback riding and fly-fishing tours are also available.

Taos and DH Lawrence

British poet and novelist David Herbert Lawrence might have only spent two years (1924–26) on the 160-acre ranch he owned here with his wife Frieda, but it was enough to declare that New Mexico 'changed me forever.' Fans of the author who wrote such classics as *Lady Chatterley's Lover* can visit **DH Lawrence Ranch** *(dhlawrenceranch.unm.edu; free but donations welcome; 9:30am-3:30pm Tue-Thu)*, 20 miles north of Taos, now administered by the University of New Mexico. If you manage to make the narrow opening window, you can visit the famous Lawrence Tree painted by Georgia O'Keeffe, the cabin Dorothy Brett stayed in when Lawrence invited her to start a utopian society and the 19th-century homesteader's cabin where the writer worked on *St Mawr, David* and *The Plumed Serpent*.

Roswell

Put on your tinfoil hat

In July 1947, two years after the first atomic bomb test in Trinity, 350 people say they witnessed an unidentified flying object crash in the desert outside Roswell. More than 75 years later, questions remain about the crash. Was it a flying saucer, as UFO fanatics believe? Or was it a weather balloon as the US government argued? Or was it something else?

Put on a tinfoil hat and investigate the answer at Roswell's **International UFO Museum & Research Center** *(roswellufomuseum.com; adult/child $7/4)*. The museum

EATING IN ROSWELL: OUR PICKS

El Coco Pirata: Probably your best meal in southeast New Mexico. All about seafood, with fresh ceviche and shrimp platters. *10am-9pm* $

Cowboy Cafe: Beloved of locals, this breakfast joint serves hearty New Mexican specialties and burgers. *6am-2pm* $

Martin's Capitol Cafe: Adobe building with Moorish arches. New Mexico classics like burritos, stuffed sopaipillas. *6am-8:30pm Mon-Sat* $

Antigua Cocina: Mexican specialties like *cochinita pibil, chile en nogada* and steak with a big tequila list. *11am-10pm Mon-Thu* $$

STEVE LAGRECA/SHUTTERSTOCK

International UFO Museum & Research Center

details accounts of the Roswell incident and what happened in the aftermath.

Continue your investigation around the corner at **Spaceport Roswell** *(spaceportroswellnm.com; adult/child $14.40/9.50)*, where you can put on VR glasses to experience what it might've been like to be on board the flying saucer that crashed outside Roswell, or join Neil Armstrong on the *Apollo 11* mission to the Moon. Across the street, walk beside aliens and try not to get abducted at **Roswell UFO Spacewalk** *(roswellspacewalk.com; $6)*, an immersive room filled with creepy dayglow decor and lights.

Las Cruces

Feel the downtown vibe

Las Cruces and its older and smaller sister city Mesilla sit in a broad desert basin beneath the striking eastern peaks of the Organ Mountains. There's something special about the combination of bright, white sunlight, glassy blue skies, flowering cacti, rippling red mountains and desert lowland landscape found here. It's worth stopping by to experience New Mexico's most Hispanic/Latinx-influenced city (60% identify as such), and explore Mesilla's cute adobe homes.

Start by walking along Main St in downtown Las Cruces on a Saturday morning and you'll see this sleepy city come to life. From 8:30am to 1pm, vendors at the **Farmers & Crafts**

CONFEDERATE CAPITAL

In July 1861, a small Confederate force from Texas humiliated a force of Union soldiers more than three times its size, between Fort Fillmore (near Mesilla) and San Augustin Pass. Mesilla went on to briefly become the capital of the Confederate Territory of Arizona, but Confederate control only lasted five weeks before soldiers fled the city and then the state.

The Civil War–era **Fort Selden Historic Site** *(museumfoundation.org; adult/child $5/free)*, 20 minutes from downtown Las Cruces, had about 1800 soldiers at its prime, including more than 400 African Americans. Inside is a detailed one-room exhibit, and outside are the fort ruins, including its jail, bakery and barracks. Entry is free with a **New Mexico Culture Pass**.

EATING IN LAS CRUCES: OUR PICKS

!Andele!: Mesilla New Mexican place with a salsa bar, homemade nachos, loaded hot dogs. *8am-9pm Tue-Sun, to 2:30pm Mon* $

La Nueva Casita: Bargain Mexican and New Mexican food, primarily for breakfast. Try the *machaca* scrambled eggs. *9am-3pm Wed-Mon* $

Chala's Wood-Fired Grill: New Mexican done right in Mesilla. Try house-smoked pulled pork. *8am-9pm Mon-Thu, to 9:30pm Fri & Sat, to 2pm Sun* $

Spotted Dog Brewery: Green-chile pesto wings, burgers, cheese, craft beer. *11:30am-10:30pm Mon-Thu, to midnight Fri & Sat, noon-8:30pm Sun* $$

BORDER PATROL

Along I-25, some 22 or so miles north of Las Cruces, signs will tell you to slow down to pass through a US border checkpoint. These types of government checkpoints are common in the southern part of the state, being so close to the border, and you're nearly guaranteed to see one if you're driving. If waved over, you'll have to answer a few questions, or you might not have to do anything at all as a green light flashes you through. Always carry ID, including a valid tourist visa if you're a foreign citizen, as well as car registration or the rental agreement. Be polite and allow them to search inside the trunk if they ask.

Market *(farmersandcraftsmarketoflascruces.com; free)* show off their hauls of local pecans and Hatch chiles, while food trucks sling tacos and churros. Local artisans are here, too, selling pottery, jewelry, fun shirts and the like. Someone might be jamming at **Downtown Blues Coffee** *(downtownbluescoffee.com)*, a cafe, record store and hub of cultural life.

Range a little further and **Mesilla**, technically its own distinct town 4 miles south of downtown, is Las Cruces' most historic neighborhood, and walking around here feels like being in 19th-century Mexico; the trial of outlaw Billy the Kid happened here in 1881. Today Mesilla is a beautifully preserved slice of history with cute adobe houses and a beautiful historic plaza with its 1855 **Basilica of San Albino** *(sanalbino.org; free)*.

The birthplace of the Space Race

Being a high-elevation desert, southern New Mexico is a great place to see the stars – and to launch spaceships.

In Alamogordo, a dusty town at the base of Lincoln National Forest's mountains an hour east of Las Cruces, is the **New Mexico Museum of Space History** *(nmspacemuseum.org; adult/child $8/6)*. Built like a space shuttle, this four-floor museum has interesting exhibits that take you from the history of Indigenous awareness of the stars to Robert H Goddard's liquid fuel rocket test in 1926 to the atomic bomb and modern space tourism.

The tradition continues at Virgin Galactic's **Spaceport America** *(spaceportamerica.com)*, the world's first commercial spaceport and an active rocket test facility, one hour north of Las Cruces. While not open for pop-ins, you can visit by booking a private tour with **Final Frontier Tours** *(spaceportamerica.com/visit; adult/child $49.99/29.99)*. Inside the facility, you'll visit mission control, speak with firefighters about potential crashes, ride the runway and test out the Multi-Axis Trainer (MAT), which prepares astronauts for zero gravity.

Truth or Consequences

Hippies and hot springs

Vying for the title of New Mexico's quirkiest town (the competition is admittedly stiff) is Truth or Consequences (also called T or C), 75 miles north of Las Cruces. Formerly known as Hot Springs, the municipality changed its name in 1950 when the then-host of a radio show called Truth or Consequences promised to air the 10th-anniversary program in the town that changed its name to the title of the show.

Today, Truth or Consequences has an artsy, transient, end-of-the-world vibe, like Joshua Tree 30 years ago. Its small downtown is packed with art galleries and eclectic gift shops. But the main reason to come to Truth or Consequences is to soak in its hot springs. Most hotels and private dwellings have them – all they need to do is dig – but the best are at **Riverbend Hot Springs** *(riverbendhotsprings.com; common pools from $25, private from $35 per 50min)*.

TOP EXPERIENCE

White Sands National Park

Fifty miles east of Las Cruces, ethereal snow-white sand dunes roll on as far as the eye can see like something out of a dream. The phenomenal 275-sq-mile White Sands National Park is nowhere near the ocean; the dunes are actually made from powdered gypsum crystals that blew from an ancient sea over the San Andres and Sacramento Mountains 4000 to 7000 years ago.

Drive

From the visitor center, drive the 16-mile scenic sandy loop (fine for cars and RVs) and stop along the way to sink your toes in the dunes. The temperature can change by 50°F in a day. Bring lots of water (1 gallon per day per person). Picnic areas along the drive offer shaded benches for lunch.

Walk (or Slide)

Walking in the silence and solitude of the dunes is almost a spiritual experience, especially at sunrise or sunset when the sea of sand sparkles. Escape the crowds on the **Alkali Flat**, a 5-mile round-trip backcountry trail through the heart of White Sands (follow the markers as it's easy to get lost). It's really a winter trail but possible to hike if you come early before it's hot. Or try the simple 1-mile loop **Dune Life Nature Trail**, which climbs two steep dunes rich with desert plant life.

Tumble down the dune or slide down on a sled or sandbar of your choice. You can buy/rent a plastic saucer ($24.99/15) at the visitor-center gift shop. You can rent a board for $25 to surf the dunes. Buy wax to make it a faster experience.

Camp

You can camp in the vast desert on the 2-mile round-trip **Backcountry Camping Loop Trail** (no water, shade or toilets). When darkness falls, the dunes mirror the night sky for ultimate blackness – the Milky Way is visible on a moonless night. At the time of research, camping was unavailable due to maintenance – check before a visit.

TOP TIPS

- Map GPS points on your trail, including where your car is. It's easy to get lost.
- The dunes get more impressive further into the park, so go to the furthest point first.
- Bring sunglasses and sunscreen – reflection can cause sunburn under your chin.
- Note that the park can close during nearby missile tests.

PRACTICALITIES

- nps.gov/whsa
- $25 per vehicle

Places We Love to Stay

$ Budget $$ Midrange $$$ Top End

Las Vegas p130

Luxor $ A pyramid-shaped, Egyptian-themed resort with cutting-edge entertainment and comfy rooms.

El Cortez $ A Fremont St icon since 1941, when the mob ran the joint. Recently revamped and adults only.

Cosmopolitan $$ These digs are the hippest on the Strip, with rooms featuring balconies, Japanese tubs and plush furnishings.

Skylofts $$$ Inside the MGM Grand, these glamorous two-story apartments have every indulgence, from spa tubs to gourmet kitchens. Butler included.

Southern Nevada p136

Baker Creek Campground $ Unfurl your tent next to an alpine stream under a canopy of aspens in Great Basin National Park.

Atlatl Rock Campground $ Gorgeous sites among sandstone formations at the heart of jaw-dropping Valley of Fire State Park.

Hidden Canyon Retreat $$ A breathtaking and historic resort tucked into a vast canyon and stretching over 375 acres near Great Basin National Park.

Grand Canyon National Park p147

Bright Angel Lodge $ Simple lodge rooms and rustic cabins on the canyon edge are excellent budget accommodations.

El Tovar $$$ Public spaces in this wooden lodge ooze old-world national-park glamor, but room aesthetics vary in appeal.

Sedona & Around p155

Wigwam Motel $ Each room at this 1937 motel on Route 66 in Holbrook is a self-contained concrete tipi.

La Posada $$ An impressively restored 1930s hacienda in Winslow with artistic, period-styled rooms named for illustrious former guests.

Jerome p160

Connor Hotel $ Twelve restored rooms capture the Victorian period, with pedestal sinks, flower wallpaper and pressed-tin ceilings.

Jerome Grand $$$ Built in 1926 as a hospital, the sturdy fortress plays up its unusual history with halls filled with relics of the past.

Prescott p160

Hotel St Michael $$ Gargoyles, ghosts and a 1925 elevator keep things offbeat at this Victorian-era hotel on Whiskey Row.

Hotel Vendome $$ This dapper inn, dating from 1917, blends up-to-date style with period touches. Ask about the ghost (Abby) in room 16.

Flagstaff p161

Americana Motor Hotel $ Revamped rooms celebrate the '70s with disco balls and space-age decor. Fun vibe and two free drinks at check-in.

Weatherford Hotel $ It's not for everyone – and potentially loud – but this historic hotel in the thick of the action downtown maintains turn-of-the-20th-century authenticity.

Canyon de Chelly p164

Thunderbird Lodge $ This ranch-style hotel with modern rooms is the only lodging in the park. Offers canyon tours.

Spider Rock Campground $ Peaceful Navajo-run campground surrounded by pinyon and juniper trees.

Tucson p169

Tuxon $ Former Motel 6 converted into a minimalist-chic dream. Immediately west of downtown off I-10.

Hotel McCoy $$ Welcoming guests with genuine friendliness and emblazoned with murals, this is our local favorite. Enjoy local craft beer at night and an oatmeal bar in the morning.

Hacienda del Sol Guest Ranch Resort $$$ This relaxing refuge has artist-designed Southwest-style rooms and teems with unique touches.

Bisbee p173

Shady Dell $ Vintage Airstreams feature mid-century decor at this retro-minded trailer park in Bisbee.

Copper Queen Hotel $$ Older than the state of Arizona itself, Copper Queen Hotel opened in 1902 and was John Wayne's Bisbee hotel of choice. Most of the original decor remains.

Torrey p187

Torrey Schoolhouse B&B $$ Sleep in the now-cozy former classrooms of this 1917 schoolhouse.

Skyview $$$ Reach the rooms, some with private hot tubs, through a 'slot canyon' art installation, or spend a starry night in a geodesic dome.

Bryce Canyon National Park & City p192

Lodge at Bryce Canyon $$ Charmingly rustic 1920s lodge; the cabins are a better pick than the generic motel-style rooms.

Bryce Canyon Grand Hotel $$ The large, clean rooms here are a step up from other hotels clustered outside the park entrance.

East Zion p194

Zion Ponderosa Ranch Resort $$ Families love this activity-rich ranch on 6.25 sq miles with swimming pools, climbing walls and mini-golf.

Zion Mountain Ranch $$$ A luxury ranch with six types of cabins, larger lodges and its own herd of roaming bison.

Albuquerque p199

Monterey Motel $ Revived Route 66 motel near Old Town with Tempur-Pedic mattresses, color-changing pool and bar.

Painted Lady $$ Former 19th-century brothel transformed into a bed and brew (beer) and backyard trolley taproom.

Hotel Chaco $$$ Modern Pueblo-style boutique hotel beautifully decorated with precious art; great rooftop bar.

Santa Fe p201

Silver Saddle Motel $ A 1958 Route 66 motel revived in 2022 with a hip California vibe and sleek modern bathrooms.

El Rey Court $$ Revived 1936 auto court with 85 stylish rooms, saltwater pool and bar with live music every Wednesday.

La Fonda $$$ Former end to Santa Fe Trail, then a Harvey House designed by John Gaw Meem and now a luxury hotel on the Plaza.

Taos p204

Doña Luz Inn $$ Each of the eight rooms in this joyful B&B is a work of Southwestern art.

Historic Taos Inn $$ Old inn with wooden furnishings, adobe fireplaces, lots of Southwest charm and a good restaurant.

Roswell Area p208

Roswell Inn $ Rare independent motel updated in 2015 with bargain prices and continental breakfast.

Home2 Suites by Hilton $$ Fresh four-floor Hilton with a pool, gym and buffet breakfast. Roswell's nicest option.

Las Cruces p209

Best Western Mission Inn $ Prettier than your typical chain hotel. Adobe walls and Hispanic art at reception.

Lundeen Inn of the Arts $ Cozy, seven-room family-run alternative to chains. Also hosts a gallery with Southwestern art.

Chandelier Bar, Cosmopolitan

TOOLKIT

The chapters in this section cover the most important topics you'll need to know about in the American Rockies. They're full of nuts-and-bolts information and valuable insights to help you understand and navigate the American Rockies and get the most out of your trip.

Canyonlands National Park (p190)

JENIFOTO/SHUTTERSTOCK

Arriving

Distances are vast and cities are far-flung. While it's easiest to fly in and out of the region, the Rockies definitely lend themselves to road-tripping and major interstates run here from across the country. Limited train services, like the *California Zephyr*, are also available. The largest airports include Las Vegas (LAS), Denver (DEN) and Phoenix (PHX), but smaller international hubs abound.

Visas

Citizens of many countries are eligible for the Visa Waiver Program, which requires prior approval via ESTA. Fill out the online form at least 72 hours prior to departure.

Cell Phones

Data and cell coverage in the West can be spotty; expect to be offline at least some of the time on road trips. The AT&T and Verizon networks have the best rural coverage.

Wi-Fi

Wi-fi is free, fast and widely available at most airports, hotels, restaurants and other public spaces across the western US.

Border Crossings

There are numerous border crossings with Canada and Mexico. Make sure your documents are in order, especially if you are not American. Avoid peak times like weekends and holidays.

From Airports to Popular Destinations

FROM	TO	DURATION
BOZEMAN	YELLOWSTONE NP	1½–2HR
DENVER	ROCKY MOUNTAIN NP	1½HR
LAS VEGAS	GRAND CANYON NP (NORTH/SOUTH RIM)	4½HR
PHOENIX	GRAND CANYON NP (SOUTH RIM)	4HR
ALBUQUERQUE	SANTA FE	1HR
BOZEMAN	GLACIER NP	5HR
DENVER	VAIL	2½HR
DENVER	MOAB	6HR
LAS VEGAS	ZION NP	2½HR
JACKSON HOLE	YELLOWSTONE NP	1HR
SALT LAKE CITY	MOAB	4HR
SALT LAKE CITY	GRAND CANYON (NORTH RIM)	6HR

Getting Around

Having your own wheels is the easiest and often least expensive way to get around. Trains and buses serve major towns but rarely get you to the top sights.

TRAVEL COSTS

Car rental **from $300/ week**

Gas **$3–4.50/gallon**

EV charging **$0.30–0.48/ kWh**

Denver ski shuttle **from $79**

Car Rental

Outside of the cities, renting a car is the way to go. Rentals are widely available at airports, and major companies offer a range of cars, from SUVs to smaller electric cars. Most require drivers to be at least 25 years old but some will rent to younger drivers for an additional fee.

Road Conditions

Road conditions vary, and many wilderness areas are only accessible via unpaved roads. It's worth considering renting a high-clearance all-wheel drive (AWD) vehicle if you plan to spend time on back roads; if you're in the mountains in the winter then AWD is a must.

TIP

Many parts of the West lack adequate cell-phone service, so make sure to download offline maps (or get a paper one) before you embark on your road trip.

THE OPEN ROAD

For decades, the open road and the West have been intertwined in the popular imagination. Route 66 was immortalized in an eponymous TV show from the early 1960s, and memorable scenes from the 1969 motorcycle-driven counterculture classic *Easy Rider* were set in New Mexico and Arizona. The climactic moment in *Thelma & Louise* occurs at the Grand Canyon (but was shot in Moab).

DRIVING ESSENTIALS

Drive on the right

Speed limit is 25–30mph on city roads, and up to 80mph on highways and interstates

Distances between gas stations can be long – watch the tank!

Weather Conditions

Summer monsoons can create flash floods while winter can bring heavy snowfall. In spring, dust storms plague the interstates in the Southwest. Many mountain passes are closed from November through Memorial Day (end of May), and even major interstates like I-70 can shut down for hours or longer because of avalanches or snow-related accidents. Always check traffic conditions before setting out.

Plane

Distances are vast, thus the fastest way to get between major cities in the West is to fly. If you're going to a ski resort or somewhat remote destination (eg Aspen), flying to a local airport may save you the stress of sitting in bumper-to-bumper traffic on the way up Vail Pass. On the flip side, smaller airports have more weather-related cancellations and fewer flights.

Train

Amtrak has three major routes through the Rockies. The *Southwest Chief* follows the general path of Route 66 through Colorado, New Mexico and Arizona. The *California Zephyr* traverses Colorado, Utah and Nevada. *Empire Builder* runs through northern Montana. Trains are relatively slow and expensive but they make for a relaxing scenic experience. Double-decker Superliner trains have spacious lounge cars with panoramic windows.

Money

CURRENCY: US DOLLAR ($)

Tipping

Tipping is not optional. Many service workers make minimum wage and rely on tips. Tip 20% in restaurants and at least $1 per drink. Add about 15% to fares for rideshares. At hotels and inns, $2 to $5 per day is typical for housekeeping.

Credit Cards

Most businesses in the West accept credit cards, debit cards and contactless phone payments, and it's easy to travel without much cash. However, some convenience stores charge a fee to use a card for a purchase under $5. Always keep some cash on you, especially small bills for tips.

ATMs

ATMs are ubiquitous. Most banks charge at least $2 per withdrawal. The Cirrus and Plus systems both have extensive ATM networks.

Taxes

Sales tax varies by state and typically falls between 6% and 9%, and is added on after the advertised price. Hotel taxes are common.

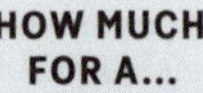

HOW MUCH FOR A...

National park entry
$35

Reusable water bottle at the Grand Canyon
$28

Museum admission
free–$35

Last-minute sun hat
$40

HOW TO... Save on National Park Admission

If you plan to visit more than two national parks, the $80 America the Beautiful Annual Pass is a no-brainer. It grants free entry to over 2000 US federal recreation areas (national parks, monuments and wildlife refuges). The pass covers one vehicle and up to four adults; seniors (62 and older) pay $20 for the Senior Pass, which has the same benefits.

Scan to find out more

GAMBLING

Expect to see casinos across the region, from the Vegas strip to remote (and not so remote) Native American reservations in all states, with the exception of Utah.

HIDDEN TREASURES

When Santa Fe art dealer Forrest Fenn was diagnosed with cancer in 2010, he filled a small bronze chest with gold coins, gold nuggets, jewelry and other items worth an estimated $2 million. Then he buried it and wrote a book laced with cryptic clues, setting off a treasure-hunting frenzy in the Southwest and Rockies. It was finally discovered in Wyoming in 2020, by a man from Michigan. The Lost Dutchman Mine, meanwhile, is a legendary gold mine hidden in the craggy Superstition Mountains east of Phoenix.

Accommodations

Camping

Camping options abound, both in state and national parks and on private property. States and counties typically have their own reservation systems, while many campsites in national parks and forests can be booked up to six months in advance at recreation.gov. Remember: camping is extremely popular in summer and if you didn't book ahead, you may be out of luck. However, some sites are walk-in only, and dispersed camping on Bureau of Land Management (BLM) and national forest land is typically free.

Resorts

Resort options vary widely, from the glittering towers of Las Vegas to the spas of Santa Fe, from dude ranches in Wyoming to Colorado ski lodges. Pick a theme that appeals to you and immerse yourself in the activities that are offered: from horseback riding and fly-fishing to skiing, mountain biking and spa days.

Offbeat Options

The West is dotted with fun and offbeat accommodations. Spend the night in an ecofriendly Earthship – built from tires, glass bottles and, yes, earth – or in a converted school bus near Taos. Or why not sleep in an Airstream or sky dome? Check vacation rental websites for other funky options.

Historic Hotels

Many cities are home to historic hotels, most dating to the turn of the 20th century. Stepping inside is like stepping back in time, with communal areas decked out in antique furnishings, Victorian-era decor and art. National parks, meanwhile, have a number of historic lodges that blend in with the spectacular surrounding landscape: an architectural style known as National Park Service Rustic.

HOW MUCH FOR A NIGHT IN A...

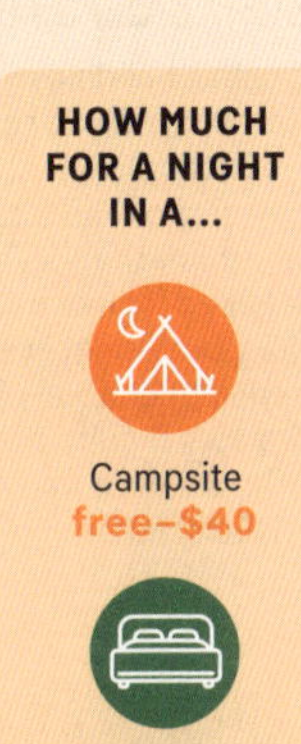

Campsite
free–$40

Motel
$100–250

Resort
from $250

Cabins, Yurts & Glamping

If you love the outdoors, but aren't keen on the idea of pitching a tent or sleeping on hard ground, you have options. Many state and national parks have cabins or yurts for rent – reserve ahead. Glamping is more often available at private resorts in spectacular locations, and offers a taste of the outdoors in luxury surrounds.

RENTALS & AIRBNBS

Across the West, you'll find thousands of vacation rentals for short- and long-term stays. Companies like Airbnb and Vrbo make it easy to find unique places to stay. Not everyone is thrilled with the ever-growing expansion, however, which has only exacerbated the housing crisis, particularly in ski resorts. Locals cite the rise in housing prices and lack of affordable rentals as more properties are taken off the market to become Airbnbs. There's also the negative effect on communities as long-term residents are displaced by transients.

CLOCKWISE FROM TOP LEFT: RUSLAN IVANTSOV/SHUTTERSTOCK, TREKANDSHOOT/SHUTTERSTOCK, CHERI ALGUIRE/SHUTTERSTOCK, SOMCHAI SOM/SHUTTERSTOCK

Family Travel

There are wolves and dinosaur bones, sand dunes and ski slopes, Ancestral Puebloan structures and giant rocks, plus tales of Billy the Kid and Geronimo. In other words, the Rockies and the Southwest are great places for a family vacation. Some of the most otherworldly landscapes jolt minds of all ages into states of wonder, remaining memorable for years.

Hydration

Keeping kids hydrated – crucial in the desert and at high altitudes – can be a challenge, so remember, it's easier to stay hydrated than to rehydrate. One good strategy is to begin each day by drinking water – set a family rule that everyone has to drink a liter or half-liter (depending on each person's size) every morning (drinking more throughout the day).

Strollers & Car Seats

Most public buildings are suitable for strollers, but baby carriers are a better option for hiking outside of short, accessible trails in some public parks. Car seats are required for infants and most children, but height, weight and age requirements vary by state. Many states require booster seats for children who are under 57in (145cm) tall.

Discounts

Children's discounts are available for everything from museum admission to ski passes. The definition of a 'child' varies, but usually means kids under 12 years old (kids under two are often free). Many restaurants also offer less-expensive children's menus.

Diaper-Changing Stations

Baby-changing tables are found in most women's restrooms and in a growing number of men's and all-gender/family restrooms. In multi-stall restrooms, tables are typically either found in the main area or in larger wheelchair-accessible stalls.

BEST ATTRACTIONS FOR FAMILIES

Dinosaur National Monument, Colorado & Utah (p79)

Touch thousands of prehistoric fossils.

Yellowstone National Park, Wyoming (p92)

Erupting geysers, bubbling mud pools and massive bison.

Grand Canyon, Arizona (p147)

Take a mule ride beneath the North Rim.

Big Sky, Montana (p101)

Big Sky is big skiing, with over 400in of powder a year.

Rafting and Mountain Biking in Moab, Utah (p183)

From white water to slickrock: yee-haw fun in a magnificent desert landscape.

BE A JUNIOR RANGER

Kids can earn a very cool badge through the Junior Ranger Program, available at numerous national park sites and countless state parks. To earn the badge, kids complete an activity book with questions and games, and for some parks complete an activity (such as a hike, while making observations along the way). The program is aimed at five- to 12-year-olds. And some parks have a range of activities for younger vs older kids, as well as particular specialties – like nighttime stargazing, paleontology or sound exploration. Adults can enjoy it too, and everyone is likely to gain a deeper understanding of the surrounding environment.

Health & Safe Travel

INSURANCE

Travel insurance to cover theft, loss and medical problems is essential, especially for international visitors. Domestic visitors should confirm they have proper coverage. Some policies do not cover 'risky' activities such as riding a motorcycle or skiing, so read the fine print. Given upheavals like COVID-19, trip-cancellation insurance is a worthwhile expense.

Heat & Altitude

During the summer, you'll need to prepare for the heat, when midday temperatures can soar. Carry plenty of water and electrolyte tablets to avoid dehydration, wear a wide-brimmed hat and use sunscreen. When arriving at high altitudes from sea level, expect some fatigue, maybe a headache and other mild symptoms. Stay hydrated and don't overdo it.

Bears

Black bears are fairly common in the Rockies, but so long as you use food-storage lockers or bear canisters in campsites, they are rarely a problem. An encounter with a more aggressive grizzly, however, is a much greater risk. In Wyoming, Montana and Idaho, always carry bear spray and make plenty of noise when hiking.

CANNABIS

Recreational marijuana is legal for adults 21 and over in most states, with the exception of Idaho, Wyoming and Utah.

WILDLIFE ROAD CROSSINGS

Bear Crossing

Cattle & Livestock Crossing

Deer Crossing

Elk Crossing

Moose Crossing

Wildfires

There's no longer a wildfire season in the West; destructive blazes can ignite at any time of year. Please respect posted campfire bans. Risks associated with wildfires go beyond the flames; wildfire smoke can cause severe health issues for both people and their pets.

RATTLESNAKES TO MEGAFAUNA

An encounter with a rattlesnake sunning itself in the middle of the trail is not uncommon. Bites are rarely fatal; stay calm and seek medical attention. In the Rockies, you'll see moose, bison and elk – all massive animals that can sprint incredibly fast. Keep your distance (no selfies) and remember that walking your dog can trigger an attack.

FROM LEFT: POR RED HERRING/SHUTTERSTOCK, LUKAS GOJDA/SHUTTERSTOCK

Food, Drink & Nightlife

When to Eat

Breakfast (7am to 10am, later on weekends) Tuck into pancakes and eggs at a diner or head to a cafe for pastries and coffee.

Lunch (noon to 2pm) Often consists of one-item dishes such as sandwiches, burritos or burgers.

Dinner (5pm to 9pm) Typically heavier than lunch and often complemented with appetizers and desserts.

MENU DECODER

Calabacitas Squash, corn and chile side dish.

Breakfast burrito Popular on-the-go meal: flour tortilla filled with scrambled eggs, potatoes, cheese, salsa and meat.

Entree Always confusing to non-Americans – the word for the main course.

Frito pie Bowl of Fritos (deep-fried corn chips) mixed with chile, cheese and onions.

Fry bread A Navajo classic that can be eaten savory ('Navajo taco') or sweet.

Huevos rancheros Fried eggs and pinto or black beans atop a corn tortilla, typically smothered in a red-chile sauce.

Posole Rich stew made with hominy (dried corn) and pork or chicken.

Sopaipilla Puffy fried dough served with honey, either eaten with a meal to cut the heat of the chile or as a dessert.

Where to Eat

Breweries and pubs Many drinking establishments also serve food, from basic bar food to more innovative dishes.

Cafes and bakeries Open during daytime, cafes are good for casual meals, sweet treats or coffee.

Food halls Typically six or more vendors; a variety of diverse cuisines.

Food trucks Kitchen on wheels, parked where hungry pedestrians are found and often at breweries.

Picnics Some of your most memorable meals may be at a picnic site with outrageous views. BYOF.

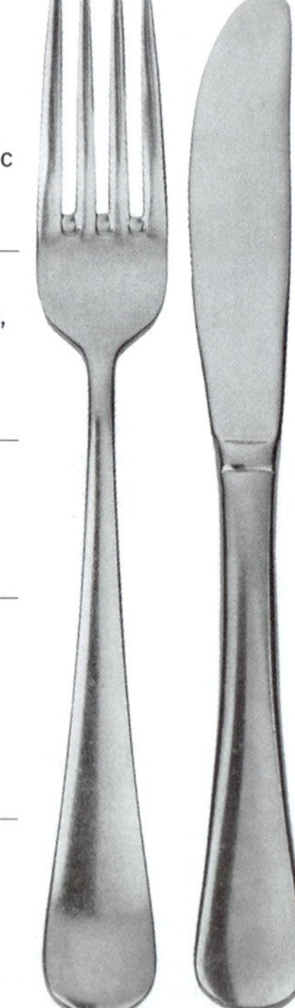

HOW TO... Order a Craft Beer

With hundreds of craft breweries throughout the West, enjoying a cold glass of beer is a quintessential experience. Across the region, beer nerds sip and savor as they would wine, and some restaurants even have 'beer sommeliers.' It's not surprising, then, that stepping into a tasting room or brewery means navigating lots of options. Here are a few tips for handling it like a local:

- Be specific about the type of beer you'd like – hoppy IPAs are a favorite, while tart farmhouse sours are more of a specialty choice.
- Specify the pour size, typically a pint or a smaller 10oz glass.
- At breweries with numerous beers, consider a 'flight': a sampler of four to six different beers in 4oz to 7oz pours.
- If you want craft beer to go, buy a six-pack or a 'growler', a 64oz glass jug.

HOW MUCH FOR A...

Coffee
$3–6

Breakfast burrito
$8–12

Food-truck meal
$10–20

Burger
$15–20

12in gourmet pizza
$18–30

Dinner for two (no drinks)
from $50

Pint of craft beer
$7–10

Margarita
$12–20

HOW TO... Order New Mexican Food

New Mexico is the only American state with an official state question – red or green? – which you will inevitably be asked every time you order a New Mexican dish, like a smothered burrito or enchilada. It refers to the kind of chile (yes, with an 'e') you want with your food. There is no rule of thumb as to which is hotter, as it depends on the particular crop, but green chiles often have slightly more kick. The red and green chiles are actually the same fruit and can come from the same plant; red has just been harvested later. You can always ask your server which might be more to your taste. You can also order Christmas-style – both red and green. While most dishes can swing either way, carne adovada is, by definition, tender pork simmered in red chile.

Some chiles are made with meat, though many are meatless; if you're a vegetarian, it's a good idea to clarify. And some are thickened with a little flour, so if you have gluten sensitivities, don't hesitate to check.

For the spice-sensitive, see if sopaipillas are on the menu – a few bites, coated with honey, do more to cut the heat than a glass of water. (Even a tortilla with honey will do, if sopaipillas are unavailable.) Sour cream and beer help, too. If you're still trepidatious, order the chile on the side.

New Mexican Chiles

Fast fact: 52,000 tons of chile were harvested in New Mexico in 2023. Over 83% were green. The state's most famous variety is the Hatch chile.

PICURIS BISON

For centuries, bison were an important part of the diet of many Native American tribes. Northern New Mexico's Picuris Pueblo, for example, would send hunters out to the plains east of the Sangre de Cristo Mountains in search of the wild herds, also known as American buffalo; the Pueblo also traded for bison products with tribes from the Plains. Then, the animals were nearly hunted to extinction with the arrival of Europeans.

The Picuris Pueblo began raising its own bison herd in the 1990s, as did other tribes around the nation; today 83 tribes belong to the Intertribal Bison Cooperative, which manages over 20,000 head – 50 of which belong to Picuris. For a time, the Pueblo sold bison meat to shops and restaurants around the region, but they were forced to suspend their business operations by government regulators. Under federal law, bison are considered an 'exotic species,' meaning that meat processing must meet certain standards above and beyond those for, say, cows, sheep and pigs. These requirements are simply too onerous for a small enterprise tucked away in the New Mexico mountains, so sales ceased. The irony seems to be lost on lawmakers that bison are in fact indigenous to North America (hence not exotic) while domesticated cows, sheep and pigs were first brought to the continent by the Spanish.

For now, while working to change the laws, Picuris distributes meat to its tribal members only, and it's typically free of charge.

Responsible Travel

Climate Change & Travel

It's impossible to ignore the impact we have when traveling; Lonely Planet urges all travelers to engage with their travel carbon footprint, which will mainly come from air travel. While there often isn't an alternative, travellers can look to minimize the number of flights they take, opt for newer aircraft and use cleaner ground transportation, such as trains. One proposed solution – purchasing carbon offsets – unfortunately does not cancel out the impact of individual flights. While most destinations will depend on air travel for the foreseeable future, for now, pursuing ground-based travel where possible is the best course of action.

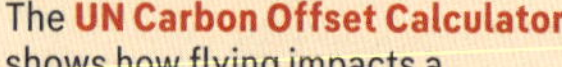

The **UN Carbon Offset Calculator** shows how flying impacts a household's emissions

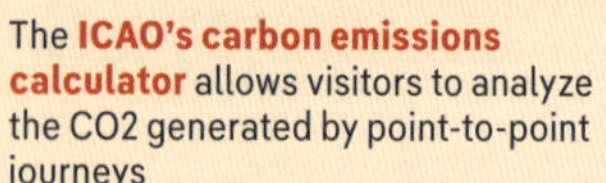

The **ICAO's carbon emissions calculator** allows visitors to analyze the CO2 generated by point-to-point journeys

Go Vegetarian

Animal husbandry is one of the major drivers of climate change. Reduce your impact by choosing plant-based meals and materials when you can, or by going vegan all together.

Go Electric

If you're renting a car, consider going electric. You'll find EV charging stations at a growing number of places, including hotels, grocery stores and campgrounds. Find the nearest charging station at chargepoint.com or chargehub.com.

You can learn the stories of individual families on tours led by local Native Americans at Monument Valley Navajo Tribal Park and at Canyon de Chelly and Bears Ears National Monuments.

There are more than 45 International Dark Sky Parks in the Rockies and the Southwest, where you can take in interstellar views. Some host ranger-led astronomy programs. Visit darkskies.com for locations.

SLEEP UNDER THE STARS

Camping is a great way to go green while also immersing yourself in nature. You'll find many enchanting settings for pitching a tent or glamping in style.

NATIVE AMERICAN ART

Some Native Americans earn a living by making art, including weavings, silverwork, ceramics and jewelry. Some of it is of world-class quality (with prices to match). Try to buy directly from the artist.

Travel by Train

Travel on Amtrak's *California Zephyr* from Chicago to San Francisco over the Rocky Mountains or the *Southwest Chief* from Chicago to LA, passing through New Mexico and Arizona.

Pack it in, pack it out: never leave behind trash when hiking or camping.

Seek out hotels with sustainability policies certified by a credible organization like LEED or EarthCheck.

Get Thrifty

Go secondhand shopping at flea markets, thrift stores and vintage shops instead of buying new. Every city and even small towns have secondhand stores packed with treasures waiting to be discovered.

Respect the Wildlife

Stay at least 50yd away from all wildlife in national parks. Never approach or feed an animal, and if your presence changes the animal's behavior in any way you're too close.

Tip Street Performers

Whether performing on the street or playing in a bar or restaurant, musicians are the lifeblood of many cities. Show your appreciation with a tip in cash or through an app.

Grand Canyon Trust

Grand Canyon Trust *(grandcanyontrust.org)* works to preserve the Colorado Plateau's landscapes and ecosystems. Volunteer with it or collect data for its studies while you travel.

The Green Crown

Renewable energy – particularly solar and wind – has grown exponentially in the West, despite efforts to cut its funding. Solar panels are a common sight throughout this sun-drenched region.

RESOURCES

happycow.net
Vegetarian and vegan restaurants across the country.

environmentamerica.org
A citizen-based environmental advocacy organization.

thedyrt.com
Top campsites across the country.

CLOCKWISE FROM TOP LEFT: TOMMASO LIZZUL/SHUTTERSTOCK, BIGTUNAONLINE/SHUTTERSTOCK, MARK YOUSO/SHUTTERSTOCK

LGBTIQ+ Travelers

Attitudes vary enormously from state to state. Big cities like Vegas, Phoenix and Denver all have welcoming LGBTIQ+ communities. Unfortunately, bigotry still exists. In rural areas – particularly Wyoming, Montana and Idaho – it's unwise to be openly out, as violence and verbal abuse do occur. When in doubt, assume locals follow a 'don't ask, don't tell' policy.

TAG-Approved Hotels

Created by the **International Gay & Lesbian Travel Association** *(iglta.org)*, the Travel Advocacy Group brings together LGBTIQ-friendly hotels, which are approved for membership based on their commitment to serving and supporting the LGBTIQ+ community. Fortunately, plenty of top-rated Southwestern hotels have joined. To find a TAG-approved hotel, it is easiest to visit city tourist-office websites as most feature LGBTIQ+ travel information pages. Thunderbird Lodge in Downtown Las Vegas is in the process of converting to an LGBTIQ+ resort. Other resources for gay-friendly accommodations include outtraveler.com, gaycities.com and travelgay.com.

VEGAS WEDDINGS

Same-sex marriage has been legal in Nevada since 2014, opening Vegas' huge wedding industry up to all couples. Now, you can get an express wedding with an Elvis impersonator to do the honors at one of Sin City's numerous chapels, including the **Gay Chapel of Las Vegas** *(gaychapeloflasvegas.com)*, which specializes in LGBTIQ+ weddings and vow renewals.

Gay Rodeo

The **Colorado Gay Rodeo Association** *(cgrarodeo.com)* is among the country's biggest and best gay-centric rodeos, featuring traditional events like bull riding and barrel racing as well as not-so-traditional events like wild drag racing and goat dressing. Any gender can compete together, a nod to non-binary and trans cowfolk. Held every July in Denver.

GROUP TRIPS

Out Of Office *(outofoffice.com)* offers some of the best gay group adventures in the Southwest, including a nine-day Grand Canyon rafting trip. It also designs upscale bespoke trips, including a self-driving trip that covers Las Vegas, northern Arizona and southern Utah. **HE Travel** *(hetravel.com)* offers a cycling tour on the Arizona Mission Trail and another trip around Salt Lake City.

LGBTIQ+ Resources

Advocate *(advocate.com/travel)* has news, LGBTIQ+ travel features and destination guides. **Damron** *(damron.com)* is a gay travel guide and app. The **LGBT National Help Center** *(lgbthotline.org)* has counseling, information and referrals. **Out Traveler** *(outtraveler.com)* is a free online magazine with travel tips, destination guides and resort reviews.

GAY STAYS

The lodging website and app **MisterB&B** lists gay-friendly hotels, apartments, private rooms and vacation homes for rent. There are numerous options all across the country, and hosts are well vetted to ensure all visitors are welcome.

NITO/SHUTTERSTOCK

Accessible Travel

If you have a physical disability, the US can be an accommodating place, though you'll need to plan your travels carefully. Bigger cities are generally more accessible, though you'll also find accessible state and national parks and other attractions sprinkled across the region.

Access Pass

The free America the Beautiful Access Pass provides no-fee entry to national parks and other federal lands for US citizens or permanent residents with disabilities. Visit store.usgs.gov/access-pass for details.

Airport

Most US airports provide barrier-free paths and accessible services throughout their terminals, including guided mobility assistance at designated locations. If a wheelchair is required upon arrival, be sure to request it in advance through your airline.

Accommodations

Hotels built since 1993 must meet modern accessibility requirements. Major chains usually have rooms adapted for accessibility needs, but you should book in advance and double-check they have what you require. Holiday rentals and older properties may not be accessible.

NATIONAL PARKS

Many national and some state parks and recreation areas have wheelchair-accessible paved, graded-dirt or boardwalk trails. Most national park websites have an accessibility page giving complete details on the park's accessible attractions.

Skiing

Many ski resorts offer programs for visitors with cognitive and physical disabilities. Ski and snowboarding instruction are provided using specialized equipment.

Santa Fe

With its historic plaza, downtown Santa Fe is a top location for wheelchair-accessible walking tours. Nearby accessible sights include the Railyard District and farmers market, and Museum Hill.

ACCESSIBLE PUBLIC TRANSIT

Public transportation in cities must be made accessible to all, including priority seating and wheelchair securement. Drivers typically are trained to assist passengers with disabilities to board or exit. Expect braille signage and stop announcements.

RESOURCES

AccessibleGO *(accessiblego.com)* provides accessibility details and community reviews for hotels, flights and more.

Society for Accessible Travel & Hospitality *(sath.org)* brings together organizations serving travelers with disabilities. It provides tons of helpful travel tips and access info.

Handiscover *(handiscover.com)* is useful for booking accessible accommodations.

Be My Eyes *(bemyeyes.com)* is an excellent app that helps blind and visually impaired travelers navigate their environment through AI and live video.

Those who want to share that they have a non-visible disability should check out the **Hidden Disabilities Sunflower Program** *(hdsunflower.com/us)*. Users wear a sunflower-emblazoned lanyard, which alerts airports and other places that they need extra help.

Severe Weather

From snowstorms to scorching UV rays and wildfires to flash floods, the Rockies and the Southwestern deserts demand that you come prepared for all types of weather. Dramatic elevation changes mean conditions change rapidly. If you use common sense and take the weather seriously, you'll be fine. But a cavalier attitude and lack of preparation can quickly turn a sudden storm into a life-threatening situation.

Snow

Snowstorms are part and parcel of life in the Rockies, and they're most common from October through May, at all elevations. Seasonal roads are typically snowed under from mid-October through Memorial Day (end of May) or even later (early July in Glacier National Park). Even places that you might not expect, like the Grand Canyon's North Rim, can remain closed well into June.

Winter road conditions can be perilous during a storm, and major interstates as far south as Arizona can shut down because of blizzards. Make sure your vehicle has AWD and snow tires, and, most importantly, beware of other drivers. Multivehicle pile-ups happen every year. If you're visiting for a ski trip, the most stress-free way of getting from the airport to your resort is to take a dedicated shuttle. It saves the hassle of renting a car and the white-knuckle driving experience.

Heat & Sun

Most places in the Rockies and the Southwest are at a higher elevation (minimum 4000ft), which means that more damaging ultraviolet (UV) rays reach the ground. At 5000ft of elevation, UV rays can be up to 20% stronger; at 9000ft, it can be up to 36% stronger, and so on. Always wear sunscreen, long sleeves, sunglasses and a wide-brimmed hat.

Heat is the number one killer across the Southwest, particularly in the Grand Canyon and the desert areas. There's little humidity in the air, which can disguise the actual temperature while at the same time sucking all the moisture out of your body. On really hot days, you won't even feel the sweat before it evaporates. Staying hydrated – you need electrolytes, too – is the critical first step in staying safe. Always carry a big jug of water (minimum 1 gallon) in your car, and avoid intense outdoor activity between 10am and 4pm.

LAYER UP

On a sunny summer day in Denver, the thermometer can top out above 100°F. But a mere 74 miles west, on top of the Mount Blue Sky Scenic Byway at 14,130ft, it can be 40°F and pelting rain, hail or snow, with the summit wrapped in thick clouds and icy winds buffeting the unprepared. There are plenty of other places in the world that love to trot out the old weather cliché 'four seasons in a day,' but the Rockies really do deliver. When you're packing for your trip, make sure to bring along lightweight rain gear (hypothermia on summer hikes and horseback rides is real) and a fleece or down puffy. It's 100°F in the shade – do you really need a puffy? Trust us, nights in both the mountains and the desert can be much colder than you expect.

Flash Floods

Local thunderstorms – sometimes known as monsoons – can dump massive amounts of water into a small area. Generally, the West's arid landscape is unable to absorb the water and so it instead flows through a wash and into the nearest stream or river, often exceeding the waterway's capacity in a matter of minutes and increasing the flow rate by a factor of 1000 or more. This is what's known as a flash flood. They are extremely common and extremely dangerous. Do not try to drive your vehicle through flowing water; it will be swept away. Do not try to wade or swim through a flood; you will be pummeled senseless, stripped of all your clothing and drown. Flash floods are most dangerous for canyon hikers in the Southwest, because you can't see the sky, and a localized storm miles away can wind up draining into your canyon with no warning. Always check flood forecasts before heading out for the day.

Altitude

No matter how in shape you are, nothing can prepare your body for the shock of oxygen-thin air. If you're coming from sea level, expect to take a day or more acclimatizing to the elevation change throughout the Rockies. Expect to feel short of breath at lower elevations like Denver (5280ft) or Salt Lake City (4226ft); you may also have a slight headache or nausea. The higher you go (eg Vail, base elevation 8120ft), the more pronounced the effects will feel. There are a few things you can do to minimize the impact, however. Drink plenty of water and avoid alcohol. Get enough sleep. And finally, take it slow. In most cases, your body will adapt with enough time. If you're planning on summiting a peak, break your ascent up into two days. Another high-altitude danger to watch out for: lightning strikes. Summer thunderstorms tend to roll in after noon, so if you're climbing a peak, be sure to turn around by lunch. Colorado and Arizona have two of the highest lightning fatality rates in the US.

Wildfires

Wildfires ravage the Western states year-round, though they're most common in summer. Decreasing precipitation, poor forest management, high winds and large stands of deadwood (generally brought on by beetle infestations) all combine to create prime conditions for blazing infernos that race across the landscape, leaving devastation in their wake and filling the sky with raining ash and a terrifying orange glow. The causes of wildfires are numerous (lightning strikes, downed power lines, arson), but some of them can be prevented. First and foremost, respect all campfire bans. Maybe you've already bought your s'mores ingredients and are tempted to ignore a local ban: please don't. Other causes range from the mundane (cigarette butts) to the surprising (blown-out tires). Wildfires are a common phenomenon and they move fast: stay abreast of blazes on your trip out West, especially if you're camping.

Nuts & Bolts

OPENING HOURS

The following is a general guideline for opening hours. Shorter hours may apply during low seasons, when some venues close completely.

Banks and offices 9am to 5pm Monday to Friday; sometimes 9am to noon Saturday

Bars and pubs 4pm to midnight, some until 2am

Casinos 24/7 in Las Vegas

Restaurants Breakfast 7am to 10am, lunch 11am to 2:30pm, dinner 5pm to 9pm

Shops 9am to 7pm Monday to Saturday; some open noon to 5pm Sunday, or until evening in tourist areas

PUBLIC HOLIDAYS

On the following holidays, banks, schools and government offices (including post offices) are closed, and transportation, museums and other services may operate on a Sunday schedule. Holidays falling on a weekend are usually observed the following Monday.

New Year's Day January 1

Martin Luther King Jr Day Third Monday of January

Presidents' Day Third Monday of February

Memorial Day Last Monday of May

Juneteenth June 19

Independence Day July 4

Labor Day First Monday of September

Indigenous Peoples' Day (Columbus Day) Second Monday of October

Veterans Day November 11

Thanksgiving Fourth Thursday of November

Christmas Day December 25

Language

Most people speak English, but Spanish is also common; over 30 Native languages are spoken in the region.

Smoking

State laws vary but, generally, smoking is not allowed in most public areas, bars, restaurants, park buildings or thermal areas.

GOOD TO KNOW

Time zones
Mountain Time (UTC-7/6), Pacific Time (UTC-8/7) or Mountain Standard Time (UTC-7)

Country calling code
+1

Emergency number
911

Population
26.17 million

Weights & Measures

The US uses the imperial system, with mountain heights measured in feet (0.3m) and road distances in miles (1.6km). Weights are measured in pounds (0.45kg) and gasoline is sold by the gallon (3.8L). Temperatures are in Fahrenheit.

Toilets

Look for free public restrooms inside national parks, campsites, public buildings, libraries, gas stations and some transportation hubs.

Electricity

Type A and B; 120V/60Hz

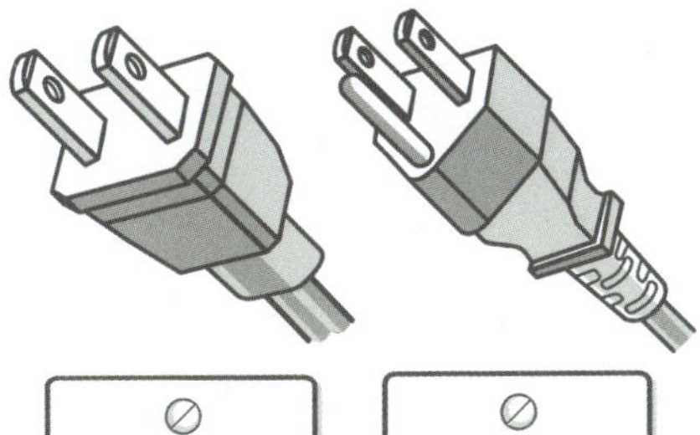

BRINGING ITEMS INTO THE US

The US has fairly strict rules regarding what you can bring into the country, so plan carefully before getting underway. In general, you're not allowed to bring any agricultural products (food, vegetables, plants etc) into the country. Bakery items and prepared foods (coffee, tea, honey) are permitted. You can bring in 1L of alcohol for personal use (but not if you're under 21). Although recreational or medical marijuana is legal in some states, it is illegal to bring marijuana and cannabis-infused products into the US. The exception is for CBD oil with less than 0.3% THC on a dry weight basis.

CLOCKWISE FROM LEFT: RILAKKUMAXX/SHUTTERSTOCK, MEGA PIXEL/SHUTTERSTOCK

STORYBOOK

Our writers delve deep into different aspects of Rockies life.

Valley outside Telluride (p77)

BRINLIETRAVELS/SHUTTERSTOCK

A HISTORY OF THE AMERICAN ROCKIES IN 15 PLACES

From snowcapped peaks to desert canyons both big and small, the centuries-old ingenuity of the Ancestral Puebloans to the get-rich-quick prospectors – and their alter ego, the environmentalists – the American Rockies have long stood apart. It's a place of big skies, big dreams and profound ties with the natural world.

IF THERE'S ONE word that sums up the history of the West, it's this: water. Long before the Europeans arrived, Ancestral Puebloans faced the same challenges that people do today: how do you feed yourself in an arid environment? Although no one knows for sure, drought seemed to be a principal driver in the migration of many Puebloans away from the Four Corners region to the banks of the Rio Grande.

The first Europeans were Spaniards moving north from Mexico. They founded Santa Fe in 1610 and established land grants as far off as present-day Colorado. But it was no more than a precarious foothold in a harsh environment, and the waves of fur trappers, miners and ranchers who arrived from the East led similarly Hobbesian lives, with an emphasis on 'brutish and short.' It wasn't until the arrival of the railroad in the 1860s, followed by the damming of major rivers, that it became possible for the region to support large numbers of people. But even as the population in the arid West continues to shoot upward today, the main issue throughout history – who gets the water from the melting snow and how do they turn it into sustenance – remains unchanged.

1. Grand Canyon National Park, Arizona

THE POWER OF EROSION

If you really want to start at the beginning, there's no better place than the Grand Canyon, which showcases a remarkably well preserved, 1.84-billion-year slice of geological history. In these exposed layers, where the Colorado River continues to carve into progressively older rock, half of the earth's lifespan is revealed. The bottom layers of Vishnu schist and Zoroaster granite are among the oldest exposed rocks on earth, with sediments offering evidence that the canyon region lay beneath an ancient sea floor two billion years ago. Learn more on a hike into the canyon, at the Yavapai Geology Museum and along the Trail of Time.

For more on the Grand Canyon National Park, see p150.

2. Dinosaur National Monument, Colorado & Utah

WHERE THE ALLOSAURUS AND THE DIPLODOCUS ROAMED

The Rockies were a very different place 150 million years ago. There were no mountains in the Jurassic, just a flat, lush plain, braided with rivers and covered with ferns and conifers. Dinosaurs of many kinds and sizes lived and died beside those rivers; their bones were covered in successive layers of sediment, forming what became known as the Morrison Formation, arguably the richest dinosaur fossil bed in the world. This site, straddling the border of Colorado and Utah, is one of the few places on earth where you can reach out and touch a dinosaur fossil, snarling in its final pose.

For more on Dinosaur National Monument, see p79.

3. Mesa Verde National Park, Colorado

NORTH AMERICA'S LARGEST CLIFF DWELLINGS

The incredible cliff dwellings of Mesa Verde National Park were built during the 12th century CE by the Ancestral Puebloans. By that time, they had already occupied the Four Corners region for over 1100 years, living and farming the valleys and mesa tops. These dwellings, built in vertiginous natural alcoves and exhibiting sophisticated masonry, were accessed via wood-pole ladders, stairways cut into the cliffs and narrow tunnels. The Puebloans abruptly left Mesa Verde in around 1300 for reasons still unknown. Today, Mesa Verde is the largest and best-known Ancestral Puebloan archaeological site, but by no means the only one.

For more on Mesa Verde National Park, see p74.

Mesa Verde National Park (p74)

NAGEL PHOTOGRAPHY/SHUTTERSTOCK

4. Indian Pueblo Cultural Center, New Mexico

SOUTHWEST HERITAGE

Today, descendants of the Ancestral Puebloans live in Pueblo communities along New Mexico's Rio Grande, and in the Acoma, Zuni and Laguna Pueblos in northwest New Mexico. Some of the oldest links with the Ancestral Puebloans are found among the Hopi tribe of northern Arizona. The mesa-top village of Old Oraibi has been inhabited since the 1100s, making it the oldest continuously inhabited settlement in North America. The lives of the Puebloans changed forever with the arrival of the Spanish in 1540, and early contact eventually turned into bloodshed at the Acoma Pueblo in 1598. In Albuquerque, you can learn more about the 19 Pueblo nations who still call New Mexico home.

For more on the Indian Pueblo Cultural Center, see p200.

5. Santa Fe, New Mexico

SPANISH EXPANSION

Originally the home of New Mexico's first Spanish governor in 1610, the one-story adobe Palace of the Governors, which overlooks the Santa Fe Plaza, is the oldest public building in continuous use in the US. It was occupied by Puebloans following a rebellion in 1680, and again by US soldiers in 1846 at the start of the Mexican-American War, after which the US annexed the entirety of the Southwest. Its Spanish Revival style is reflected in the architecture across downtown Santa Fe, and the plaza it overlooks has a long history as a marketplace.

For more on Santa Fe, see p201.

6. The Lewis and Clark Interpretive Center, Montana

THE LOUISIANA PURCHASE

In 1803 Thomas Jefferson paid $15 million to Napoleon and with the stroke of a pen doubled the size of the United States. The very next year, Lewis and Clark were dispatched to map 'Louisiana,' establish sovereignty over the Native tribes, and find a river passage between the Great Plains and the Pacific. Along the way they picked up a Canadian trapper and his Shoshone wife, Sacagawea, who famously served as an interpreter for the group. Learn more about the hardships they faced on the Upper

Missouri River at the Lewis and Clark National Historic Trail Interpretive Center.

For more on Lewis and Clark, see p108.

7. Temple Square, Salt Lake City

THE MORMON CHURCH

On July 24, 1847, Brigham Young, soon after entering the Salt Lake Valley, famously declared, 'This is the place.' Facing persecution and prosecution (for polygamy) in the East, Mormon settlers fled the United States and began establishing communities in what was then Mexican territory. Temple Square in downtown Salt Lake City is still the center of the Church of Jesus Christ of Latter-day Saints. Anchored by the soaring Salt Lake Temple (open only to church members in good standing), this 35-acre area encompasses religious and historic buildings, as well as museums that are free to visit and open to all.

For more on Temple Square, see p179.

8. Pikes Peak, Colorado

THAR'S GOLD IN THEM THAR HILLS

In January 1859, gold was discovered in Colorado's snowy Front Range, and the race for the nugget was on. Prospectors crossing the Great Plains repeated the mantra 'Pikes Peak or Bust,' as the mountain was a key landmark for those traveling West. But even though it gave its name to one of the largest gold rushes in American history – it drew an estimated 100,000 people to the new territory – Pikes Peak was, in fact, gold-free. Today you can hike, drive or take a train up to the summit of the mountain that went on to inspire the lyrics to 'America the Beautiful.'

For more on Pikes Peak, see p81.

9. Yellowstone National Park, Wyoming, Montana & Idaho

THE WORLD'S FIRST NATIONAL PARK

President Ulysses S Grant signed the Yellowstone National Park Protection Act in 1872, establishing Yellowstone as the world's first national park. The park's creation was spurred on not just by conservationists, but also by lobbyists for the Northern Pacific Railroad, who had their eyes on the almighty tourist dollar. And indeed, this unlikely partnership went on to influence the creation of several other Western parks, like the Grand Canyon. While the establishment of the park system was a victory for the environment and public lands, it also had a dark side: the eviction of the Native peoples who originally lived there.

For more on Yellowstone National Park, see p92.

10. Shootout at the OK Corral, Arizona

ACCURACY IS EVERYTHING

'Here lies Lester Moore. Four slugs from a .44. No Les, no more.' The epitaphs at Boothill Cemetery tell you everything you need to know about living – and dying – in Tombstone in the late 1800s. In 1877 prospector Ed Schieffelin struck it rich after being told the only rock he'd find out here would be his own tombstone, and the name stuck. Like all boomtowns, it had its fair share of showdowns at high noon, none more famous than the 30-second gunfight between the lawman Wyatt Earp and the Clanton-McLaury gang. See it reenacted daily.

For more on the OK Corral, see p175.

11. The Mob Museum, Las Vegas

BRIGHT LIGHTS, SIN CITY

Yes, America's favorite party town owes much of its existence (surprise, surprise) to organized crime. After Nevada legalized gambling in 1931, more and more criminals began to drift in to this back-of-beyond railroad hub, using their business expertise – gambling, prostitution, debt collection and money laundering – to turn it into the world's foremost gaming resort. Early movers and shakers were small-time crooks and crooked cops, but once New Yorker Bugsy Siegel built the Flamingo in 1946, the big boys took over and Vegas never looked back. Learn more about the Mob connection at this engaging museum.

For more on the Mob Museum, see p135.

12. Route 66, Kingman, Arizona

GET YOUR KICKS

Stretching from Chicago to Los Angeles, Route 66 was established in 1926 as one of America's first interstate roads. It rose to national attention during the Dust Bowl (1930–39), when some 2.5 million displaced farmers from the Great Plains set off down the Mother Road. In the prosperous 1950s,

Maroon Bells (p70), Aspen

Route 66 took on a new identity as families with flashy new automobiles drove to the Pacific on what has since become a hallowed American tradition: the road trip. Decommissioned in 1984, the now legendary highway was saved from obscurity by a small-town barber in Seligman, Arizona. Learn all about it at Kingman's Route 66 Museum.

For more on Route 66, see p167.

13. Minidoka National Historic Site, Idaho

THE CASUALTIES OF WARTIME

During WWII, concentration camps were a tragic part of the political landscape, from Nazi Germany to the Japanese Empire to the United States. In response to the Japanese bombing of Pearl Harbor in 1941, President Franklin D Roosevelt signed an order that led to the internment of some 120,000 Japanese Americans and immigrants in 10 camps across the West, like this one in Idaho. As in WWI, German Americans were also designated as 'enemy aliens' and deported or held in camps, but in far fewer numbers. A visit here is a sobering reminder of how war – and its handmaiden, fear – impact us all, even when we're thousands of miles away.

For more on Minidoka National Historic Site, see p119.

14. Aspen, Colorado

IN POWDER WE TRUST

In 1899 miners trapped by record snowfall decided to have a little fun: for the fee of one ham sandwich, prospectors could enter a 15-mile ski race from the town of Independence down to Aspen. It was hardly the first ski event in Colorado, but it was a fitting start for what went on to become one of the world's most famous ski resorts. American industrialist Walter Paepcke, WWII vets from the 10th Mountain Division (America's only battalion on skis) and Austrian Bauhaus artist Herbert Bayer endowed Aspen with its unique flair in the postwar years, from the mind-body-spirit ethos to the beloved network of backcountry huts modeled after those in the Alps.

For more on Aspen, see p68.

15. Hoover Dam, Nevada

THE CHANGING CLIMATE

At the time of its completion in 1936, the 726ft Hoover Dam was a world marvel, providing both drinking water and electricity for the desert cities of California, Nevada and Arizona. Fast-forward to the 21st century, and all that human ingenuity is suddenly looking a little more precarious. A decades-long drought, a rapidly growing population and a century-old miscalculation in how much water really flows in the Colorado River all combined to reduce the water stored in the Lake Mead reservoir to its lowest levels ever: 26.63% capacity. Rival states are now scrambling to hammer out new water-use agreements before it's too late.

For more on the Hoover Dam, see p137.

MEET THE MONTANANS

The fourth-largest state in the nation, Montana is a place that defies the stereotypes you so often see on the screen. MARK SCHOENFELD introduces the Montanans.

ANYTIME MONTANA POPS up in popular culture – a phenomenon that seems to occur at least once a decade – folks around here will have opinions about their portrayal.

For instance, Montanans will point out that the television series *Yellowstone* was not filmed in the Paradise Valley, but rather in yet another picturesque stretch of river land south of Missoula, hundreds of miles and a Continental Divide away from the show's namesake river. And no, it wasn't the Big Blackfoot River where Brad Pitt dazzled trout in *A River Runs Through It*. You'd have to visit three different blue-ribbon trout streams to reproduce the Oscar-winning cinematography.

Montana has tens of thousands of miles of rivers, but do not ask a Montanan where their favorite place to fish is. This rule also applies to where they hunt deer, elk, upland game birds, ducks or morels. Don't ask about huckleberry patches or stands of saskatoons (another type of berry). The pleasure, Montanans will tell you, is in finding your own places to enjoy such delights. After all, it's home to more than 30 million acres of public land in addition to about 7 million acres of private land made accessible by the state's Block Management program. Upwards of a third of Montana is publicly owned.

Though the state's politics have listed rightward over the past decade, protection of public lands remains a bipartisan issue, and groups that you could imagine in conflict – snowmobilers and cross-country skiers, or fly anglers and tubers – by and large manage to cohabitate the public lands peacefully, if not begrudgingly.

In my early days in the state, I naively thought that Montanans didn't care about culinary diversity, as evidenced by the proliferation of burger and pizza restaurants (both efficient vessels for calories to fuel recreational pursuits). I've since learned Montana hosts no shortage of diverse fare. Sure, you may need to visit a gas station in East Missoula for authentic Native food or a bus stop in Dillon for your favorite tacos, but just imagine the landscapes you'll pass on the way there. I have friends who will drive an hour and a half to hike a box canyon and pick up frozen tamales on their way home. And since Montana has far more cows than people, the beef we eat is phenomenal. Another pair of friends once drove from Bozeman to a Pearl Jam show in Missoula almost entirely on gravel roads. Their waypoints were burger joints, dive bars and hot springs, and they camped for free on public land.

How Many

Montana is vast, encompassing 93 million sweeping acres of big sky country. And despite what the locals might tell you, it is definitely not crowded. The human population is a mere 1.1 million; the bovine population is 2.2 million. An estimated 15,000 to 20,000 bears live here, too.

CLOCKWISE FROM TOP LEFT: GOODLUZ/SHUTTERSTOCK, COUNTER/GETTY IMAGES, JORDAN SIEMENS/GETTY IMAGES, JORDAN SIEMENS/GETTY IMAGES

MY CONNECTION

I fell in love with the state during a summer graduate program in Bozeman. Every minute not spent in the classroom found me exploring rivers and peaks and the valleys between. I went home to Texas and proceeded to fall in love with a Montanan who was attending graduate school in my hometown. We were engaged two years later on the frozen banks of the Clark Fork River, a few miles downstream from where we now live with our two kids.

You might see a bumper sticker here that says: MONTANA IS FULL. You can imagine that same sentiment expressed on wagon trains crossing vast plains, the granite peaks of the northern Rockies backlit by the setting sun. It seems that as soon as someone new arrives in Montana, the urge arises to keep it to themselves. I understand the attitude, though, and do my best to give more than I get from this magical place. And I don't even begrudge the driver who flicked me off my first summer here, before I replaced my Texas license plates.

Navajo woman, Navajo Nation
SERGII FIGURNYI/SHUTTERSTOCK

VISITING THE NAVAJO NATION: A GUIDE TO RESPECTFUL TRAVEL

To appreciate and get more out of your visit to the Navajo Nation, you should arrive prepared to be a respectful visitor. By George Joe, a Navajo writer with his own travel guide, NavajoGuide.com.

THE NAVAJO NATION is the largest American Indian reservation in the United States, spanning three states – New Mexico, Arizona and Utah – and covering an area nearly the size of West Virginia. In many areas of the reservation, there is no electricity, running water or cell phones, residents 65+ do not speak English, and centuries-old ceremonies are still conducted.

The very first thing first-time visitors ask is: 'Is it similar to a Tony Hillerman novel?' You can get a sense of Navajo culture by reading Hillerman's mystery novels, but they are fictional and many things he writes about are not entirely accurate, which he does so as not to give away tribal secrets. Watching the TV series *Dark Winds* can also offer a glimpse into Navajo life in the 1970s.

Visiting Sites & Attractions

When visiting the Navajo Nation, it's crucial to follow local rules, such as staying on designated roads and trails. For example, in Monument Valley, visitors must remain on Valley Dr and not wander into areas where Navajo families live. The only authorized hiking trail without a guide is the 3.9-mile Wildcat Trail.

- Always check if a guide is required before visiting specific locations. A list is usually available on the tribe's discovernavajo.com website.
- Avoid off-road driving or causing damage to natural areas.
- Do not drive too fast as it stirs up dirt.
- Respect restrictions like 'no bicycles' in certain areas like Monument Valley.

Forrest Gump Hill near Monument Valley is at Mile 13 on Hwy 163. It's famous as the place where Forrest Gump ended his run in the movie. The view is stunning, but be

mindful of oncoming traffic when taking photos.

If visiting the Navajo Nation Council Chambers, be quiet inside and turn off your cell phone, especially if a meeting is taking place. If attending a chapter meeting, also be quiet. Since you are an outsider (not tribal member), you do not need to sign in.

Attending Public Events & Ceremonies

If you attend a Navajo Council meeting inside the Navajo Council Chambers, remember that food is not allowed, and attendees are expected to remain silent. Similarly, if you attend a chapter meeting, which is public, treat it like attending a city council meeting.

When visiting sacred sites or attending ceremonies, like the Kinaaldá (a coming-of-age ceremony for girls), it is crucial to observe with respect and silence. Modest attire is recommended, and guests should bring a gift of food if invited. For ceremonies like the Yei Bi Chei (a traditional nine-day ceremony), it's best to attend with a Navajo companion to ensure you follow proper protocols.

While traveling on reservation roads, you might see signs for cultural events such as 'Ndaah' or 'Squaw Dance.' These events are often for Navajo community members and should be treated with the same respect as a church service. Confirm whether visitors are welcome before attending, and remember that certain ceremonies are private, unless a Navajo invites you.

During prayers, songs and talks, one should not interrupt and should remain respectfully silent and out of the way when inside the ceremonial hogan or home site area. Appropriate attire means dressing modestly – covering your skin is recommended. If you are uncertain, you may ask for guidance on how to proceed or act.

If you meet a medicine man, be respectful of their time and purpose. Many are elderly and may not speak English. Avoid pressing them with questions, as they may be engaged in important cultural responsibilities.

National Parks & Archaeological Sites

When visiting national parks within the reservation, follow these guidelines.

- Do not enter or alter archaeological sites.
- Avoid entering private property without permission.
- Do not deface rock walls or structures.
- Ask permission before photographing Navajo people, their homes or their animals.

Photography Etiquette

If you are taking photos for personal use, no permit is needed. However, for any commercial photography or video, you must obtain a permit from the Navajo Parks & Recreation Department in Window Rock. Certain events, like ceremonies or Native American Church gatherings, are off-limits for photography.

Respectful Behavior & Attire

While visiting the Navajo Nation, maintain modest dress and avoid clothing that is revealing or tight. Avoid loud and boisterous behavior, as it can be considered disrespectful. Displays of affection, such as hugging or touching, should only be done with permission.

Direct eye contact can be considered impolite in some contexts.

Navajo people often have a reserved demeanor, especially around strangers.

Navajo cuisine

CLASSICSTOCK/GETTY IMAGES

Respect their space and limit unnecessary conversation.

How to Respectfully Purchase Authentic Navajo Arts & Crafts

When buying Navajo arts and crafts, it's important to be courteous. Avoid questioning craftspeople aggressively about the authenticity of their silver or stones because it is a big concern. Most are dedicated artisans, and there is a strong tradition of self-regulation among them. Refer to reputable guides like *navajo guide.com* for tips on where to find authentic goods and how to buy directly from the source. Many well-established trading posts and stores offer genuine items both on and off the reservation.

- Do not raise your voice or make accusations.
- Learn how to distinguish quality artisanship, but trust that most sellers operate with integrity.

WHEN VISITING SACRED SITES OR ATTENDING CEREMONIES, IT IS CRUCIAL TO OBSERVE WITH RESPECT AND SILENCE.

Turquoise jewelry

GRANDRIVER/GETTY IMAGES

Handling Panhandlers

If you plan to spend time on the reservation, you might encounter individuals asking for money, similar to city life. Often, such requests may be related to purchasing alcohol, which the tribe disapproves of but cannot fully control. If you feel uncomfortable, a polite 'no' usually suffices. In some cases, it may be best to walk away to avoid confrontation.

To avoid further interactions, offering a small amount of change can sometimes deter continued requests.

Avoiding Stereotypes

There are common misconceptions about Navajo life. For instance, Navajos do not live in tipis; traditional homes include hogans – eight-sided structures with the entrance facing east – or modern housing. While most Navajos speak English, older residents in remote areas may be more comfortable speaking in Navajo, and an interpreter may be needed. It is worth noting that fewer than 0.5% of Navajo children today enter school speaking the language.

Navajo Cultural Taboos

Navajo culture includes many taboos, and it's helpful to be aware of a few, for example, do not look at an eclipse or eat or sleep during one. If a convenience store suddenly closes at noon with a sign that says 'Reopens after Eclipse,' you will know why. Respect these traditions, as they are deeply meaningful to many Navajo people.

- Don't point at a rainbow with your index finger. You might lose it. Instead, use your thumb.
- Don't throw objects at a dust devil (whirlwind). Don't curse at a whirlwind or run into one, because it will affect your heart.
- Do not touch trees or rocks struck by lightning.

Navajo Cuisine: What to Expect

There are many safe and delicious dining options throughout the reservation, from restaurants in larger towns to roadside stands offering traditional Navajo dishes. For those curious about authentic flavors, the Window Rock Food Pavilion is a great place to try Navajo cuisine.

Roadside stands and food booths must have a permit, and tribal health workers frequently inspect them. Usually, they post their permit. Please do not make disparaging comments about the smell of the food or how it is cooked.

Be respectful when trying traditional foods, like mutton stew or frybread, even if they seem unfamiliar.

By following these guidelines, you can enjoy a respectful and enriching visit to the Navajo Nation, while appreciating the rich history, culture and traditions of the Navajo people.

PUBLIC LAND & POLITICS IN UTAH

More than 70% of Utah is owned by the federal or state governments – but how should the land be used? By Lauren Keith

WHEN PRESIDENT BARACK Obama created Bears Ears National Monument in 2016, Utah found itself back at the center of a long-simmering controversy: how should vast tracts of public land in the West be managed? Should they be set aside for recreation and preservation or sold to private interests to grow local economies?

Buying – & Taking – the West

The federal government owns nearly half of the land in the West, and Utah ranks second in the country for the most government-owned acres, after neighboring Nevada. As the 19th-century idea of 'manifest destiny' pushed Euro-American settlers to move west and stake their claims, the US government bought or took land, including from Native people, to fuel its expansion.

Homesteading and land grants put land into farmers' hands, and ranchers were often permitted the free use of 'unclaimed' areas. While this method worked in the flat and fertile Midwest, the mountain-filled and arid stretches of the West were not always suited for agriculture. Over time, environmental conservation became a higher public priority, and some of the land became protected wilderness and parks.

Pictured clockwise from top left: Double Arch (p189); Zion National Park (p194); Petroglyphs, Bears Ears National Monument (p185); Grand Staircase–Escalante National Monument

National Park vs National Monument

The difference between a national park and a national monument is simply how the site is established. An act of Congress designates a national park, while a national monument can be created by presidential proclamation or by Congress. National monuments established by a president can become national parks with congressional approval.

The 1906 Antiquities Act, brought into law by conservationist President Theodore Roosevelt, authorized presidents to create national monuments. The act was passed in response to the looting of Native archaeological sites, and it permitted the president to preserve 'historic landmarks, historic and prehistoric structures, and other objects of historic or scientific interest' as national monuments, 'the limits of which in all cases shall be confined to the smallest area compatible with the proper care and management of the objects to be protected.'

A few months after the act passed, Roosevelt created the first national monument, Devils Tower in Wyoming, followed by the Petrified Forest and Grand Canyon in Arizona. Even then, the protection of the Grand Canyon was contentious – a mining claimant sued in federal court, arguing that Roosevelt had overstepped his power by setting aside the entire canyon. The Supreme Court ruled unanimously in Roosevelt's favor.

Since then, seven Republican and nine Democratic presidents have created more than 140 national monuments, including four of Utah's five national parks.

The Controversy of Grand Staircase–Escalante & Bears Ears

In 1996, President Bill Clinton created Grand Staircase–Escalante (GSENM). It was the country's second-largest national monument at the time, covering nearly 2 million acres. In 2017, just a year after Bears Ears was established, the Trump administration shrank the new monument by 85%, the biggest cutback of federal land protection in US history, igniting a political firestorm. And no wonder – Bears Ears has come to represent many hot-button topics in US political debates: federal versus state power, the influence of industry lobbyists among politicians, racism and Indigenous rights, and climate change versus natural resource extraction. GSENM was downsized by almost half at the same time.

Within hours of Trump's proclamation, five Native tribes, environmental groups such as the Natural Resources Defense Council and the Southern Utah Wilderness Alliance, and outdoor outfitter Patagonia filed lawsuits in federal court. One of President Joe Biden's first acts was ordering a review of these national monuments, and in 2021, both were expanded back to their original boundaries. What will happen to these areas during Trump's second term as president? Only time will tell.

Separately, Utah sued the federal government in 2024 in an attempt to wrest control of some land in the state from the Bureau of Land Management (BLM). The areas it seeks to take are not part of any national parks or monuments, and the lawsuit is seen as a longshot.

Are Tourists Loving Utah to Death?

Regardless of the political battle, one thing is clear: everyone loves Utah's parks. Visitation hit record highs in 2021, when 11.2 million people traveled to the state's five national parks. Zion leads the way, breaking records with more than five million visitors in 2021, becoming the fourth national park to ever reach that number.

While more visitors means more awareness of the need to protect Utah's wild lands and more funds for the National Park Service (NPS), the sheer numbers have put strain on popular destinations. Finding a solution to increased visitation has not been easy: proposals have included increasing entrance fees by more than 100% during peak season, mandating a reservation system for park entry or creating a permit system for hiking certain trails. Some of these initiatives have been put into action: since 2022, the NPS has required hikers to Angels Landing to get a permit, and travelers to Arches National Park must have timed-entry tickets from 7am to 4pm from April through October. Both the NPS and some visitors say these restrictions are working.

The first paintings of Western landmarks such as Zion Canyon were instrumental in sparking the US conservation movement during the late 19th century, which in turn brought about the establishment of the NPS. But who controls Utah's land and how its beautiful spaces should be enjoyed are enduring questions, with no easy answers.

CLOCKWISE FROM TOP LEFT: JROBI8926/SHUTTERSTOCK, ANNA ABRAMSKAYA/SHUTTERSTOCK, AURORA OPEN/GETTY IMAGES, FOTOGRO/SHUTTERSTOCK

Colorado River
MAREK ULIASZ/ALAMY

COLORADO'S CHANGING CLIMATE

In the parched Rocky Mountains, water is everything. How is climate change impacting the region's long-term prospects? By Christopher Pitts

THE MOST VISIBLE indication of the effects of climate change in Colorado are not in the state itself, but further downstream along the Colorado River. In 2022 water levels at Lake Mead, the massive reservoir formed by the Hoover Dam outside Las Vegas, fell to their lowest level ever, at just one-fourth of its capacity.

The infamous bathtub ring, a chalky white coating on the reservoir's cliffs, is a reminder of just how far the water's surface has dropped in the past two decades. At its all-time low in 2022, the ring extended 150ft down to the water's surface – or 26.63% capacity. Even after two historically wet winters, in 2024 the reservoir had only risen to 34% capacity. If the water in the Colorado River continues to be used at the same rate as today, the US Bureau of Reclamation concluded that the water level in the reservoir will soon drop so low that Hoover Dam will no longer be able to generate electricity. And after that? There remains the possibility that one day, the reservoir could reach 'dead pool,' when the level in the dam drops so low that the river stops flowing entirely, and Arizona, Nevada, southern California and northwestern Mexico will be cut off from their main source of water.

The Colorado River

But what does all this have to do with Colorado? In a word: snowpack. The Colorado River, whose headwaters lie on the western slope of Rocky Mountain National Park and whose tributaries are scattered across the Rockies, is largely fed by snowmelt. Approximately 90% of all the water in the river comes from the mountains of Colorado, Wyoming and Utah, with the lion's share coming from Colorado watersheds. The equation is simple: the less snow that falls in the Rockies, the less water there is in the river, and less water that's available for one of the most important agricultural regions in the country – not to mention the 40 million people who live in the Colorado River basin (including Los Angeles, San Diego, Las Vegas and Phoenix).

Of course, as any skier will tell you, snowpack varies from year to year. Some years may be above average, others below. But data from the Environmental Protection Agency (EPA) indicates that overall, there has been a downward trend over time: across the West, snowpack has declined an average 23% since 1955. More importantly, the date of peak snowpack has been moving steadily backward. That is, the largest amount of snow in the Colorado

Rockies used to be measured in mid-April; over the past decade, that date has been inching toward March.

What does that tell us? That because of climate change, winters are slowly getting shorter. Meanwhile, summer temperatures in the Southwest have risen faster than in any other part of the United States. In Colorado, they've risen by 2.5°F since the beginning of the 20th century. Higher temperatures mean increased aridity and higher rates of evaporation throughout the landscape. Soils in particular have dried out to such an extent that when the spring runoff begins, much of that snowmelt is sucked straight into the ground, leaving increasingly less water that makes it into the river system – even in years when snowpack is average.

Factor in the 20-plus-year megadrought that is currently gripping the region (the worst in 1200 years), and a flawed seven-state compact that draws more water from the Colorado River than there is annual flow, and you have all the ingredients for what has become a monumental crisis – albeit in slow motion. At this point, it seems highly unlikely that nature will replenish the Lake Mead or Lake Powell (on the Utah–Arizona border) reservoirs on its own. Barring an end to the drought, the only other way to avoid dead pool is to reduce consumption.

Wildfire-fighting efforts in Boulder (p188), 2022

MICHAEL CIAGLO/GETTY IMAGES

Considering that roughly one-half of all the water that flows out of the spigots in Los Angeles, San Diego and Phoenix comes directly from the Colorado River (in Vegas it's upwards of 90%), drastically reducing consumption in what is one of the fastest-growing regions in the US may seem like a tall order. But city dwellers aren't even the primary consumers. That would be agriculture, which sucks up 80% of the allotted river flow. And yet, reducing agricultural demand for irrigated water is easier said than done. With only 3in of annual rainfall, Yuma (Arizona) and the Imperial Valley (southern California) might seem like some of the world's most improbable farmland, but they're actually the nation's primary producer of winter fruit and vegetables. When farmland in the rest of the nation is on winter vacation, 90% of all the carrots, lettuce and other greens you find at the supermarket are being grown in the always-sunny desert, irrigated directly with Colorado River water.

Climate change is not the only reason the Southwest's most important water source is drying up. Flawed planning, stubborn special-interest groups, outdated water rights and a naturally occurring drought cycle all play their own role. But as in so many other situations, climate change makes an already serious problem that much worse. As the Colorado snowpack continues to decline and summer temperatures continue to rise, eventually, there can only be one outcome. And sure enough, in 2023 an agreement on the first round of water restrictions was finally reached: the three Lower Basin states agreed to cut 3 million acre-feet of water use per year through 2026, in return for $1.2 billion in payments from the federal government. A critical first step in establishing a permanent agreement when the temporary deal expires.

Wildfires

Beyond the consequences for all the people who live downstream, climate change has a direct impact on Coloradans as well.

Colorado's mainstay of the tourism economy, skiing ($5 billion in annual revenue), seems to be headed for a day of reckoning, though the impacts of warming weather are less immediately visible for high-altitude ski resorts in the Rockies than in lower-elevation resorts in the Alps or along the East Coast, where winter rainfall is already commonplace. While Colorado ski resorts are nonetheless preparing for shortened seasons and less natural snowfall, there is another less obvious threat on the near horizon: wildfire.

In 2021, just miles from the residential sprawl around Lake Tahoe, California, the Caldor Fire raced through the mountains with such startling speed and ferocity that it's a miracle that firefighters were able to stop the blaze before it reached the lakeside settlements. One of the casualties of the fire, however, was the Sierra-at-Tahoe ski resort, where roughly 80% of the terrain was burned; the shocking photos of empty ski lifts being swallowed up by a raging orange inferno seemed to encapsulate all fire-mitigation challenges the West is currently facing.

THE LESS SNOW THAT FALLS IN THE ROCKIES, THE LESS WATER THERE IS IN THE RIVER, AND THE LESS WATER THAT'S AVAILABLE FOR ONE OF THE MOST IMPORTANT AGRICULTURAL REGIONS IN THE COUNTRY.

FRANCISCO BLANCO/SHUTTERSTOCK

While California's fires may get more coverage in the media, this is a region-wide phenomenon. Over the past decade, unusually hot and dry conditions have led to an increase not only in the number of wildfires per year, but also in their intensity. Warming conditions have stressed forests, making them more susceptible to disease and infestations of spruce, fir and pine beetles. Huge stands of dead trees – anyone who drives up Trail Ridge Rd in Rocky Mountain National Park will spot the gray- and rust-colored stands of deadwood – combined with exceptionally dry grasses, low humidity and high winds have resulted in increasingly massive fires. Of the 20 largest fires in Colorado history, 16 occurred after 2011, and the other four took place in the 2000s. The three largest ever, Cameron Peak, East Troublesome and Pine Gulch, all took place in 2020, filling the skies outside several major cities with raining ash and a terrifying red glow.

Another change is that there is no longer a wildfire season. What used to be a late-summer event might now happen at any time of year, as evidenced by the most destructive fire in Colorado history, the Marshall Fire, which sprang up at the edge of Boulder on December 30, 2021. Fueled by 115mph gusting winds and a complete absence of snowfall that year, the grassland fire swept through a dense residential community in a matter of hours, completely destroying over 1000 homes and businesses, taking two lives and causing $2 billion in damages.

There's no question that decades of overly aggressive fire suppression on public lands is partially to blame for the blazes, as the Smokey the Bear strategy resulted in the accumulation of huge amounts of fuel and dense understory vegetation throughout the West. While no one wants unplanned fires to happen (campfires are off-limits in many places throughout Colorado), local officials today are passing on a different sort of message. It's no longer one of fire suppression, but fire adaptation. As the Boulder City Wildfire Preparedness Guide reminds its residents: 'We live in a location where the wildfire threat is real. Wildfires happen frequently. A wildfire that threatens your home is not a matter of if, but when.' Residents in the West are learning to be prepared, because they are now living in an environment where people have to accept wildfires and mandatory evacuations as an inevitable part of their lives.

INDEX

Map Pages **000**

"The Grand Canyon lives up to the hype: its immensity, its grandeur, its beauty and its very age, all scream for superlatives."

"Come late September, Colorado's roads fill with leaf peepers, out in search of the glorious golden hues that wash across the mountainsides."

FROM LEFT: CANADASTOCK/SHUTTERSTOCK, MATTHEW ANDERSEN/SHUTTERSTOCK

Mapping data sources:
© Lonely Planet
© OpenStreetMap http://openstreetmap.org/copyright

THIS BOOK

The 4th edition of Lonely Planet's *American Rockies* guidebook was written and researched by Christopher Pitts, Anthony Ham and Liza Prado. This guidebook was produced by the following:

Destination Editor Melissa Yeager

Production Editor Kate Chapman

Image Editor Compton Sheldon

Cartographer Valentina Kremenchutskaya

Coordinating Editor Andrea Dobbin

Assisting Editors Janet Austin

Cover Researcher Giada de Agostinis

Thanks Amy Balfour, Imogen Bannister, Jade Bremner, Nicole Hagg, Ashley Harrell, Lauren Keith, Sarah Kezele, Saralinda Turner

Paper in this book is certified against the Forest Stewardship Council™ standards. FSC™ promotes environmentally responsible, socially beneficial and economically viable management of the world's forests.

Published by Lonely Planet Global Limited
CRN 554153
4th edition – Feb 2026
ISBN 978 1 83758 816 9

10 9 8 7 6 5 4 3 2 1
Printed in China